AWS Security Cookboo..

Practical solutions for managing security policies, monitoring, auditing, and compliance with AWS

Heartin Kanikathottu

BIRMINGHAM - MUMBAI

AWS Security Cookbook

Commissioning Editor: Karan Sadawna
Acquisition Editor: Shrilekha Inani
Content Development Editor: Pratik Andrade
Senior Editor: Arun Nadar
Technical Editor: Mohd Riyan Khan
Copy Editor: Safis Editing
Project Coordinator: Neil Dmello
Proofreader: Safis Editing
Indexer: Tejal Daruwale Soni
Production Designer: Nilesh Mohite

First published: February 2020

Production reference: 1260220

Published by Packt Publishing Ltd.
Livery Place
35 Livery Street
Birmingham
B3 2PB, UK.

ISBN 978-1-83882-625-3

www.packt.com

To God Almighty, for allowing me to take up this opportunity and complete it successfully. To my wife, Sneha Heartin, for being a loving and supportive wife and a great reviewer; and to my baby girl, June Grace, for sacrificing a lot of dada time. To our parents, and our siblings and their families, for their unconditional love and support.

– Heartin Kanikathottu

Contributors

About the author

Heartin Kanikathottu is an author, architect, and tech evangelist with over 12 years of IT experience. He has worked for companies including VMware, IG Infotech, Software AG, SAP Ariba, American Express, and TCS. His degrees include a B-Tech in computer science, an MS in cloud computing, and an M-Tech in software systems. He has over 10 professional certifications in the areas of the cloud, security, coding, and design from providers such as AWS, Pivotal, Oracle, Microsoft, IBM, and Sun. His blogs on computer science, the cloud, and programming have followers from countries across the globe. He mentors others and leads technical sessions at work, meetups, and conferences. He likes reading and maintains a big library of technical, fictional, and motivational books.

Thank you God Almighty for allowing me to take up this authoring opportunity and to complete it successfully. I want to thank all the people who have been close to me and have supported me, especially my wife Sneha who was also the official reviewer for the book; my baby girl June, who sacrificed a lot of her dada time; our parents, Dr. Gresamma, Jacob, Chinnamma, and Thomas; and our siblings and their families. The additional review efforts of my friends, Jayasree, Anitha, Jyothi, Raj, Rajni, Rijo, Saurabh, and Ashutosh, in making this a valuable book was significant. I would not have completed this book without the support of my current employer, VMware, and many colleagues who provided support in various forms, especially P Ramani, Rajneesh, Kyle, Chandana, Casey, and Cathal. Last, but not least, the support from Packt, with some amazing people and great tools, helped me a lot in completing this book on time.

About the reviewers

Sneha Thomas is a senior software engineer with around 10 years of IT experience. She is currently working at Australia and New Zealand Banking Group Limited (ANZ) as a technical lead. She has a master's degree with a specialization in cloud computing and a bachelor's degree in electronics and communications. She has very good knowledge of the AWS cloud as well as many other public clouds. She currently works as a full-stack developer and has worked on various technologies such as Java, Spring, Hibernate, and Angular, along with various web technologies such as HTML, JavaScript, and CSS. She was the reviewer for the book Serverless Programming Cookbook from Packt Publishing. She also likes writing blogs, and her Java blog has a good number of followers.

Michael J. Lewis currently works in the Cloud Enablement practice at Slalom Consulting in Atlanta, Georgia, specializing in AWS and DevSecOps. A computer science major and a U.S. naval submarine veteran with over 25 years' experience in the computer industry, he has been at the forefront of emerging technologies, from the internet boom to the latest trends in serverless and cloud computing. He and his wife Julie reside in Georgia with their three wonderful children.

Packt is searching for authors like you

If you're interested in becoming an author for Packt, please visit `authors.packtpub.com` and apply today. We have worked with thousands of developers and tech professionals, just like you, to help them share their insight with the global tech community. You can make a general application, apply for a specific hot topic that we are recruiting an author for, or submit your own idea.

Table of Contents

Preface

AWS Security Cookbook discusses practical solutions to the most common problems faced by security consultants while securing their infrastructure. This book discusses services and features within AWS that can help us to achieve security models such as the CIA triad (confidentiality, integrity, and availability), the AAA triad (authentication, authorization, and availability), and non-repudiation.

The book begins by getting you familiar with IAM and S3 policies; then, it dives deeper into data security, application security, monitoring, and compliance. Over the course of this book, you will come across AWS Security services such as Config, GuardDuty, Macie, Glacier Vault Lock, Inspector, and Security Hub. Lastly, this book covers essential security areas per chapter and progresses toward cloud security best practices and integrating additional security services.

By the end of this book, you will be adept with all of the techniques pertaining to securing AWS deployments along with having help to prepare for the AWS Certified Security – Specialty certification.

Who this book is for

If you are an IT security professional, cloud security architect, or a cloud application developer working on security-related roles and are interested in using the AWS infrastructure for secure application deployment, then this book is for you. This book will also benefit individuals interested in taking up the AWS Certified Security – Specialty certification. Prior knowledge of AWS and cloud computing is required.

What this book covers

`Chapter 1`, *Managing AWS Accounts with IAM and Organizations*, covers recipes for working with **Identity and Access Management** (**IAM**) users, groups, roles, and permission policies. This chapter also discusses recipes to create and manage multiple user accounts from a single master account using the AWS Organizations service.

`Chapter 2`, *Securing Data on S3 with Policies and Techniques*, discusses recipes related to securing **Simple Storage Service** (**S3**) data with **Access Control Lists** (**ACLs**), bucket policies, pre-signed URLs, encryption, versioning, and cross-region replication.

`Chapter 3`, *User Pools and Identity Pools with Cognito*, focuses mostly on application security with Cognito and discusses recipes related to concepts such as user pools, user signups, authentication and authorization flows, and federated identity logins.

`Chapter 4`, *Key Management with KMS and CloudHSM*, discusses recipes for managing encryption keys with AWS **Key Management Service** (**KMS**), which uses shared **Hardware Security Modules** (**HSMs**), as well as CloudHSM, which uses dedicated HSMs for enhanced security.

`Chapter 5`, *Network Security with VPC*, discusses recipes to secure your AWS infrastructure by creating **Virtual Private Clouds** (**VPCs**). We discuss topics such as public and private subnets, configuring route tables and network gateways, and using security mechanisms such as security groups and **Network Access Control Lists** (**NACLs**) to secure incoming and outgoing traffic.

`Chapter 6`, *Working with EC2 Instances*, covers additional recipes for securing Amazon **Elastic Compute Cloud** (**EC2**) instances, such as launching them into custom VPCs, using security groups, using the Systems Manager Parameter Store, and bootstrapping an EC2 instance with user data. We will also learn to encrypt data in **Elastic Block Store** (**EBS**).

`Chapter 7`, *Web Security Using ELBs, CloudFront, and WAF*, discusses recipes for securing web traffic and improving availability with different types of load balancers, the CloudFront service, and features such as instance-level TLS termination. We will also learn how to configure and use **Web Application Firewalls** (**WAFs**) within AWS.

`Chapter 8`, *Monitoring with CloudWatch, CloudTrail, and Config*, covers recipes to help us in troubleshooting, achieving compliance and accountability, and more through continuous monitoring, alerting, and regular auditing. We will learn about services such as CloudWatch, CloudTrail, Config, and **Simple Notification Service** (**SNS**).

`Chapter 9`, *Compliance with GuardDuty, Macie, and Inspector*, discusses recipes related to checking for compliance and notifying us about non-compliance. We will learn about services, such as GuardDuty, Macie, and Inspector, that use machine learning and advanced algorithms to help us to check compliance.

`Chapter 10`, *Additional Services and Practices for AWS Security*, discusses additional services and features that you can use to secure your AWS infrastructure, such as Security Hub, **Single Sign-On** (**SSO**), Resource Access Manager, Secrets Manager, Trusted Advisor, Artifact, and S3 Glacier vaults. We will also learn how to use additional security products from AWS Marketplace.

To get the most out of this book

- You will need a working AWS account for practicing the recipes within this book.
- You should already have some basic knowledge of AWS services such as IAM, S3, EC2, and VPC.
- Basic knowledge of cloud computing, computer networking, and IT security concepts can help you to grasp the contents of this book faster.

Download the example code files

You can download the example code files for this book from your account at `www.packt.com`. If you purchased this book elsewhere, you can visit `www.packtpub.com/support` and register to have the files emailed directly to you.

You can download the code files by following these steps:

1. Log in or register at `www.packt.com`.
2. Select the **Support** tab.
3. Click on **Code Downloads**.
4. Enter the name of the book in the **Search** box and follow the onscreen instructions.

Once the file is downloaded, please make sure that you unzip or extract the folder using the latest version of:

- WinRAR/7-Zip for Windows
- Zipeg/iZip/UnRarX for Mac
- 7-Zip/PeaZip for Linux

The code bundle for the book is also hosted on GitHub at `https://github.com/PacktPublishing/AWS-Security-Cookbook`. In case there's an update to the code, it will be updated on the existing GitHub repository.

We also have other code bundles from our rich catalog of books and videos available at `https://github.com/PacktPublishing/`. Check them out!

Download the color images

We also provide a PDF file that has color images of the screenshots/diagrams used in this book. You can download it here: `https://static.packt-cdn.com/downloads/9781838826253_ColorImages.pdf`.

Conventions used

There are a number of text conventions used throughout this book.

`CodeInText`: Indicates code words in text, database table names, folder names, filenames, file extensions, pathnames, dummy URLs, user input, and Twitter handles. Here is an example: "Verify that our `testuser` user can now list the files in the S3 bucket."

A block of code is set as follows:

```
"Condition": {
    "StringEquals": {
        "s3:x-amz-acl": [
            "public-read"
        ]
    }
}
```

When we wish to draw your attention to a particular part of a code block, the relevant lines or items are set in bold:

```
"Condition": {
    "StringEquals": {
        "s3:x-amz-acl": [
            "public-read"
        ]
    }
}
```

Any command-line input or output is written as follows:

```
aws iam attach-group-policy \
--group-name testusergroup \
--policy-arn arn:aws:iam::135301570106:policy/MyS3ListPolicyCLI \
--profile awssecadmin
```

Bold: Indicates a new term, an important word, or words that you see on screen. For example, words in menus or dialog boxes appear in the text like this. Here is an example: "Go to the **Organize accounts** tab."

Warnings or important notes appear like this.

Tips and tricks appear like this.

Sections

In this book, you will find several headings that appear frequently (*Getting ready*, *How to do it...*, *How it works...*, *There's more...*, and *See also*).

To give clear instructions on how to complete a recipe, use these sections as follows.

Getting ready

This section tells you what to expect in the recipe and describes how to set up any software or any preliminary settings required for the recipe.

How to do it...

This section contains the steps required to follow the recipe.

How it works...

This section usually consists of a detailed explanation of what happened in the previous section.

There's more...

This section consists of additional information about the recipe in order to make you more knowledgeable about the recipe.

See also

This section provides helpful links to other useful information for the recipe.

Get in touch

Feedback from our readers is always welcome.

General feedback: If you have questions about any aspect of this book, mention the book title in the subject of your message and email us at `customercare@packtpub.com`.

Errata: Although we have taken every care to ensure the accuracy of our content, mistakes do happen. If you have found a mistake in this book, we would be grateful if you would report this to us. Please visit `www.packtpub.com/support/errata`, selecting your book, clicking on the Errata Submission Form link, and entering the details.

Piracy: If you come across any illegal copies of our works in any form on the internet, we would be grateful if you would provide us with the location address or website name. Please contact us at `copyright@packt.com` with a link to the material.

If you are interested in becoming an author: If there is a topic that you have expertise in and you are interested in either writing or contributing to a book, please visit `authors.packtpub.com`.

Reviews

Please leave a review. Once you have read and used this book, why not leave a review on the site that you purchased it from? Potential readers can then see and use your unbiased opinion to make purchase decisions, we at Packt can understand what you think about our products, and our authors can see your feedback on their book. Thank you!

For more information about Packt, please visit `packt.com`.

1
Managing AWS Accounts with IAM and Organizations

The security of an application or a platform is generally considered as providing authentication, authorization, integrity, and confidentiality. Availability and accounting are two other aspects of security that are often overlooked. The **Confidentiality, Integrity, and Availability** (**CIA**) model and **Authentication**, **Authorization**, and **Accounting** (**AAA**) model are two popular models related to cloud security. CIA is generally referred to as the CIA triad. Apart from these, we should also consider non-repudiation while securing our application or platform.

In this chapter, we will learn about the AWS **Identity and Access Management** (**IAM**) service, the primary service in AWS for managing users, groups, roles, and permissions. We will learn how to write security policies. We will also discuss using the AWS Organizations service to create multiple accounts from within a single master account. We can use the AWS Organizations service to switch between the associated accounts without logging out of AWS, which helps to work with multiple accounts easily. We will also discuss core security concepts related to the cloud.

This chapter will cover the following recipes:

- Configuring IAM for a new account
- Creating IAM policies
- Creating a master account for AWS Organizations
- Creating a new account under an AWS Organization
- Switching roles with AWS Organizations

Technical requirements

We need a working AWS account to practice the recipes within this chapter. We should install and configure the AWS **Command-Line Interface** (**CLI**) in our local machine. It's assumed that you have basic knowledge of S3.

The AWS Management Console is generally used for one-time activities. For repetitive tasks, we should use **Application Programming Interfaces** (**APIs**). I will be providing CLI API usages for most cases with code files. You may follow these CLI API usages and implement them in a programming language of your choice using the AWS SDK or automate them using CloudFormation templates, as applicable.

The code files for this book are available at `https://github.com/PacktPublishing/AWS-Security-Cookbook`. The code files for this chapter are available at `https://github.com/PacktPublishing/AWS-Security-Cookbook/tree/master/Chapter01`.

Configuring IAM for a new account

IAM is the primary service in AWS for managing access to AWS services. IAM is a universal service and is not region-specific. After creating an AWS account, we should do some basic IAM configuration in order to secure our AWS account. IAM provides a checklist for these activities. Though not part of this checklist, we will also provide an account alias and create a billing alarm.

Getting ready

We need a newly created AWS account to complete all the steps in this recipe. Our IAM dashboard should look as follows. Even if you do not have a new account, you can still follow this recipe and verify whether everything has been configured correctly:

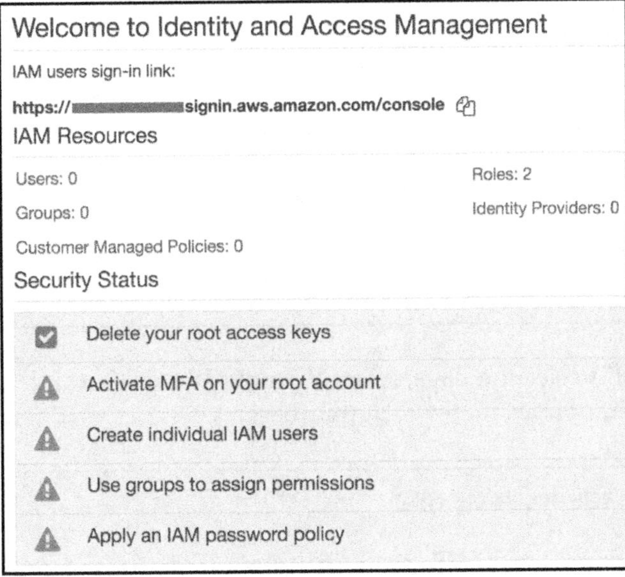

You need to install an authenticator app on your mobile if you are planning to set up **multi-factor authentication** (**MFA**) using a virtual MFA device. Google Authenticator is one popular option. You can also use a YubiKey U2F security key, any U2F-compliant device, or a hardware MFA device.

Universal 2nd Factor (**U2F**) is an authentication standard for securely accessing online services with only a security key without any drivers or client software.

How to do it...

Follow these steps on a new IAM dashboard. If your account isn't new, verify whether everything has been configured correctly:

1. Give a unique and meaningful alias for the account within the IAM users sign-in link.

   This is not a security requirement, but it makes it easier for our IAM users to log in to our account. By default, the account ID is used. Next, we will follow the IAM security checklist and make all the fields of the checklist green.

2. Activate MFA on our root account. Expand the **Activate MFA** checklist item and click on **Manage MFA**:

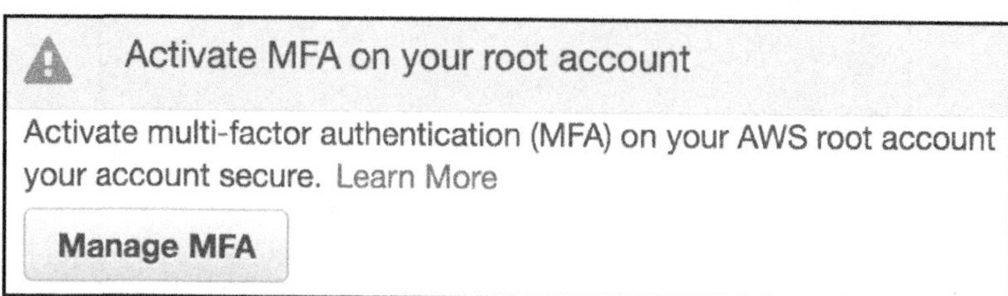

3. On the MFA selection page, select **Virtual MFA device** and click **Next**. You may select other options if they're applicable:

AWS will now provide a QR code.

4. Scan the QR code using an authenticator app (installed in the *Getting ready* section) and enter two successful token keys to activate it. After MFA has been activated, we will need to provide a token from this app, along with a username and password, to log in to the AWS console.

You should save the QR code image in a secure place if you ever want to reconfigure the authenticator app without accessing the current authenticator app setup; for example, in the event that your current mobile stops working. Alternatively, you can contact AWS support in case of such an event and they can help you reset the authenticator app configuration.

5. Create a user after expanding the **Create Individual IAM Users** checklist. We can also use the left menu item to go to the **Users** page.
6. Provide a username by using the option to add the user to a group.
7. Create a group.
8. Assign some policies to the group.

Policies are JSON documents that are used by IAM that authorize us to use various AWS services. It is good practice to assign policies to groups rather than to individual users.

9. Expand the checklist item for the password policy and set a decent password policy.
10. Go back to the IAM dashboard and check that all the checkmarks are green:

Now, let's create a billing alarm.

Creating a billing alarm

In this section, we will set up a billing alarm that will let us know when we exceed a set limit:

1. Go to your billing dashboard from the drop-down menu next to your account name on the upper-right corner of the screen:

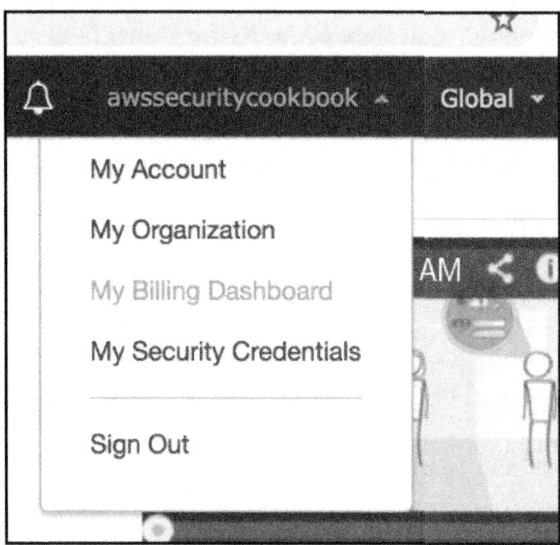

2. From the billing dashboard, click on **Billing preferences**, select the **Receive Billing Alerts** checkbox, and click **Save preferences**:

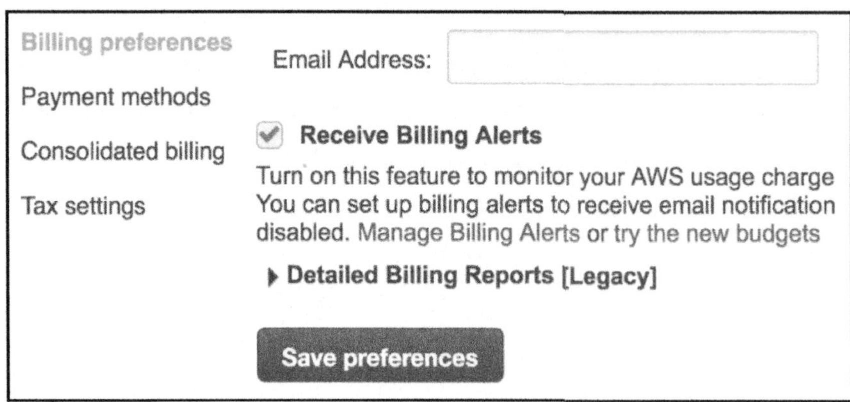

3. Go to the CloudWatch service dashboard and click on **Billing** on the left. From the **Billing alarm** page, click on **Create alarm**. On the **Create alarm** page, provide our usage limit and an email for sending notifications:

Billing alarm

You can create a billing alarm to receive e-mail alerts when your AWS charges exceed a threshold you choose. Simply:

1. Enter a spending threshold
2. Provide an email address
3. Check your inbox for a confirmation email and click the link provided

When my total AWS charges for the month

exceed: 5 USD

send a notification to: awsseccookbook@gmail.com

At the time of writing this book, only AWS allows us to create a billing alarm if our region is set to US East (N. Virginia).

How it works...

IAM is the AWS service that helps us manage the identity of users within AWS in order to verify their identity (authentication) and their permissions to AWS services (authorization).

IAM has four core concepts:

- **Users**: A user can be created in IAM and given the necessary permissions to access AWS resources.
- **Groups**: Users can be added to groups. Permissions can now be given to groups instead of individual users. This is a recommended best practice.
- **Policies**: Policies are JSON documents that define the permissions for users or groups.
- **Roles**: Roles are generally used for giving users temporary permissions to access an AWS service. For example, we can attach a role with S3 permissions to an EC2 service.

The IAM dashboard provides a set of checklist items to keep our account secure. It is good practice to keep them all green. The first checklist item checks whether we have active access keys for our root account that can be used for programmatic access. The **root** account is the account that we log into using the primary email and has access to everything in our account. It is good practice to use root for creating other accounts and then use those accounts for our day-to-day activities.

The next checklist item checks whether we have enabled MFA for our root account. MFA will enforce an additional level of authentication, apart from the username and password, using tokens from a virtual or hardware MFA device. The next two checklist items make sure that we create at least one user and a group. The last checklist item is for setting a password rotation policy for our account.

Finally, we also set up a billing alarm. Though not part of the IAM checklist, it is good practice to set a billing alarm. This will trigger an alarm and let us know when we exceed the set limit.

There's more...

Let's quickly go through some important concepts related to IAM and security:

- **Authentication** is the process of verifying a user's identity with a username and password, or credentials such as the access key and the secret access key.
- There are primarily two types of access credentials in AWS for authenticating users:
    - **Access key ID and secret access key**: This is used for programmatic access, and is used with AWS APIs, CLI, SDK, and any development tools.
    - **Username and password**: For managing console access.
- **Authorization** is the process of checking whether a user has the right permissions to perform an action and is usually defined using the permission's policies.
- **Confidentiality** is done to make sure the data that's sent from the source is not read by anyone in between. This can be made possible using cryptography.
- **Data integrity** is done to make sure the data has come from the right person and has not been tampered in between. This is also generally made possible using cryptography.
- **Availability** makes sure the service can be used when it is needed.
- **Accounting** helps us identify the responsible parties in case of a security event.

- **Non-repudiation** prevents a user from denying an activity. Cryptography comes to our aid here.
- The **AWS shared responsibility model** defines the responsibilities of AWS and its customers in securing our solutions on the AWS cloud. In summary, it states that the security of the cloud, for example, securing the global infrastructure, hardware, networking, and so on is AWS's responsibility; while security in the cloud, for example, updates and security patches for the servers we provision, protecting credentials and keys, and so on is the customer's responsibility.
- AWS IAM supports **Payment Card Industry Data Security Standard** (**PCI-DSS**) compliance. This is an information security standard required for organizations that handle credit cards.

See also

- You can read more about the AWS shared responsibility model here: `https://aws.amazon.com/compliance/shared-responsibility-model`.
- This book does not cover AWS basics beyond the security domain. If you are new to AWS, you can read about cloud computing, AWS basics, and CLI configurations here: `https://cloudmaterials.com/en/book/getting-started-cloud-computing-and-aws`.

Creating IAM policies

In this recipe, we will learn how to create IAM policies from the Management Console, as well as the AWS CLI. We will create an IAM policy for an S3 bucket.

Getting ready

We need a working AWS account with the following resources configured:

- A user with no permissions and a user with administrator permissions. Add these users to two groups. We should configure CLI profiles for these users. I will be calling the users and their CLI profiles `testuser` and `awssecadmin` and the groups `awstestusergroup` and `awssecadmingroup`, respectively.

`awssecadmin` is a user with full administrator permissions. In real-world projects, we won't have a single user with all permissions. Instead, we will segregate permissions into different user groups. If we are practicing these recipes from an office account, it is unlikely that we will be provided with full administrative permissions. We may have to list the exact permissions that we need. Therefore, I will also be providing the minimal permissions needed by the administrator user for each applicable recipe with the code files.

- An S3 bucket with default permissions. I will be using a bucket name of `awsseccookbook`. S3 bucket names are globally unique. Therefore, select an available name and replace my bucket with your bucket name wherever applicable.
- Check the contents of the S3 bucket from the CLI using `testuser` and verify that it has no permissions:

```
$ aws s3 ls awsseccookbook --profile testuser

An error occurred (AccessDenied) when calling the ListObjectsV2
operation: Access Denied
```

How to do it...

First, we will create IAM policies from the Management Console using the IAM policy editor. Then, we will create the same policy from the AWS CLI.

Creating policies with the IAM visual editor

We can create a policy using the IAM visual editor as follows:

1. Log in to the console as an administrator and go to the IAM dashboard.
2. Click on **Policies** from the left sidebar.
3. Click on **Create Policy**. This will provide us with a visual editor:

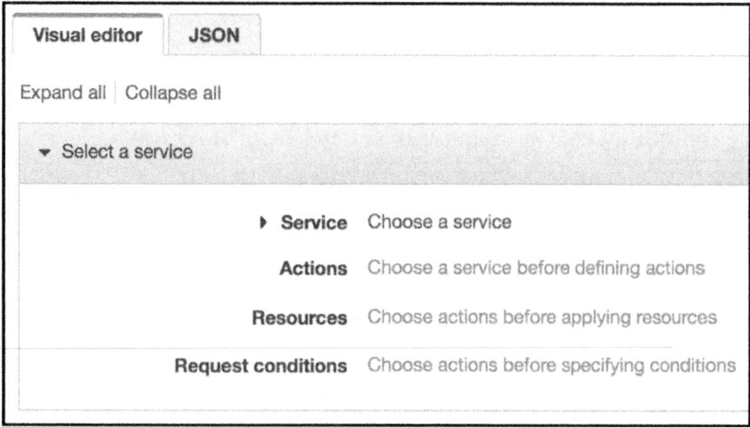

We can also click on the **JSON** tab and enter the JSON directly if we have already created the policy JSON.

4. Set the **Service** to S3.
5. Select **ListBucket** under **Actions**.
6. Under **Resources**, select **Specific**, click on **Add ARN**, and enter our bucket's ARN in the format `arn:aws:s3:::<bucket_name>`.
7. Under **Request conditions**, click **Add condition** and add a condition, as follows, with an EPOCH time from the future (we can find many online tools that do the time conversion for us):

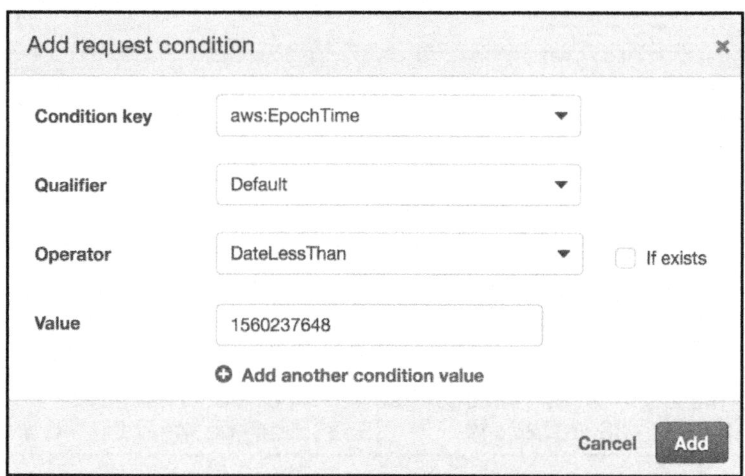

Click **Add**.

8. Click **Review Policy**.
9. Provide a name (for example, `MyS3ListPolicy`), add a description (for example, `My S3 ListPolicy`), and click **Create Policy**.
10. Verify the policy that was generated from the **JSON** tab:

Permissions | Policy usage | Policy versions | Access Advisor

Policy summary | {} JSON | Edit policy

```
{
    "Version": "2012-10-17",
    "Statement": [
        {
            "Sid": "VisualEditor0",
            "Effect": "Allow",
            "Action": "s3:ListBucket",
            "Resource": "arn:aws:s3:::awsseccookbook",
            "Condition": {
                "DateLessThan": {
                    "aws:EpochTime": "1560237648"
                }
            }
        }
    ]
}
```

11. Click on **Groups** from the left sidebar of the IAM dashboard and go to our `testuser` group. Click on **Attach Policy** and attach the policy we created in the previous step.

You can also attach policies to groups or users from the **Policy** tab of the IAM dashboard.

12. Verify this by running the `s3 ls` command from the command line with the `testuser` profile name (the same command from the *Getting ready* section). We should see a successful response, as follows:

```
$ aws s3 ls awsseccookbook --profile testuser
2019-06-08 18:27:49     155335 image-heartin-k.png
```

Now, let's look at how to create policies using the AWS CLI.

Creating policies using the AWS CLI

In this section, we will create a policy with the JSON we generated in the previous recipe. If you are following along from the previous section, detach the current policy from the group (or user) and confirm that the `testuser` user cannot list the contents of the bucket. Let's get started:

1. Create a file called `my-s3-list-bucket-policy.json` with the following JSON policy:

```
{
  "Version": "2012-10-17",
  "Statement": [
    {
      "Sid": "MyS3ListBucketPolicy",
      "Effect": "Allow",
      "Action": "s3:ListBucket",
      "Resource": "arn:aws:s3:::awsseccookbook",
      "Condition": {
        "DateLessThan": {
          "aws:EpochTime": "1609415999"
        }
      }
    }
  ]
}
```

The preceding policy will only allow access if the current EPOCH timestamp is less than the EPOCH timestamp represented by the value of `aws:EpochTime`. The value of `1609415999` in the preceding policy denotes **Thursday, 31 December 2020 11:59:59 GMT**. We can use one of the free EPOCH time converters available online to generate an EPOCH time corresponding to a date we want to test the policy with.

2. Create the policy using the `create-policy` subcommand:

```
aws iam create-policy \
--policy-name MyS3ListPolicyCLI \
--policy-document file://resources/my-s3-list-bucket-
policy.json \
--profile awssecadmin
```

This should return the policy's details, along with its ARN:

```
{
    "Policy": {
        "PolicyName": "MyS3ListPolicyCLI",
        "PolicyId": "ANPAR7AE2DY5CXZZ65PIF",
        "Arn": "arn:aws:iam::135301570106:policy/MyS3ListPolicyCLI",
        "Path": "/",
        "DefaultVersionId": "v1",
        "AttachmentCount": 0,
        "PermissionsBoundaryUsageCount": 0,
        "IsAttachable": true,
        "CreateDate": "2019-06-11T07:11:45Z",
        "UpdateDate": "2019-06-11T07:11:45Z"
    }
}
```

3. Attach the policy to the group using the `attach-group-policy` subcommand while providing the policy ARN from the previous command:

```
aws iam attach-group-policy \
--group-name testusergroup \
--policy-arn arn:aws:iam::135301570106:policy/MyS3ListPolicyCLI
\
--profile awssecadmin
```

4. Verify that our `testuser` user can now list the files in the S3 bucket:

```
$ aws s3 ls awsseccookbook --profile testuser
2019-06-08 18:27:49     155335 image-heartin-k.png
```

How it works...

In this recipe, we created an IAM policy from the console and the CLI. IAM policies are JSON documents and follow a structure that is followed by most policy types within AWS, with the exception of **access control lists (ACLs)**, which are XML-based.

The policy document is composed of statements that are added as arrays to the `Statement` element. A `Statement` element for an IAM policy may contain the following subelements:

- `Sid` is the statement ID, which is optional. This can be used to provide a description of the policy.

- `Effect` specifies whether we want to allow or deny access to a resource. The supported values are `Allow` and `Deny`.
- `Action` specifies the permission or permissions (`s3:ListBucket`) for which this statement has been applied:

```
"Action": [
  "s3:ListAllMyBuckets",
  "s3:ListBucket"
],
```

We can also specify `*` to denote any action.

- `Resource` specifies the ARN of the resource (for example, S3 bucket) that the statement is applied to. For S3 buckets, ARN should follow the following format: `arn:aws:s3:::<bucket_name>/<key_name>`.
  We can use a comma to separate multiple values. We can specify `*` to denote any resources.
- `Condition` allows us to conditionally execute policies. We use Boolean operators to match the condition against values in the request. For example, the following condition checks whether a canned ACL of `"public-read"` is used in the request:

```
"Condition": {
    "StringEquals": {
        "s3:x-amz-acl": [
            "public-read"
        ]
    }
}
```

There are conditional keys that are common to all AWS services that support policies: those that are specific to S3 bucket operations and those that are specific to S3 object operations. In this recipe, we added a condition to check whether the current time is less than a particular time as an EPOCH timestamp. This is an optional element. We will look at conditions in a bit more detail in `Chapter 2`, *Securing Data on S3 with Policies and Techniques*.

There's more...

Let's quickly go through some important concepts related to policies in AWS:

- **Types of AWS policies** include identity-based policies (for example, IAM policies), resource-based policies (for example, S3 bucket policies and IAM role trust policies), permissions boundaries, an organization's **service control policy** (**SCP**), ACLs, and session policies.
- An **AWS IAM policy's type** can be either **AWS managed**, **Job function**, or **Customer managed**. We can check the type from the console on the **Policies** page within IAM:

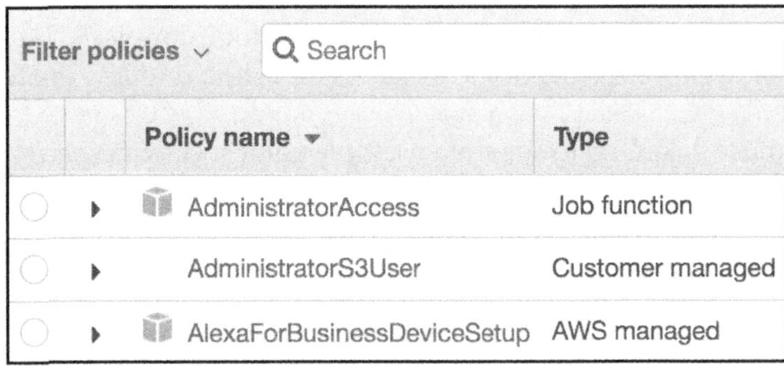

- **Job function** is a subset of **AWS managed** and is designed to align with common IT job functions. The current list of job functions includes Administrator, Billing, Database Administrator, Data Scientist, Developer Power User, Network Administrator, Security Auditor, Support User, System Administrator, and View-Only User.
- **AWS Policy Generator** can generate the following policies: IAM Policy, S3 Bucket Policy, SNS Topic Policy, a VPC Endpoint Policy, and an SQS Queue Policy. It is currently available at `https://awspolicygen.s3.amazonaws.com/policygen.html`.
- If there is an allow and deny effect for the same action and resource in a policy, deny will always take precedence.
- An IAM policy cannot be used to grant permissions for anonymous users, unlike S3 ACL and the Bucket Policy.

- The IAM policy cannot be applied to a root user and can only be applied to IAM users.
- The `NotPrincipal` policy element denotes the principal entity to deny access.
- `NotAction` excludes the specified list of actions.
- The following are some of the predefined condition keys that are supported by all AWS services that support IAM access control: `aws:CurrentTime`, `aws:EpochTime`, `aws:MultiFactorAuthAge`, `aws:MultiFactorAuthPresent`, `aws:PrincipalOrgID`, `aws:PrincipalArn`, `aws:RequestedRegion`, `aws:SecureTransport`, and `aws:UserAgent`.

See also

- You can read more about AWS policies and permissions here: `https://docs.aws.amazon.com/IAM/latest/UserGuide/access_policies.html`.
- S3 also supports two other policy types, namely the Bucket Policy and ACLs, as we will see in `Chapter 2`, *Securing Data on S3 with Policies and Techniques*.

Creating a master account for AWS Organizations

In this recipe, we will learn how to set up an AWS master account for AWS Organizations. Many organizations have multiple AWS accounts for development, deployment (production), and more. The AWS Organizations service helps us centrally manage all our AWS accounts.

Getting ready

We'll need a working AWS account to complete this recipe.

How to do it...

We can create a master account with AWS Organizations as follows:

1. Log in to the console as an administrator and go to the AWS Organizations service dashboard:

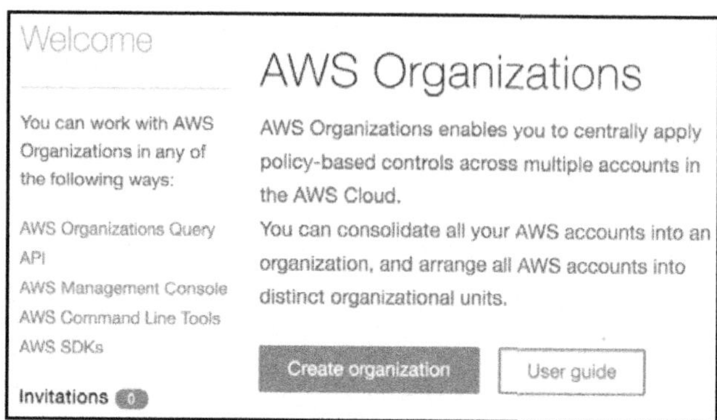

2. Click on **Create organization**. We will be shown a popup containing important details and restrictions:

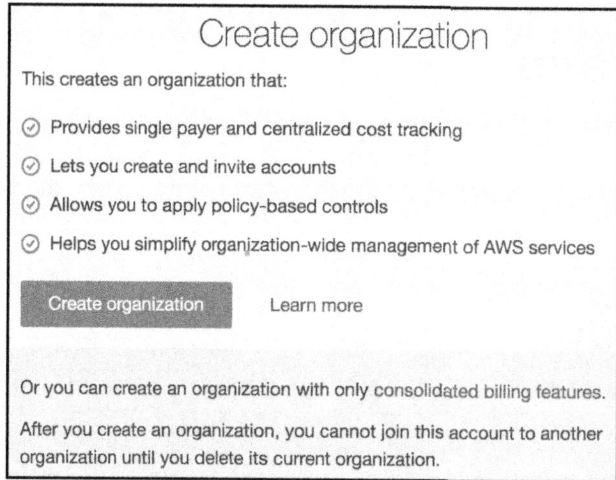

3. Click on **Create organization** in the popup.
4. AWS will now send a verification email to the account's registered email address. Verify your email to finish setting up the master account. The master account will be denoted by a star next to the account name in the **Accounts** tab.

5. Go to the **Organize accounts** tab. Click on the **New organizational unit** tab and create two **organizational units (OUs)**:

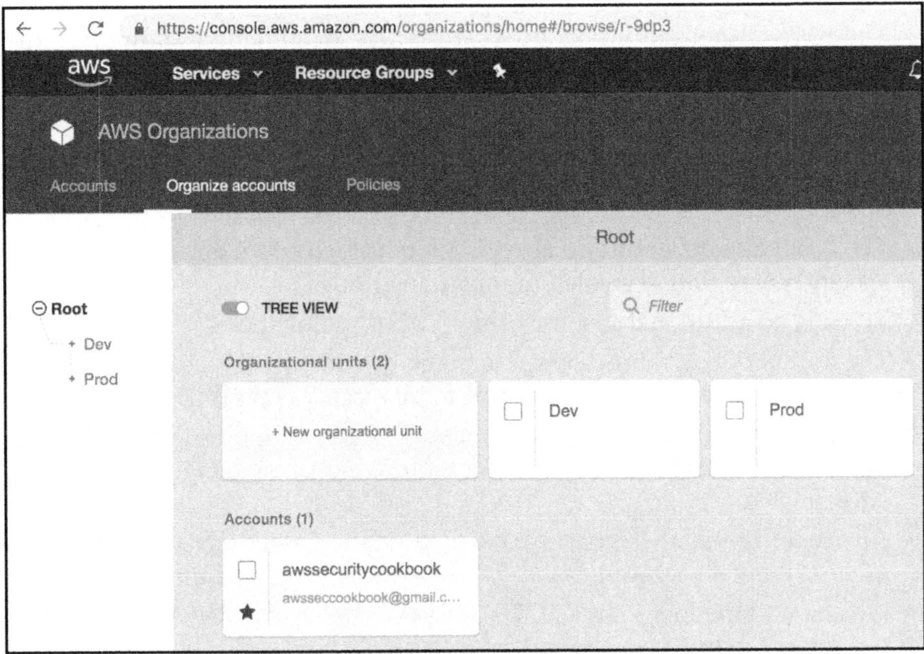

We will create accounts under the OUs in the next recipe.

How it works...

In this recipe, we created an AWS Organizations master account and a few OUs under it. The AWS Organizations service dashboard has three tabs now. The **Accounts** tab contains the account name, email, account ID, and status for all accounts, including the master account. The master account is denoted by a star next to the account name. We can create OUs and manage the hierarchy structure of OUs and accounts in the **Organize accounts** tab.

We can create sub-OUs within an OU. We can move an account to an OU by navigating to the root or OU that currently contains the account, selecting the account, and choosing **Move**. The third tab, **Policies**, within the Organizations dashboard allows us to create and manage policies. We can attach a policy to an OU by going to the **Organize accounts** tab, selecting the OU from the list, and then attaching the policy in the details pane.

There's more...

Let's quickly go through some important details about the AWS Organizations service:

- The AWS Organizations service is supported in all regions; however, the endpoints are located in US East (N. Virginia) for commercial organizations and AWS GovCloud (US-West) for AWS GovCloud (US) organizations.
- We can use the AWS Organizations service using one of the following: AWS Management Console, the AWS Organizations Query API, AWS CLI, or AWS SDKs.
- The AWS Organizations service is a global service. We don't need to select or specify any region to create organization entities.
- There is no additional cost for using AWS Organizations.
- The number of accounts we can manage within an AWS Organization varies for accounts. We can ask AWS Support to increase this limit.
- We can only initiate the creation of a new organization from an AWS account that is not a member of any organization. We cannot change the master account once created.
- An account can only be part of one organization at a time and within an organization, an account can only be part of one OU at a time.
- We can nest the hierarchy of OUs and accounts up to 5 levels (including root).
- We can use SCPs to restrict AWS service actions to root accounts, IAM users, and IAM roles in the accounts of our organization.
- SCPs can only deny access; they cannot allow access.
- When both the permissions boundary (an IAM feature) and SCP are present, the action is only allowed if the permission boundary, the SCP, and the identity-based policy all allow the action.
- We can integrate supported services with AWS Organizations to manage services across accounts. The current supported list of services that can be integrated includes AWS Artifact, AWS CloudTrail, Amazon CloudWatch Events, AWS Config, AWS Directory Service, AWS Firewall Manager, AWS License Manager, AWS RAM, AWS Service Catalog, and AWS Single Sign-On. We can enable integration from the supported service's dashboard.

We can enable SCP for our organization as follows:

1. Go to the AWS Organizations service in the master account's console.
2. Go to the **Organize accounts** tab.

3. Click on **Root** from the left sidebar. We should see the **ENABLE/DISABLE POLICY TYPES** section on the right pane.
4. Click **Enable** for **Service control policies**.

After enabling SCP for an organization, we can add an SCP as follows:

1. Go to the AWS Organizations service in the master account's console.
2. Go to the **Policies** tab.
3. Click on **Service control policies**.
4. Click on **Create policy**.
5. Provide a **Policy name** and **Description**.
6. Add a policy, as follows:

```
{
  "Version": "2012-10-17",
  "Statement": [
    {
      "Effect": "Deny",
      "Action": "cloudtrail:StopLogging",
      "Resource": "*"
    }
  ]
}
```

   This policy will restrict anyone within the OU.

7. Click on **Create policy**.
8. Click on **Root** or an OU from the left sidebar.
9. Click on **Service control policies** on the right pane.
10. Click on **Attach** against our new policy.

See also

- For the limitations of the AWS Organizations service, you can refer to `https://docs.aws.amazon.com/organizations/latest/userguide/orgs_reference_limits.html`.
- You can find examples of SCPs here: `https://docs.aws.amazon.com/organizations/latest/userguide/orgs_manage_policies_example-scps.html`.

Creating a new account under an AWS Organization

In this recipe, we will create a new OU called **Test**. We will create an AWS account from the CLI under one of those OUs. We will also look at account creation from the console.

Getting ready

You'll need to create an AWS Organization account with a master account to complete this recipe. Follow the *Creating a master account for AWS Organizations* recipe to do so.

For executing the command from the CLI, we need to configure AWS CLI with credentials for a user with administrator access in your master account. I will be using a user with a CLI profile called `awssecadmin`.

How to do it...

In this recipe, we will create accounts using CLI commands. After that, we will discuss account creation from the console.

Creating an account and OU from the CLI

Follow these steps from the AWS CLI:

1. We can create an AWS account from the CLI using the `create-account` subcommand, like so:

```
aws organizations create-account \
--email awsseccookbook1@gmail.com \
--account-name awsseccookbookchild1 \
--profile awssecadmin
```

   This should give us the following response:

```
{
    "CreateAccountStatus": {
        "Id": "car-bb6f15308b7311e98b7112a0c7517226",
        "AccountName": "awsseccookbookchild1",
        "State": "IN_PROGRESS",
        "RequestedTimestamp": 1560166479.627
    }
}
```


2. We can check the status of our request using the `describe-create-account-status` subcommand by providing the request ID we received in the previous step:

```
aws organizations describe-create-account-status \
--create-account-request-id car-
bb6f15308b7311e98b7112a0c7517226 \
--profile awssecadmin
```

If the request succeeded, we should get the following response:


```
{
    "CreateAccountStatus": {
        "Id": "car-bb6f15308b7311e98b7112a0c7517226",
        "AccountName": "awsseccookbookchild1",
        "State": "SUCCEEDED",
        "RequestedTimestamp": 1560166479.726,
        "CompletedTimestamp": 1560166483.721,
        "AccountId": "380701114427"
    }
}
```


3. We can verify that the account was created under `ROOT` and get the root's ID using the `list-parents` subcommand using the account ID we received in the previous step:

```
aws organizations list-parents \
--child-id 380701114427 \
--profile awssecadmin
```

This should give us the following response:


```
{
    "Parents": [
        {
            "Id": "r-9dp3",
            "Type": "ROOT"
        }
    ]
}
```


4. Create an OU called `Test` under root using the `create-organizational-unit` subcommand using the ID of the root we received in the previous step:

```
aws organizations create-organizational-unit \
--parent-id r-9dp3 \
--name Test \
--profile awssecadmin
```

This should give us the following response:


```
{
    "OrganizationalUnit": {
        "Id": "ou-9dp3-moeksvq4",
        "Arn": "arn:aws:organizations::135301570106:ou/o-971vdyppdh/ou-9dp3-moeksvq4",
        "Name": "Test"
    }
}
```


5. Move our new account from root into our new OU while providing the account ID, root's ID, and OU's ID from the previous steps using the `move-account` subcommand, like so:

```
aws organizations move-account \
--account-id 380701114427 \
--source-parent-id r-9dp3 \
--destination-parent-id ou-9dp3-moeksvq4 \
--profile awssecadmin
```

This command does not return anything.

6. Check the parent for our account using the `list-parents` subcommand, as we did in *step 3*. We should get a response with the OU as the parent:

```
{
    "Parents": [
        {
            "Id": "ou-9dp3-moeksvq4",
            "Type": "ORGANIZATIONAL_UNIT"
        }
    ]
}
```

7. We can list all the OUs under root using the `list-children` subcommand with the child type set to `ORGANIZATIONAL_UNIT`:

```
aws organizations list-children \
--parent-id r-9dp3 \
--child-type ORGANIZATIONAL_UNIT \
--profile awssecadmin
```

   This should give us the following response if we have a total of three OUs, assuming we created two in the previous recipe:

```
{
    "Children": [
        {
            "Id": "ou-9dp3-moeksvq4",
            "Type": "ORGANIZATIONAL_UNIT"
        },
        {
            "Id": "ou-9dp3-k78re8mv",
            "Type": "ORGANIZATIONAL_UNIT"
        },
        {
            "Id": "ou-9dp3-o4qre2dw",
            "Type": "ORGANIZATIONAL_UNIT"
        }
    ]
}
```

To get details of the OU, along with its name, we can use the `describe-organizational-unit` subcommand with a single parameter named `organizational-unit-id` by passing in the ID.

Creating and moving an account from the console

Since we already saw how to create OUs from the console in the previous recipe, we will only discuss creating an account in this section. Let's get started:

1. Log in as an administrator in the master account and go to the AWS Organizations dashboard.
2. Go to the **Accounts** tab and click on **Add Account**. We will be provided with options to either invite an account or create one.
3. Click on **Create Account** and enter values for **Full name** and **Email**. Note that the default role is populated as `OrganizationAccountAccessRole`:

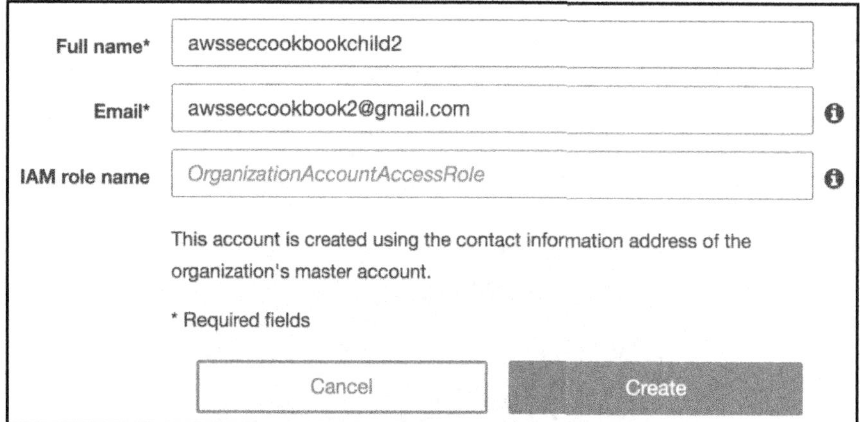

Full name here will be our account name. We can change the account name later by logging into the account with the root user email. We can reset the password using the **Forgot password** option the first time we sign in as the root account.

4. Click on **Create** to create the account. If you are unable to create the account due to the limit being reached, please contact AWS support. This limit varies from account to account. If successful, we should see all three accounts (`master`, `child1`, and `child2`) under the **Accounts** tab.

Removing an account from an organization lets us run the account as a standalone account. If we try to remove the newly created account now, we will get an error stating that the sign-in process for the account hasn't been completed. To work as a standalone account, we need to sign in as a root user and provide additional information, including credit card details.

5. We can add the newly created account under the **Prod** OU as follows:
    1. Go to the **Organize Accounts** tab.
    2. Select the account to move (`child2`, in this case) and click **Move**.
    3. From the popup, select **Prod** and click **Move**.
    4. Go inside the configuration for the **Prod** OU by clicking on it and verifying whether the account is under it.

How it works...

In this recipe, we created an account from the CLI using the `create-account` subcommand. This command works asynchronously and returns immediately with a request ID. We can check the status of our request using the `describe-create-account-status` subcommand while providing the request ID. To check whether an account was created, we can check the AWS CloudTrail log for the `CreateAccountResult` event.

The `create-account` subcommand also accepts other parameters, namely `role-name` and `iam-user-access-to-billing`. The `role-name` parameter is used to specify the name of an IAM role that will be automatically pre-configured in the new member account. This role provides administrator permissions to the member account and trusts the master account. This means that users in the master account can assume the role, provided the master account administrator allows this. The default value is **OrganizationAccountAccessRole**. If we log in to the child account and check the `OrganizationAccountAccessRole` role, we will see that it has the **Administrator Access** policy attached to it. If we check the **Trust relationships** section, we will see that our master account has been added as a trusted entity. An administrator from the master account can now switch roles to the child account and have administrator access.

The `iam-user-access-to-billing` parameter needs to be set to `ALLOW` for IAM users to access account billing information. If it is set to `DENY`, only the root user can access account billing information. The default value is **ALLOW**. We also created an OU and moved our account under the OU. Within the examples, we used the `list-children` subcommand with the child type as `ORGANIZATIONAL_UNIT` to list all the OUs under root. We can set `child-type` to **ACCOUNT** to list all the accounts instead.

There's more...

Let's quickly go through some of the other useful AWS CLI subcommands for AWS Organizations:

- `create-gov-cloud-account` can be used to create accounts in the AWS GovCloud (US) region if we are authorized to do so.
- `invite-account-to-organization` sends an invitation to another account to join our organization.
- `remove-account-from-organization` removes an account from the organization.
- `create-organization` creates an AWS Organization, while `delete-organization` deletes an AWS Organization.
- `leave-organization` removes an account from its parent organization.
- `create-organizational-unit` creates an OU, while `delete-organizational-unit` deletes an OU. To delete an OU, we must remove all accounts and child OUs.
- `update-organizational-unit` renames an OU.
- `describe-account` retrieves information about that account and should be called from the master account. `describe-organization` retrieves information about the organization. `describe-organizational-unit` retrieves information about an OU.
- `list-accounts` lists all the accounts in the organization. `list-accounts-for-parent` lists the child accounts of the given target root or OU. `list-create-account-status` lists the account creation requests that match the given status. `list-roots` lists the roots that are defined in the current organization.
- `tag-resource` and `untag-resource` can be used for managing tags.

See also

- Please refer to the AWS CLI documentation for organizations to learn about all the commands that we can use to work with the AWS CLI: `https://docs.aws.amazon.com/cli/latest/reference/organizations/index.html`.

Switching roles with AWS Organizations

In this recipe, we will learn how to switch from the master account to a member account from within the console. Switching between accounts from the console without having to log out from AWS is a great feature that is used extensively in many organizations. For example, a user may be given a basic user in one account and they can switch to other accounts with the appropriate roles (for example, Admin for Dev and ReadOnly for Prod).

Getting ready

We need to create a master account and a child account with AWS Organizations. We can do this by following the *Creating a master account for AWS Organizations* and *Creating a new account under an Organization* recipes of this chapter.

How to do it...

First, we'll learn how to switch between accounts as an administrator user in the master account and then allow a non-admin user to switch accounts.

Switching as an administrator

An administrator from the master account can switch into a child account by following these steps:

1. Log in to the master account as an IAM user with administrator permissions.

2. Click on the drop-down menu next to username and click on **Switch Role**:

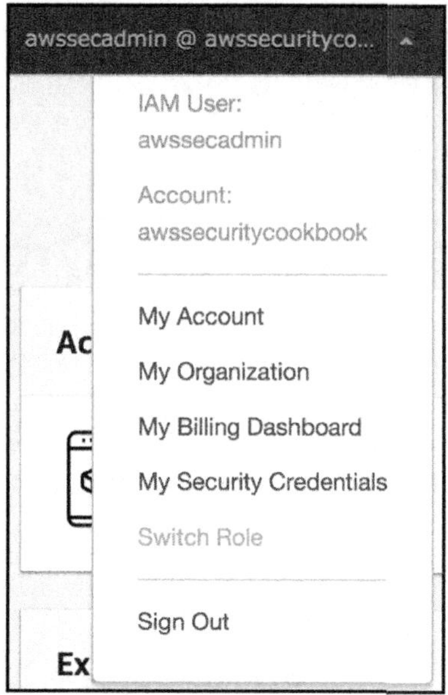

3. On the role switch page, click **Switch Role**.
4. On the next screen, enter the following:
    1. Enter the account ID of the child account (available from AWS Organization's **Account** tab).
    2. Set the **Role** to `OrganizationAccountAccessRole`.
    3. Enter a value for **Display Name** (for example, `AwsSecAdmin@OrganizationAccountAccessRole`):

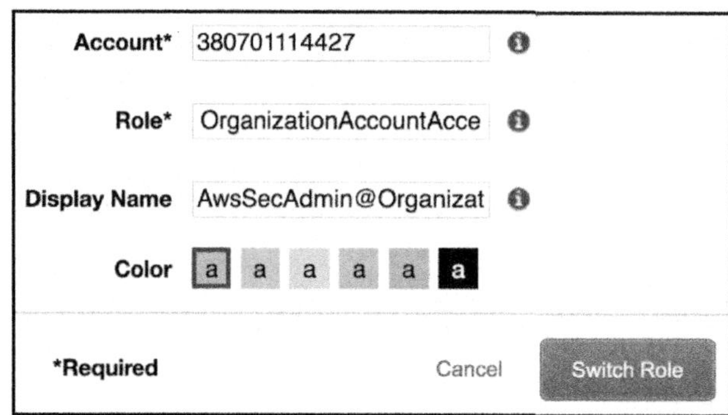

We should be logged in to our child account with the specified role. We can verify these details from the dropdown next to our account name:

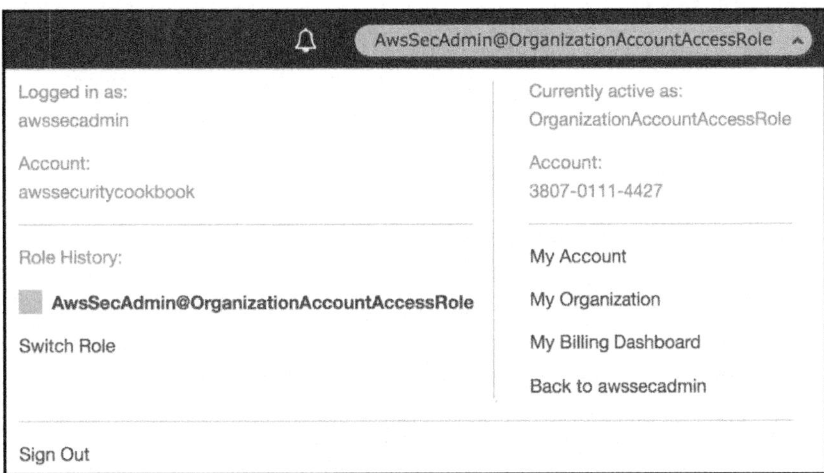

5. Switch back to the parent account by clicking on the **Back to awssecadmin** link from the dropdown. If we try to switch roles with a non-admin user by following the preceding steps (with no permissions attached), switching roles will fail with an error, as follows:

Could not switch roles using the provided information. Please check your settings and try again. If you continue to have problems, contact your administrator.

Now, let's look at how to grant permission for a non-admin user in order to switch roles.

Granting permission for a non-admin user to switch roles

For switching role, the non-admin user should be given the `AssumeRole` permission for the role on the master account. Let's take a look:

1. Sign in to the master account as an administrator.
2. Create a policy that allows `AssumeRole` on the child account role, that is, `OrganizationAccountAccessRole`:

```
{
 "Version": "2012-10-17",
```

```
"Statement": [
{
"Sid": "AssumeRoleForChildAccount",
"Effect": "Allow",
"Action": "sts:AssumeRole",
"Resource":
"arn:aws:iam::380701114427:role/OrganizationAccountAccessRole"
}
]
}
```

Save this policy as `AssumeRolePolicyChild1`.

3. Attach this policy to our `testusergroup` group.
4. Sign out and sign back in as `testuser` user.
5. Follow the steps in the previous section and enter the following details on the **Switch Role** screen:

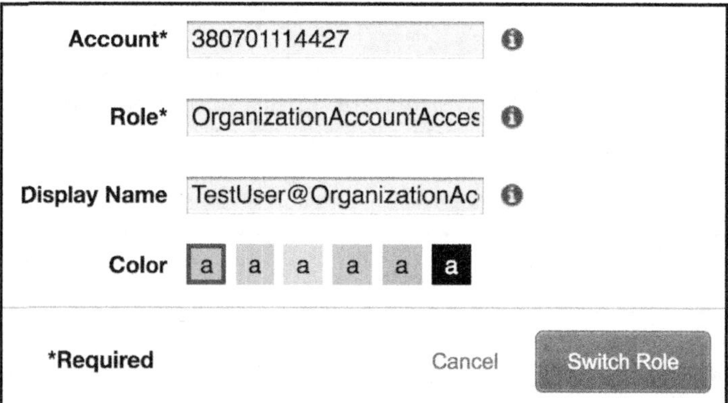

6. Click on **Switch Role**.

This time, we should be able to switch role into the new account. We can verify this from the drop-down menu next to our account name in the taskbar:

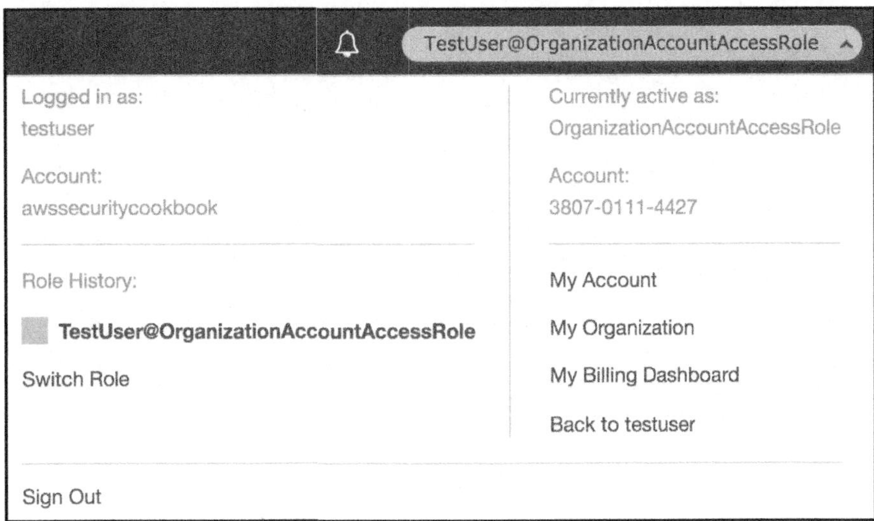

In this recipe, a user with no permission in the master account received full administrator access in the child account. In the real world, administrators will create different roles in different child accounts (for example, Dev, Testing, Prod, and so on) and then the user groups in the master account will be granted access to the respective roles in those accounts.

Granting permission for a non-admin user to switch roles using the CLI

We can grant permission for a non-admin user from the CLI as follows:

1. Create a policy document that allows `AssumeRole` on the child account role, that is, `OrganizationAccountAccessRole` and save it as `assume-role-policy-document.json`. Refer to the previous section for the JSON document structure.
2. Create the policy, as follows:

```
aws iam create-policy \
--policy-name MyAssumeRolePolicyCLI \
--policy-document file://resources/assume-role-policy-
document.json \
--profile awssecadmin
```

We should get the following response:


```
{
    "Policy": {
        "PolicyName": "MyAssumeRolePolicyCLI",
        "PolicyId": "ANPAR7AE2DY5FLMD6BVL6",
        "Arn": "arn:aws:iam::135301570106:policy/MyAssumeRolePolicyCLI",
        "Path": "/",
        "DefaultVersionId": "v1",
        "AttachmentCount": 0,
        "PermissionsBoundaryUsageCount": 0,
        "IsAttachable": true,
        "CreateDate": "2019-06-11T12:47:14Z",
        "UpdateDate": "2019-06-11T12:47:14Z"
    }
}
```


3. Attach this policy to the user group:

```
aws iam attach-group-policy \
--group-name testusergroup \
--policy-arn
arn:aws:iam::135301570106:policy/MyAssumeRolePolicyCLI \
--profile awssecadmin
```

We should now be able to switch roles.

How it works...

In this recipe, we switched roles from our master account to a child account within an AWS Organization without any additional configuration. Then, we granted permission for another non-admin user's group to assume the default role, that is, `OrganizationAccountAccessRole`, that was created by AWS as part of creating the child account.

Both roles and users are AWS identities with permission policies that specify what they can do. Users have standard credentials such as password or access keys. However, users, groups, applications, or other AWS services can assume a role and will be provided with temporary security credentials for the role session.

Granting permissions to allow access to resources that we control is called delegation. To perform delegation, we need to set up a trust between the account that owns the resource (the trusting account) and the account with users that need access (the trusted account). The trusting and trusted accounts can be the same account or different accounts.

While delegating permission, in addition to the standard permissions policy that grants the user the needed permissions, the IAM role in the trusting account will also have a trust policy defined. The trust policy specifies which accounts are allowed to assume the role. The trust policy is written in JSON format according to the rules of the IAM policy language.

As we saw in the previous recipe, the master account is added as a trusted entity by default when we created the member under our organization. In this recipe, the trusted account (master account) granted further permission for the `testusergroup` to assume the default role from the member account through a policy. This policy granted the `AssumeRole` permission of the **Security Token Service** (**STS**) service.

In this recipe, we didn't create any role since AWS already created one for us. The `create-role` CLI command can be used to create a role. The `get-role` command gathers information about a role, while `delete-role` can be used to delete a role. `update-role` can be used to update the description or maximum session duration for the role.

Switching roles between any two accounts

Please note that it is not necessary for the accounts to be a part of an AWS Organization to perform role switching. This can be configured between any two accounts. To allow a user group, for example, `testusergroup`, from account A to switch role to account B, we can follow these steps:

1. Create a policy in account B with required access permissions to resources in account B.
2. Create a role in account B with the trusted entity as account A and attach the policy we created in the previous step.
3. Account A's admin should grant the `STS:AssumeRole` permission for the role we created in the previous step by providing the complete role ARN to the required users or groups in account A so that they can assume that role from account B.
4. Verify the setup by signing in as a user from `testusergroup` into account A and switch roles to account B.

There's more...

Let's quickly go through some important details about IAM roles:

- The trust policy for a role allows a user in the trusted account to switch to or assume that role.
- A wildcard (*) cannot be specified as a principal for a trust policy.
- When a user assumes a role, it temporarily gives up its own permissions until the user stops using the role.
- Some services allow **attaching a policy directly to a resource without needing to use a role** as a proxy. These resources include S3 buckets, Glacier vaults, Amazon **simple notification service** (**SNS**) topics, and Amazon **simple queue service** (**SQS**) queues.
- Roles can be used by the **external users authenticated by an external identity provider** service to get access to AWS resources. Roles allow mobile apps to use AWS resources without embedding AWS keys within the app.
- **Role chaining** is the process where a role assumes a second role through the AWS CLI or API.
- To pass the role information to an EC2 instance when the instance starts, we can add the role within an instance profile. An instance profile can be considered a container for an IAM role. The `list-instance-profiles-for-role` CLI command lists the instance profiles for a role.
- The **permissions boundary** is a feature we can use to set the maximum permissions that an identity-based policy can grant to an IAM entity such as a user or role. The `put-role-permissions-boundary` CLI command creates or updates the permissions boundary for a role, while `delete-role-permissions-boundary` deletes the permissions boundary for the role.
- The `attach-role-policy` CLI command attaches a policy to a role, while `detach-role-policy` detaches a policy from a role.
- The `put-role-policy` CLI command creates or updates an inline policy, `get-role-policy` retrieves the specified inline policy in a role, and `delete-role-policy` deletes the specified inline policy.

See also

- The steps to create roles and attach permissions are also discussed in the *Implementing S3 cross-region replication within the same account* and *Implementing S3 cross-region replication across accounts* recipes in `Chapter 2`, *Securing Data on S3 with Policies and Techniques*.
- You can read more about delegating access across AWS accounts without using AWS Organizations here: `https://docs.aws.amazon.com/IAM/latest/UserGuide/tutorial_cross-account-with-roles.html`.
- For more recipes on AWS IAM and AWS Organizations, you can refer to `https://cloudmaterials.com/en/book/advanced-account-management-aws-iam-and-aws-organizations`.
- A detailed example of switching roles between two accounts that are not part of AWS Organizations is available at `https://cloudmaterials.com/en/recipe/recipes-how-switch-between-2-accounts-aws`.

2
Securing Data on S3 with Policies and Techniques

Amazon S3 is an object store on the AWS platform. In simple terms, an object store is a key-value store for objects with a name as the key and an object as the value, unlike a filesystem store, which is hierarchical. In this chapter, we will learn to secure S3 data with **access control lists** (**ACLs**), bucket policies, pre-signed URLs, encryption, versioning, and cross-region replication. We have already seen how to secure S3 data using an IAM policy in `Chapter 1`, *Managing AWS Accounts with IAM and Organizations*.

This chapter will cover the following recipes:

- Creating S3 access control lists
- Creating an S3 bucket policy
- S3 cross-account access from the CLI
- S3 pre-signed URLs with an expiry time using the CLI and Python
- Encrypting data on S3
- Protecting data with versioning
- Implementing S3 cross-region replication within the same account
- Implementing S3 cross-region replication across accounts

Technical requirements

We need a working AWS account. We should install and configure the AWS CLI on our local machine.

Code files for this chapter are available at `https://github.com/PacktPublishing/AWS-Security-Cookbook/tree/master/Chapter02`.

Creating S3 access control lists

In this recipe, we will learn to grant permissions to the public (everyone) using ACLs from a console, using predefined groups from the CLI, and using canned ACLs from the CLI. ACLs can be used to grant basic read/write permissions to buckets, objects, and their ACLs. ACL grantees can be either an AWS account or a predefined group.

Getting ready

We need a working AWS account with the following resources configured:

1. **A bucket with a file**: I will be using a bucket name `awsseccookbook` with a file named `image-heartin-k.png`. Replace these with your own bucket name and filename.
2. **A user with no permission and a user with administrator permission**: Configure CLI profiles for these users. I will name users and their profiles `testuser` and `awssecadmin`, respectively.

It is good practice to add users to groups and give permissions to these groups instead of directly assigning permissions to users.

3. Uncheck the two **Block all public access** settings related to ACLs. Leave the other settings checked and click **Save**:

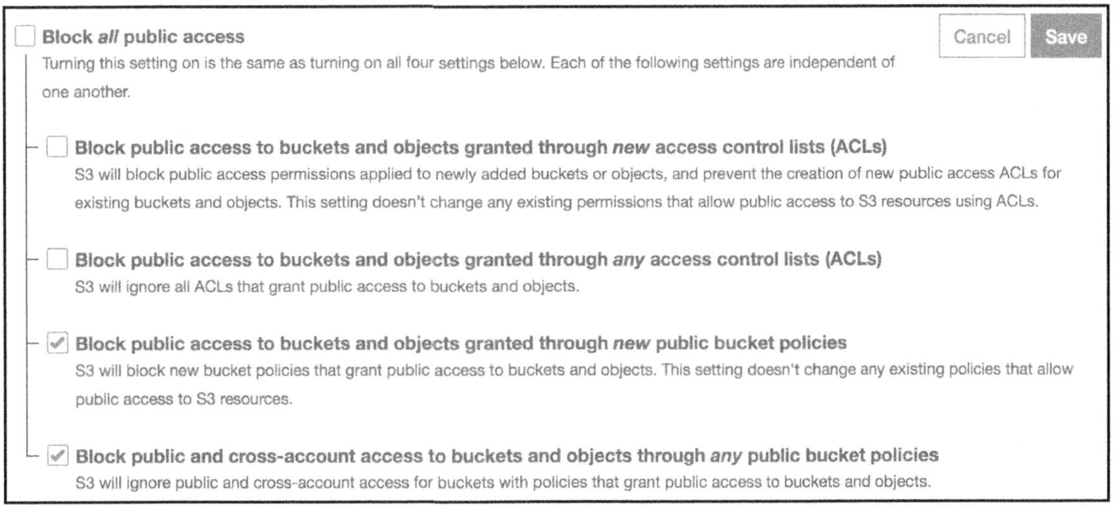

Block *all* public access

Cancel Save

Turning this setting on is the same as turning on all four settings below. Each of the following settings are independent of one another.

Block public access to buckets and objects granted through *new* access control lists (ACLs)

S3 will block public access permissions applied to newly added buckets or objects, and prevent the creation of new public access ACLs for existing buckets and objects. This setting doesn't change any existing permissions that allow public access to S3 resources using ACLs.

Block public access to buckets and objects granted through *any* access control lists (ACLs)

S3 will ignore all ACLs that grant public access to buckets and objects.

Block public access to buckets and objects granted through *new* public bucket policies

S3 will block new bucket policies that grant public access to buckets and objects. This setting doesn't change any existing policies that allow public access to S3 resources.

Block public and cross-account access to buckets and objects through *any* public bucket policies

S3 will ignore public and cross-account access for buckets with policies that grant public access to buckets and objects.

We can manage block public access settings for a bucket by going to **Block public access** under the bucket's **Permissions** tab. We can also manage these settings at account level from the S3 dashboard sidebar.

How to do it...

We will discuss various usages of S3 ACLs in this section.

Granting READ ACLs for a bucket to everyone from the console

Perform the following steps to allow everyone to list the bucket's contents:

1. Go to the S3 service in the console.
2. Go to the **Access Control List** tab under the bucket's **Permissions** tab of the bucket, click on **Everyone,** select **List objects**, and then click **Save**.

3. Access the bucket from the browser and we should be able to list the contents of the bucket:

```
https://s3.amazonaws.com/awsseccookbook/

This XML file does not appear to have any style information associated with it.

<ListBucketResult xmlns="http://s3.amazonaws.com/doc/2006-03-01/">
  <Name>awsseccookbook</Name>
  <Prefix/>
  <Marker/>
  <MaxKeys>1000</MaxKeys>
  <IsTruncated>false</IsTruncated>
  <Contents>
    <Key>image-heartin-k.png</Key>
    <LastModified>2019-06-08T12:57:49.000Z</LastModified>
    <ETag>"070f3d6245efcb633898c923c8b421ae"</ETag>
    <Size>155335</Size>
    <StorageClass>STANDARD</StorageClass>
  </Contents>
</ListBucketResult>
```

Next, we will learn to grant `READ` for AWS users using predefined groups.

Granting READ for AWS users using predefined groups from the CLI

We can grant `READ` for any AWS user using the `AuthenticatedUser` predefined group by performing the following steps:

1. If you followed along with the previous section, remove the **List objects** permission for the bucket that was granted to **Everyone**.
2. Create a policy that grants access to the `AuthenticatedUsers` group and save it as `acl-grant-authenticated-users.json`:

```
{
  "Owner": {
    "DisplayName": "awsseccookbook",
    "ID":
"5df5b6014ae606808dcb64208aa09e4f19931b3123456e152c4dfa52d38bf8
fd"
  },
  "Grants": [
    {
      "Grantee": {
        "Type": "Group",
```

```
            "URI":
"http://acs.amazonaws.com/groups/global/AuthenticatedUsers"
          },
          "Permission": "READ"
        }
    ]
}
```

Here, the `Owner` element has the current account's display name and canonical ID. The `Grants` element grants the `READ` permission to the `AuthenticatedUsers` group.

3. Execute the `put-bucket-acl` command by providing the preceding policy document:

```
aws s3api put-bucket-acl \
    --bucket awsseccookbook \
    --access-control-policy file://resources/acl-grant-
authenticated-users.json \
    --profile awssecadmin
```

4. The `testuser` user should now be able to list the contents of the S3 bucket. However, we won't be able to list the bucket contents from the browser.

Granting public READ for an object with canned ACLs from the CLI

We can upload an object and grant public read access using a canned ACL as follows:

1. Download the image file using the admin user profile. On this occasion, downloading should be successful:

```
$ aws s3 cp s3://awsseccookbook/image-heartin-k.png image-heartin-k.png \
> --profile awssecadmin
download: s3://awsseccookbook/image-heartin-k.png to ./image-heartin-k.png
```

2. Upload the same file as an administrator, providing the canned ACL for `public-read`:

```
aws s3 cp image-heartin-k.png s3://awsseccookbook/image-
heartin-new.png \
--acl public-read \
--profile awssecadmin
```

3. Download the new file using the `testuser` profile:

```
$ aws s3 cp s3://awsseccookbook/image-heartin-new.png image-heartin-new.png \
> --profile testuser
download: s3://awsseccookbook/image-heartin-new.png to ./image-heartin-new.png
```

We should now be able to download the file successfully.

How it works...

In this recipe, we learned about ACLs.

In the *Granting READ ACLs for a bucket to everyone from the console* section, we granted the `READ` permission to everyone through ACLs. In the *Granting READ for AWS users using predefined groups from the CLI* section, we granted the `READ` permission using a predefined group: `AuthenticatedUsers`.

The policy document for granting access through ACLs has the following structure:

```
{
  "Grants": [
    {
      "Grantee": {
        "DisplayName": "string",
        "EmailAddress": "string",
        "ID": "string",
        "Type": "CanonicalUser"|"AmazonCustomerByEmail"|"Group",
        "URI": "string"
      },
      "Permission": "FULL_CONTROL"|"WRITE"|"WRITE_ACP"|"READ"|"READ_ACP"
    }
    ...
  ],
  "Owner": {
    "DisplayName": "string",
    "ID": "string"
  }
}
```

The grantee can be specified in one of the following ways:

- With `Type` as `AmazonCustomerByEmail`, along with the canonical ID of the account in the `EmailAddress` field
- With `Type` as `CanonicalUser`, along with the email for the account in the `ID` field
- With `Type` as `Group`, along with the URI for a predefined group in the `URI` field

The account can be specified using an email address or the canonical ID of the account. We can get the canonical ID of an account from the **Security Credentials** page of our account.

The following are globally the URIs for predefined groups and should be used in the JSON policy:

- `AuthenticatedUser`: `http://acs.amazonaws.com/groups/global/AuthenticatedUsers`
- `AllUsers`: `http://acs.amazonaws.com/groups/global/AllUsers`
- `LogDelivery`: `http://acs.amazonaws.com/groups/s3/LogDelivery`

ACLs can be used to grant the following permissions to buckets/objects:

- `READ`: List objects for a bucket. Read an object and its metadata.
- `WRITE`: Create, overwrite, or delete objects for a bucket. Not applicable for an object.
- `READ_ACP`: Read the ACL of a bucket or object.
- `WRITE_ACP`: Write the ACL for a bucket or object.
- `FULL_CONTROL`: All the previous permissions.

In the *Granting public READ for an object with canned ACLs from the CLI* section, we used a canned policy, `pubic-read`, which allows everyone to read that object. Canned ACLs are short-hand ACL permissions that can be used to provide permission for a resource from the command line. Currently, the following canned ACLs are supported: `private`, `public-read`, `public-read-write`, `aws-exec-read`, `authenticated-read`, `bucket-owner-read`, `bucket-owner-full-control`, and `log-delivery-write`.

In the case of cross-account access, if a user from account A uploads an object to a bucket in account B (owned by account B), account B will have no access to that object even if it is the bucket owner. Account A can, however, grant permission to the bucket owner while uploading the document using the `bucket-owner-read` or `bucket-owner-full-control` canned ACL.

We used the `put-bucket-acl` sub-command of the `aws s3api` command in this recipe to set permissions on a bucket using ACLs. Similarly, `put-object-acl` sets permission for an object. If we forget the policy structure for a `put` policy, we can execute a `get` policy to get the structure and modify it for our purpose. The `get-bucket-acl` sub-command of the `aws s3api` command gets the bucket's ACL policy, and `get-object-policy` gets an object's ACL policy.

There's more...

S3 is considered to be secure by default. A new object will have no access except for the account owner. An account owner of an S3 resource is the account that created that resource.

Let's go through some important concepts related to ACLs:

- ACLs provide basic read/write permission to buckets, objects, and their ACLs.
- ACLs can only grant access to AWS accounts and predefined groups.
- ACLs, by default, allow full control to the owner of the resource and nothing to everyone else.
- ACLs can only grant permission; they cannot deny access.
- ACLs are represented internally as XML documents.
- ACLs are generally considered legacy and, wherever possible, it is preferable to use either an IAM policy or a bucket policy. However, there are some scenarios where ACLs are the best, or the only, choice:
    - ACLs can be used to grant access to objects not owned by the bucket owner. For example, when a user in one account uploads an object to another accounts' bucket, canned ACLs can be used to provide access to the bucket owner.
    - ACLs are used to grant permission to an S3 log delivery group for a bucket.
    - ACLs can be used to grant individual permissions to many objects. Even though this can be done with a bucket policy, it is easier to achieve this with ACLs.
- While ACLs are specified per resource, bucket policies are specified per bucket and prefixes. IAM policies have resources specified in a similar way to bucket policies, but are applied to IAM users.

Let's quickly go through some more important concepts related to canned ACLs:

- The `bucket-owner-read` and `bucket-owner-full-control` canned ACLs are only applicable to objects and are ignored if specified while creating a bucket.
- The `log-delivery-write` canned ACL only applies to a bucket.
- With the `aws-exec-read` canned ACL, the owner gets the `FULL_CONTROL` permission and Amazon EC2 gets `READ` access to an **Amazon Machine Image** (**AMI**) from S3.
- With the `log-delivery-write` canned ACL, the `LogDelivery` group gets `WRITE` and `READ_ACP` permissions for the bucket. This is used for S3 access logging.
- When making an API call, we can specify a canned ACL in our request using the `x-amz-acl` request header.

Comparing ACLs, bucket policies, and IAM policies

ACLs differ from IAM policies and bucket policies in the following ways:

- ACLs provide only basic read/write permission to buckets, objects, and their ACLs. IAM policies and bucket policies provide more fine-grained permissions than ACLs.
- ACLs can only grant access to AWS accounts and predefined groups. ACLs cannot grant permissions to IAM users. IAM policies and bucket policies can be used to grant access to IAM users.
- ACLs, by default, allow full control to the owner of the resource and nothing to everyone else. Bucket policies and IAM policies are not attached to a resource by default.
- ACLs can only grant permissions. Bucket policies and IAM policies can explicitly deny access.
- ACLs cannot conditionally allow or deny access. Bucket policies and IAM policies can conditionally allow or deny access.
- ACLs are represented internally as XML documents. Bucket policies and IAM policies are represented as JSON documents, and the maximum size of such a JSON document is 20 KB.

IAM policies differ from ACLs and bucket policies in the following ways:

- IAM policies are user-based and are applied to users. ACLs and bucket policies are resource-based policies and are applied to resources.
- IAM policies can be inline (embedded directly into a user, group, or role) or standalone (can be attached to any IAM user, group, or role). ACLs and bucket policies are sub-resources of a bucket.
- IAM policies can only give access to an IAM user. Bucket policies and ACLs can be used to provide anonymous access as well as access to a root user.

We can mix ACLs, bucket policies, and IAM policies. All policies are evaluated at the same time if the bucket and user are within the same account.

See also

- You can read about IAM policies in the *Creating IAM policies* recipe in `Chapter 1`, *Managing AWS Accounts with IAM and Organizations*.

Creating an S3 bucket policy

In this recipe, we will learn to create bucket policies for our S3 buckets. Whenever possible, it is preferable to use a bucket policy or IAM policy instead of ACLs. The choice between bucket and IAM policies is mostly a personal preference. We can also create bucket policies using prefixes. S3 is an object store with no concept of folders, but prefixes can be used to imitate folders. Prefixes can represent objects as well.

Getting ready

We need a working AWS account with following resources configured:

1. **A bucket and a file in it**: I will be using a bucket name `awsseccookbook` with a file named `image-heartin-k.png`. Replace them with your bucket name and filename.
2. **A user with no permission and a user with administrator permission**: Configure CLI profiles for these users. I will be calling users and their profiles `testuser` and `awssecadmin`, respectively.

3. Uncheck the two **Block all public access** settings related to bucket policies. Leave the the other settings checked, as shown in the following screenshot, and click **Save**:

☐ **Block *all* public access**
Turning this setting on is the same as turning on all four settings below. Each of the following settings are independent of one

☑ **Block public access to buckets and objects granted through *new* access control lists (ACLs)**
S3 will block public access permissions applied to newly added buckets or objects, and prevent the creation of new public permissions that allow public access to S3 resources using ACLs.

☑ **Block public access to buckets and objects granted through *any* access control lists (ACLs)**
S3 will ignore all ACLs that grant public access to buckets and objects.

☐ **Block public access to buckets and objects granted through *new* public bucket policies**
S3 will block new bucket policies that grant public access to buckets and objects. This setting doesn't change any existing

☐ **Block public and cross-account access to buckets and objects through *any* public bucket policies**
S3 will ignore public and cross-account access for buckets with policies that grant public access to buckets and objects.

4. Verify that your bucket does not allow listing for everyone by going to the bucket URL from the browser.

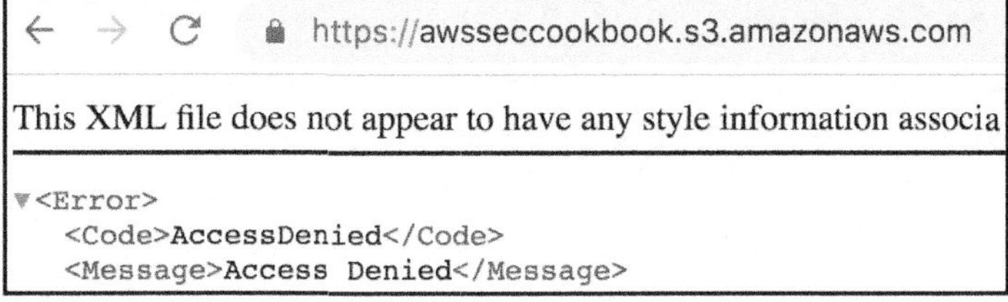

Next, we will use bucket policies to give permissions to everyone to list the contents of our bucket and then retry this step.

How to do it...

We will first generate a policy from the console using the policy generator. Later, we will execute the policy from the CLI.

Bucket public access with a bucket policy from the console

We can give public access to list the contents of a bucket as follows:

1. Go to the S3 service in the console, click on your bucket's name, go to the **Permissions** tab, and then go to **Bucket Policy**.
2. Click on **Policy generator** in the lower-left corner.
3. Within **Policy generator**, select/enter data as follows:
    - Select **Type of Policy** as **Bucket Policy**.
    - Select **Principal** as `*`.
    - Select **AWS Service** as **Amazon S3**.
    - Select **Actions** as **ListBucket**.
    - Select **Amazon Resource Name (ARN)** as `arn:aws:s3:::awsseccookbook`.
4. Click on **Add Conditions (Optional)**.
5. Click **Add Condition** and enter the following:
    - **Condition** as **DateLessThan**
    - **Key** as **aws:EpochTime**
    - **Value** as a future date in epoch format (for example, `1609415999`)
6. Click **Add Condition**.
7. Click **Add Statement**.
8. Click **Generate Policy**. The policy should look similar to the following. I have changed the `Sid` to a meaningful name:

```
{
    "Id": "Policy1560413644620",
    "Version": "2012-10-17",
    "Statement": [
        {
            "Sid": "ListBucketPermissionForAll",
            "Action": [
                "s3:ListBucket"
              ],
            "Effect": "Allow",
            "Resource": "arn:aws:s3:::awsseccookbook",
            "Condition": {
                "DateLessThan": {
                    "aws:EpochTime": "1609415999"
                }
            },
```

```
                    "Principal": "*"
                }
            ]
        }
```

9. Copy and paste the policy from the policy generator into the bucket policy editor, and click **Save**. The contents of the bucket should now be listed:

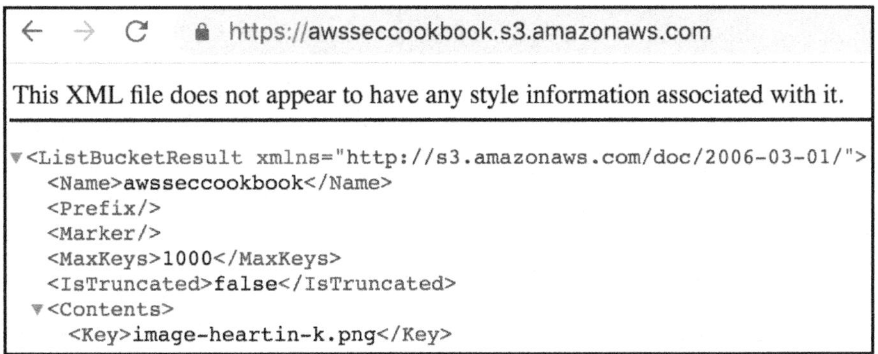

10. In the bucket policy, change the value of `Action` to `s3:GetObject` and `Resource` to `arn:aws:s3:::awsseccookbook/*`, and then click **Save**. Access any object from within the bucket from the browser. We should be able to successfully retrieve the object:

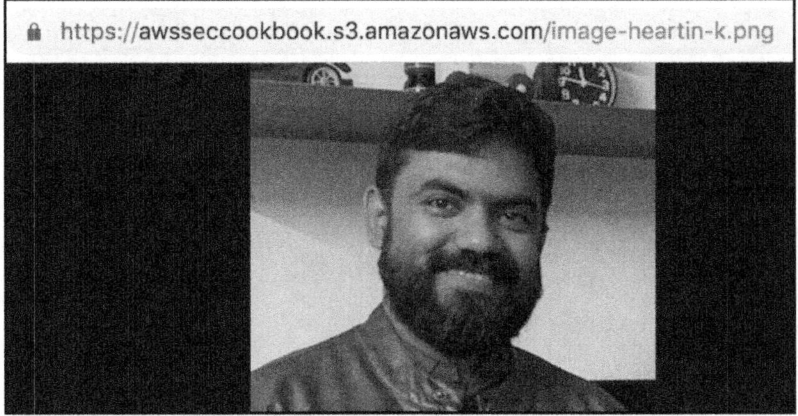

If we change the resource to `arn:aws:s3:::awsseccookbook/*` without an object operation such as `s3:GetObject`, we will get an error stating that the action does not apply to any resource. This is because, when we add any prefix to the bucket, it is considered an object operation and we have not defined any object operations yet.

Bucket list access with a bucket policy from the CLI

In this section, we will see how to add a bucket policy from the CLI:

1. If you are following along from the previous section, remove the bucket policy that was added. Verify that you do not have access to list the bucket or get the object from the browser.
2. Create a bucket policy to allow our test user to access it and save it as `bucket-policy-allow-test-user.json`:

```
{
    "Id": "Policy1560416549842",
    "Version": "2012-10-17",
    "Statement": [
        {
            "Sid": "ListAllBuckets",
            "Action": [
                "s3:ListBucket"
            ],
            "Effect": "Allow",
            "Resource": "arn:aws:s3:::awsseccookbook",
            "Principal": {
                "AWS":
"arn:aws:iam::135301570106:user/testuser"
            }
        }
    ]
}
```

The condition element is an optional element.

3. Attach the policy to the bucket:

```
aws s3api put-bucket-policy \
 --bucket awsseccookbook \
 --policy file://resources/bucket-policy-allow-test-user.json \
 --profile awssecadmin
```

4. List the contents of the bucket using the `testuser` user from the command line, as shown in the following screenshot:

```
$ aws s3 ls awsseccookbook     --profile testuser
2019-06-12 21:08:05     155335 image-heartin-k.png
```

Now that you have seen how to create policies from the console and the CLI, practice more scenarios with each of the available actions and conditions.

How it works...

In this recipe, we created S3 bucket policies. A bucket policy statement can have the following components: **Sid**, **Principal**, **Effect**, **Action**, **Resource**, and **Condition**. All of these except **Principal** are the same as an IAM policy and we explored them in the *Creating IAM policies* recipe in `Chapter 1`, *Managing AWS Accounts with IAM and Organizations.*

Principal for a bucket policy can be an account, user, or everyone (denoted by `*`). Principals can contain an ARN for a resource (specified using the **ARN** element) or a canonical ID (specified using the **CanonicalUser** element).

Resource in the case of a bucket policy is a bucket or object and is denoted using a bucket ARN. The bucket ARN should be in the form: `arn:aws:s3:::bucket_name`. An object resource is represented in the form: `arn:aws:s3:::bucket_name/key_name`. To denote all objects within a bucket, we can use `arn:aws:s3:::bucket_name/*`. We can denote every resource in every bucket as `arn:aws:s3:::*`.

Conditions allow us to conditionally execute policies. We used conditions in one of the examples. We will see further practical uses of conditions in the next recipe.

There's more...

Bucket policies follow the same JSON document structure as IAM policies, but have an additional principal field. The principal is the user or entity for which a policy statement is applicable. There is no principal for an IAM policy as it is attached to an IAM user. The IAM user who executes that policy is the principal in the case of an IAM policy.

Consider the following examples when using `Principal` in bucket policies:

- A root user can be represented as follows:

```
"Principal" : {
    "AWS": "arn:aws:iam::135301570106:root"
}
```

- An IAM user can be represented as follows:

```
"Principal" : {
    "AWS": "arn:aws:iam::135301570106:user/testuser"
}
```

- A canonical user ID can be represented as follows:

```
"Principal" : {
"CanonicalUser":"5df5b6014ae606808dcb64208aa09e4f19931b3123456e
152c4dfa52d38bf8fd"
}
```

  Canonical IDs were used in the previous recipe, *Creating S3 access control lists.*

- An anonymous user can be represented as follows:

```
"Principal" : "*"
```

Let's quickly go through some more important details relating to S3 bucket policies:

- Currently, we have around 50 bucket policy actions, including those that work on an object (for example, `s3:PutObject`), a bucket (for example, `s3:CreateBucket`), or a bucket sub-resource (for example, `PutBucketAcl`).
- The current list of bucket sub-resources with permissions includes **BucketPolicy**, **BucketWebsite**, **AccelerateConfiguration**, **BucketAcl**, **BucketCORS**, **BucketLocation**, **BucketLogging**, **BucketNotification**, **BucketObjectLockConfiguration**, **BucketPolicyStatus**, **BucketPublicAccessBlock**, **BucketRequestPayment**, **BucketTagging**, **BucketVersioning**, **EncryptionConfiguration**, **InventoryConfiguration**, **LifecycleConfiguration**, **MetricsConfiguration**, **ReplicationConfiguration**, and **AnalyticsConfiguration**.
- We cannot specify an IAM group as a principal in an S3 bucket policy. If we add a group instead of a user, we will get an error: `Invalid principal in policy`.

- Here are some S3-specific condition keys available for use in conditions within a policy: `s3:x-amz-acl`, `s3:x-amz-copy-source`, `s3:x-amz-metadata-directive`, `s3:x-amz-server-side-encryption`, `s3:VersionId`, `s3:LocationConstraint`, `s3:delimiter`, `s3:max-keys`, `s3:prefix`, `s3:x-amz-server-side-encryption-aws-kms-key-id`, `s3:ExistingObjectTag/<tag-key>`, `s3:RequestObjectTagKeys`, `s3:RequestObjectTag/<tag-key>`, `s3:object-lock-remaining-retention-days`, `s3:object-lock-mode`, `s3:object-lock-retain-until-date`, and `s3:object-lock-legal-hold`.

See also

- You can read about IAM policies in the *Creating IAM policies* recipe in `Chapter 1`, *Managing AWS Accounts with IAM and Organizations*.
- For a detailed comparison of ACLs, bucket policies, and IAM policies, refer to the *There's more* section in the *Creating S3 access control lists* recipe.

S3 cross-account access from the CLI

In this recipe, we will allow cross-account access to a bucket in one account (let's call this account A) to users in another account (let's call this account B), both through ACLs and bucket policies. Logging is a common use case for cross-account access. We can store our logs in a different account to provide access to an auditor or to secure them in case the account is compromised.

Getting ready

We need two working AWS accounts (let's call them account A and account B), configured as follows:

1. **Note down the canonical ID of account B**: I have noted down mine as `e280db54f21834544a8162b8fc5d23851972d31e1ae3560240156fa14d66b952`.
2. **A bucket in account A with a file in it**: I will be using a bucket name `awsseccookbook`, with a file named `image-heartin-k.png`. Replace them with your bucket name and filename.

3. **A user with administrator permission in account A and account B**: We'll create profiles for these users in the CLI. I am using the `awssecadmin` and `awschild1admin` CLI profiles, respectively.
4. **A user or group with no permission in account B**: I have created a group, `testusergroup`, and added the `testuser` user to the group. I will call this user's CLI profile `child1_testuser`.

Verify that both the administrator user and the non-administrator user from account B have no permission to upload to the bucket in account A.

We can make use of the AWS Organizations service to manage multiple accounts and switch between them with ease.

How to do it...

We will implement cross-account access using CLI commands. You can follow the CLI commands and the tips provided within the following recipe to implement the cross-account access in the console or by using APIs.

Uploading to a bucket in another account

Perform the following steps to upload files as a user from account B to a bucket in account A:

1. Create an access control policy document that grants access to account B and save it as `acl-write-another-account.json`:

```
{
  "Owner": {
    "DisplayName": "awsseccookbook",
    "ID":
"5df5b6014ae606808dcb64208aa09e4f19931b3123456e152c4dfa52d38bf8
fd"
  },
  "Grants": [
    {
      "Grantee": {
        "Type": "CanonicalUser",
        "ID":
"e280db54f21834544a8162b8fc5d23851972d31e1ae3560240156fa14d66b9
```

```
52"
            },
            "Permission": "WRITE"
        }
    ]
}
```

The canonical ID of account A is provided under the `Owner` section, and the canonical ID of account B is provided under the `Grants` section.

2. Update the ACL on the bucket owned by account A, as an administrator of account A:

```
aws s3api put-bucket-acl \
    --bucket awsseccookbook \
    --access-control-policy file://resources/acl-write-another-
account.json \
    --profile awssecadmin
```

We should now be able to upload objects to the bucket as an administrator from account B. However, a non-administrator from account B will not be able to upload files:

```
$ aws s3 cp image-heartin-k.png s3://awsseccookbook/image-from-b-admin.png \
>     --profile awschild1admin
upload: ./image-heartin-k.png to s3://awsseccookbook/image-from-b-admin.png
$
$ aws s3 cp image-heartin-k.png s3://awsseccookbook/image-from-b-user.png \
>     --profile child1_testuser
upload failed: ./image-heartin-k.png to s3://awsseccookbook/image-from-b-user.png An
error occurred (AccessDenied) when calling the PutObject operation: Access Denied
```

To grant permissions from the console, go to the bucket's ACL, click **Add account**, enter the canonical ID, and give the required permissions.

3. Create a policy to delegate `s3:PutObject` access and the `s3:PutObjectAcl` action to administrator users in account B, and save this file as `iam-policy-s3-put-obj-and-acl.json`:

```
{
  "Version": "2012-10-17",
  "Statement": [
    {
      "Sid": "DelegateS3WriteAccess",
```

```
            "Effect": "Allow",
            "Action": [
              "s3:PutObject",
              "s3:PutObjectAcl"
            ],
            "Resource": "arn:aws:s3:::awsseccookbook/*"
          }
        ]
      }
```

The `s3:PutObjectAcl` action is required to use canned ACLs later.

4. Create a policy in account B using the preceding policy document as an administrator in account B:

```
aws iam create-policy \
    --policy-name MyS3PutObjAndAclPolicy \
    --policy-document file://resources/iam-policy-s3-put-obj-
and-acl.json \
    --profile awschild1admin
```

We should get a response as follows:


```
{
    "Policy": {
        "PolicyName": "MyS3PutObjAndAclPolicy",
        "PolicyId": "ANPAVRI4OAA52LAMKDSEE",
        "Arn": "arn:aws:iam::380701114427:policy/MyS3PutObjAndAclPolicy",
        "Path": "/",
        "DefaultVersionId": "v1",
        "AttachmentCount": 0,
        "PermissionsBoundaryUsageCount": 0,
        "IsAttachable": true,
        "CreateDate": "2019-06-14T00:07:38Z",
        "UpdateDate": "2019-06-14T00:07:38Z"
    }
}
```

5. Attach the preceding policy to the test user's group:

```
aws iam attach-group-policy \
    --group-name testusergroup \
    --policy-arn
arn:aws:iam::380701114427:policy/MyS3PutObjAndAclPolicy \
    --profile awschild1admin
```

We may also attach the policy directly to the user instead; however, using a group is a recommended practice.

6. Upload the object to the bucket as a non-administrator user in account B:

```
aws s3 cp image-heartin-k.png s3://awsseccookbook/image-from-b-
user.png \
    --profile child1_testuser
```

We should be able to upload the file successfully.

If we try to download the object as an administrator in account A, the request will fail as follows:

```
$ aws s3 cp s3://awsseccookbook/image-from-b-user.png image-from-b.json \
>     --profile awssecadmin
fatal error: An error occurred (403) when calling the HeadObject operation: Forbidden
```

7. Upload the object to the bucket as a user in account B with the `bucket-owner-full-control` canned ACL:

```
aws s3 cp image-heartin-k.png s3://awsseccookbook/image-from-b-
user.png \
    --acl bucket-owner-full-control \
    --profile child1_testuser
```

Account A should now be able to download the file successfully:

```
$ aws s3 cp s3://awsseccookbook/image-from-b-user.png image-from-b.json \
>     --profile awssecadmin
download: s3://awsseccookbook/image-from-b-user.png to ./image-from-b.json
```

In the next section, we will learn to enforce the situation whereby account B should always give this permission to account A, with the bucket owner using bucket policies.

Uploading to a bucket in another account with a bucket policy

If you followed along with the previous section, remove the ACL granted on account A before proceeding with the following steps:

1. Create a bucket policy that explicitly allows our non-administrator user, `testuser`, from account B to perform a `PutObject` action. Also, make sure that the user gives full control to the bucket owner through a canned ACL. Save the file as `bucket-policy-write-another-account-user.json`:

```
{
  "Id": "SomeUniqueId1",
  "Version": "2012-10-17",
  "Statement": [
    {
      "Sid": "AllPutForOtherAccountUser",
      "Action": [
        "s3:PutObject"
      ],
      "Effect": "Allow",
      "Resource": "arn:aws:s3:::awsseccookbook/*",
      "Condition": {
        "StringEquals": {"s3:x-amz-acl":"bucket-owner-full-
control"}
      },
      "Principal": {
        "AWS": [
          "arn:aws:iam::380701114427:user/testuser"
        ]
      }
    }
  ]
}
```

2. Attach the bucket policy to the bucket:

```
aws s3api put-bucket-policy \
 --bucket awsseccookbook \
 --policy file://resources/bucket-policy-write-another-account-
user.json \
 --profile awssecadmin
```

3. Attach a policy in account B to the non-administrator user, `testuser`, which allows the `s3:PutObject` and `s3:PutObjectAcl` actions. This step has already been performed in the previous section. If you haven't already done this in the previous section (or if you deleted the policy), work through the previous section to complete it.

4. Upload image as `testuser` from account B to a bucket in account A with and without canned ACLs:

```
$ aws s3 cp image-heartin-k.png s3://awsseccookbook/image-from-b-user.png \
>     --profile child1_testuser
upload failed: ./image-heartin-k.png to s3://awsseccookbook/image-from-b-user.png An
 error occurred (AccessDenied) when calling the PutObject operation: Access Denied
$
$ aws s3 cp image-heartin-k.png s3://awsseccookbook/image-from-b-user.png \
>     --acl bucket-owner-full-control \
>     --profile child1_testuser
upload: ./image-heartin-k.png to s3://awsseccookbook/image-from-b-user.png
```

Here, we used a bucket policy to ensure that the user from account B provides full control to the bucket owner in account A using canned ACLs; otherwise the upload will fail.

How it works...

In the *Uploading to a bucket in another account* section, we first granted permissions to account B through a policy in account A. Later, the account B administrator delegated the permission to an administrator user through the user's group. We also saw that the account A administrator won't have access to an object uploaded by the user of account B, even though account A is the bucket owner, unless account B explicitly grants permission.

For account A to have access, the user of account B should grant permission while uploading the file, and this can be done using canned ACLs. An account B user with `s3:PutObjectAcl` permission can grant permission to account A, the bucket owner, using the `bucket-owner-read` or `bucket-owner-full-control` canned ACLs. With ACLs, there is no way to enforce a constraint, such as that account B should always give permission to account A, the bucket owner. This can, however, be enforced with bucket policies.

In the *Uploading to a bucket in another account with a bucket policy* section, we directly gave permission to the account B user through a bucket policy. We also added a `Condition` element to our bucket policy to ensure that the user in account B should always use the `bucket-owner-full-control` ACL to give complete control to account A, the bucket owner. The `s3:PutObjectAcl` permission is required for account B to specify a canned ACL.

There's more...

Account A can grant access to its S3 resources to account B in one of the following ways:

- The account A administrator grants access to account B through a bucket policy or ACL. The account B administrator delegates that permission to a user using a user policy. The user in account B can then access the S3 resources in account A according to the permissions granted to them. In this recipe, we followed this approach using ACL in the *Uploading to a bucket in another account* section, and the same is also possible with a bucket policy.
- The account A administrator grants access directly to a user in account B through a bucket policy. The account B administrator still has to delegate permission to the user using a policy. The user in account B can then access the S3 resources in account A according to the permissions granted to them. In this recipe, we followed this approach in the *Uploading to a bucket in another account with a bucket policy* section.
- The account A administrator creates a role with the required permissions to its S3 resources in account A. The role will have a trust relationship with account B as a trusted entity and account A as the trusting entity. The account B administrator delegates that permission to a user using user policy. The user in account B can then assume that role and access the S3 resources in account A in accordance with the permissions granted to them. We saw a variation of IAM role-based, cross-account access in `Chapter 1`, *Managing AWS Accounts with IAM and Organizations*, in the *Switching role with AWS organizations* recipe.

Let's quickly go through some scenarios to understand cross-account policies better:

- Account A created a bucket and gave `PutObject` ACL permissions to everyone (public access):
    - Can a user from the same AWS account with no permissions (no policies attached) upload a file to that bucket from the AWS CLI? *Yes.*

    - Can a user from another AWS account with no permissions (no policies attached) upload a file to that bucket from the AWS CLI? *No.*
    - Can an administrator user from another AWS account upload a file to that bucket from the AWS CLI? *Yes.*
- Account A created a bucket and gave `PutObject` ACL permissions to account B using the account's canonical ID:
    - Can a user with no permissions (no policies attached) from account B upload a file to that bucket from the AWS CLI? *No.*
    - Can an administrator user from account B upload a file to that bucket from the AWS CLI? *Yes.*
- Account B uploaded a file to account A with cross-account access and no canned ACL (equivalent to the canned private ACL).
    - Can a user with no permissions (no policies attached) from the bucket owner account read that object? *No.*
    - Can an administrator user from the bucket owner account read that object? *No.*
    - Can an administrator user from the bucket owner account delete that object? *Yes.*
- Account A created a bucket and gave the `PutObject` permission directly to a user, `testuser`, in account B through a bucket policy.
    - Can `testuser` upload to a bucket in account A without additional permissions in account B? *No, they still need to have the* `PutObject` permission to the bucket assigned through a user policy within account B.
    - Can an administrator in account B upload to a bucket in account A? *No, we have explicitly granted permission to* `testuser`.
- Can the account B administrator delegate more access to its users than it was granted by account A? *This will not result in an error, but it will not have any impact as the permissions will be evaluated again from account A.*
- Can we enforce the usage of canned ACL through a bucket policy? *Yes, using a condition that checks the value of the* `s3:x-amz-acl` condition key, *for example, for the* `bucket-owner-full-control` value.

See also

- We saw a variation of IAM role-based, cross-account access in `Chapter 1`, *Managing AWS Accounts with IAM and Organizations*, in the *Switching Role with AWS Organizations* recipe.

S3 pre-signed URLs with an expiry time using the CLI and Python

In this recipe, we will learn to use pre-signed URLs from the CLI and then via the Python SDK. We can grant temporary permission to access S3 objects using pre-signed URLs with an expiry time. Currently, we cannot do this from the console. We have to do it through APIs from the CLI or by using an SDK.

Getting ready

We need a working AWS account with the following resources configured:

1. **A bucket and a file in it**: I will be using a bucket name `awsseccookbook` with a file named `mission-impossible.txt`. Replace them with your bucket name and filename.
2. **A user with administrator permission on S3**: We will configure a CLI profile for this user. I will be calling both the user and the CLI profile `awssecadmin`.

To execute the Python code, we need to install Python and Boto3 in the following order:

1. Install `python3`.
2. Install `boto3` (if `pip3` is installed, you can install `boto3` as follows:

```
pip3 install boto3
```

How to do it...

We will first create a pre-signed URL from the CLI and then use the Python SDK.

Generating a pre-signed URL from the CLI

We can create a pre-signed URL from the CLI and test it as follows:

1. Pre-sign a URL from the CLI as follows:

```
aws s3 presign s3://awsseccookbook/image-heartin-k.png \
    --expiry 100 \
    --profile awssecadmin
```

   This command will output a signed URL with an expiry time:

```
$ aws s3 presign s3://awsseccookbook/mission-impossible.txt \
>     --expires-in 300 \
>     --profile awssecadmin
https://awsseccookbook.s3.amazonaws.com/mission-impossible.txt?AWSAccessKeyId=AKIAR7
AE2DY5NZX6NNPN&Signature=VwQ61zSbRipJlvXxWK1K6RkZ8No%3D&Expires=1560483746
```

2. Copy and paste the URL and run it from a browser within the specified time. We should be able to see the contents of our file:

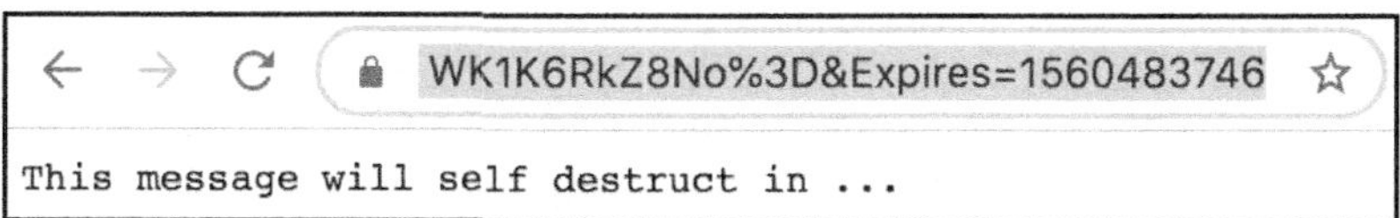

   If we run the URL after the specified time, we should get an *access denied* error message:

Next, we will look at how to do pre-signing using the Python SDK.

Generating a pre-signed URL using the Python SDK

We can create a pre-signed URL using the Python SDK and test it as follows:

1. Create a file named `s3presign.py` with the following code:

```
import boto3

boto3.setup_default_session(profile_name='awssecadmin')
s3_client = boto3.client('s3')

url = s3_client.generate_presigned_url('get_object',
Params={'Bucket': 'awsseccookbook', 'Key': 'mission-
impossible.txt'}, ExpiresIn=300)
print(url)
```

2. Execute the code as `python3 s3presign.py`:

   This will return the pre-signed URL:

```
$ python3 s3presign.py
https://awsseccookbook.s3.amazonaws.com/mission-impossible.txt?AWSAccessKeyId=AK
IAR7AE2DY5NZX6NNPN&Signature=w4GajRADHtU7neiHy4eMxAOBcZk%3D&Expires=1560491940
```

Run the URL from a browser (much as we did in the previous section) before and after the specified time.

How it works...

In the *Generating a pre-signed URL from the CLI* section, we pre-signed a URL from the CLI. In the *Generating a pre-signed URL using the Python SDK* section, we pre-signed a URL using the Python SDK. We used the `boto3` library for our Python SDK demo. Boto is the AWS SDK for Python. It facilitates the creation, configuration, and management of AWS services, such as EC2 and S3 using Python.

Most APIs related to pre-signing will accept the following data for generating pre-signed, timed URLs:

- Bucket and object
- Expiry date and time
- HTTP method
- Security credentials

In this recipe, we specified the bucket, object, and expiry in code. The HTTP operation was `GET`. For security credentials, we specified a user profile that has permissions for the operation, which was `get_object` in our case. Anyone with valid credentials can generate a pre-signed URL. However, if the user does not have permission to perform the intended operation (for example, `get_object`), then the operation will eventually fail.

There's more...

In this recipe, we generated pre-signed URLs using both CLI commands and Python code. The following code snippet shows how pre-signing can be done from Java:

```
GeneratePresignedUrlRequest generatePresignedUrlRequest = new
    GeneratePresignedUrlRequest(bucketName, objectKey)
         .withMethod(HttpMethod.PUT)
         .withExpiration(expiration);
 URL url = s3Client.generatePresignedUrl(generatePresignedUrlRequest);
```

You can follow the AWS documentation to do the same with other supported SDKs as well.

See also

- Refer to the following link for more use cases for Python and Boto3 related to pre-signed URLs: `https://boto3.amazonaws.com/v1/documentation/api/latest/guide/s3-presigned-urls.html`.

Encrypting data on S3

In this recipe, we will learn to encrypt data on S3 at rest using server-side encryption techniques. Encryption on the server side can be done in three ways: server-side encryption with S3-managed keys (SSE-S3), server-side encryption with KMS-managed keys (SSE-KMS), and server-side encryption with customer-provided keys (SSE-C). In client-side encryption, data is encrypted on the client side and then sent to the server.

Getting ready

We need a working AWS account with the following resources configured:

1. **A bucket**: I will be using a bucket with the name `awsseccookbook`. Replace it with your bucket name.
2. **A user with administrator permission on S3**: Configure a CLI profile for this user. I will be calling both the user and the profile on the `awssecadmin` CLI.
3. **A customer-managed key created in KMS**: Follow the *Creating keys in KMS* recipe in `Chapter 4`, *Key Management with KMS and CloudHSM*, to create a key. I have created one named `MyS3Key`.

How to do it...

In this recipe, we will learn about various use cases for server-side encryption.

Server-side encryption with S3-managed keys (SSE-S3)

We can upload an object from the console with SSE-S3 as follows:

1. Go to the S3 bucket.
2. Click **Upload**, click **Add Files**, select your file, and then click **Next**, selecting the defaults in the **Set Properties** tab.
3. In the **Set Properties** tab, scroll down and select **Amazon S3 master key** under **Encryption**. Follow the on-screen options to complete the upload. We can verify this from the object's properties:

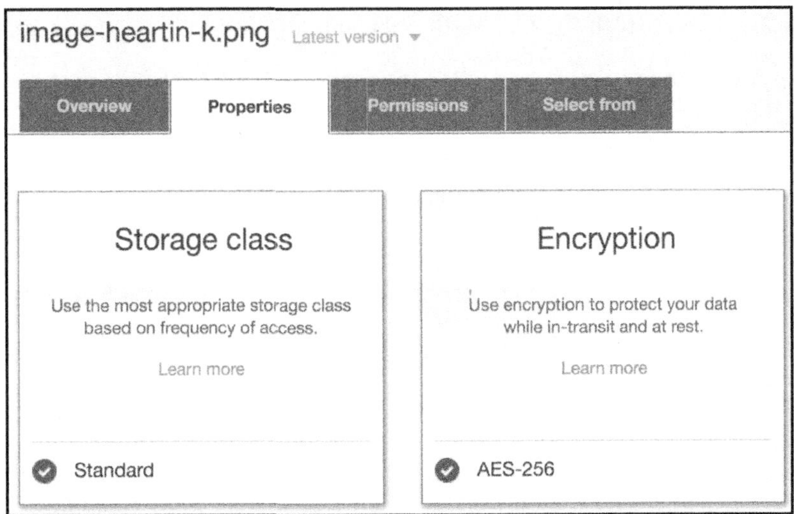

It is important to note that, if we try to open or download the object, we will still be able to see the object as-is because S3 will decrypt the object using the same key.

We can change encryption for an existing object to SSE-S3 as follows:

1. Go to the object's **Properties** tab.
2. Go to **Encryption**, select **AES-256**, and then click **Save**:

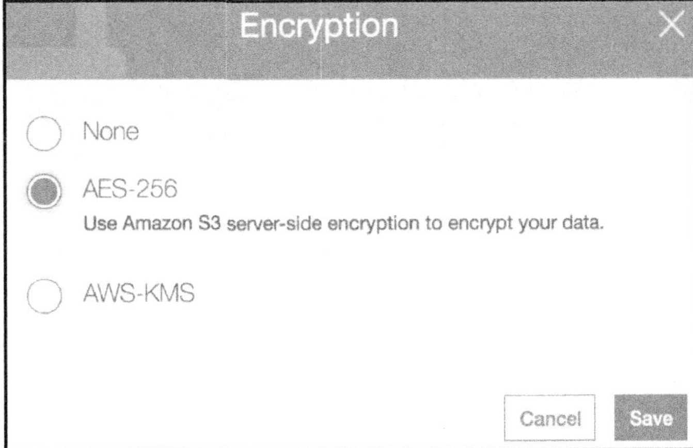

We can upload an object from the CLI with SSE-S3 using the following command:

```
aws s3 cp image-heartin-k.png s3://awsseccookbook/image-heartin-k.png \
--sse AES256 \
--profile awssecadmin
```

Next, we will execute SSE with KMS managed keys.

Server-side encryption with KMS-managed keys (SSE-KMS)

We can upload an object from the console with SSE-KMS as follows:

1. Go to the bucket.
2. Click **Upload**, click **Add Files**, select your file, and then click **Next**, selecting the defaults in the **Set Properties** tab.
3. In the **Set Properties** tab, scroll down, select **AWS KMS master key**, and then select our KMS key (refer to the *Getting ready* section). Follow the options on the screen to complete the upload:

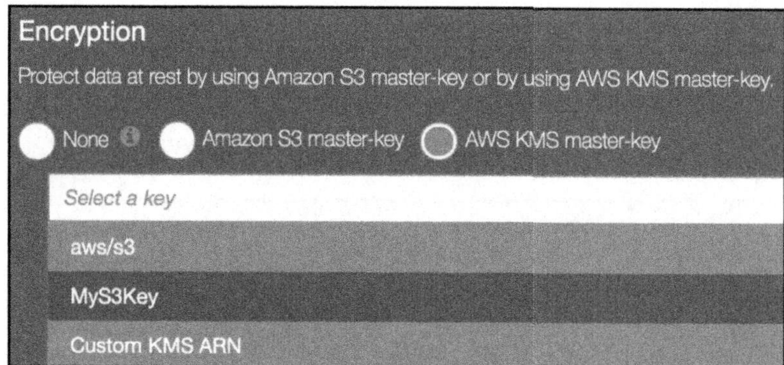

We can change encryption for an existing object to SSE-KMS as follows:

1. Go to the object's **Properties** tab.
2. Go to **Encryption**, select **AWS-KMS**, then select your KMS key (refer to the *Getting ready* section), and then click **Save**:

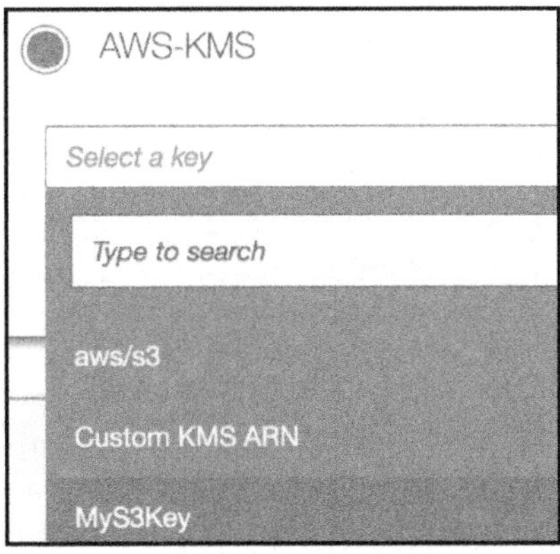

We can upload an object from the CLI with SSE-KMS using the following command:

```
aws s3 cp image-heartin-k.png s3://awsseccookbook/image-heartin-k.png \
--sse aws:kms \
--sse-kms-key-id cd6b3dff-cfe1-45c2-b4f8-b3555d5086df \
--profile awssecadmin
```

`sse-kms-key-id` is the ID of the KMS key you created (refer to the *Getting ready* section).

Server-side encryption with customer-managed keys (SSE-C)

We can upload an object from the CLI with SSE-C as follows:

1. Upload an object from the CLI with SSE-C by using the following command:

```
aws s3 cp image-heartin-k.png s3://awsseccookbook/image-
heartin-k.png \
--sse-c AES256 \
--sse-c-key 12345678901234567890123456789012 \
--profile awssecadmin
```

2. Retrieve the object encrypted using SSE-C, providing the same key we used in the previous command, as follows:

```
aws s3 cp s3://awsseccookbook/image-heartin-k.png image-
heartin-k1.png \
--sse-c AES256 \
--sse-c-key 12345678901234567890123456789012 \
--profile awssecadmin
```

If we do not specify the `sse-c` option while downloading an object encrypted with SSE-C, we will get an exception as follows: *fatal error: An error occurred (400) when calling the HeadObject operation: Bad Request.* If we do not specify the correct key that was used for encryption (using the `sse-c-key` option) while downloading an object encrypted with SSE-C, we will get an exception as follows: *fatal error: An error occurred (403) when calling the HeadObject operation: Forbidden.*

How it works...

In the *Server-side encryption with S3-managed keys (SSE-S3)* section, we uploaded an object from the console with SSE-S3 encryption. We changed the encryption for an existing object to SSE-S3 encryption. We also uploaded an object with SSE-S3 encryption. When performing SSE-S3 encryption from the CLI, the value of the `sse` parameter is optional. The default is `AES256`.

In the *Server-side encryption with KMS-managed keys (SSE-KMS)* section, we uploaded an object with SSE-KMS encryption. We changed encryption for an existing object to SSE-KMS encryption. We also uploaded an object from the CLI with SSE-KMS encryption. When performing SSE-KMS encryption from the CLI, the value of the `sse-c` parameter is optional. The default is `AES256`.

In the *Server-side encryption with customer-managed keys (SSE-C)* section, we uploaded an object from the CLI with SSE-C encryption. Unlike the other two server-side encryption techniques `SSE-S3` and `SSE-KMS`, the console does not currently have an explicit option for SSE-C. We will need to execute this using APIs. In this recipe, we used a 32-digit number as the key. However, in the real world, keys are generally generated using a key generation tool. We will learn more about keys when we discuss KMS later in this book.

There's more...

Let's quickly go through some important concepts related to S3 encryption:

- Data on S3 can be encrypted while at rest (stored on AWS disks) or in transit (moving to and from S3). Encryption at rest can be done using server-side encryption or by uploading encrypted data from the client.
- S3 server-side encryption techniques for data at rest use symmetric keys for encryption.
- Encryption of data in transit using SSL/TLS (HTTPS) uses asymmetric keys for encryption.
- S3 default encryption (available as bucket properties) provides a way to set the default encryption behavior for an S3 bucket with SSE-S3 or SSE-KMS. Enabling this property does not affect existing objects in our bucket, and applies only for new objects uploaded.
- With client-side encryption, we need to manage keys on our own. We can also use KMS to manage keys through SDKs. However, it is not currently supported by all SDKs.
- Encryption in transit can be achieved with client-side encryption or by using SSL/TLS (HTTPS).
- Server-side encryption types, SSE-S3 and SSE-KMS, follow envelope encryption, while SSE-C does not use envelope encryption.
- Some important features of SSE-S3 include the following:
    - AWS takes care of all key management.
    - It follows envelope encryption.
    - It uses symmetric keys to encrypt data.
    - Each object is encrypted with a unique key.
    - It uses the AES-256 algorithm.
    - A data key is encrypted with a master key that is automatically rotated periodically.
    - It is free.
- Some important features of SSE-KMS include the following:
    - Keys are managed by AWS KMS.
    - Keys can be shared by multiple services (including S3).
    - As customers, we get more control over keys, such as creating master and data keys, and disabling and rotating master keys.

    - It follows envelope encryption.
    - It uses symmetric keys to encrypt data.
    - A data key is encrypted with a master key.
    - It uses the AES-256 algorithm.
    - We can choose which object key to encrypt while uploading objects.
    - We can use CloudTrail to monitor KMS API calls, enabling better auditing.
    - It is not free.
- Some important features of SSE-C include the following:
    - Keys are managed by us (customers).
    - The customer provides a key along with data. S3 uses this key for encryption and deletes the key.
    - The key must be supplied for decryption as well.
    - It does not use envelope encryption.
    - It uses symmetric keys to encrypt data.
    - It uses the AES-256 algorithm.
    - AWS will force you to use HTTPS while uploading data since you are uploading your symmetric key as well.
    - It is free.
- By default, S3 allows both HTTP and HTTPS access to data. HTTPS can be enforced with the help of a bucket policy with the following condition element:

```
"Condition": {
    "Bool": {
        "aws:SecureTransport": "false"
    }
}
```

  Any requests without HTTPS will fail with this condition.

See also

- You can read more about encryption at https://heartin.tech/en/blog-entry/important-points-remember-about-encryption.

Protecting data with versioning

In this recipe, we will learn to enable versioning on an S3 bucket. If versioning is enabled for a bucket, S3 keeps a copy of every version of the file within the bucket. Versioning protects data by providing a means to recover it in the case of unintentional actions such as deletes and overwrites.

Getting ready

We need a working AWS account with the following resources configured:

1. **A bucket**: I will be using a bucket name `awsseccookbook`. Replace it with your bucket name.
2. **A user with administrator permission on S3**: Configure a CLI profile for this user if you want to execute this recipe from the CLI. I will be calling both the user and the `awssecadmin` CLI profile.

How to do it...

We can enable versioning as follows:

1. Go to the S3 bucket's **Properties** tab, click on **Versioning**, select **Enable Versioning**, and then click **Save**.
2. Suspend versioning from the same screen by selecting **Suspend versioning** and click **Save**.

How it works...

In this recipe, we enabled and suspended versioning from the console. After we enable versioning, S3 stores every version of the object with a version ID. While making a `GET` request, we can specify the ID of the version to be returned. If you do not specify any version while making a `GET` request, S3 will return the latest version of the object.

We can restore an S3 version using either of the following ways:

- Retrieve the version we want to restore and add it to the bucket with a `PUT` request (recommended).
- Delete every version of the object available from the present version until the required version becomes the current version.

When you delete an object with versioning enabled, a delete marker is added as the latest version of the object. If you delete the delete marker, another version of the delete marker is created. We can delete a specific version of an object by specifying the version ID. When we delete a version, no delete markers are inserted.

Once versioning is enabled, it cannot be disabled, only suspended. No further versions are created when versioning is suspended. However, all previous versions will still be present. Once versioning is suspended, any new object will be stored with a `NULL` version ID and becomes the current object.

There's more...

We can enable and suspend versioning from the CLI using the `put-bucket-versioning` sub-command providing that `bucket` and `versioning-configuration`. `versioning-configuration` contain two parameters: `MFADelete`, which denotes the required state of MFA Delete (`Enabled` or `Disabled`), and `Status`, which denotes the required state of versioning (`Enabled` or `Suspended`). For versioning configuration, we can either use the shorthand form, `--versioning-configuration MFADelete=Disabled,Status=Enabled`, or we can specify a JSON file with the configuration as `--versioning-configuration file://resources/versioning-configuration.json`; the JSON file will look as follows:

```
{
  "MFADelete": "Disabled",
  "Status": "Enabled"
}
```

Complete CLI commands for enabling and suspending versioning are available with the code files.

Let's quickly go through some important concepts related to S3 versioning:

- Versioning is a sub-resource of an S3 object.
- A delete request on a suspended bucket will work as follows:
    - If there is a version with the `NULL` version ID(this is present only if the object was modified after suspending versions), it is deleted and then a delete marker with the `NULL` version ID is inserted.
    - If there is no version with the `NULL` version ID, a delete marker with the `NULL` version ID is inserted.
- We can use life cycle management rules to transition older versions to other S3 storage tiers (archives) or even delete them.
- We can protect versions by enabling MFA Delete. With MFA Delete for versioning, an extra level of authentication is required to delete versions. The MFA Delete configuration is stored within the versioning sub-resource.

Let's also quickly go through some scenario-based questions to understand versioning better:

- We enabled versioning and `PUT` the same object twice (with modifications). We then disabled versioning and `PUT` the same object twice (with modifications). How many versions of the object will now be available if you check? 3.
- We enabled versioning and `PUT` the same object twice, creating two versions as version 1 and version 2. We then disabled versioning and `PUT` the same object again, creating version 3. Later, we deleted the object. Can we restore this object? If yes, which version will be the latest? We can restore the object and the latest one following the restoration will be version 2.

See also

- You can enable MFA Delete to protect versions further by following this link: `https://docs.aws.amazon.com/AmazonS3/latest/dev/UsingMFADelete.html`.

Implementing S3 cross-region replication within the same account

In this recipe, we will learn to implement cross-region replication with S3 buckets. If cross-region replication is enabled for a bucket, the data in a bucket is asynchronously copied to a bucket in another region. Cross-region replication provides better durability for data and aids disaster recovery. Replicating data may be also done for compliance and better latency.

Getting ready

We need a working AWS account with the following resources configured:

- A user with administrator permission for S3 for a source bucket's account. I will be calling the user `awssecadmin`.
- Create two buckets, one each in two regions, with versioning enabled. I will be using the `awsseccookbook` bucket in the us-east-1 (N. Virginia) region and the `awsseccookbookmumbai` bucket in ap-south-1 (Mumbai).

How to do it...

We can enable cross-region replication from the S3 console as follows:

1. Go to the **Management** tab of your bucket and click on **Replication**.
2. Click on **Add rule** to add a rule for replication. Select **Entire bucket**. Use the defaults for the other options and click **Next**:

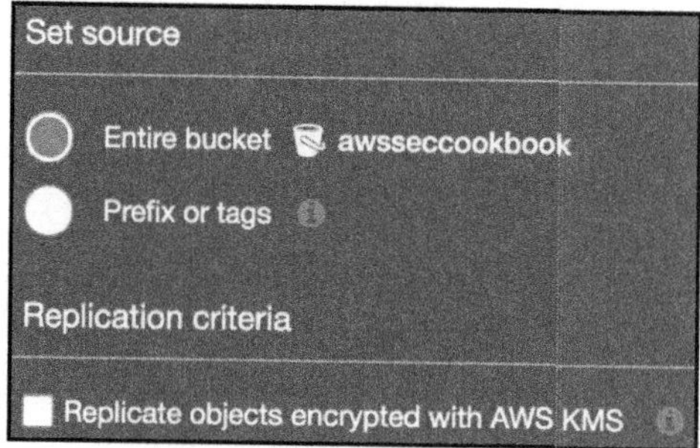

3. In the next screen, select the **Destination bucket**. Leave the other options as-is and click **Next**:

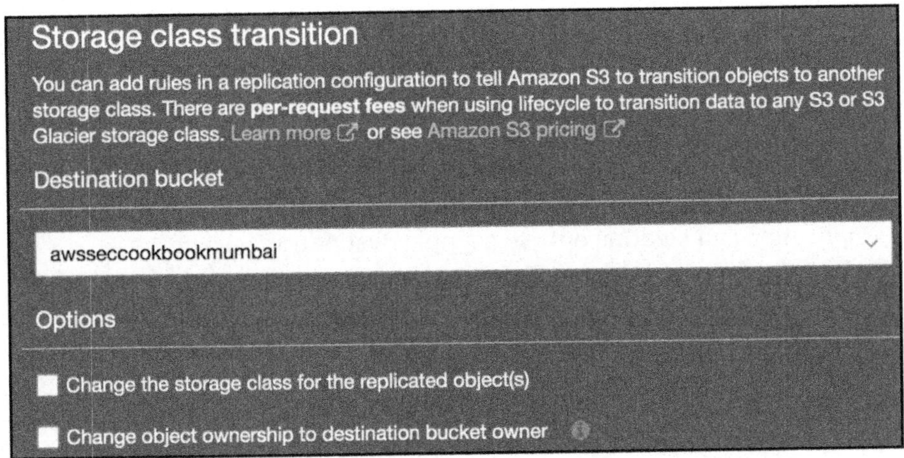

4. In the the **Configure options** screen, ask S3 to create the required IAM role, name your rule (by selecting the relevant option), and then click **Next**:

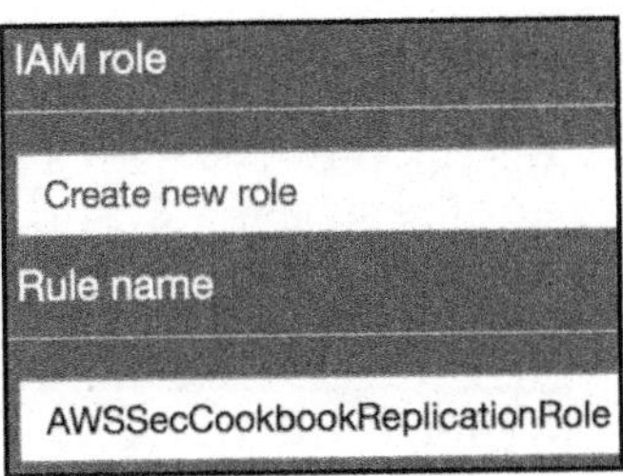

5. In the next screen, **review** the rule and click **Save**.
6. Upload an object to the source bucket and verify whether the object is replicated in the destination bucket. Also, verify that the value of the **Replication Status** field of the object in the object's **Overview** tab is **COMPLETE** once replication is completed.

The autogenerated role's permissions policy document and trust policy document are available with code files as `replication-permissions-policy.json` and `assume-role-policy.json`.

How it works...

In this recipe, we enabled cross-region replication within the same account. We replicated the entire bucket. We can also specify a subset of objects using a prefix or tags. We did not change the storage class of replicated objects in this recipe even though we can.

Here are the prerequisites for cross-region replication:

1. Source and destination buckets must be version-enabled and should be in different regions.
2. Replication can be done only to a single destination bucket.
3. S3 should have permission to replicate to a destination bucket.

We asked S3 to create the required role for replication. The autogenerated role has a permissions policy with `s3:Get*` and `s3:ListBucket` permissions on the source bucket, and `s3:ReplicateObject`, `s3:ReplicateDelete`, `s3:ReplicateTags`, and `s3:GetObjectVersionTagging` permissions on the destination bucket.

There's more...

The steps to enable cross-region replication from the CLI can be summarized as follows:

1. Create a role that can be assumed by S3, with a permissions policy with the `s3:Get*` and `s3:ListBucket` actions for the source bucket and objects, and the `s3:ReplicateObject`, `s3:ReplicateDelete`, `s3:ReplicateTags`, and `s3:GetObjectVersionTagging` actions for the destination bucket objects.
2. Create (or update) a replication configuration for the bucket using the `aws s3api put-bucket-replication` command providing a replication configuration JSON.

Complete CLI commands and policy JSON files are available with the code files.

Let's quickly go through some more details related to S3 cross-region replication:

- Cross-region replication is done via SSL.
- Only objects that were added after enabling cross-region replication are replicated.
- If the source bucket owner does not have read object or read ACL permission, objects are not replicated.

- By default, the source object's ACLs are replicated. However, changing ownership to the destination bucket owner can be configured.
- Objects with SSE-C encryption are not currently replicated.
- To replicate objects with SSE-KMS encryption, we need to provide one or more KMS keys as required for S3 to decrypt the objects. KMS requests related to S3 in the source and destination regions can cause us to exceed the KMS request limit for our account. We can request an increase in our KMS request limit from AWS.
- Since replication happens asynchronously, it might take some time (even up to hours for larger objects) to replicate.
- Sub-resource changes are not currently replicated. For example, automated life cycle management rules are not replicated. However, we can configure a change in the current storage class of the object during replication.
- We cannot replicate from a replica bucket.
- Deleting a version in the source bucket does not delete the version in the destination bucket. This adds additional protection to data. A delete marker was replicated with the old schema if `DeleteMarkerReplication` is enabled. However, the new schema does not support delete marker replication, which would prevent any delete actions from replicating.

See also

- You can read more about S3 cross-region replication here: `https://docs.aws.amazon.com/AmazonS3/latest/dev/replication.html`.

Implementing S3 cross-region replication across accounts

In this recipe, we will implement cross-region replication across accounts.

Getting ready

We need a working AWS account with the following resources configured:

- A user with administrator permission for S3 for a source bucket's account. I will be calling this user `asawssecadmin`.

- Create one bucket each in two accounts with two different regions and versioning enabled. I will be using the `awsseccookbook` bucket for the us-east-1 (N. Virginia) region in the source account and the `awsseccookbookbackupmumbai` bucket with ap-south-1 (Mumbai) in the destination account.

How to do it...

We can enable cross-region replication from the S3 console as follows:

1. Go to the **Management** tab of your bucket and click on **Replication**.
2. Click on **Add rule** to add a rule for replication. Select **Entire bucket**.

Screens that do not change for those shown in previous sections are not shown again. Refer to earlier sections if you have any doubts.

3. In the next screen, select a destination bucket from another account, providing that account's account ID, and click **Save**:

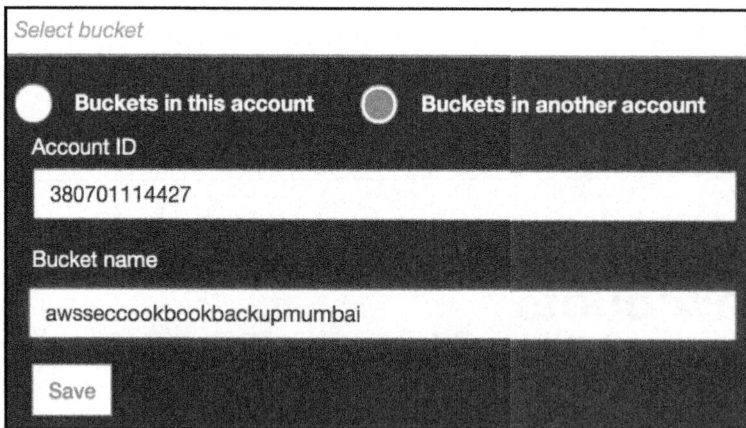

4. Select the option to change ownership of the object destination bucket owner and click **Next**:

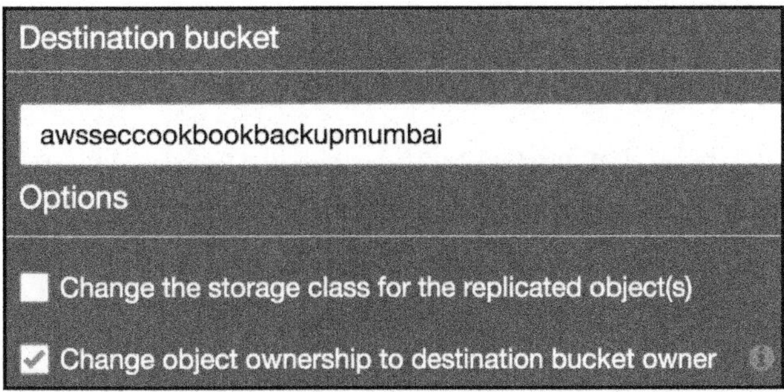

5. In the **Configure options** screen, ask S3 to create the required IAM role for replication (as we did in previous recipes). Also, copy the bucket policy that is provided by S3 and apply it to the destination bucket:

Amazon S3 requires you to put the following policy in the destination bucket.

Bucket policy Copy

```
{
    "Version": "2008-10-17",
    "Id": "S3-Console-Replication-Policy",
```

The bucket policy for the destination bucket should appear as follows:

```
{
  "Version": "2008-10-17",
  "Id": "S3-Console-Replication-Policy",
  "Statement": [
    {
      "Sid": "S3ReplicationPolicyStmt1",
      "Effect": "Allow",
      "Principal": {
        "AWS": "arn:aws:iam::135301570106:root"
      },
      "Action": [
        "s3:GetBucketVersioning",
        "s3:PutBucketVersioning",
        "s3:ReplicateObject",
        "s3:ReplicateDelete",
        "s3:ObjectOwnerOverrideToBucketOwner"
      ],
      "Resource": [
        "arn:aws:s3:::awsseccookbookbackupmumbai",
        "arn:aws:s3:::awsseccookbookbackupmumbai/*"
      ]
```

```
        }
    ]
}
```

6. Review the rule and click **Save**. The autogenerated role's permissions policy document and trust policy document are available with the code files as `replication-permissions-policy-other-account.json` and `assume-role-policy.json`, respectively.

7. Log in to the account where the destination bucket is present and update the bucket policy copied in *step 5* on the destination bucket.
8. Upload an object to the source bucket and verify whether the object is replicated in the destination bucket. Also, verify that the destination account is the owner of the uploaded file.

How it works...

We enabled cross-region replication across accounts. For general work on cross-region replication, refer to the *Implementing S3 cross-region replication within the same account* recipe. Replicating objects in another AWS account (cross-account replication) will provide additional protection for data against situations such as someone gaining illegal access to the source bucket and deleting data within the bucket and its replications.

We asked S3 to create the required role for replication. The autogenerated role has a permissions policy with `s3:Get*` and `s3:ListBucket` permissions on the source bucket, and `s3:ReplicateObject`, `s3:ReplicateDelete`, `s3:ReplicateTags`, and `s3:GetObjectVersionTagging` permissions on the destination bucket. Given that we selected the option to change object ownership to the destination bucket owner, which is required for cross-region replication across accounts, the destination policy included the `s3:ObjectOwnerOverrideToBucketOwner` action. These actions are required for owner override. Without owner override, the destination bucket account won't be able to access the replicated files or their properties.

With cross-region replication across accounts, the destination bucket in another account should also provide permissions to the source account using a bucket policy. The generated trust relationship document has `s3.amazonaws.com` as a trusted entity. The trust policy (assume role policy) allows the trusted entity to assume this role through the `sts:AssumeRole` action. Here, the trust relationship document allows the S3 service from the source account to assume this role in the destination account. For reference, the policy is provided with the code files as `assume-role-policy.json`.

There's more...

The steps to implement cross-region replication across accounts from the CLI can be summarized as follows:

1. Create a role that can be assumed by S3 and has a permissions policy with the `s3:Get*` and `s3:ListBucket` actions for the source bucket and objects, and the `s3:ReplicateObject`, `s3:ReplicateDelete`, `s3:ReplicateTags`, `s3:GetObjectVersionTagging` and `s3:ObjectOwnerOverrideToBucketOwner` actions for the destination bucket objects.
2. Create (or update) the replication configuration for the bucket using the `aws s3api put-bucket-replication` command by providing a replication configuration JSON. Use the `AccessControlTranslation` element to give ownership of the file to the destination bucket.
3. Update the bucket policy of the destination bucket with the `put-bucket-policy` sub-command.

Complete CLI commands and policy JSON files are provided with the code files for reference.

Now, let's quickly go through some more concepts and features related to securing data on S3:

- The S3 **Object Lock** property can be used to prevent an object from being deleted or overwritten. This is useful for a **Write-Once-Read-Many** (**WORM**) model.
- We can use the **Requester Pays** property so that the requester pays for requests and data transfers. While **Requester Pays** is enabled, anonymous access to this bucket is disabled.
- We can use **tags** with our buckets to track our costs against projects or other criteria.
- By enabling **Server Access Logging** for our buckets, S3 will log detailed records for requests that are made to a bucket.
- We can **log object-level API activity** using the CloudTrail data events feature. This can be enabled from the S3 bucket's properties by providing an existing CloudTrail trail from the same region.

- We can configure **Events** under bucket properties to receive notifications when an event occurs. Events can be configured based on a prefix or suffix. Supported events include `PUT`, `POST`, `COPY`, multipart upload completion, object create events, object lost in RSS, permanently deleted, delete marker created, all object delete events, restore initiation, and restore completion.
- S3 **Transfer Acceleration** is a feature that enables the secure transfer of objects over long distances between a client and a bucket.
- We can configure our bucket to allow cross-origin requests by creating a **CORS** configuration that specifies rules to identify the origins we want to allow, the HTTP methods supported for each origin, and other operation-specific information.
- We can enable **storage class analysis** for our bucket, prefix, or tags. With this feature, S3 analyzes our access patterns and suggests an age at which to transition objects to Standard-IA.
- S3 supports two types of **metrics**: the daily storage metric (free and enabled by default) and request and data transfer metrics (paid and need to be opted in to). Metrics can be filtered by bucket, storage type, prefix, object, or tag.

See also

- In this chapter, we learned about important security-related features that are present in S3. You may learn more about S3 from `https://cloudmaterials.com/en/book/amazon-s3-and-overview-other-storage-services`.

3
User Pools and Identity Pools with Cognito

In this chapter, we will learn about Amazon Cognito. Cognito is Amazon's serverless user identity management service. Amazon Cognito can be used as an identity provider and an identity broker. As an identity provider, Cognito enables us to manage our own user pools. As an identity broker, Cognito helps us to make use of other identity providers such as Amazon, Google, Facebook, and Twitter. While most other chapters in this book discuss services related to infrastructure security on AWS, this chapter focuses mostly on application security concepts such as user pools, user signups, authentication and authorization flows, and federated identity logins.

In this chapter, we will cover the following recipes:

- Creating Amazon Cognito user pools
- Creating an Amazon Cognito app client
- User creation and user signups
- Implementing an admin authentication flow
- Implementing a client-side authentication flow
- Working with Cognito groups
- Federated identity with Cognito user pools

Technical requirements

We need a working AWS account. A basic knowledge of security concepts related to user management, such as authentication and authorization, will be beneficial in understanding the recipes within this chapter.

Code files for this chapter are available at `https://github.com/PacktPublishing/AWS-Security-Cookbook/tree/master/Chapter03`.

Creating Amazon Cognito user pools

In this recipe, we will create a Cognito user pool from the console.

Getting ready

We require a working AWS account.

How to do it...

We can create a Cognito user pool from the AWS management console as follows:

1. Go to the Cognito service in the console. We should see options to manage user pools and identity pools:

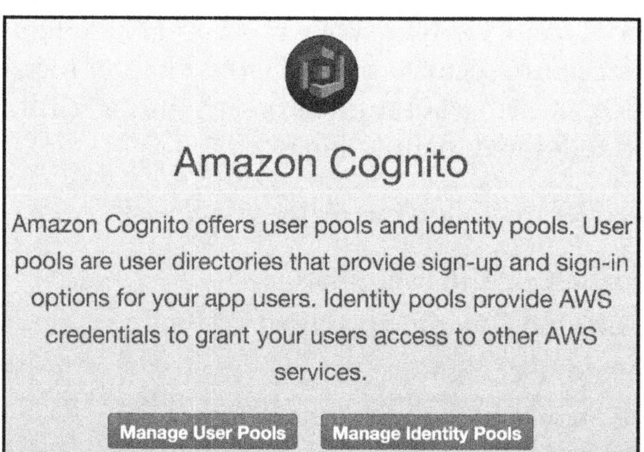

2. Click on **Manage User Pools**.
3. Click on **Create a user pool**. Currently, the console provides two ways to create a user pool: **Review defaults** (change only the ones that need to be changed) or **Step through settings** (review/change each setting one by one):

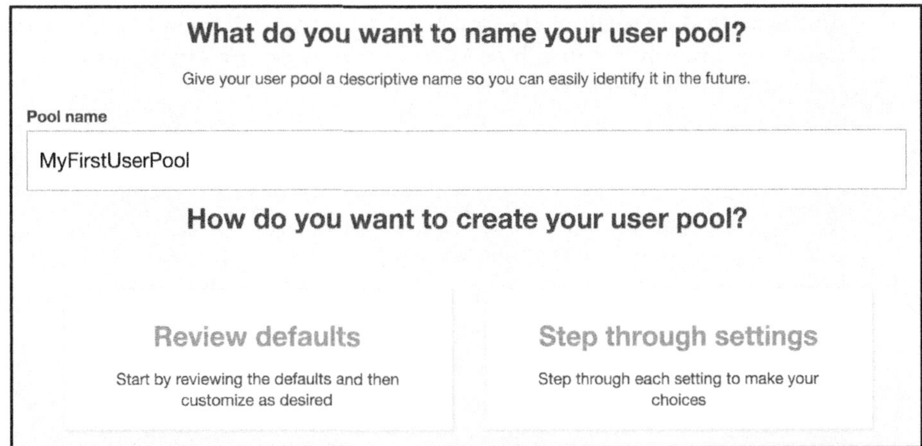

4. Provide a pool name as shown in the previous step and click on **Review defaults**. We should see sections for **Pool name**, attributes (**Required attributes**, **Alias attributes**, **Username attributes**, **Custom attributes**), password policy (**Minimum password length**, **Password policy**, **User sign ups allowed**), email settings (**FROM email address**, **Email Delivery through Amazon SES**), verification settings (**MFA**, **Verifications**), tags, app clients, and triggers. We will use the default values and selections for password settings and other sections. Refer to the *There's more...* section to see the defaults.

5. Add alias attributes that can be used alongside the username for logging in from the attributes section:

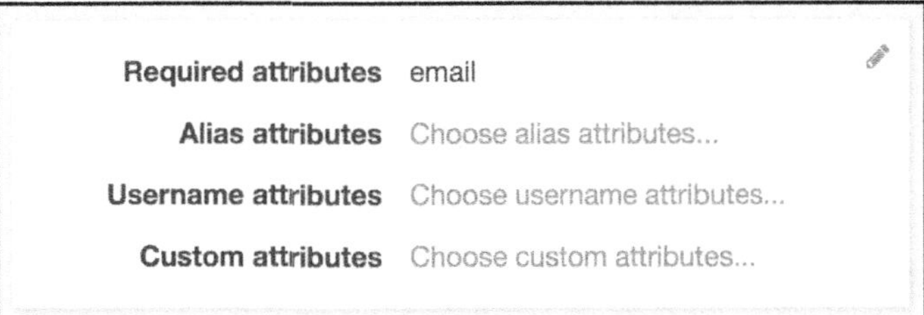

Within the attributes section, click on the edit icon or click on the **Choose alias attributes** (or any other) hyperlink to go to the configure attributes step. After that, add alias attributes as follows:

How do you want your end users to sign in?

You can choose to have users sign in with an email address, phone number, username or preferred username plus their password. Learn more.

- (●) **Username** - Users can use a username and optionally multiple alternatives to sign up and sign in.
  - [x] Also allow sign in with verified email address
  - [x] Also allow sign in with verified phone number
  - [x] Also allow sign in with preferred username (a username that your users can change)
- ( ) **Email address or phone number** - Users can use an email address or phone number as their "username" to sign up and sign in.
  - Allow email addresses
  - Allow phone numbers
  - Allow both email addresses and phone numbers (users can choose one)

6. Click on the **Next** step at the end of the page and then click **Review** from the left to see the updated attributes section in the review. It should now appear as follows:

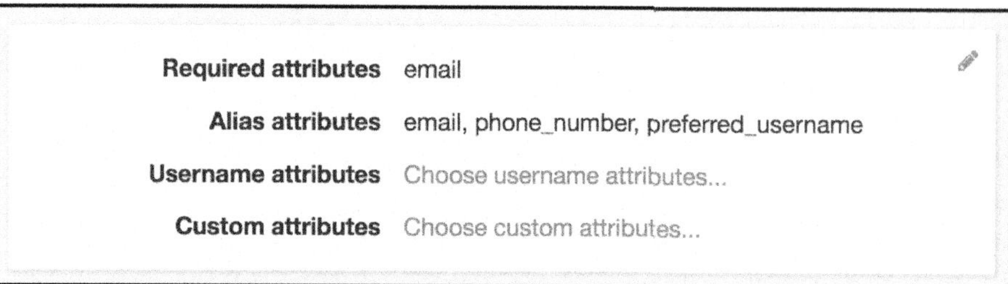

7. Click on **Create pool** to create the user pool. If successful, we should get a success message:

Your user pool was created successfully.

Since we have not configured SES to send email, we may also see a warning as follows:

FROM email address	Default
Email Delivery through Amazon SES	No
	Note: You have chosen to have Cognito send emails on your behalf. Best practices suggest that customers send emails through Amazon SES for production User Pools due to a daily email limit.
	Learn more about email best practices.

For production user pools, it is recommended sending SMS messages through Amazon SES.

8. Go to the Cognito dashboard's home, click on **Manage user pools**, and verify the user pool.

How it works...

In this recipe, we created an Amazon Cognito user pool retaining most of the defaults, but changing the user attributes' configuration. We created a few alias attributes.

By default, we can sign in using a username. We can add additional attributes as alias attributes and then use these to sign in. Allowed values for alias attributes are email, phone, or preferred username. We can also use one or both of email or phone number as the username and then use these to sign in instead of username, as shown in the following screenshot:

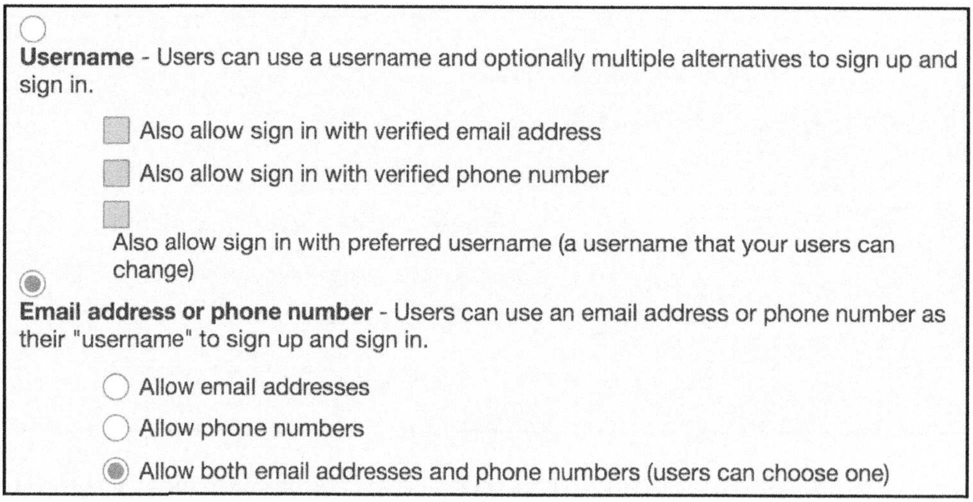

Username - Users can use a username and optionally multiple alternatives to sign up and sign in.

Also allow sign in with verified email address

Also allow sign in with verified phone number

Also allow sign in with preferred username (a username that your users can change)

Email address or phone number - Users can use an email address or phone number as their "username" to sign up and sign in.

Allow email addresses

Allow phone numbers

Allow both email addresses and phone numbers (users can choose one)

We can only specify either the alias attributes or username attributes, but not both. Within the console, this is enforced by using radio buttons. When we are using APIs (using the AWS CLI or AWS SDK), we need to make sure we specify only one of them.

There's more...

In this recipe, we selected the **Review defaults** option to create the user pool. Let's quickly go through the sections in the review page.

The pool name in our case is `MyFirstUserPool`:

Pool name MyFirstUserPool

In the attributes section, by default, **email** is selected as a **Required attributes** with no **Alias attributes**, **Username attributes**, or **Custom attributes**:

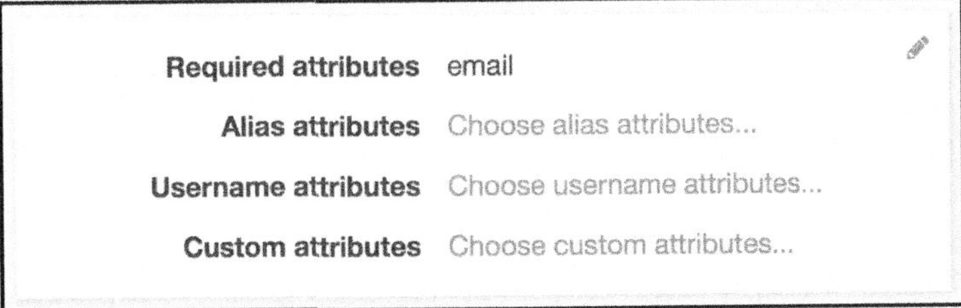

Current defaults for password settings are as follows:

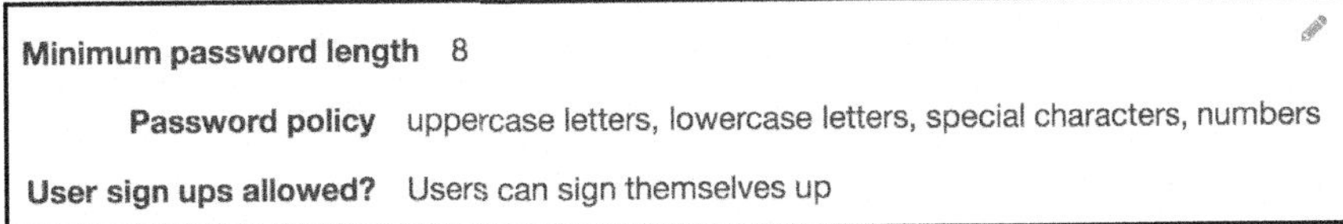

The remaining sections in the review page currently have the following values, followed by the **Create pool** button:

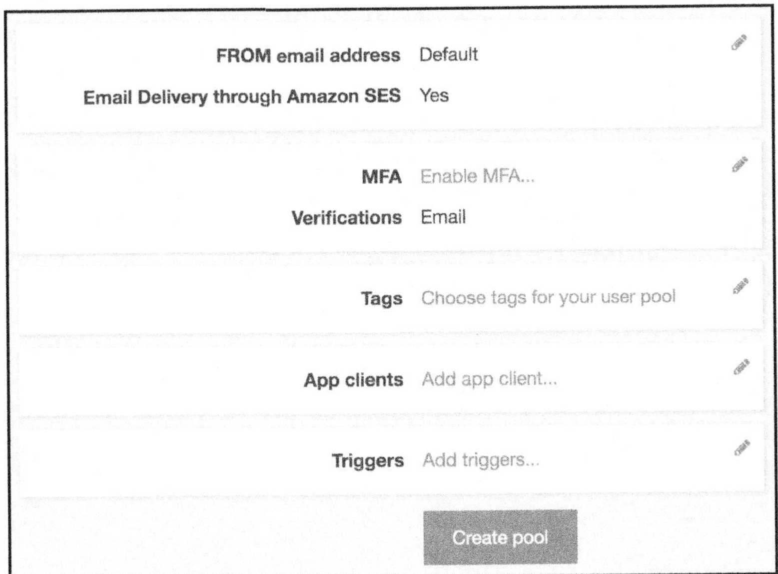

We created a user pool from the console in this recipe. We can create a user pool with default configurations with the `aws cognito-idp create-user-pool` command, passing `pool-name` and `region`.

Even though we can directly specify all user pool settings from the command line by referring to the documentation, it is an easier and safer approach to use an input JSON file with all the configurations specified. The sample input CLI JSON file for an AWS CLI command can be generated using the `generate-cli-skeleton` sub-command. We can then fill in the template and create a user pool by using the `aws cognito-idp create-user-pool` command, passing the JSON file as a `cli-input-json` parameter instead of `pool-name`. For example, we can create a user pool with email verification using the following JSON file:

```
{
  "PoolName": "MyUserPoolWithEmailVerification",
  "AutoVerifiedAttributes": [
    "email"
  ]
}
```

It is generally a good practice to add email and/or phone verification, as it allows self-confirmation of user accounts and also enables us to reset passwords if forgotten. Without any forms of verification, users will have to contact the administrators for user confirmations or password resets.

In our user pool, we executed customization of attributes only. We can do customization for other parameters from the left sidebar after selecting our user pool. The following is a list of all the current options available. Under **General Settings**, we have **Users and groups**, **Attributes**, **Policies**, **MFA and verification**, **Advanced Security**, **Message customizations**, **Tags**, **Devices**, **App clients**, **Triggers**, and **Analytics**. Under **App integration**, we have **App client settings**, **Domain name**, **UI customization**, and **Resource servers**. Under **Federation**, we have **Identity providers** and **Attribute mapping**.

See also

- You can read about basic security concepts related to user identity here: `https://cloudmaterials.com/en/blog-entry/basic-security-concepts-related-user-identity`

Creating an Amazon Cognito app client

In this recipe, we will create an app client for a user pool. An app client is needed to perform unauthenticated calls such as sign in, sign up, and forgot password. This is a small recipe, but this recipe and the previous one form the basis for further recipes in this chapter.

Getting ready

We need to create a user pool based on the *Creating Amazon Cognito user pools* recipe.

How to do it...

We can create an app client for an existing user pool as follows:

1. Go to the Amazon Cognito dashboard, click on **Manage user pools**, and then click on our user pool.

We can also create an app client when we create the user pool by going to the app client menu item in the sidebar.

2. Click on **App Client** from the sidebar.
3. Click on **Add an app client**.

4. Uncheck the **Generate client secret** option and select **ADMIN_NO_SRP_AUTH** and **USER_PASSWORD_AUTH**:

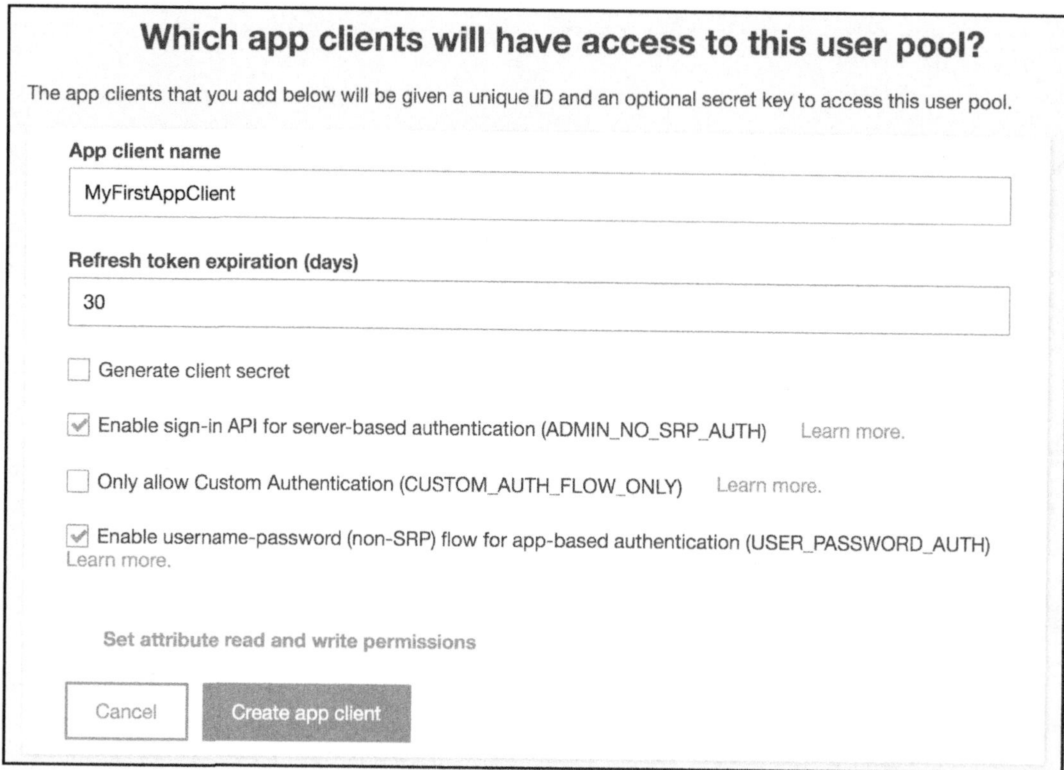

If needed, we can set attribute read and write permissions for this app client by clicking on the **Set attribute read and write permissions** link.

5. Click on **Create app client** to create the client.

How it works...

In this recipe, we created an API client with the following settings:

1. An unchecked **Generate client secret** option
2. **With Enable sign-in API for server-based authentication (ADMIN_NO_SRP_AUTH)** selected

3. With **Enable username-password (non-SRP) flow for app-based authentication (USER_PASSWORD_AUTH)** selected

There's more...

In this recipe, we created a Cognito user pool client from the console. We can also create a client from the CLI by using the `create-user-pool-client` sub-command of the `cognito-idp` CLI command.

Let's quickly go through a number of further concepts related to Cognito user authentication flows:

- Here are the different types of authentication flows supported by Cognito:
    - Client-side authentication flow
    - Server-side authentication flow
    - Custom authentication flow
    - Admin authentication flow
    - User migration authentication flow
- The custom authentication flow works with other authentication flows in parallel, unless you specify otherwise by selecting **only allow custom authentication flow** from the console while creating the app client, or through the `CUSTOM_AUTH_FLOW_ONLY` enum in the `ExplicitAuthFlows` user pool client property.
- We can customize Cognito authentication flows using AWS Lambda triggers.

Customizing workflows with triggers

We can customize Cognito workflows with AWS Lambda functions that trigger in response to various events. The following are the triggers currently available: **Pre sign-up**, **Pre authentication**, **Custom message**, **Post authentication**, **Post confirmation**, **Define Auth Challenge**, **Create Auth Challenge**, **Verify Auth Challenge Response**, **User Migration**, and **Pre Token Generation**.

We can configure AWS Lambda functions as triggers from the **Triggers** tab of our user pool:

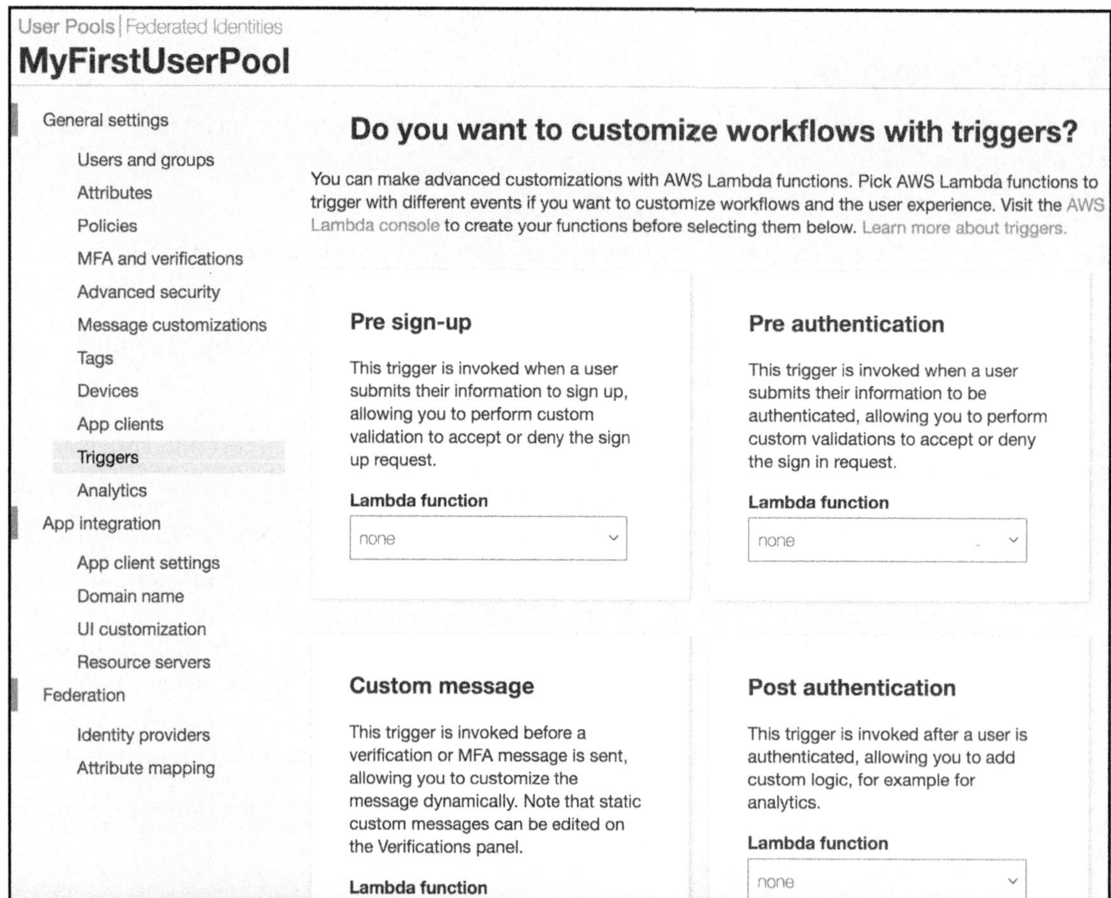

Scroll down to see more triggers:

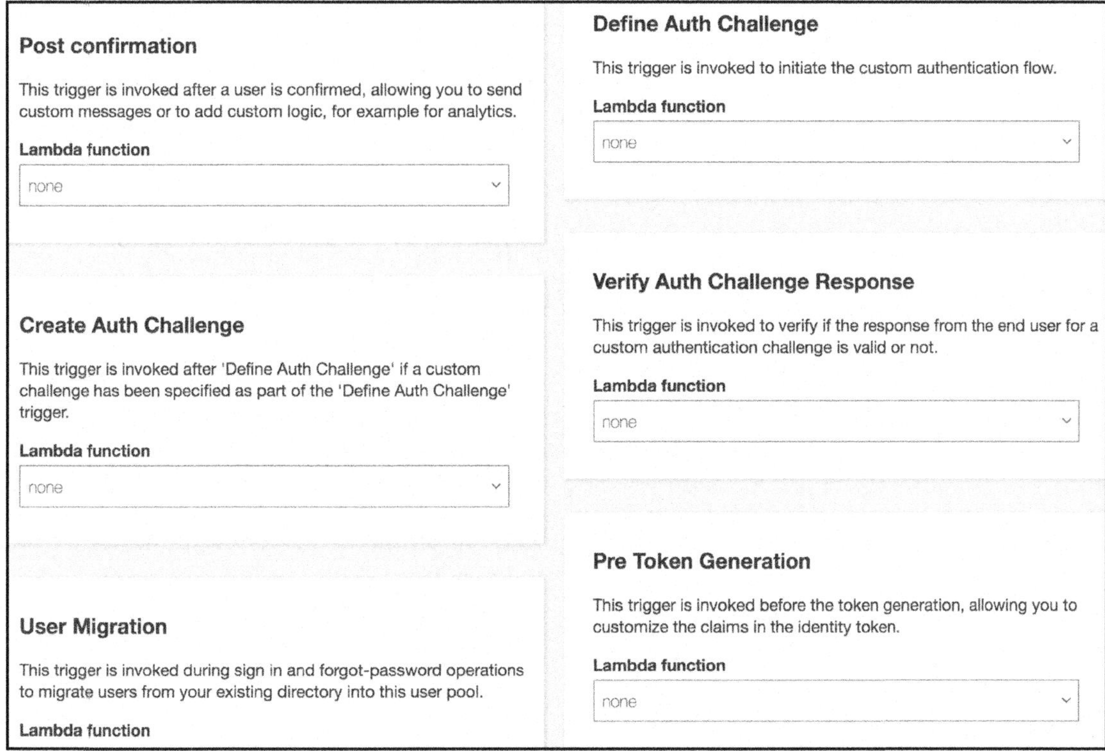

You may experiment with these triggers to improve your expertise with Cognito.

See also

- A list of supported triggers for working with Cognito identity pools can be found here: `https://docs.aws.amazon.com/cognito/latest/developerguide/cognito-user-identity-pools-working-with-aws-lambda-triggers.html`

User creation and user signups

In this recipe, we will see user creation by an administrator as well as user creation through self-signup.

Getting ready

Create a user pool with a default configuration on the basis of the *Creating Amazon Cognito user pools* recipe. Steps to create a user pool from the CLI are provided with code files. I have created a user pool with default configurations and its ID is `us-east-1_Q1cydt6I0`. Replace it with your ID within the recipe.

For user signups with self approval, we need a user pool with email verification. I have created a user pool from the CLI with email verification, as discussed within the *There's more* section of the *Creating Amazon Cognito user pools* recipe, with the ID `us-east-1_cRtc8peWU`. Replace it with your ID within the recipe.

We need an administrator user and should configure a profile in the AWS CLI for this user. I have created a user and a CLI profile with the name `awssecadmin`. Replace it with your CLI profile name within the recipe.

How to do it...

We will first create a user as an administrator and then create a user through self-signup.

Creating a user by an administrator

Create a user using `admin-create-user`, providing our admin user profile name as follows:

```
aws cognito-idp admin-create-user \
     --user-pool-id us-east-1_Q1cydt6I0 \
     --username testuser \
     --temporary-password Passw0rd$ \
     --profile awssecadmin
```

We should get the following response:


```
{
    "User": {
        "Username": "testuser",
        "Attributes": [
            {
                "Name": "sub",
                "Value": "3c309173-99f5-442f-a3c8-f533a0490259"
            }
        ],
        "UserCreateDate": 1569393053.452,
        "UserLastModifiedDate": 1569393053.452,
        "Enabled": true,
        "UserStatus": "FORCE_CHANGE_PASSWORD"
    }
}
```


In the next section, we will create a user through self-signup with admin confirmation.

Creating a user through self-signup with admin confirmation

To create users through self-signup, we need to first create an app client. An app client may be created based on the authentication flows you would like to support.

1. Create an app client by running the following command:

```
aws cognito-idp create-user-pool-client \
    --user-pool-id us-east-1_Q1cydt6I0 \
    --client-name UserPoolClientForSignUp \
    --profile awssecadmin
```

We should get back the following response:


```
{
    "ChallengeParameters": {},
    "AuthenticationResult": {
        "AccessToken": "eyJraWQiOiJKcUdKTW1TVXd4QWdZQ09YbXlcL1Z
ZDY0OTIwLTRjZmEtNGVkZi04MjNjLWYwMjczMTU0YjA2ZSIsInRva2VuX3VzZSI
C51cy1lYXN0LTEuYW1hem9uYXdzLmNvbVwvdXMtZWFzdC0xX1ExY3lkdDZJMCIs
MzOGpzZ2pnczYzYmUwY2lkcSIsInVzZXJuYW1lIjoidGVzdHVzZXIifQ.jOF7CU
CNEzHOpigX2PZo_H1cWH-QwP0oeGBYfV7IS_i18BQ4xTp8j94KBMACAbAvwx280
Kdt2Q",
        "ExpiresIn": 3600,
        "TokenType": "Bearer",
        "IdToken": "eyJraWQiOiI4QitKSndcL2tPNVV1UFVMcmpxMDg2enJ
OGpzZ2pnczYzYmUwY2lkcSIsImV2ZW50X2lkIjoiYjRkNjQ5MjAtNGNmYS00ZWR
W1hem9uYXdzLmNvbVwvdXMtZWFzdC0xX1ExY3lkdDZJMCIsImNvZ25pdG86dXNl
ENiXUS0oZ7I6EalHhQJhTJRmEDeV_FwORQjcXPUtCfUh8gXAczoXv9Ns0_gPlJe
JyBhxLsDQS4XKCa3fQpZbN_3ZYG1wFcHFph0E5mgoFhBuc0fMKA_R7drW1oeis5
    }
}
```


2. Sign up a user using the app client specified in the previous step:

```
aws cognito-idp sign-up \
    --client-id 7bb4jnd3mdva5hmkodkghrraog \
    --username testuser2 \
    --password Passw0rd$
```

We should get the following response:


```
{
    "ChallengeParameters": {},
    "AuthenticationResult": {
        "AccessToken": "eyJraWQiOiJKcUdKTW1TVXd4QWdZQ09YbXlcL1Z
ZDY0OTIwLTRjZmEtNGVkZi04MjNjLWYwMjczMTU0YjA2ZSIsInRva2VuX3VzZSI
C51cy1lYXN0LTEuYW1hem9uYXdzLmNvbVwvdXMtZWFzdC0xX1ExY3lkdDZJMCIs
MzOGpzZ2pnczYzYmUwY2lkcSIsInVzZXJuYW1lIjoidGVzdHVzZXIifQ.jOF7CU
CNEzHOpigX2PZo_H1cWH-QwP0oeGBYfV7IS_i18BQ4xTp8j94KBMACAbAvwx280
Kdt2Q",
        "ExpiresIn": 3600,
        "TokenType": "Bearer",
        "IdToken": "eyJraWQiOiI4QitKSndcL2tPNVV1UFVMcmpxMDg2enJ
OGpzZ2pnczYzYmUwY2lkcSIsImV2ZW50X2lkIjoiYjRkNjQ5MjAtNGNmYS00ZWR
W1hem9uYXdzLmNvbVwvdXMtZWFzdC0xX1ExY3lkdDZJMCIsImNvZ25pdG86dXNl
ENiXUS0oZ7I6EalHhQJhTJRmEDeV_FwORQjcXPUtCfUh8gXAczoXv9Ns0_gPlJe
JyBhxLsDQS4XKCa3fQpZbN_3ZYG1wFcHFph0E5mgoFhBuc0fMKA_R7drW1oeis5
    }
}
```

3. Confirm the user account as an admin:

```
aws cognito-idp admin-confirm-sign-up \
    --user-pool-id us-east-1_Q1cydt6I0 \
    --username testuser2 \
    --profile awssecadmin
```

We can now log in with this user using any of the authentication flows, such as admin authentication (server-side) or client-side authentication flows (using SRP or a password with a username).

Creating a user through self-signup with self-confirmation

To create a user through self-signup and self-confirmation, observe the following steps:

1. Create an app client for our user pool. The user pool should support email verification:

```
aws cognito-idp create-user-pool-client \
    --user-pool-id us-east-1_cRtc8peWU \
    --client-name UserPoolClientForSignUp \
    --profile awssecadmin
```

We should get the following response:


```
{
    "UserPoolClient": {
        "UserPoolId": "us-east-1_cRtc8peWU",
        "ClientName": "UserPoolClientForSignUp",
        "ClientId": "5r4f3tpvi026j51atur29uqlme",
        "LastModifiedDate": 1569408972.854,
        "CreationDate": 1569408972.854,
        "RefreshTokenValidity": 30,
        "AllowedOAuthFlowsUserPoolClient": false
    }
}
```

2. Create a user account through signup, providing an email:

```
aws cognito-idp sign-up \
    --client-id 5r4f3tpvi026j51atur29uqlme \
    --username testuser3 \
    --password Passw0rd$ \
    --user-attributes Name=email,Value=awsseccookbook@gmail.com
```

We should get the following response:

```
{
    "UserConfirmed": false,
    "CodeDeliveryDetails": {
        "Destination": "a***@g***.com",
        "DeliveryMedium": "EMAIL",
        "AttributeName": "email"
    },
    "UserSub": "1157998d-9f1e-4624-b3a2-fbc003a89b81"
}
```

We should also get a confirmation code via email, shown as follows:

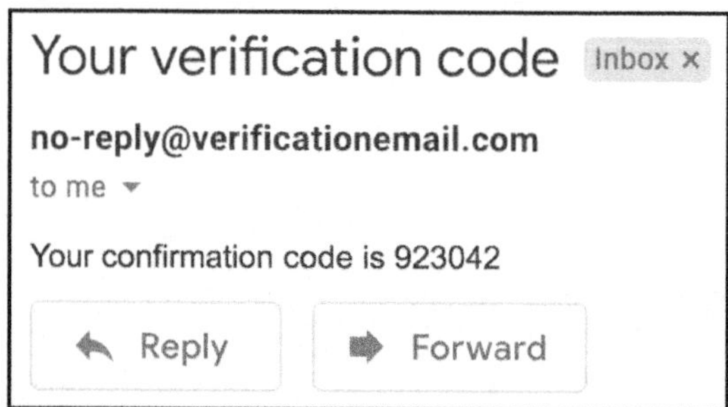

3. Self-confirm the account with the confirmation code received:

```
aws cognito-idp confirm-sign-up \
    --client-id 5r4f3tpvi026j51atur29uqlme \
    --username testuser3 \
    --confirmation-code 923042
```

We can now log in with this user using any of the authentication flows, such as admin authentication (server-side) or client-side authentication flows (using SRP or a password with a username), while using an appropriate app client.

How it works...

There is no need to specify the app client when an administrator creates or confirms a user. However, when a user does a self-signup or self-confirm, we need to use an app client of the user pool to which the user is added. Also, an administrator operation such as user creation or user approval will require AWS administrator developer credentials. However, no profile is needed for user self-signup or user self-confirmation.

When a user is created by an administrator with a temporary password, their user status is set as **FORCE_CHANGE_Status**. The user needs to change their password when next signing in. When a user signs up, the account is not confirmed until an administrator approves the account or the user self-confirms it. An email and/or password is optional when we execute admin approval. When we do self-confirmation, the parameter to be used for self-confirmation, such as email, needs to be specified.

There's more...

In this recipe, we used app clients that support only basic authentication flows. We will see some of the different authentication flows available to use with Cognito user pools in further recipes.

See also

- You can find all the supported options for the Cognito self-signup API here: `https://docs.aws.amazon.com/cli/latest/reference/cognito-idp/sign-up.html`

Implementing an admin authentication flow

In this recipe, we will implement a server-side authentication flow with admin authentication APIs from the AWS CLI with AWS developer credentials.

Getting ready

Create a user pool with a default configuration on the basis of the *Creating Amazon Cognito user pools* recipe. Steps to create a user pool from the CLI are provided with code files. I have created a user pool with default configurations whose ID is `us-east-1_Q1cydt6I0`. Replace it with your ID within the recipe.

We need an administrator user and should configure a profile in the AWS CLI for this user. I have created a user and profile with the name `awssecadmin`. Replace it with your CLI profile name within the recipe.

How to do it...

We can create a user pool client with **ADMIN_NO_SRP_AUTH** enabled and use it for server-side admin authentication flow as follows:

1. Create a user pool client with an explicit authentication flow as `ADMIN_NO_SRP_AUTH`:

```
aws cognito-idp create-user-pool-client \
    --user-pool-id us-east-1_Q1cydt6I0 \
    --client-name MyClientForServerSideFromCLI \
    --explicit-auth-flows ADMIN_NO_SRP_AUTH \
    --region us-east-1 \
    --profile awssecadmin
```

This should provide a response as follows:


```
{
    "UserPoolClient": {
        "UserPoolId": "us-east-1_Q1cydt6I0",
        "ClientName": "MyClientForServerSideFromCLI",
        "ClientId": "6c5f8dn6s38jsgjgs63be0cidq",
        "LastModifiedDate": 1569392010.067,
        "CreationDate": 1569392010.067,
        "RefreshTokenValidity": 30,
        "ExplicitAuthFlows": [
            "ADMIN_NO_SRP_AUTH"
        ],
        "AllowedOAuthFlowsUserPoolClient": false
    }
}
```

2. Create a user:

```
aws cognito-idp admin-create-user \
    --user-pool-id us-east-1_Q1cydt6I0 \
    --username testuser \
    --temporary-password Passw0rd$ \
    --profile awssecadmin
```

We should get the following response:

```
{
    "User": {
        "Username": "testuser",
        "Attributes": [
            {
                "Name": "sub",
                "Value": "3c309173-99f5-442f-a3c8-f533a0490259"
            }
        ],
        "UserCreateDate": 1569393053.452,
        "UserLastModifiedDate": 1569393053.452,
        "Enabled": true,
        "UserStatus": "FORCE_CHANGE_PASSWORD"
    }
}
```

We may also reuse a user created from the previous recipe.

3. Initiate an authentication flow as an admin:

```
aws cognito-idp admin-initiate-auth \
    --user-pool-id us-east-1_Q1cydt6I0 \
    --client-id 6c5f8dn6s38jsgjgs63be0cidq \
    --auth-flow ADMIN_NO_SRP_AUTH \
    --auth-parameters USERNAME=testuser,PASSWORD=Passw0rd$ \
    --profile awssecadmin
```

We should get the following response:


```
{
    "ChallengeName": "NEW_PASSWORD_REQUIRED",
    "Session": "N02drbF3ldLJd91x4m7_iTRYiMSy9uuKpYHgHxMGb4qX1JMM
xDYVOODUP4VxIMsCPv370IfCKqgbC4Umazkd4K99ASKyg7M00My5l490yE6dJVyN
S68enmgXkPSaFGiYFvmnvQLK7DVBO7dwHaBubGYFJYzgR7BYOkzWDRTfS3Uqr3at
IHGuKnFulYe2-1i_UuWOjfhg6dYK2JX2oGyZE6_jSiRXCEfAimTyul8jdaw6ILvk
aO9cJAq544ocAyjwJBaqM1sKmutwVhVRu_UkVKIjxyBEAzt4VHFJR1ZV06lyiyYp
    "ChallengeParameters": {
        "USER_ID_FOR_SRP": "testuser",
        "requiredAttributes": "[]",
        "userAttributes": "{}"
    }
}
```


4. Respond to the authentication challenge with a new password:

```
aws cognito-idp admin-respond-to-auth-challenge \
    --user-pool-id us-east-1_fYsb1Gyec \
    --client-id 6c5f8dn6s38jsgjgs63be0cidq \
    --challenge-name NEW_PASSWORD_REQUIRED \
    --challenge-responses
USERNAME=testuser,NEW_PASSWORD=NewPassw0rd$ \
    --session <session-id> \
    --profile awssecadmin
```

We should get back the following response:


```
{
    "ChallengeParameters": {},
    "AuthenticationResult": {
        "AccessToken": "eyJraWQiOiJKcUdKTW1TVXd4QWdZQ09YbXlcL1ZJ
ZTAwZjQ1LTdkNjUtNDM3OC04ZTBkLTJlNTE2NmM5ZDA4MyIsInRva2VuX3VzZSI6
C51cy1lYXN0LTEuYW1hem9uYXdzLmNvbVwvdXMtZWFzdC0xX1ExY3lkdDZJMCIsI
MzOGpzZ2pnczYzYmUwY2lkcSIsInVzZXJuYW1lIjoidGVzdHVzZXIifQ.lVJ3g8B
J9Bl6jk0hgDjlyXAbsH4NhOTszZUt6Us9Vxrtc1iwXI2vvK9zTJFLhlKa4460RE4
aBsRA",
        "ExpiresIn": 3600,
        "TokenType": "Bearer",
        "RefreshToken": "eyJjdHkiOiJKV1QiLCJlbmMiOiJBMjU2R0NNIiw
CvurNmt33yO6eLLy-gu29SO_DV7ArZnBHQcDbkaCr5A8PLQzPzGaZdx8EAh3Niu6
w-gAB0tsBWydcqCISRb9zgAWnvwni8QjAV4A.Sczo1GJg5xy1q243.DYSZKQxK67
ckD6A1snBHDOq2BdXaQeYPM4ocicnhoepPz9XgvyAMn7BcEKpCWHZ90hrLya040e
DZXGonrx58rbfm8bZXSh-TnaHlOZj6SJWTGV_HhEX2THvpnRy18wWGFCYlsFQGet
UcJTZeX4syWQLC9IPQgpKd9bdyeWBK1GuYyeLcWdPq-HRqhQiTFghJvFMbLTCWwX
Q8JqVuEmvWt6OxvE2f3XzL-fYkSymquMaFmbA0K8swYGv4iDUYXMrHEBAOmdki9m
OIJnICXXcjtXh8UPpBU7cDCP04uBjf1IE-716-AZO6pn55oi0K_8oqPzDSqT39ge
RCx-bkMGFMlKmrISahGEd0FPlmqhKy5Rn0-8HVsmNap2VMnEeWDThqL7ZYCfSYds
        "IdToken": "eyJraWQiOiI4QitKSndcL2tPNVV1UFVMcmpxMDg2enJs
OGpzZ2pnczYzYmUwY2lkcSIsImV2ZW50X2lkIjoiMjVlMDBmNDUtN2Q2NS00Mzc4
W1hem9uYXdzLmNvbVwvdXMtZWFzdC0xX1ExY3lkdDZJMCIsImNvZ25pdG86dXNlc
p8Hvt-32z14BcIL2vJrNygaJzmc4tG3eULqAYcjqqUeswBslv_DDtYGMKbfAITON
mCQ8pnk15zd4Hp3mrHSWtzxLp9PRNHvG4_LuJ5RT36ZU7Sp_pQ-lY7gzzSduq-xP
    }
}
```

5. Log in with your new password:

```
aws cognito-idp admin-initiate-auth \
    --user-pool-id us-east-1_Q1cydt6I0 \
    --client-id 6c5f8dn6s38jsgjgs63be0cidq \
    --auth-flow ADMIN_NO_SRP_AUTH \
    --auth-parameters USERNAME=testuser,PASSWORD=NewPassw0rd$ \
    --profile awssecadmin
```

If successful, we should get `AccessToken`, `RefreshToken`, and `IdToken`, similar to the previous command.

6. Use `RefreshToken` to generate `AccessToken`:

```
aws cognito-idp admin-initiate-auth \
    --user-pool-id us-east-1_Q1cydt6I0 \
    --client-id 6c5f8dn6s38jsgjgs63be0cidq \
    --auth-flow REFRESH_TOKEN_AUTH \
    --auth-parameters REFRESH_TOKEN=<RefreshToken> \
    --profile awssecadmin
```

We should get the following response:


```
{
    "ChallengeParameters": {},
    "AuthenticationResult": {
        "AccessToken": "eyJraWQiOiJKcUdKTW1TVXd4QWdZQ09YbXlcL1Z
ZDY0OTIwLTRjZmEtNGVkZi04MjNjLWYwMjczMTU0YjA2ZSIsInRva2VuX3VzZSI
C51cy1lYXN0LTEuYW1hem9uYXdzLmNvbVwvdXMtZWFzdC0xX1ExY3lkdDZJMCIs
MzOGpzZ2pnczYzYmUwY2lkcSIsInVzZXJuYW1lIjoidGVzdHVzZXIifQ.jOF7CU
CNEzHOpigX2PZo_H1cWH-QwP0oeGBYfV7IS_i18BQ4xTp8j94KBMACAbAvwx280
Kdt2Q",
        "ExpiresIn": 3600,
        "TokenType": "Bearer",
        "IdToken": "eyJraWQiOiI4QitKSndcL2tPNVV1UFVMcmpxMDg2enJ
OGpzZ2pnczYzYmUwY2lkcSIsImV2ZW50X2lkIjoiYjRkNjQ5MjAtNGNmYS00ZWR
W1hem9uYXdzLmNvbVwvdXMtZWFzdC0xX1ExY3lkdDZJMCIsImNvZ25pdG86dXNl
ENiXUS0oZ7I6EalHhQJhTJRmEDeV_FwORQjcXPUtCfUh8gXAczoXv9Ns0_gPlJe
JyBhxLsDQS4XKCa3fQpZbN_3ZYG1wFcHFph0E5mgoFhBuc0fMKA_R7drW1oeis5
    }
}
```

7. Perform a cleanup.

   Delete the app client:

```
aws cognito-idp delete-user-pool-client \
    --user-pool-id us-east-1_Q1cydt6I0 \
    --client-id 6c5f8dn6s38jsgjgs63be0cidq \
    --profile awssecadmin
```

   Then, delete the user:

```
aws cognito-idp admin-delete-user \
     --user-pool-id us-east-1_Q1cydt6I0 \
     --username testuser \
     --profile awssecadmin
```

If you are planning to use the app client and user pool, you may not perform the cleanup until you have finished all the recipes within this chapter.

How it works...

An admin authentication flow uses admin-specific authentication APIs and requires administrator credentials to execute. Admin APIs are generally used in secure server-side applications that are written using a server-side programming language such as Java or .Net.

By default, with no explicit authentication flows, Cognito uses SRP-based authentication. We enabled `ADMIN_NO_SRP_AUTH`, which allows admin APIs to pass a username and password without SRP.

Let's quickly go through the API commands that we used in this recipe:

- We created a user pool from the CLI using the `create-user-pool-client` sub-command.
- We created a user using the `admin-create-user` sub-command.
- We initiated the authentication flow with admin APIs using the `admin-initiate-auth` sub-command.
- We responded to authentication challenges by using the `admin-respond-to-auth-challenge` sub-command.

- Finally, we did the cleanup by deleting the user pool client using the `delete-user-pool-client` sub-command and then deleting the user using the `cognito-idp admin-delete-user` sub-command.

There's more...

SRP stands for **Secure Remote Password** (**SRP**) protocol and is a password-authenticated key agreement method for establishing cryptographic keys with one or more party's knowledge of a password. SRP-based authentication is supported by iOS-, Android-, and JavaScript-based SDKs. Currently, server-based programming language SDKs do not support SRP.

We saw three types of token within this recipe: `RefreshToken`, `AccessToken`, and `IdToken`. These tokens are in the **JSON Web Token** (**JWT**) format defined as per the **OpenID Connect** (**OIDC**) open standard. `IdToken` consist of claims about the identity of the user, including name, email, and phone number, while `AccessToken` is used to grant access to resources. While `AccessToken` and `IdToken` are short-lived, `RefreshToken` is long-lived, and is used to obtain a new `IdToken` or `AccessToken`.

See also

- You can find supported options and usage for the Cognito user pool client API at `https://docs.aws.amazon.com/cli/latest/reference/cognito-idp/create-user-pool-client.html`.

Implementing a client-side authentication flow

In this recipe, we will use client-side authentication with the non-admin APIs. We will execute this recipe from the AWS CLI with username- and password-based authentication. In a real-world app based on iOS, Android, or JavaScript, you may use SRP instead of the password.

Getting ready

Create a user pool with a default configuration on the basis of the *Creating Amazon Cognito user pools* recipe. Steps to create a user pool from the CLI are provided with code files. I have created a user pool with default configurations and its ID is `us-east-1_Q1cydt6I0`. Replace it with your ID within the recipe.

We need an administrator user and should configure a profile in the AWS CLI for this user. I have created a user and profile with the name `awssecadmin`. Replace it with your CLI profile name within the recipe.

How to do it...

We can implement client-side authentication flow from the AWS CLI with `USER_PASSWORD_AUTH` authentication flow as follows:

1. Create an app client with the authentication flow as `USER_PASSWORD_AUTH`:

```
aws cognito-idp create-user-pool-client \
    --user-pool-id us-east-1_Q1cydt6I0 \
    --client-name my-user-pool-client \
    --explicit-auth-flows USER_PASSWORD_AUTH \
    --profile awssecadmin
```

We should get the following response:

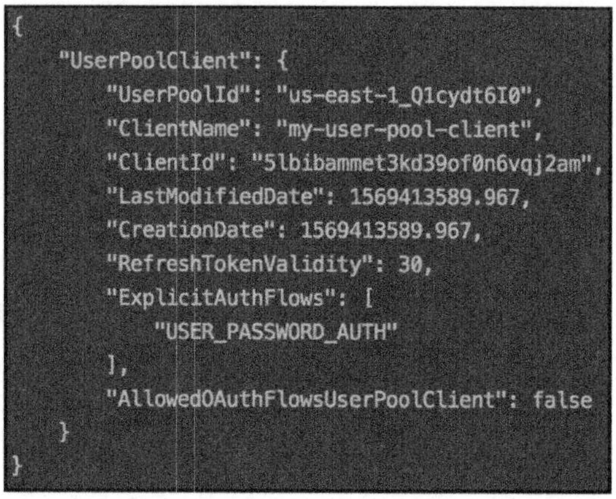

```
{
    "UserPoolClient": {
        "UserPoolId": "us-east-1_Q1cydt6I0",
        "ClientName": "my-user-pool-client",
        "ClientId": "5lbibammet3kd39of0n6vqj2am",
        "LastModifiedDate": 1569413589.967,
        "CreationDate": 1569413589.967,
        "RefreshTokenValidity": 30,
        "ExplicitAuthFlows": [
            "USER_PASSWORD_AUTH"
        ],
        "AllowedOAuthFlowsUserPoolClient": false
    }
}
```

2. Create a user:

```
aws cognito-idp admin-create-user \
    --user-pool-id us-east-1_Q1cydt6I0 \
    --username testuser4 \
    --temporary-password Passw0rd$ \
    --profile awssecadmin
```

We should get the following response:

```
{
    "User": {
        "Username": "testuser4",
        "Attributes": [
            {
                "Name": "sub",
                "Value": "68b42d94-28bb-4b0e-ad2c-33c077a66c41"
            }
        ],
        "UserCreateDate": 1569414353.672,
        "UserLastModifiedDate": 1569414353.672,
        "Enabled": true,
        "UserStatus": "FORCE_CHANGE_PASSWORD"
    }
}
```

We can create a user following any of the ways described in the *User creation and user signups* recipe.

3. Initiate an authentication flow with a username and password:

```
aws cognito-idp initiate-auth \
    --client-id 5lbibammet3kd39of0n6vqj2am \
    --auth-flow USER_PASSWORD_AUTH \
    --auth-parameters USERNAME=testuser4,PASSWORD=Passw0rd$
```

We should get the following response:

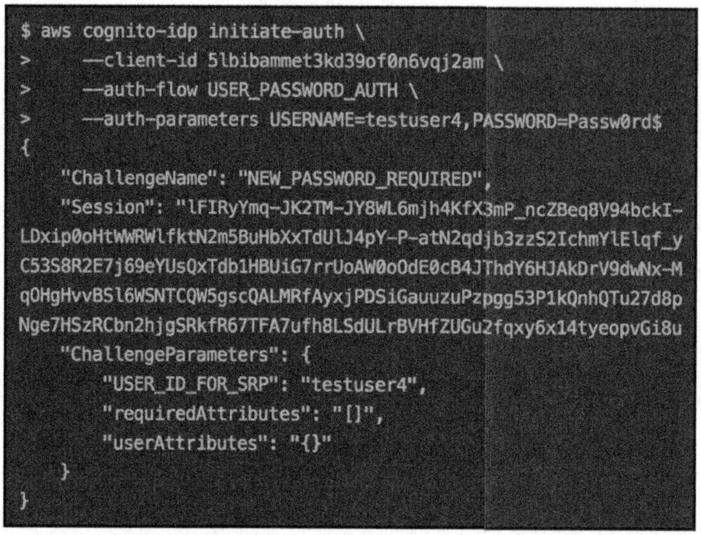

```
$ aws cognito-idp initiate-auth \
>     --client-id 5lbibammet3kd39of0n6vqj2am \
>     --auth-flow USER_PASSWORD_AUTH \
>     --auth-parameters USERNAME=testuser4,PASSWORD=Passw0rd$
{
    "ChallengeName": "NEW_PASSWORD_REQUIRED",
    "Session": "lFIRyYmq-JK2TM-JY8WL6mjh4KfX3mP_ncZBeq8V94bckI-
LDxip0oHtWWRWlfktN2m5BuHbXxTdUlJ4pY-P-atN2qdjb3zzS2IchmYlElqf_y
C53S8R2E7j69eYUsQxTdb1HBUiG7rrUoAW0oOdE0cB4JThdY6HJAkDrV9dwNx-M
qOHgHvvBSl6WSNTCQW5gscQALMRfAyxjPDSiGauuzuPzpgg53P1kQnhQTu27d8p
Nge7HSzRCbn2hjgSRkfR67TFA7ufh8LSdULrBVHfZUGu2fqxy6x14tyeopvGi8u
    "ChallengeParameters": {
        "USER_ID_FOR_SRP": "testuser4",
        "requiredAttributes": "[]",
        "userAttributes": "{}"
    }
}
```

4. Create a new password by responding to the authentication challenge:

```
aws cognito-idp respond-to-auth-challenge \
    --client-id 5lbibammet3kd39of0n6vqj2am \
    --challenge-name NEW_PASSWORD_REQUIRED \
    --challenge-responses
USERNAME=testuser4,NEW_PASSWORD=NewPassw0rd$ \
    --session <session-id>
```

Replace `session-id` with the session ID you received in the previous step. If successful, we should get the following response:

```
{
    "ChallengeParameters": {},
    "AuthenticationResult": {
        "AccessToken": "eyJraWQiOiJKcUdKTW1TVXd4QWdZQ09YbXlcL1ZJ
Yzg4OGQwLWEzY2UtNGY1My1hZmZiLTBhOTc2NzIwYTQzYyIsInRva2VuX3VzZSI6
C51cy1lYXN0LTEuYW1hem9uYXdzLmNvbVwvdXMtZWFzdC0xX1ExY3lkdDZJMCIsI
V0M2tkMzlvZjBuNnZxajJhbSIsInVzZXJuYW1lIjoidGVzdHVzZXI0In0.dPnt-P
0drrxVduUo4eudJd7XT2M1DG6t0sfE7qRILpCsoC_bHtTrQ7IbATMFtK7WlPZIZJ
9Izt5g",
        "ExpiresIn": 3600,
        "TokenType": "Bearer",
        "RefreshToken": "eyJjdHkiOiJKV1QiLCJlbmMiOiJBMjU2R0NNIiw
j3s6SX8o_A6jdVi3CySi1oMnz5bqei_6nvKpKbV2TXlJJwtaqABjQDdh9Qz45g7s
38ujBbi6Fx1fypA5MmL6NsQS8SaN-rP1Pbqg.Js9-D0V7mszVjDmA.LerhS1x1HR
ILCxeGBGRby-4UlcnM9VR_UVGllATWNzIbL-kfmfJjoKgh4pW7jiwnKlr4rNgW50
h0hg7XAlI1ezq0FECPNyhJd2THqWrQ5r7UNu_PDShAuRH-QZzWqs6IQnzCC5FoLe
uRj_OBPhMrX8QrNyTPc-w5eiaZy5AnPw2ip2-12fzOYzH6EBADNUli07MvL6iloe
E1bOBrMGhdHQOicOYiVaaYeZKurTd63qKq4_5e1siwiPn32nS8blrEZDW2hUfr_f
P1LM7NcqeNrvOj3EISKAgLC_Qzm_6uoxWtPQwrCHeZ_OWXbkdzZ_yLYD_hQz6Cwz
fApv6aEa_HJCKkCfMQt0Y9Jh_EkFGfkBvGl_9vMN2NKgt10gs0Do5u_-eseiYrMP
        "IdToken": "eyJraWQiOiI4QitKSndcL2tPNVV1UFVMcmpxMDg2enJs
M2tkMzlvZjBuNnZxajJhbSIsImV2ZW50X2lkIjoiNWNjODg4ZDAtYTNjZS00ZjUz
W1hem9uYXdzLmNvbVwvdXMtZWFzdC0xX1ExY3lkdDZJMCIsImNvZ25pdG86dXNlc
H6HfTzNwDtxNvRIQjnLJSQ4LIRlGWfG5ofjfuLNvKfYSYUkqv7hLp8-339uCE1uY
QZk04LUVu3yXIIPBI3qAAAtXRNxLPwqV3aZkJyqCRpddw2O9q9SJPHKuHzzyidTT
    }
}
```

We may use the refresh token to generate other tokens, as we saw in the previous recipe.

5. Sign in using the new username and password:

```
aws cognito-idp initiate-auth \
    --client-id 5lbibammet3kd39of0n6vqj2am \
    --auth-flow USER_PASSWORD_AUTH \
    --auth-parameters USERNAME=testuser4,PASSWORD=NewPassw0rd$
```

We should get `AccessToken`, `RefreshToken`, and `IdToken` as per the previous step. You may also clean up the user and app client, as we saw in the previous recipe.

How it works...

In this recipe, we first created an app client with the authentication flow as `USER_PASSWORD_AUTH` using the `create-user-pool-client` sub-command. Next, we created the user using administrator credentials with the `admin-create-user` sub-command. You may use a user created through self-signup as well.

After that, we initiated the authentication flow using the `initiate-auth` sub-command. As we saw, the forced change in the password is required when users are created using admin APIs. Therefore, we changed the password using the `respond-to-auth-challenge` sub-command. We also signed in using the new username and password.

There's more...

We can use Amazon Cognito SDK for iOS, Android, or JavaScript standalone for developing client-side apps. We could also make use of Amazon Amplify, which is a framework that combines many other frameworks and SDKs for developing client-side applications on iOS, Android, web, or React platforms.

See also

- More details regarding Cognito client-side authentication flow scan be found here: `https://docs.aws.amazon.com/cognito/latest/developerguide/amazon-cognito-user-pools-authentication-flow.html#amazon-cognito-user-pools-client-side-authentication-flow`
- Read more about AWS Amplify here: `https://aws.amazon.com/amplify`

Working with Cognito groups

In this recipe, we will create two groups and assign users to those groups.

Getting ready

Create a user pool with a default configuration on the basis of the *Creating Amazon Cognito user pools* recipe. Steps to create a user pool from the CLI are provided with code files. I have created a user pool with default configurations and its ID is `us-east-1_Q1cydt6I0`. Replace it with your ID within the recipe.

We require an administrator user and should configure a profile in the AWS CLI for this user. I have created a user and profile with the name `awssecadmin`. Replace it with your CLI profile name within the recipe.

We require three users: `testuser1`, `testuser2`, and `testuser3`. We can create the users from the console or from the CLI on the basis of previous recipes within this chapter.

How to do it...

We will create groups from the console and assign users to the groups by following these steps:

1. Go to the Cognito dashboard and then go to our user pool.
2. Click on **Users and groups**.
3. Click on the **Groups** tab.
4. Click on **Create group**.
5. Enter **Name**, **Description**, and then click on **Create group**:

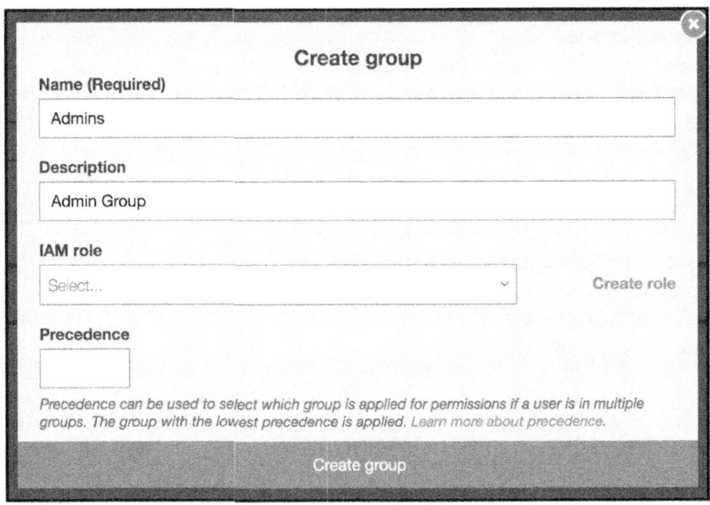

6. Create another group called `CAdmins` and its description as `Content Admins`.
7. Click on the **Admins** group from the list of groups.
8. Click on **Add user** and add `testuser1` using the plus(+) button.
9. Click on **Add user** and add `testuser2` using the plus(+) button.
10. Go back and click on the `CAdmins` group from the list of groups.
11. Click on **Add user** and add `testuser2` using the plus(+) button.
12. Click on **Add user** and add `testuser3` using the plus(+) button.

How it works...

We can categorize users into groups with Amazon Cognito user pools. A single user can be part of multiple groups. We can also go within the user console and click on **Add to group** to add the user to a group.

In this recipe, we created groups without associating any role. In the real world, the groups can be associated with an AWS role and provide selective access to AWS services. Within our applications, we can have custom roles or permissions based on these group names.

There's more...

In this recipe, we created groups from the console. We can also create groups from the CLI using the following command:

```
aws cognito-idp create-group \
    --group-name 'Admins' \
    --user-pool-id us-east-1_Q1cydt6I0 \
    --description 'Admins Group' \
    --profile awssecadmin
```

We can add a user to a group from the CLI with the following command:

```
aws cognito-idp admin-add-user-to-group \
    --user-pool-id us-east-1_Q1cydt6I0 \
    --username testuser4 \
    --group-name Admins \
    --profile awssecadmin
```

We can list the groups for a user as follows:

```
aws cognito-idp admin-list-groups-for-user \
    --username testuser4 \
    --user-pool-id us-east-1_Q1cydt6I0 \
    --profile awssecadmin
```

This will give a response similar to the one shown here:

```
{
    "Groups": [
        {
            "GroupName": "Admins",
            "UserPoolId": "us-east-1_Q1cydt6I0",
            "Description": "Admin Group",
            "LastModifiedDate": 1569428801.371,
            "CreationDate": 1569428801.371
        },
        {
            "GroupName": "CAdmins",
            "UserPoolId": "us-east-1_Q1cydt6I0",
            "Description": "Content Admins",
            "LastModifiedDate": 1569429006.324,
            "CreationDate": 1569429006.324
        }
    ]
}
```

From the application, we can check for a user's groups and then provide special privileges.

See also

- More details about Cognito user pool groups can be found here: `https://docs.aws.amazon.com/cognito/latest/developerguide/cognito-user-pools-user-groups.html`

Federated identity with Cognito user pools

In this recipe, we will log in to our application using Amazon credentials. We can do the same with other supported providers such as Facebook, Google, and Twitter. While the steps within Cognito will be similar to all the providers, configurations that have to be done at the provider side may be different for different providers. Nevertheless, working with one provider will help us to improve our understanding of the complete process.

Getting ready

We need a working AWS account and an account with an AWS developer portal.

How to do it...

We need to first create a security profile ID for our application through the Amazon developer portal and then do the configurations within Cognito using that ID.

Configuring within the Amazon developer portal

We can create a security profile ID for our application as follows:

1. Log in to `https://developer.amazon.com/loginwithamazon/console/site/lwa/overview.html` using our AWS credentials:

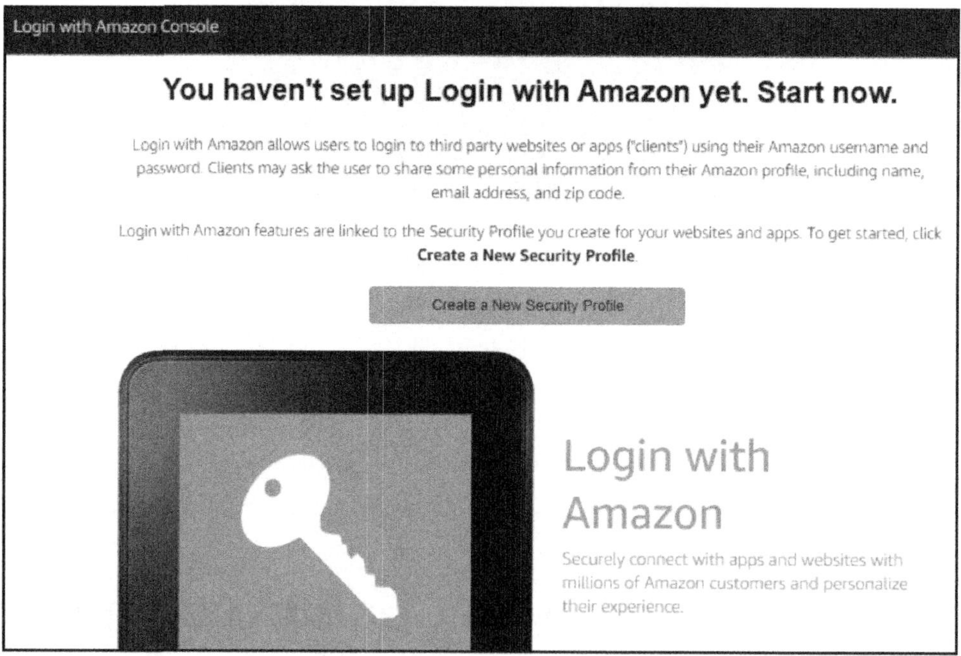

2. Click on **Create a New Security Profile**, enter the profile details, such as **Security Profile Name**, **Security Profile Description**, **Consent Privacy Notice URL**, and **Consent Logo Image**, and then click **Save**:

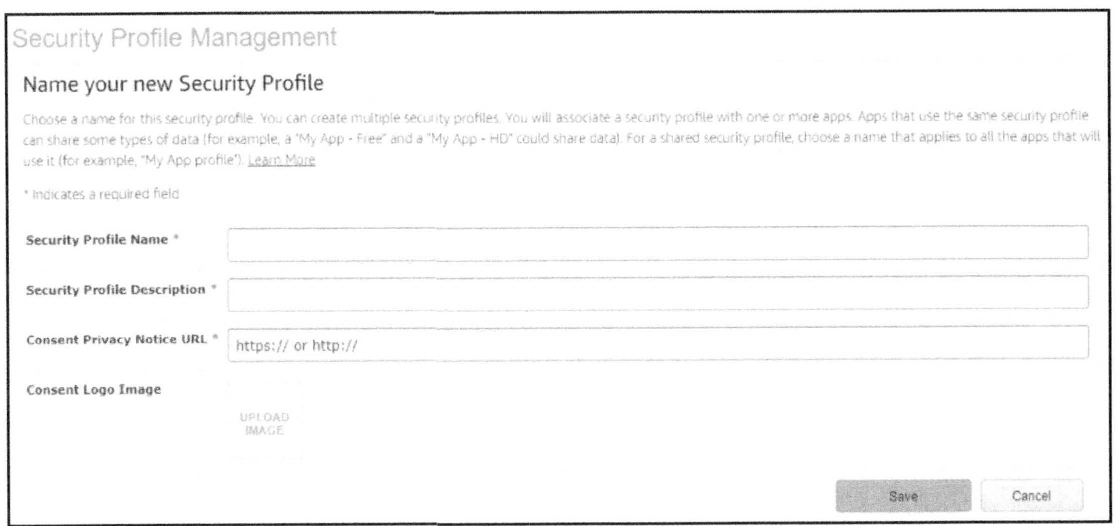

Once saved, we should get a success message similar to the one shown here:

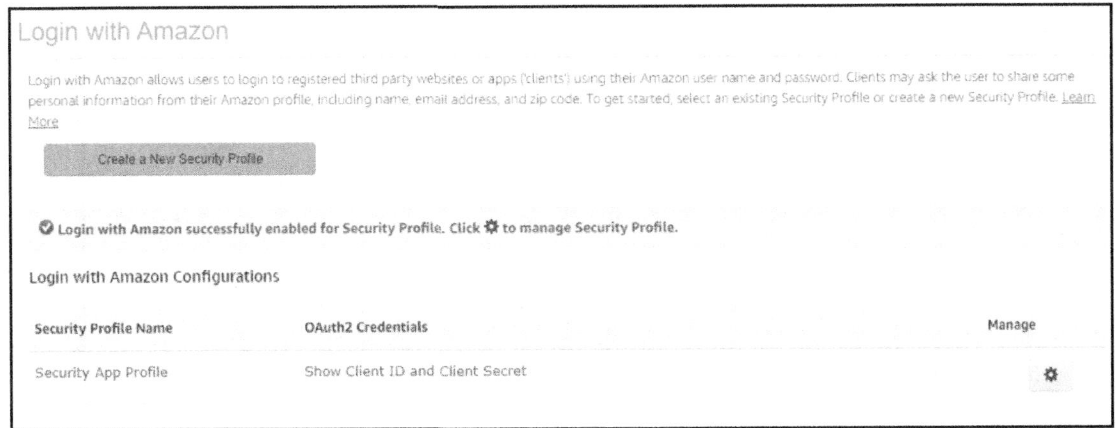

3. Click the settings button on the right-hand side under the **Manage** tab. We can see the details of the profile and edit any details if needed. We can also get the **Security Profile ID** from this page, which is required while configuring in Cognito:

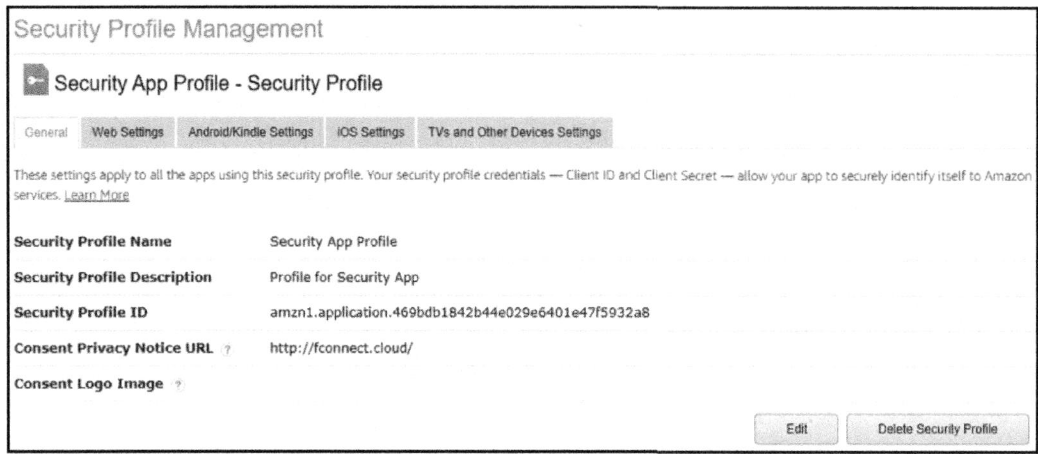

4. Click on the **Web Settings** tab and provide the value for **Allowed Origins**, the URL of our domain where we will be using the AWS login:

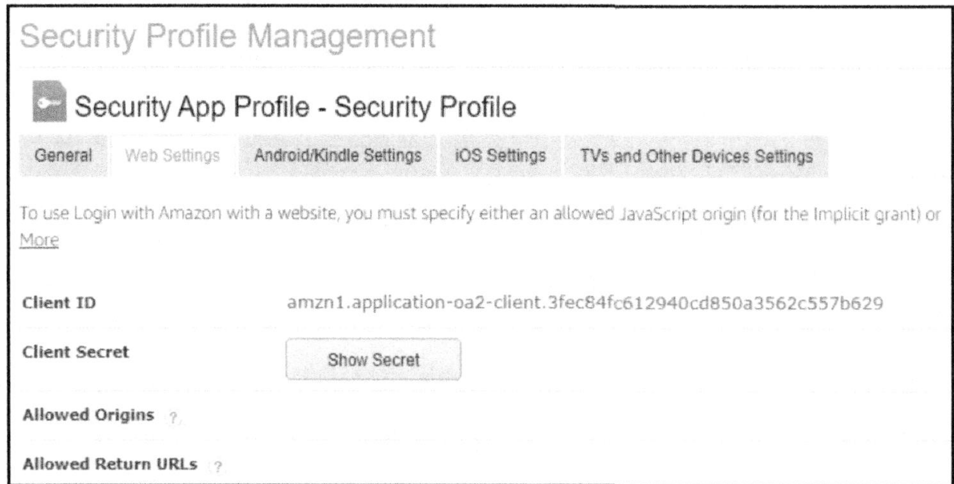

Next, we will configure Cognito from the AWS management console.

Configuring in Cognito

Once we have configured a security profile within the Amazon developer portal, we can configure it within the Cognito console as follows:

1. Go to the Cognito service in the console.
2. Click on **Manage Identity Pools**.
3. Click on **Create New Identity Pool**.
4. Provide a name for the pool:

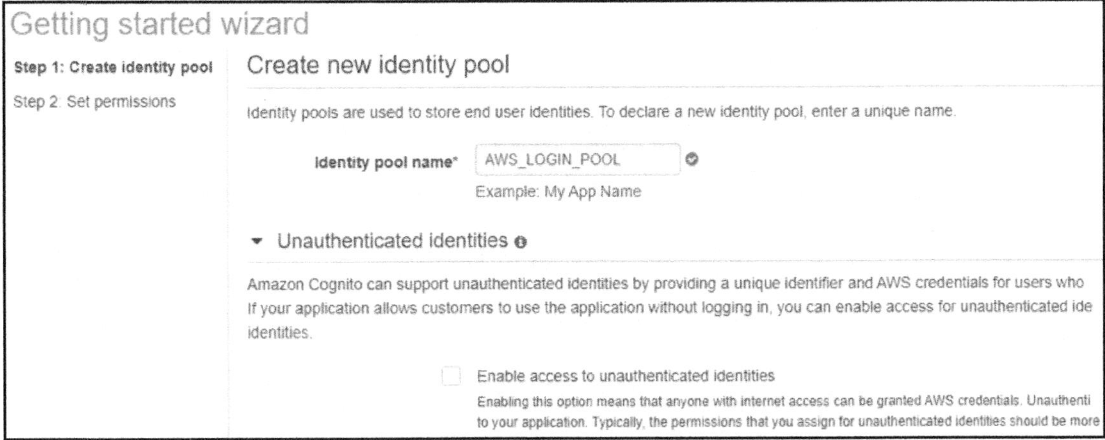

5. Expand the **Authentication providers** section, select the **Amazon** tab, and enter the **Amazon App ID** received from the AWS developer portal:

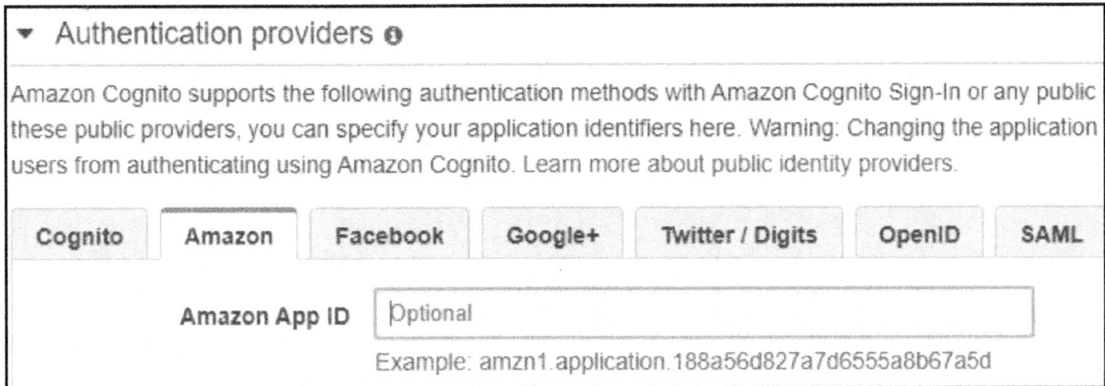

6. Create an HTML file with a button and the JavaScript code to do the login as follows:
    1. The following code will provide a button within the `index.html` file:

```
<a href="#" id="LoginWithAmazon">
 <img border="0" alt="Login with Amazon"
src="https://images-na.ssl-images-amazon.com/images/G/
01/lwa/btnLWA_gold_156x32.png" width="156" height="32"
/>
</a>
```

    2. Add a login with an Amazon (LWA) SDK for JavaScript:

```
<div id="amazon-root"></div>
```

    3. The `amazon-root` element needs to be present in the page for the LWA SDK for JavaScript:

```
<script type="text/javascript">
window.onAmazonLoginReady = function() {
 console.log("amazon on ready");
 amazon.Login.setClientId('amzn1.application-oa2-
client.3fec84fc612940cd850a3562c557b629');
 console.log("client id is" +
amazon.Login.getClientId());
 };
 (function(d) {
 var a = d.createElement('script'); a.type =
'text/javascript';
 a.async = true; a.id = 'amazon-login-sdk';
 a.src =
'https://assets.loginwithamazon.com/sdk/na/login1.js';
 d.getElementById('amazon-root').appendChild(a);
 })(document);;
</script>
```

4. Replace `CLIENT-ID` with your client ID from the AWS developer portal.
5. Add the code required to retrieve the token within the `onClick` handler of the button:

```
script type="text/javascript">
document.getElementById('LoginWithAmazon').onclick =
function() {
 options = { scope : 'profile' };
amazon.Login.authorize(options, function(response) {
 if ( response.error ) {
 alert('oauth error ' + response.error);
 return;
 }
 alert('success: ' + response.access_token);
 AWS.config.region = 'us-east-1';
 if (true) { // logged in
 AWS.config.credentials = new
AWS.CognitoIdentityCredentials({
 IdentityPoolId: 'us-east-1:30cf7838-5877-4c67-
b591-1093faa416ea',
 Logins: {
 'www.amazon.com': response.access_token,
 }
 });
```

6. After retrieving the access token, use the same token to authenticate against AWS Cognito. Set the region to `us-east-1`. Use the `IdentityPoolID` obtained while creating the identity pool:

```
AWS.config.credentials = new
AWS.CognitoIdentityCredentials({
 IdentityPoolId: 'us-east-1:30cf7838-5877-4c67-
b591-1093faa416ea',
 Logins: {
 'www.amazon.com': response.access_token,
 }
```

Once we have successfully authenticated against Cognito, the following method receives the `sessionToken` variable.

```
AWS.config.credentials.get(function(){
 console.log("inside aws credentials get");
 // Credentials will be available when this function is called.
 var accessKeyId = AWS.config.credentials.accessKeyId;
 var secretAccessKey = AWS.config.credentials.secretAccessKey;
```

```
var sessionToken = AWS.config.credentials.sessionToken;
console.log('You are now logged in.' +sessionToken );
alert('success: and the session token is ' + sessionToken);
});

} else {
console.log('There was a problem logging you in.');
}
});
<code> </code>
```

The completed `index.html` file is present with the code files. Do remember to replace the ID wherever necessary.

7. Upload the file to the domain's or subdomain's folder, access it from the browser, and click the button to initiate the login process. Once the login process is complete, we can verify the tokens from the console (if using Chrome, this is accessible from developer tools). We can also confirm the use of a federated entity by looking into the Cognito console:

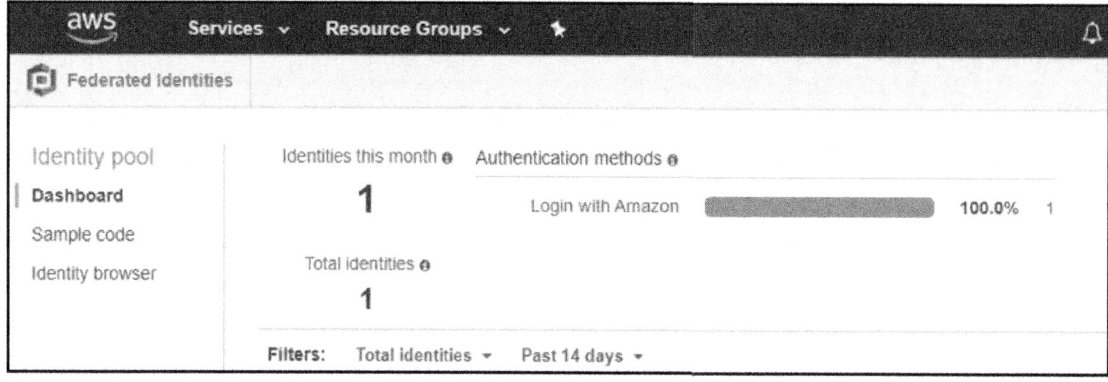

Experiment more with different identity providers by following the steps we discussed here.

How it works...

In this recipe, we created a security profile within the Amazon developer portal and configured it as a Cognito identity pool with a federated login. Amazon and most other identity providers require us to invoke them only from authorized domains that are HTTPS enabled and, hence, we will need a domain with HTTPS for this recipe. We created an HTML file with JavaScript code to do the required login process. A detailed explanation of the JavaScript code is beyond the scope of this book.

We explored the use of Amazon as an identity provider. Other supported identity providers for Cognito user pools are as follows: public providers such as **Login with Amazon, Facebook, Google, and Twitter**, **Cognito User Pools**, **Open ID Connect Providers**, **SAML Identity Providers**, and **Developer Authenticated Identities**.

There's more...

We can also use SAML identity provider configurations in AWS IAM to establish trust between AWS and SAML-compatible identity providers, such as Shibboleth or Microsoft **Active Directory Federation Service** (**ADFS**). Steps to set up federated sign-in with ADFS in IAM can be summarized as follows:

1. Download the `FederationMetadata.xml` file from our ADFS server.
2. Go to the IAM dashboard.
3. Create an identity provider as follows:
    1. Click on **Identity providers** from the left sidebar.
    2. Click on **Create Provider**.
    3. For **Provider Type**, select **SAML**.
    4. For **Provider Name**, give a meaningful name.
    5. For **Metadata Document**, click **Choose File** and upload the `FederationMetadata.xml` file we downloaded in *step 1*.
    6. Click **Next Step**.
    7. Review and click **Create** to complete creation of the authentication provider.

4. Create a role in IAM that federated users can assume via SAML 2.0 as follows:
    1. Click on **Roles** from the left sidebar of the IAM dashboard.
    2. Click on **Create role**.
    3. For **Select type of trusted entity**, select **SAML 2.0 federation**.
    4. For **SAML provider**, select the identity provider we created in *step 3*.
    5. Select **Allow programmatic and AWS Management Console access**. The values for the **Attribute** and **Value** fields will be populated automatically. Click **Next: Permissions**.
    6. Choose one or more permission policies for our new role. Click **Next: Review**.
    7. For **Role name** and **Role description**, provide a meaningful name and description for our role.
    8. Create further roles as per *steps 1* to *8*, as required.

Users (as defined in the identity provider) should assume an AWS role during the sign-in process. You need to follow the documentation for **Active Directory** (**AD**) and ADFS to complete the preceding steps for setting up a federated sign-in through AD and ADFS.

See also

- You can read more about Cognito identity pools here: `https://docs.aws.amazon.com/cognito/latest/developerguide/cognito-identity.html`
- You can read about enabling SAML 2.0 federated users to access the management console here: `https://docs.amazonaws.cn/en_us/IAM/latest/UserGuide/id_roles_providers_enable-console-saml.html`.

4
Key Management with KMS and CloudHSM

Encryption is the process of converting plaintext into ciphertext using a key. We can get the original plain text from the ciphertext using the same key, and this is referred to as decryption. AWS **Key Management Service** (**KMS**) helps us create and manage encryption keys while making use of shared **hardware security modules** (**HSMs**). CloudHSM is another service within AWS that allows us to manage encryption keys but uses dedicated HSMs for enhanced security. We will look at recipes for working with both AWS KMS and AWS CloudHSM within this chapter.

In this chapter, we will cover the following recipes:

- Creating keys in KMS
- Using keys with external key material
- Rotating keys in KMS
- Granting permissions programmatically with grants
- Using key policies with conditional keys
- Sharing customer-managed keys across accounts
- Creating a CloudHSM cluster
- Initializing and activating a CloudHSM cluster

Technical requirements

You will need a working AWS account to complete the recipes in this chapter. Basic knowledge of encryption, including symmetric keys, asymmetric keys, and **public key infrastructure** (**PKI**) will be helpful for understanding the recipes within this chapter.

The code files for this chapter are available at `https://github.com/PacktPublishing/AWS-Security-Cookbook/tree/master/Chapter04`.

Creating keys in KMS

In this recipe, we will create a key using AWS KMS. Usually, the keys will be created for a particular use case, such as encrypting data in S3, and they will be named accordingly. Technically, we can reuse the key for other service use cases as well, and in such cases it is advised that we name the key appropriately.

Getting ready

We need a working AWS account to complete this recipe.

How to do it...

We can create a CMK in KMS from the console as follows:

1. Go to **KMS service** in the console.
2. Select **Customer managed keys** from the left sidebar (if it's not already selected) and click **Create Key**.
3. Provide an **Alias** and **Description**, leave the other selections as is, and click **Next**:

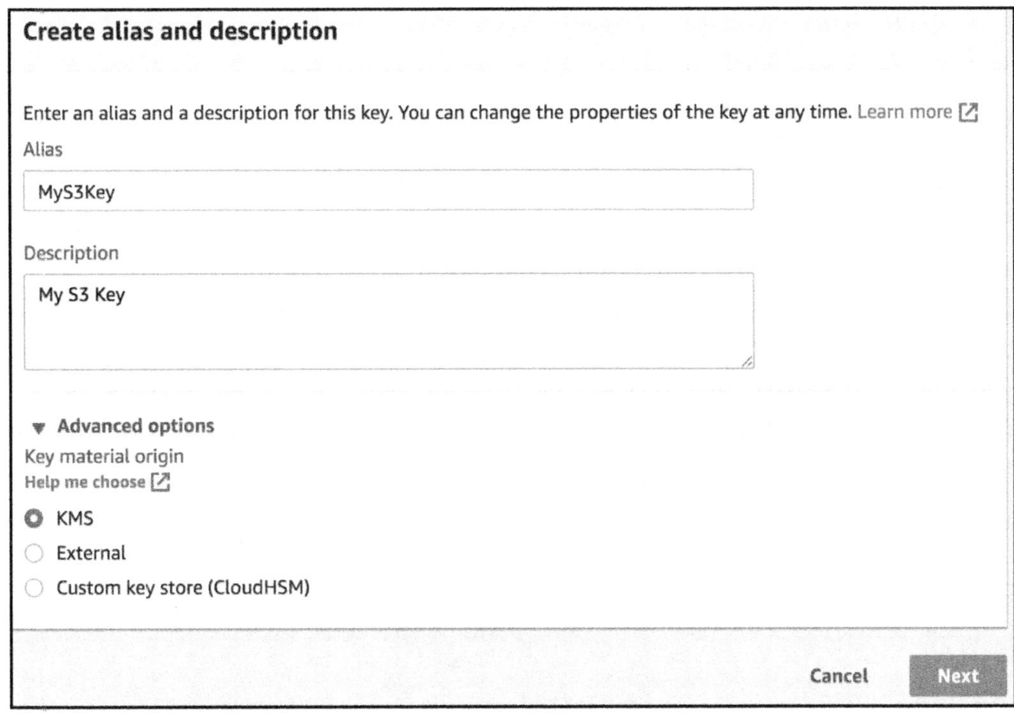

4. Click **Next** until you reach the **Key administrators** page. Select the users and roles who can administer this key using the KMS API:

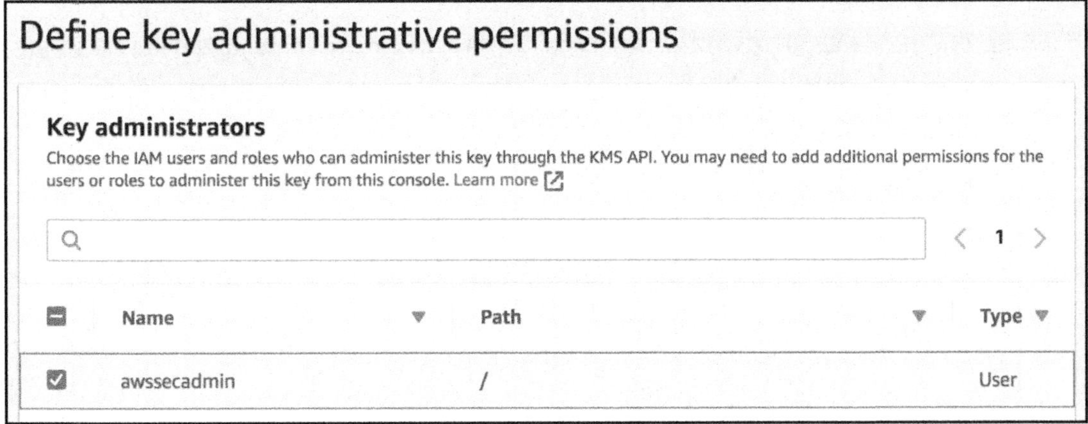

On the same page, leave the selection to allow key administrators to delete this key and click **Next**:

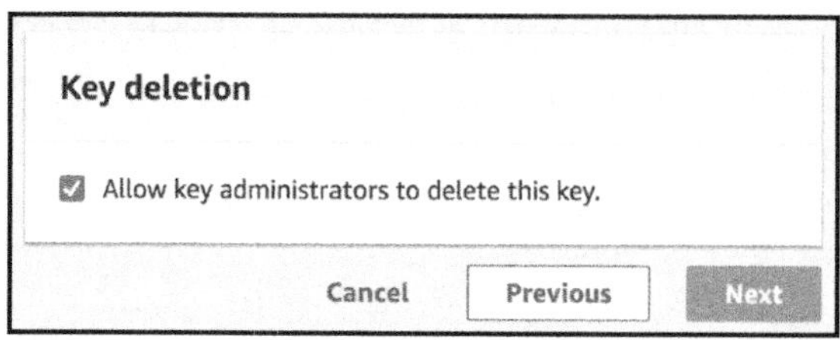

5. On the **Define key usage permissions** page, select the **Identity and Access Management** (**IAM**) users and roles who can use the customer-managed key to encrypt and decrypt data:

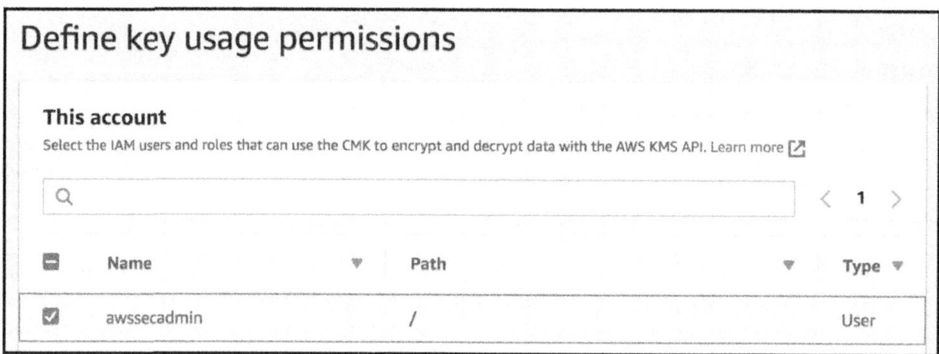

6. On the same page, we can add other AWS accounts to manage the keys. Leave that as is and click **Next**:

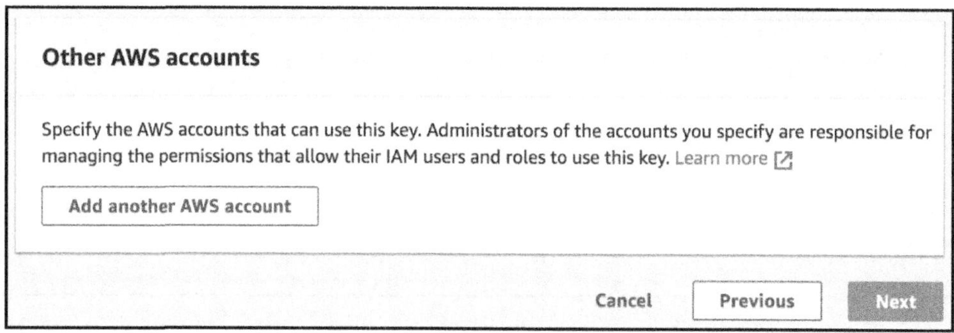

7. Review the policy and click **Next**. We should see a message stating that the key has been generated successfully. The policy that's generated by AWS is kept within the code files for reference as `review-generated-policy.json`.

How it works...

In this recipe, we defined an alias and description for our key. On the next screen, we can add **tags** to our recipes. We skipped this step. Furthermore, we can add IAM users or roles as key administrators. While key administrators can manage keys, they do not have permission to encrypt or decrypt data using those keys by default.

After that, we added users who can use these keys. Unless added to this list, even a key administrator won't be able to use this key. Key administrators, however, can add themselves as key users. We can also allow other AWS accounts to use these keys. Doing so will allow the administrators of those accounts to delegate permissions to the users or roles within that account.

Next, we reviewed our key policy settings and clicked on **Finish**. We can edit these settings if we need to from this screen. Now, we should see our key listed under CMK.

There's more...

In this recipe, we created a key using the standard options available with KMS. We can configure these options based on our requirements. For example, in this recipe, we choose the option to allow key administrators to delete the key. Based on our security requirements, we may unselect this option to not allow key administrators to delete the key.

Play around with all the options available within KMS and get familiar with them. This will help you decide on what options to choose when you are faced with a scenario at work, in an exam, or an interview.

Let's quickly go through some important points about the AWS KMS service:

- A master key is represented in AWS KMS using the **customer master key (CMK)** entity and is the primary resource within the AWS KMS service.
- AWS KMS CMKs can encrypt data up to 4 KB in size and are generally used to encrypt other keys, such as data keys. These data keys are used to encrypt the actual data. The data keys are not created and managed within the AWS KMS service.
- KMS is a region-specific service and, hence, the keys managed by KMS are region-specific. Therefore, to use KMS keys, the respective services should also be in the same region. For example, to use the key that we created for encrypting an S3 data, the S3 bucket needs to be in the same region.
- A user with S3 administrator permissions won't have permission to view a file encrypted using a KMS key encryption unless they are a key user for the key being used to encrypt that file.
- A user with `AdministratorAccess` permission (full administrator access) will have permission to view a file that's been encrypted using a KMS key encryption.
- A user with `AdministratorAccess` permission (full administrator access) will have permission to add themselves as a key administrator or key user.
- A user with `SystemAdministrator` permission will not have permission to view a file encrypted using a KMS key encryption.
- A user with `SystemAdministrator` permission will not have permission to add themselves as a key administrator or key user.
- Key administrators do not have permission to encrypt or decrypt data using those keys. Key administrators, however, can modify the key policy to add themselves as key users. This is where the audit and logging services become more relevant.
- We cannot directly delete a key. A key administrator can disable and/or schedule a key for deletion. Currently, the administrator can specify a waiting period between 7 and 30 days inclusive while scheduling a key deletion.
- Once a key has been disabled, we cannot decrypt any data that's encrypted with that key until we enable that key again.
- Once a key has been deleted, we cannot decrypt any data encrypted with that key.

See also

- Refer to the following link for important concepts related to encryption: `https://heartin.tech/en/blog-entry/important-points-remember-about-encryption`.
- You can read more about the key policies in AWS KMS at `https://docs.aws.amazon.com/kms/latest/developerguide/key-policies.html`.
- You can read about important cryptography concepts within AWS that are useful for working with KMS effectively at `https://docs.aws.amazon.com/crypto/latest/userguide/cryptography-concepts.html`.
- The *KMS Cryptographic Details* white paper is a good document for learning about the cryptography details for KMS: `https://d0.awsstatic.com/whitepapers/KMS-Cryptographic-Details.pdf`.

Using keys with external key material

When we create keys within AWS KMS, AWS creates and manages the key material for that key. We can also create keys using our own key material that has been created outside of AWS. In this recipe, we will learn how to import our own key material into AWS KMS.

Getting ready

We need a working AWS account to complete this recipe.

How to do it...

We will start by creating our key from AWS KMS by setting the key material origin to **External**. Then, we will download the key import wrapper from the AWS KMS service, generate the key in our local machine, and wrap it with the import wrapper. Finally, we will upload our key material that's been wrapped with the import wrapper to finish key creation.

Creating key configuration for an external key

We can create key configuration for an external key as follows:

1. Go to **KMS service** in the console.
2. Click on **Create Key**.
3. Provide an **Alias** and **Description**. Expand the **Advanced options** menu and select **External**. Here, we can read the security, availability, and durability implications while using an external key, select the corresponding checkbox, and click **Next**:

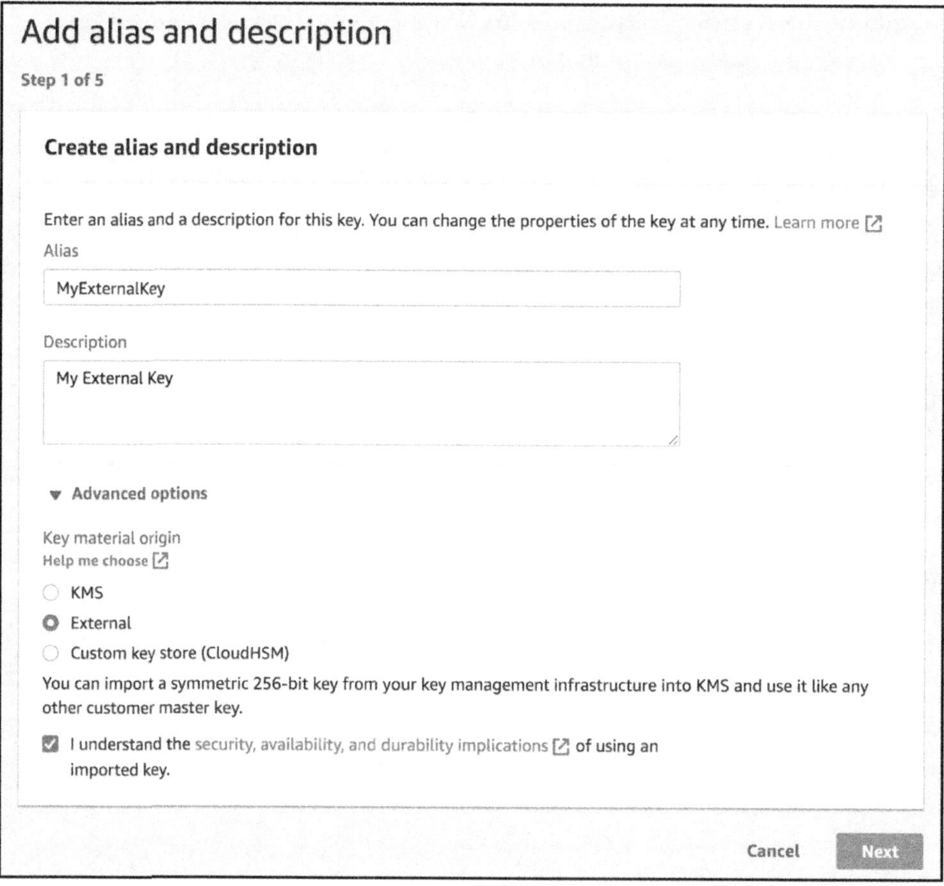

4. On the screen for **Add tags**, add any tags if required.
5. On the screen for **Define key administrative permissions**, add your key administrators.
6. On the screen for **Define key usage permissions**, define your key users. If required, we can also add external accounts within this screen.
7. On the **Review and edit key policy** screen, review the policy document and click **Finish**. This will take us to the screen for downloading the wrapping key and importing the token.
8. On the **Download wrapping key and import token** screen, select a wrapping algorithm and click on **Download wrapping key and import token**:

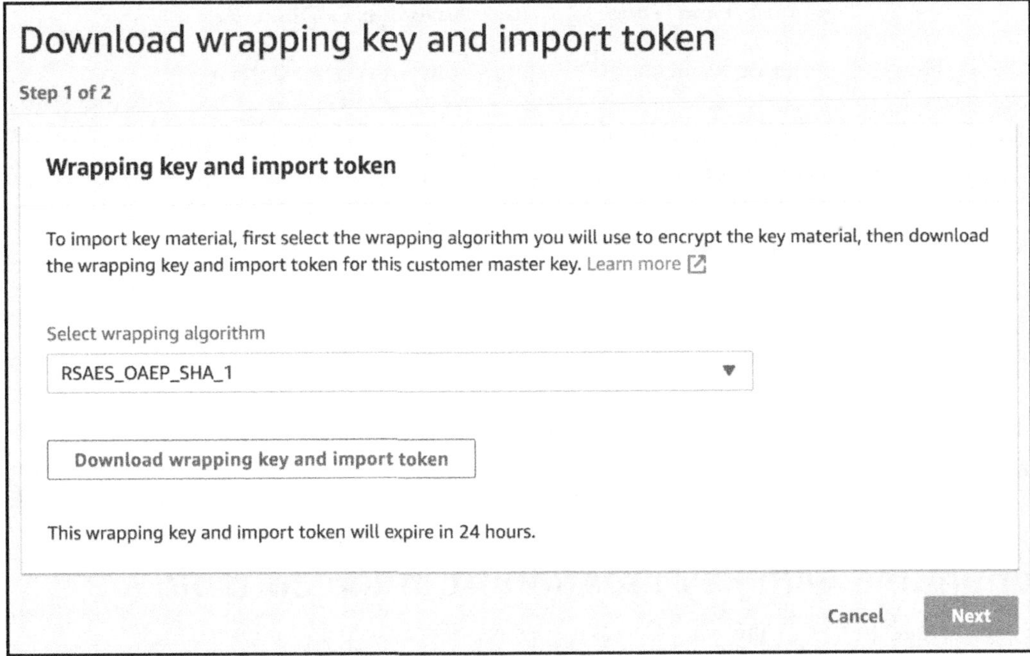

I have used **SHA_1** here, but you can use a more secure one that is available. Refer to the *There's more...* section for more details.

Keep the `ImportParameters.zip` file for the steps we will follow in the next section. Once we click **Next**, we will be taken to the screen for uploading our key material. First, we will generate our key material and return to AWS KMS in the *Rotating Keys in KMS* section.

Generating our key material using OpenSSL

We can generate our key material using OpenSSL as follows:

1. Go to the OpenSSL website and download the latest version of OpenSSL. I've downloaded `openssl-1.0.2t.tar.gz`. The current link to the website is `www.openssl.org`.
2. Uncompress the downloaded OpenSSL file into a folder.
3. Uncompress the `ImportParameters.zip` file and copy the wrapping key into the OpenSSL directory.
4. Go to the OpenSSL folder and run the following command:

```
openssl rand -out PlaintextKeyMaterial.bin 32
```

This will generate a file called `PlaintextKeyMaterial.bin`.

5. Execute the following command from the same folder while providing the name of our wrapping key for the `inkey` parameter:

```
openssl rsautl -encrypt \
 -in PlaintextKeyMaterial.bin \
 -oaep \
 -inkey wrappingKey_f963711d-c91e-49ae-
b923-4722926e2b85_10281245 \
 -keyform DER \
 -pubin \
 -out EncryptedKeyMaterial.bin
```

This will generate a file called `EncryptedKeyMaterial.bin`.

Continuing with key creation from the console

We can upload our key material from the AWS KMS console as follows:

1. Click on **Choose file** under **Wrapped key material** and select the `EncryptedKeyMaterial.bin` file.
2. Click on **Choose file** under **Import token** and select the import token we downloaded from KMS on the previous screen:

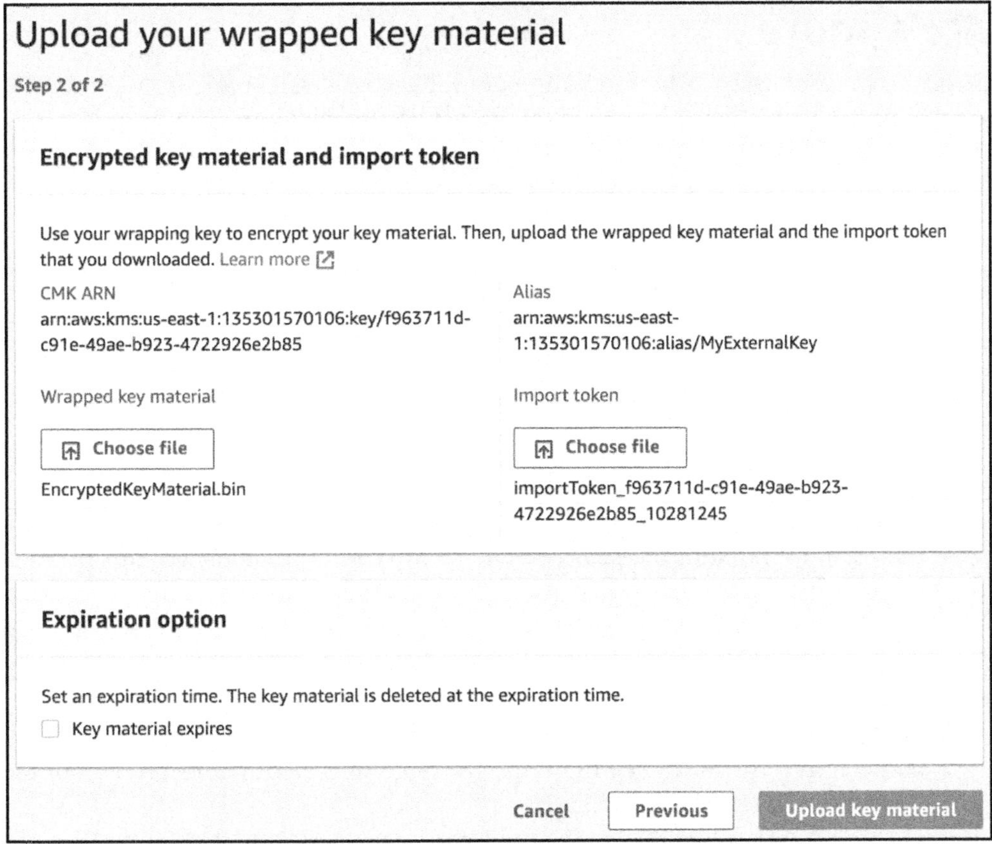

3. Leave the **Key material expires** option unchecked and click on **Upload key material**. You can choose this option if this is a requirement. The key is now ready for use.

How it works...

In this recipe, we created a **customer master key** (**CMK**) by setting the key material origin to **External**. After that, we selected one of the allowed encryption schemes for the key wrapper and downloaded the key wrapper. This key wrapper is the public key that is used to encrypt and securely upload our key material to the AWS KMS service. An import token from the AWS KMS service was also downloaded, along with the key wrapper. The import token is used to make sure the key that's uploaded is the right one for the right key that we downloaded the wrapper token for.

There's more...

In this recipe, we used **SHA_1** to wrap our external key material before uploading it. You can select a more secure alternative from the **Select wrapping algorithm** drop-down menu:

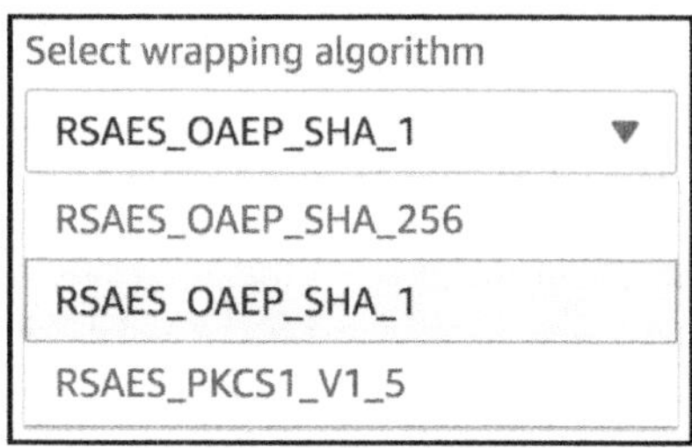

Let's quickly go through some more details regarding importing keys into AWS KMS:

- When we import our own key material, we are responsible for generating the key material with randomness, as per our security requirements. We are also responsible for the durability of the key material.
- With an imported key material, we can set an expiration date for the key material and also manually delete the key material. We can make the key available again in the future by importing the key material into the CMK.
- We cannot delete the key material for a CMK with AWS key material. When using CMK with AWS key material, we can only schedule the deletion of the CMK with 7-30 days notice.
- Once a CMK has been deleted, any data that's been encrypted by it cannot be decrypted. This is true for both CMKs with AWS key material and CMKs with imported key material.
- A key material imported into a CMK is permanently associated with that CMK.
- We can only reimport the key material. We cannot import a different key material again for that CMK.
- A ciphertext encrypted with a CMK with an external key material cannot be decrypted by another CMK, even if we use the same key material.
- A CMK with an imported key material must be deleted before you reimport the key material again into another CMK.

- We can reimport the key material into an existing CMK if the key material is deleted.
- In the case of region-wide failures that affect CMKs, AWS won't automatically restore any imported key material. In such scenarios, we need to have a copy of our key material in order to reimport it.

See also

- Detailed steps and commands for key generation and imports for AWS KMS can be found here: `https://docs.aws.amazon.com/kms/latest/developerguide/importing-keys-import-key-material.html`.

Rotating keys in KMS

Rotating keys regularly is a best practice that needs to be followed while using keys. Key rotation may also be a requirement based on regulatory rules or corporate policies. These rules and policies may also provide guidelines on the key rotation frequencies. We will look at the different cases of key rotation within this recipe.

Getting ready

We need a working AWS account to complete this recipe. Follow the *Creating Keys in KMS* recipe and create a CMK with AWS key material.

How to do it...

We can specify automatic key rotation every year (365 days) for CMKs with AWS key material as follows:

1. Go to **KMS service** in the console.
2. Click on the **Alias** or **Key ID** of our CMK.
3. Click on the **Key rotation** tab.

4. Select **Automatically rotate this CMK every year**:

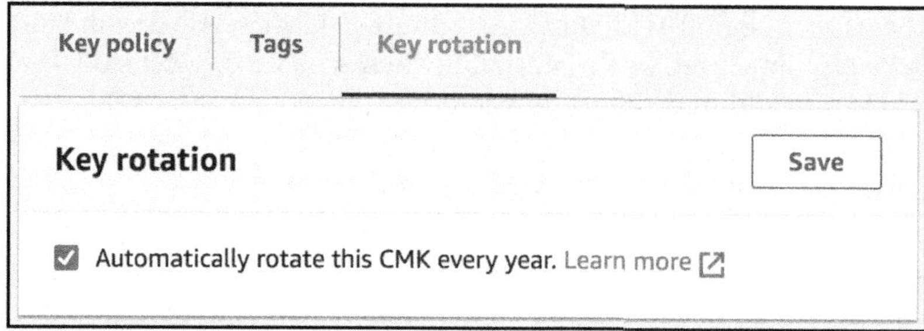

5. Click **Save**.

How it works...

When we specify the option to automatically rotate this CMK every year, AWS will rotate the CMK every year, but keeps a copy of the old backing key in order to decrypt any data that was encrypted with the old backing key. AWS keeps the older backing keys until we delete them.

With automatic rotation, only the backing key of a CMK is rotated. This means that the CMK ID, ARN, region, policies, permissions, and other properties remain the same. Therefore, we do not need to change applications or aliases that use a CMK.

There's more...

Let's quickly go through some of the important points related to AWS KMS key rotation:

- Automatic key rotation every year (365 days) is only supported for CMKs with AWS key materials.
- We can do a manual key rotation for CMKs with AWS key material if we want a different duration for the key rotation.
- With automatic key rotation, only CMK is rotated and not the data keys.
- With automatic key rotation, new encryptions are made using the new backing key. However, data encrypted using an older backing key is decrypted using that key. For this purpose, AWS keeps all backing keys available until we delete the CMK.

- With automatic key rotation, even if we disable key rotation, old backing keys will still be available to decrypt data that was encrypted using that key.
- With automatic key rotation, if you disable rotation and reenable it again, it will continue with the old key rotation schedule if the backing key is less than a year old. If the backing key is older than 365 days, it is changed immediately and then rotated every 365 days.
- With automatic key rotation, key rotation will not happen if a key is pending for deletion. If deletion is canceled, it will continue with the old key rotation schedule if the backing key is less than a year old. If the backing key is older than 365 days, it is changed immediately and then rotated every 365 days.
- Automatic key rotation is not supported for custom key stores backed by AWS CloudHSM clusters. For such CMKs, the value of the **Origin** field is `AWS_CloudHSM`. In this case, we need to manually rotate keys and change any encrypted data or aliases to use the new key.
- For AWS-managed keys, we cannot change the rotation frequency, which is currently 3 years.
- Automatic key rotation can be monitored using the KMS CMK rotation event in Amazon CloudWatch Events.
- We can use the AWS KMS API to enable and disable automatic key rotation.
- It is good practice to use aliases to refer to CMKs when we do manual key rotation. We can update the alias so that it points to the new target CMK instead of the old CMK.
- Even with manual rotation, AWS KMS can identify the right backing key that was used for encryption and use it for decryption as long as we keep the older CMKs available.
- We can update aliases using the `update-alias` subcommand of the AWS KMS API.

See also

- You can read more about rotating keys here: `https://docs.aws.amazon.com/kms/latest/developerguide/rotate-keys.html`.

Granting permissions programmatically with grants

KMS grants can be used to give temporary granular permissions to AWS KMS API operations such as encrypt, decrypt, describe keys, and more. We can use grants to provide access to a user in their own account or even another account. In this recipe, we will grant access to a user so that they can encrypt and decrypt files using AWS KMS.

Getting ready

We need a working AWS account and two users: an administrator user and a user with no permissions. The CLI profiles should be configured for these users. I will be calling these users and their CLI profiles `awssecadmin` and `testuser`, respectively.

Create a KMS key by following previous recipes in this chapter. Alternatively, use the following command to create a KMS key from the AWS CLI:

```
aws kms create-key --profile awssecadmin
```

This will provide an output similar to the following:


```
{
    "KeyMetadata": {
        "AWSAccountId": "135301570106",
        "KeyId": "1ab77c7a-7ca4-4387-a4c5-2fba3cb5c0f5",
        "Arn": "arn:aws:kms:us-east-1:135301570106:key/1ab77c7a-7ca4-4387-a4c5-2fba3cb5c0f5",
        "CreationDate": 1572327372.686,
        "Enabled": true,
        "Description": "",
        "KeyUsage": "ENCRYPT_DECRYPT",
        "KeyState": "Enabled",
        "Origin": "AWS_KMS",
        "KeyManager": "CUSTOMER"
    }
}
```


Next, we will check whether our test user has any permissions by running the following command:

```
aws kms encrypt \
    --plaintext "hello 3" \
    --key-id 1ab77c7a-7ca4-4387-a4c5-2fba3cb5c0f5 \
    --profile testuser
```

We should get an error message similar to the one shown in the following screenshot:

```
An error occurred (AccessDeniedException) when calling the Encrypt operation: User:
 arn:aws:iam::135301570106:user/testuser is not authorized to perform: kms:Encrypt
on resource: arn:aws:kms:us-east-1:135301570106:key/1ab77c7a-7ca4-4387-a4c5-2fba3cb
5c0f5
```

In the preceding command, we can specify the key ID alone, as follows, the complete key ARN, or an alias (if one is available).

How to do it...

We can grant encrypt permission to `testuser` and then use it to encrypt as follows:

1. Grant encrypt permission to `testuser` using the `create-grant` subcommand by providing the user's ARN:

    ```
    aws kms create-grant \
        --key-id 1ab77c7a-7ca4-4387-a4c5-2fba3cb5c0f5 \
        --grantee-principal arn:aws:iam::135301570106:user/testuser
    \
        --operations "Encrypt" \
        --profile awssecadmin
    ```

    We should get a response similar to the one shown in the following screenshot:


```
{
    "GrantToken": "AQpAZTZmYjE0NTAzZTA4MzE1ZmY0NGJjYWE2MTM0M2RjY2ZhNjAyYjc1OGRkZGQ0
MjhhMTdmZWQyMTdkNjBiODQyNyKIAgEBAgB45vsUUD4IMV_0S8qmE0Pcz6YCt1jd3UKKF_7SF9YLhCcAAAD
fMIHcBgkqhkiG9w0BBwaggc4wgcsCAQAwgcUGCSqGSIb3DQEHATAeBglghkgBZQMEAS4wEQQMReW8CIXsPO
Ah1kW1AgEQgIGXgcA_BfKYkjNhrOPJTJ1JAX-xl8YrQeMl-c4gpGA8dvxdUsIcx7QLfPoJrQWHRNEqOSbxa
yTZmgUhNSnnHOzWghDn0hhvVWQsoMlRiAhKG9V2e-ziu_zlYnJYWadlNbKPna0m7JoB2WMtNnbZ8hq_lArz
WtdiWqJwSnyoY0q5yLPJEYhXawuI6r0Ra1CK2e-MnH-wBAe7dyogOhKOSJMuu2Y-0MwsgoXefh0DFx3NmrL
8N8-6FgW-ov4",
    "GrantId": "3a128e48932ebb663ed0cc2c8285de7e1d03171dcd9ab2fc37cfba1605bea2fe"
}
```

We can get the user's ARN from the IAM dashboard or prepare one based on the preceding format. We can also use the following command to get the user's ARN from the console:

```
aws iam get-user \
    --user-name testuser \
    --profile awssecadmin
```

This command will return a response similar to the following:


```
{
    "User": {
        "Path": "/",
        "UserName": "testuser",
        "UserId": "AIDAR7AE2DY5LQZJINX3D",
        "Arn": "arn:aws:iam::135301570106:user/testuser",
        "CreateDate": "2019-06-11T05:40:03Z",
        "PasswordLastUsed": "2019-06-11T10:45:44Z"
    }
}
```


2. Encrypt data with the `testuser` user:

```
aws kms encrypt \
    --plaintext "hello 3" \
    --key-id 1ab77c7a-7ca4-4387-a4c5-2fba3cb5c0f5 \
    --profile testuser
```

This time, we should get a successful response, as follows:


```
{
    "CiphertextBlob": "AQICAHh+JhXUvzoC5jvshclLNQLN4hURhxRnwL6kpkSXVXmg8AGghVEmYYUD
tO6KbfnBBKVgAAAAZTBjBgkqhkiG9w0BBwagVjBUAgEAME8GCSqGSIb3DQEHATAeBglghkgBZQMEAS4wEQQ
MZVZhOWlRNd/P6+ojAgEQgCLfNqlfHLsd1QktOK5NM/ETomCKtp7oVzGuPh7QZpTO7c4m",
    "KeyId": "arn:aws:kms:us-east-1:135301570106:key/1ab77c7a-7ca4-4387-a4c5-2fba3c
b5c0f5"
}
```


3. Verify the grants for the key using the following command:

```
aws kms list-grants \
    --key-id 1ab77c7a-7ca4-4387-a4c5-2fba3cb5c0f5 \
    --profile awssecadmin
```

This should return a response similar to the following:


```
{
    "Grants": [
        {
            "KeyId": "arn:aws:kms:us-east-1:135301570106:key/1ab77c7a-7ca4-4387-a4c5-2fba3cb5c0f5",
            "GrantId": "3a128e48932ebb663ed0cc2c8285de7e1d03171dcd9ab2fc37cfba1605bea2fe",
            "Name": "",
            "CreationDate": 1572338941.0,
            "GranteePrincipal": "arn:aws:iam::135301570106:user/testuser",
            "IssuingAccount": "arn:aws:iam::135301570106:root",
            "Operations": [
                "Encrypt"
            ]
        }
    ]
}
```


4. Revoke the grant by providing the grant ID:

```
aws kms revoke-grant \
    --key-id 1ab77c7a-7ca4-4387-a4c5-2fba3cb5c0f5 \
    --grant-id
3a128e48932ebb663ed0cc2c8285de7e1d03171dcd9ab2fc37cfba1605bea2f
e \
    --profile awssecadmin
```

5. Verify that the grant has been revoked by trying to encrypt it using `testuser` and by running the `list-grants` subcommand.

   Running the `encrypt` command from *step 2* will provide the following output:

```
An error occurred (AccessDeniedException) when calling the Encrypt operation: User:
arn:aws:iam::135301570106:user/testuser is not authorized to perform: kms:Encrypt on
 resource: arn:aws:kms:us-east-1:135301570106:key/1ab77c7a-7ca4-4387-a4c5-2fba3cb5c0
f5
```

   Running the `encrypt` subcommand from *step 3* will provide the following output:

Similarly, we can also grant permission for other operations as well.

How it works...

In this recipe, we granted permission to the `testuser` user using the `create-grant` subcommand of the `aws kms` CLI command. We verified that the user could not perform encryption before granting permission. We verified that `testuser` could perform encryption after granting permission.

Then, we revoked the grant using the `revoke-grant` subcommand of the `aws kms` CLI command. We also used other subcommands, such as `list-grants` to list the grants for a particular key ID and `encrypt` to encrypt the plain text.

There's more...

In this recipe, we granted permission to only one operation. We can grant permission to multiple operations like so:

```
aws kms create-grant \
    --key-id 1ab77c7a-7ca4-4387-a4c5-2fba3cb5c0f5 \
    --grantee-principal arn:aws:iam::135301570106:user/testuser \
    --operations "Encrypt" "Decrypt" \
    --profile awssecadmin
```

Let's quickly go through some important concepts related to granting and revoking permissions programmatically within AWS:

- The supported grant operations are `Encrypt`, `Decrypt`, `GenerateDataKey`, `GenerateDataKeyWithoutPlaintext`, `ReEncryptFrom`, `ReEncryptTo`, `CreateGrant`, `RetireGrant`, and `DescribeKey`.
- We can use the `encrypt` subcommand of the AWS KMS API to convert plain text into ciphertext with the help of a key.
- We can use the `decrypt` subcommand of AWS KMS API to convert ciphertext into plain text with the help of the same key that was used for encryption.
- We can use the `re-encrypt` subcommand of the AWS KMS API to decrypt and re-encrypt data on the server-side with a new CMK without exposing the plain text on the client-side. This subcommand can also be used to change the encryption context of a ciphertext.

- Encryption context is an optional additional set of key-value pairs that form an additional authentication check. The same encryption context that is used for encryption needs to be used for decryption and re-encryption. Since the encryption context is not a secret, it will appear in plain text within AWS CloudTrail logs, making it useful for monitoring and auditing cryptographic operations.
- Grants are an alternative to the key policies.
- Within the same account, we can use the key ID or key ARN with the `create-grant` subcommand. For users in other accounts, ARN needs to be specified.
- The `create-grant` subcommand has a constraints parameter that accepts an encryption context.
- When we create grants, the permissions may not be reflected immediately due to the eventual consistency model followed by AWS. By using the grant tokens received from the create grant command in further requests, we can avoid any delay due to eventual consistency.
- The `list-grants` subcommand is used to list all the grants for a key and provides the following additional parameters for paginating the result: `starting-token`, `page-size`, and `max-items`.
- The AWS CLI pagination parameters, `starting-token`, `page-size`, and `max-items`, have the following functions:
    - The `max-items` parameter states the maximum number of items that need to be returned by the API.
    - If there are more results from the API calls than specified by `max-items`, then a `NextToken` is provided in the response, which needs to be passed as `starting-token` in the next request.
    - The `page-size` parameter specifies the maximum number of elements to retrieve in a single API call. For example, if `page-size` is 10 and `max-items` is 100, 10 API calls will be made in the background and then 100 items will be returned.
- The `revoke-grant` subcommand can be run by the root user of the account that created it, `RetiringPrincipal` of the grant, or `GranteePrincipal` if they've been given the grant for the `RetireGrant` operation.

- The AWS documentation recommends that, when cleaning up, we retire a grant when we're done using it using the `retire-grand` subcommand, but should revoke a grant using the `revoke-grand` subcommand when we intend to actively deny operations that depend on it.
- The `list-retirable-grants` subcommand can be used to list all grants with the specified `RetiringPrincipal`.
- The `list-retirable-grants` subcommand provides the following parameters to limit the retriable grants that need to be returned: `limit` and `marker`. `limit` is the maximum items that need to be returned, while `marker` is the value of the `NextMarker` that is returned with the previous request when more items than specified by the limit parameter need to be returned.

See also

- For more details on creating grants from the CLI, you can refer to `https://docs.aws.amazon.com/cli/latest/reference/kms/create-grant.html`.

Using key policies with conditional keys

In this recipe, we will learn how to use key policies, especially with key policy conditions. Resource-based policies attached to CMKs are called key policies. For managing access to KMS resources, we can use key policies alone, or we can use IAM policies and grants along with key policies.

In general, permissions policies specify the resources that access has to be provided to, what actions are provided, and who gets those permissions. We can attach policies to IAM identities such as users, groups, roles, and more, called IAM policies, or to services such as S3, KMS, and more, which are known as resource-based policies.

Getting ready

We need an S3 bucket to complete this recipe. I will be using a bucket called `awscookbook` that was created in us-east-1.

How to do it...

We can demonstrate the use of key policies with condition keys as follows:

1. Create a key with the default configuration from the console, as follows:
    1. Provide an **Alias** and **Description** on the first screen. I have provided `testkey` and `test key`, respectively.
    2. Optionally, you can add any **Tags** on the next screen.
    3. On the next screen, do not add any key administrators.
    4. Do not add any key users either.
    5. Review the policy and click **Finish**:

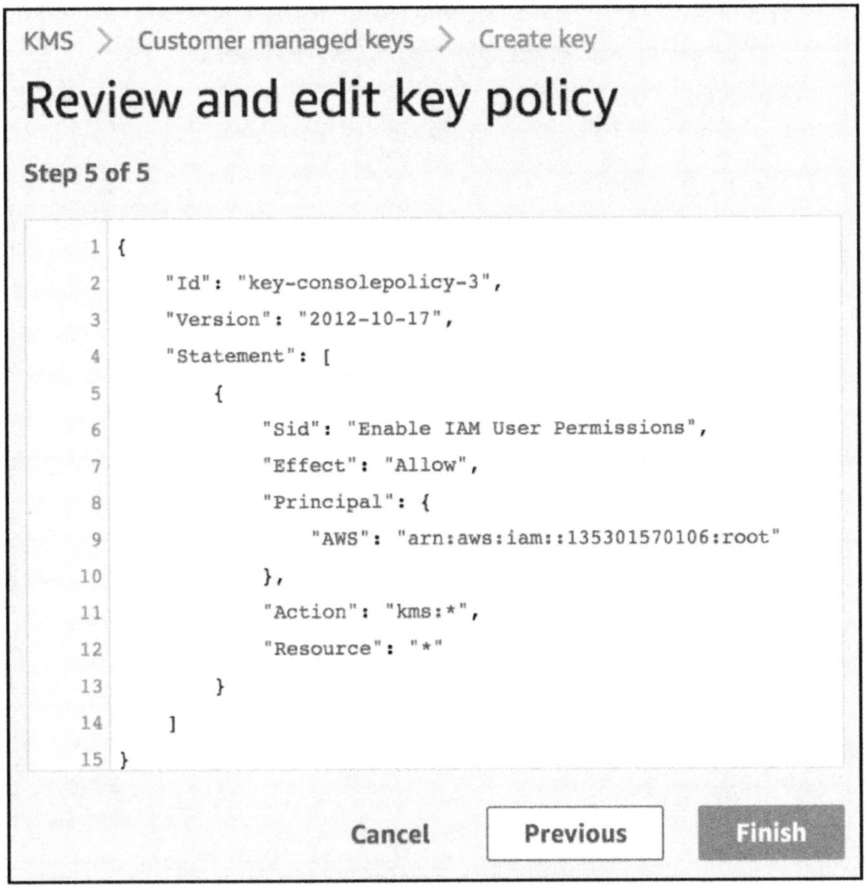

KMS > Customer managed keys > Create key

Review and edit key policy

Step 5 of 5

```
{
    "Id": "key-consolepolicy-3",
    "Version": "2012-10-17",
    "Statement": [
        {
            "Sid": "Enable IAM User Permissions",
            "Effect": "Allow",
            "Principal": {
                "AWS": "arn:aws:iam::135301570106:root"
            },
            "Action": "kms:*",
            "Resource": "*"
        }
    ]
}
```

Cancel | Previous | Finish

2. You can add this KMS CMK as the encryption key for an S3 bucket in the same region as follows:
    1. Go to the **Properties** tab of an S3 bucket.
    2. Click on **Default encryption**.
    3. Select **AWS-KMS** as the encryption method.
    4. Select the key we created.
    5. Click **Save**:

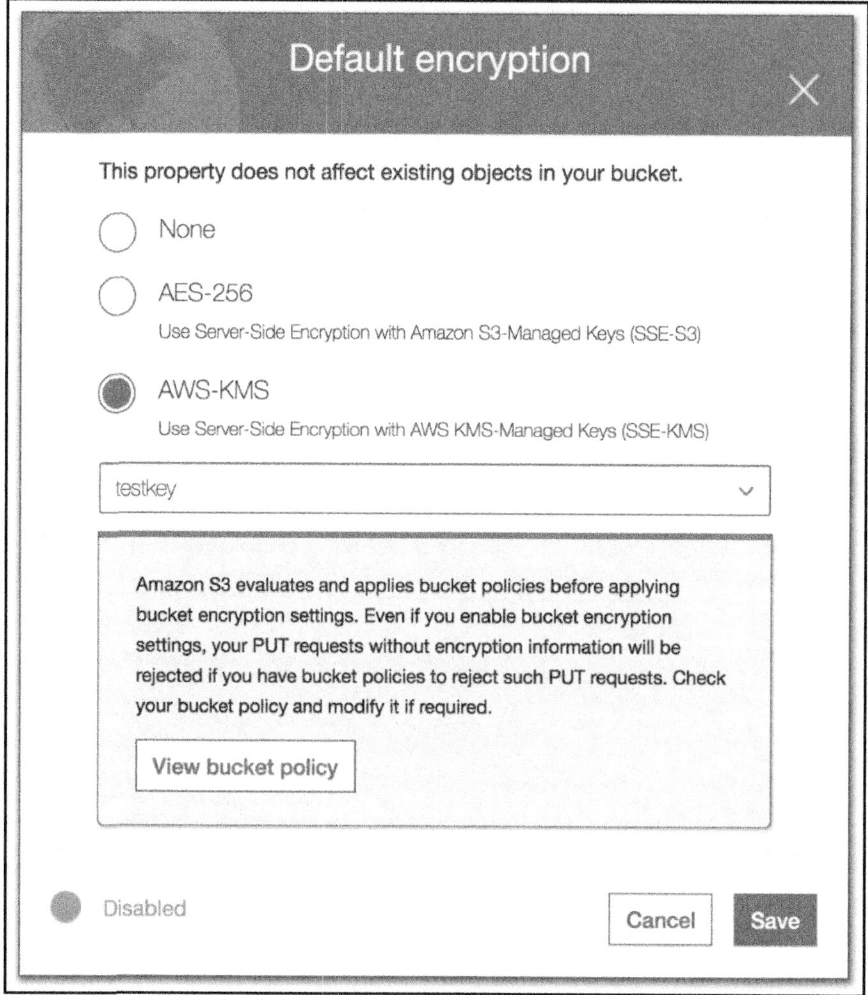

3. Upload a file into S3 and verify that encryption and decryption are working, like so:
    1. Upload a file into S3.
    2. Click on that file and click **Open** to view the file's contents:

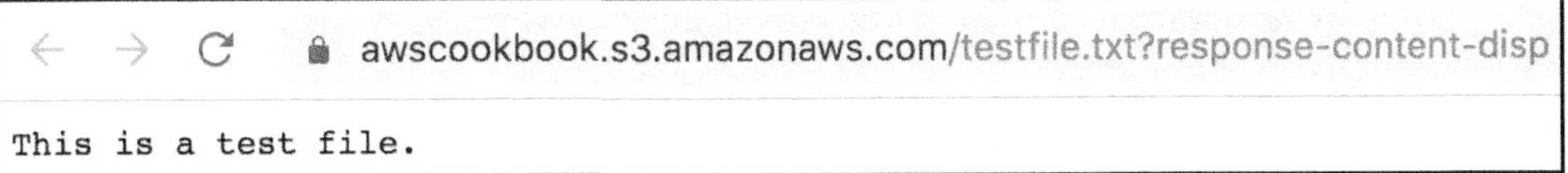

4. Deny key usages from the S3 service by adding the following key policy statement:
    1. Go to the KMS dashboard.
    2. Click on the key policy we need to modify.
    3. Click on the **Key policy** tab.
    4. Click on **Switch to policy view**.
    5. Click **Edit**, add the following statement with proper commas, and click **Save**:

```
{
    "Effect":"Deny",
    "Principal":{
        "AWS":"arn:aws:iam::135301570106:root"
    },
    "Action":[
        "kms:Encrypt",
        "kms:Decrypt",
        "kms:ReEncrypt*",
        "kms:GenerateDataKey*",
        "kms:CreateGrant",
        "kms:ListGrants",
        "kms:DescribeKey"
    ],
    "Resource":"*",
    "Condition":{
        "StringEquals":{
            "kms:ViaService":"s3.us-east-1.amazonaws.com"
        }
    }
}
```

5. Go back to the same file we opened in *step 3* and click on **Open** to open the file. We won't be able to view the file now and will get the following error. This has happened because S3 doesn't have permission to use the key to perform decryption:

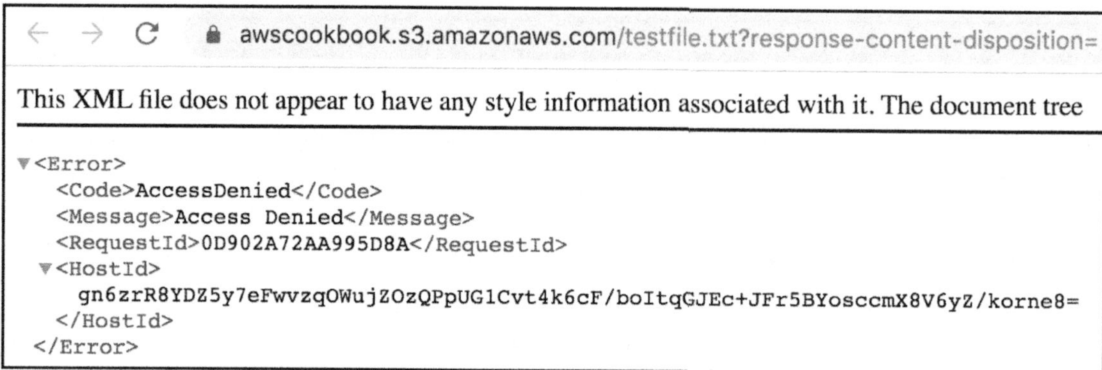

If we try to run the URL directly on a browser without clicking **Open from S3 console**, the file won't be displayed with or without the key condition policy since decryption will not be attempted.

How it works...

In this recipe, we created a key with default permissions and tried encrypting and decrypting files in the bucket with that key. We were able to successfully encrypt and decrypt. Then, we added an explicit **Deny** for S3 service using the `kms:ViaService` condition key and tried decrypting the same file again. This time, we weren't able to decrypt.

As we saw in *step 1*, the default key policy gives full permission to the owner account's root user and enables the IAM policies that are required to access the CMK. It also allows key administrators to administrate the CMK and key users to use the CMK. Also, we need to specify the region for the S3 service while using it within the ViaService API. I used us-east-1 since my bucket is present in us-east-1.

In our key policy JSON, we used the following elements:

- **Effect**: Specifies whether to allow or deny permissions.
- **Principal**: Specifies who gets the permissions. Allowed values include AWS accounts (root), IAM users, IAM roles, and supported AWS services.
- **Action**: Specifies the operations (for example, `kms:Encrypt`) to allow or deny.
- **Resource**: Specifies the resource to apply the policy. We specified `*` to denote all the resources.
- **Condition**: Used to specify any condition for the key policy to take effect. This is an optional element.

We can also specify an optional `Sid` parameter. **Sid** stands for **statement identifier** and can contain a string value that describes our policy.

There's more...

Let's quickly go through some important concepts about using key policies:

- For managing access to KMS resources, we can use key policies alone, or we can use IAM policies and grants along with key policies.
- To allow access to KMS CMK, we always need to use key policies, either alone or along with IAM policies or grants.
- The primary resource within KMS is the CMK.
- A CMK's ARN has the following form: `arn:aws:kms:<region>:<account ID>:key/<key ID>`.
- Some KMS operations also allow the use of an alias as a resource. An alias ARN has the following form: `arn:aws:kms:<region>:<account ID>:alias/<alias name>`.
- Any user, including the root user, can access CMK, but only if the key policy allows it.
- The default key policy when a CMK is created from the console gives full permission to the owner's account root user and also enables IAM policies that are required to access the CMK. It will also allow key administrators to administrate the CMK and key users to use the CMK. The default key policy when a CMK is created programmatically gives full permission to the owner's account root user. It also enables IAM policies that are required to access CMK.

- When we add key administrators, the key administrator's details are added to the policy document statement for key administrators.
- The following are the important operations that are included in the key administrator's policy document statement: `kms:Create*`, `kms:Describe*`, `kms:Enable*`, `kms:List*`, `kms:Put*`, `kms:Update*`, `kms:Revoke*`, `kms:Disable*`, `kms:Get*`, `kms:Delete*`, `kms:TagResource`, `kms:UntagResource`, `kms:ScheduleKeyDeletion`, and `kms:CancelKeyDeletion`.
- AWS has added a wildcard to some of the default permissions so that, if AWS creates a new action that starts with the same prefix, the administrators will get the permission automatically.
- When we add key users, the key user details are added to the policy document statement for the key users.
- The following are the important operations that are included in the key user's policy document statement: `kms:Encrypt`, `kms:Decrypt`, `kms:ReEncrypt*`, `kms:GenerateDataKey*`, and `kms:DescribeKey`.
- AWS provides global condition keys, as well as service-specific keys.
- The global condition keys include `aws:PrincipalTag`, `aws:PrincipalType`, `aws:RequestTag`, `aws:SourceIp`, `aws:SourceVpc`, `aws:SourceVpce`, `aws:TagKeys`, `aws:TokenIssueTime`, `aws:userid`, and `aws:username`.
- The AWS KMS condition keys include `kms:BypassPolicyLockoutSafetyCheck`, `kms:CallerAccount`, `kms:EncryptionContext`, `kms:EncryptionContextKeys`, `kms:ExpirationModel`, `kms:GrantConstraintType`, `kms:GrantIsForAWSResource`, `kms:GrantOperations`, `kms:GranteePrincipal`, `kms:KeyOrigin`, `kms:ReEncryptOnSameKey`, `kms:RetiringPrincipal`, `kms:ValidTo`, `kms:ViaService`, `kms:WrappingAlgorithm`, and `kms:WrappingKeySpec`.

See also

- You can read more about key policies at `https://docs.aws.amazon.com/kms/latest/developerguide/key-policies.html`.
- Details about KMS condition keys can be found here: `https://docs.aws.amazon.com/kms/latest/developerguide/policy-conditions.html`.

Sharing customer-managed keys across accounts

In this recipe, we will learn how to use a CMK from one account in another account.

Getting ready

We need two AWS accounts to complete this recipe. I am reusing the accounts we created using AWS organizations in `Chapter 1`, *Managing AWS Accounts with IAM and Organizations*, with the account ID of the first account set to `135301570106` and the account ID of the second account set to `380701114427`.

How to do it...

First, we will create a new CMK in the first account. After that, we will provide permissions to use it from the second account. Finally, we will test the first account from the second account using the CMK.

Creating a key and giving permission to the other account

In this section, we will create a key with key usage permission to account 2, as follows:

1. Go to the KMS dashboard, click on **Create key**, and start creating a CMK by providing an **Alias** and **Description**.
2. Optionally, add any **Tags** on the next screen.
3. On the next screen, we can add any key administrators if we want to.

4. On the **Define key usage permissions** screen, scroll down to the **Other AWS accounts** section:

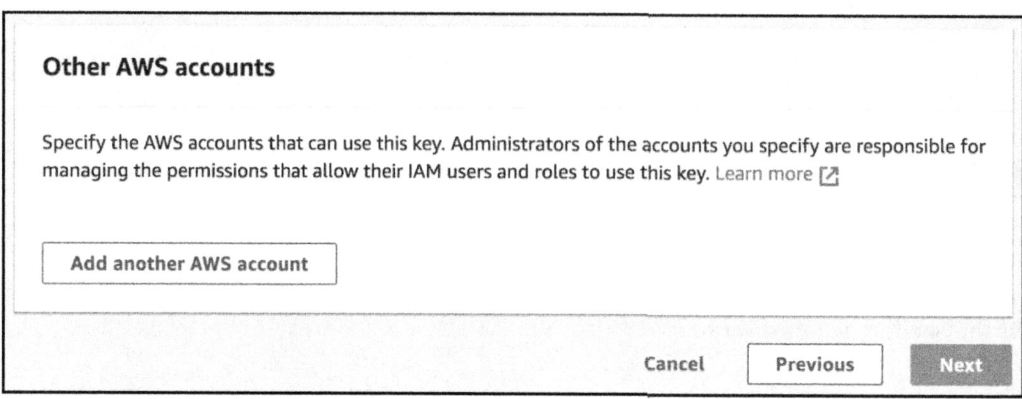

5. Click on **Add another AWS account**.
6. Enter the account ID of the second AWS account and click **Next**:

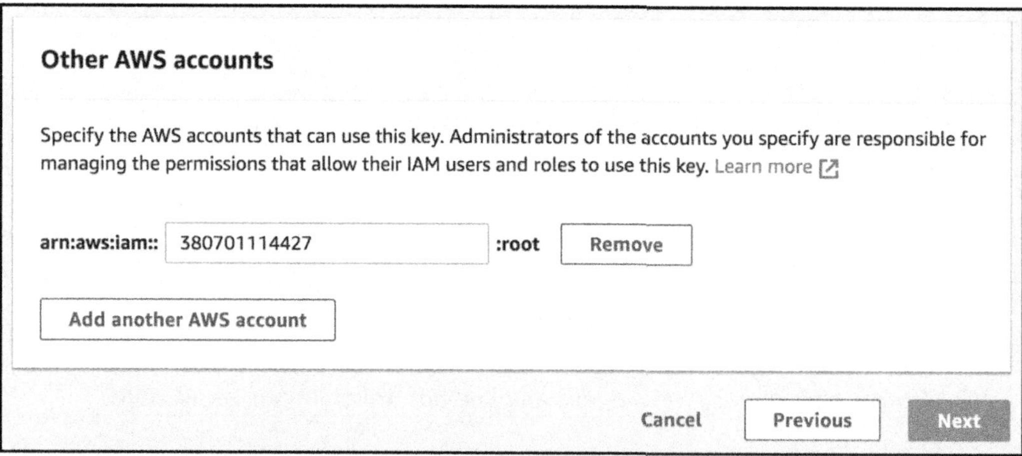

7. On the **Review and edit key policy** screen, click **Finish**. We should see that the following statement has been added to the key policy:

```
{
   "Sid":"Allow attachment of persistent resources",
   "Effect":"Allow",
   "Principal":{
      "AWS":"arn:aws:iam::380701114427:root"
   },
```

```
            "Action":[
                "kms:CreateGrant",
                "kms:ListGrants",
                "kms:RevokeGrant"
            ],
            "Resource":"*",
            "Condition":{
                "Bool":{
                    "kms:GrantIsForAWSResource":"true"
                }
            }
        }
```

The ARN for our newly created key is as follows: `arn:aws:kms:us-east-1:135301570106:key/d791248f-c742-4ed9-a081-cfa314dd6903`.

Using the key as an administrator user from account 2

Now, let's try using the key as a user with the administrator permission from account 2. Follow these steps:

1. Encrypt the data with the profile of an administrator user from account 2 from the CLI:

```
aws kms encrypt \
     --plaintext "hello 4" \
     --key-id arn:aws:kms:us-east-1:135301570106:key/d791248f-
c742-4ed9-a081-cfa314dd6903 \
     --profile awschild1admin
```

   We should see the following response:


```
{
    "CiphertextBlob": "AQICAHgAn+wuJ5cOyzgLN21IJKa50Jcy2hJTTmILJbmxbp392wE92OZRG6baitBiM
pD/0aijAAAAZTBjBgkqhkiG9w0BBwagVjBUAgEAME8GCSqGSIb3DQEHATAeBglghkgBZQMEAS4wEQQMW9jzsbPNp
JAvGd+aAgEQgCL4VAqVMNcnLmOPcdM+/m0zFPFxZ66pjeRMb4zVKbgQwpxt",
    "KeyId": "arn:aws:kms:us-east-1:135301570106:key/d791248f-c742-4ed9-a081-cfa314dd690
3"
}
```


In the next section, we will use the key as a non-admin user from account 2.

Using the key as a non-admin user from account 2

To use the CMK as a non-admin user, the root or the admin user of account 2 has to delegate the permission to the non-admin user by following these steps:

1. Go to the IAM dashboard.
2. Click on **Policies**.
3. Click on **Create policy**.
4. Go to the **JSON** tab.
5. Enter the following policy:

```
{
  "Version": "2012-10-17",
  "Statement": [
    {
      "Sid": "Delegate CMK access from 135301570106",
      "Effect": "Allow",
      "Action": [
        "kms:Encrypt",
        "kms:Decrypt",
        "kms:ReEncrypt*",
        "kms:GenerateDataKey*",
        "kms:DescribeKey"
      ],
      "Resource": "arn:aws:kms:us-
east-1:135301570106:key/d791248f-c742-4ed9-a081-cfa314dd6903"
    }
  ]
}
```

6. Click on **Review policy**.
7. Provide a name and description for our policy.
8. Click on **Create policy**.
9. Click **Users**.
10. Click on the non-admin user that we want to delegate permission to.
11. Click on **Add permissions**.
12. Click on **Attach existing policies directly**.

13. Search and select our new policy. Click on **Next:Review**.
14. Click on **Add permissions**.
15. Encrypt the data with the profile of a non-administrator user from account 2 from the CLI:

```
aws kms encrypt \
    --plaintext "hello 5" \
    --key-id arn:aws:kms:us-east-1:135301570106:key/d791248f-
c742-4ed9-a081-cfa314dd6903 \
    --profile child1_testuser
```

We should see the following response:


```
{
    "CiphertextBlob": "AQICAHgAn+wuJ5cOyzgLN21IJKa50Jcy2hJTTmILJbmxbp392wHeifaQJMSxhFz5c
W0TgNQEAAAAZTBjBgkqhkiG9w0BBwagVjBUAgEAME8GCSqGSIb3DQEHATAeBglghkgBZQMEAS4wEQQMc6KZwgWQ0
0Ut6TUMAgEQgCKevCclS+xpt7x90SttjsMlGBNw2qxk4FoTYhrlED1CSCSp",
    "KeyId": "arn:aws:kms:us-east-1:135301570106:key/d791248f-c742-4ed9-a081-cfa314dd690
3"
}
```


In this recipe, we created a new CMK. You can also edit an existing CMK and add another account's details.

How it works...

In this recipe, we created a CMK in account 1 with permissions for account 2. After that, we successfully encrypted data on the other account with an administrator user's profile from CLI.

To encrypt using a non-administrator user, an administrator user of account 2 needs to delegate permissions to the user or role that needs access. We did this through an IAM policy. The policy was created from the console. Then, we added this policy to our non-administrator user, `testuser`.

For more details on the policy document's structure, refer to the *Using key policies with conditional keys* recipe.

There's more...

In this recipe, we tried encrypting data from the AWS CLI. Even though delegating key permissions across accounts is supported for most integrated services, such as S3 and EC2, their support for selecting the key automatically from the console may not be supported. Check out each service's console documentation for more details. If there is a limitation from the console, then we will need to do this through the API by specifying the ARN of the key.

See also

- You can read more about cross-account access to CMKs at `https://docs.aws.amazon.com/kms/latest/developerguide/key-policy-modifying-external-accounts.html`.

Creating a CloudHSM cluster

In this recipe, we will create an AWS CloudHSM cluster. CloudHSM is a dedicated **hardware security module** (**HSM**) on the AWS Cloud that we can use to generate and use our own encryption keys. AWS KMS, on the other hand, uses shared HSM. While KMS only allows us to use symmetric keys, CloudHSM supports both symmetric and asymmetric keys.

Getting ready

We need a working AWS account to complete this recipe.

CloudHSM usage costs more than KMS, and CloudHSM doesn't have a free tier either. If you are following these recipes for learning purposes, you should clean up the resources that you created after completing all the recipes related to CloudHSM.

How to do it...

In this recipe, we will create a CloudHSM cluster using the default VPCs, as follows:

1. Go to the **CloudHSM service** in the console.

2. Click on **Create Cluster**.
3. Select the VPC that you want to use:

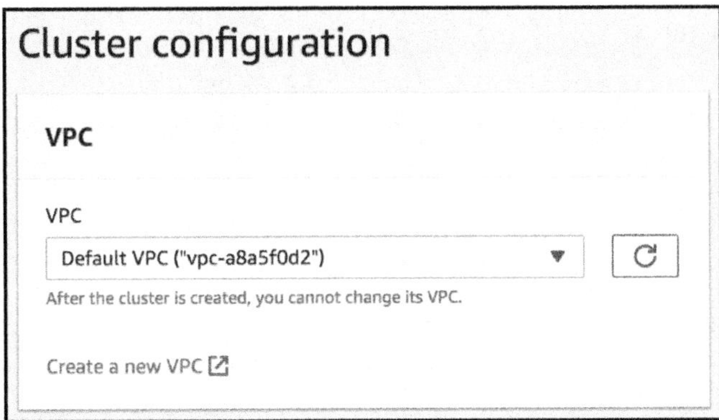

You may also create a custom VPC with private and public subnets and use them instead of the default VPCs that we're using in this chapter, if you are configuring CloudHSM for production. We will be covering VPCs in-depth in the next chapter.

4. Select one subnet per availability zone, for three availability zones. You can choose more or fewer availability zones as per your requirements:

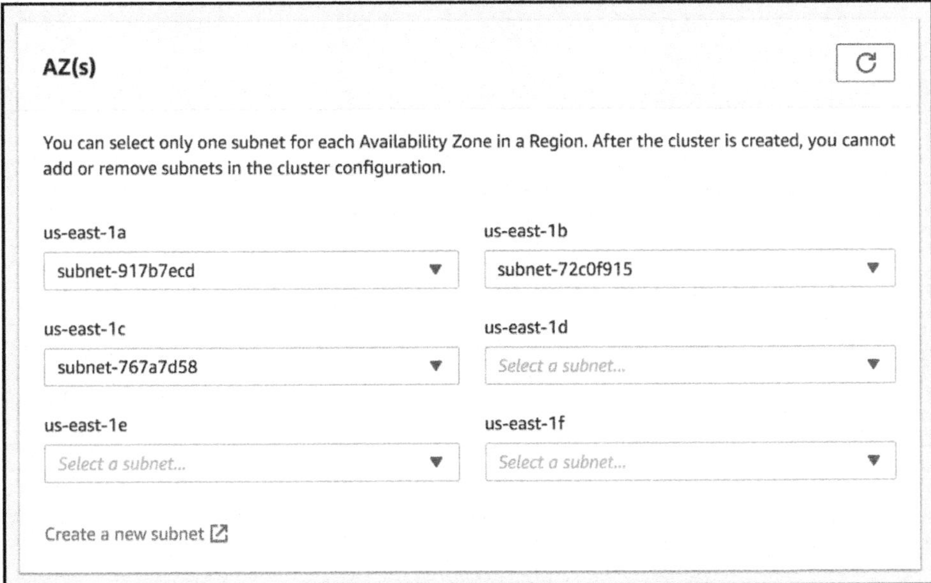

5. Select the **Create a new cluster** option and click on **Review**:

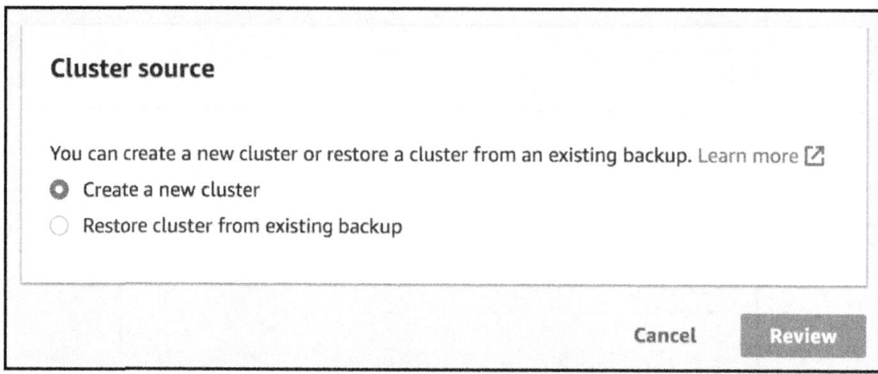

6. Review the details on the **Review** screen and click **Create cluster**:

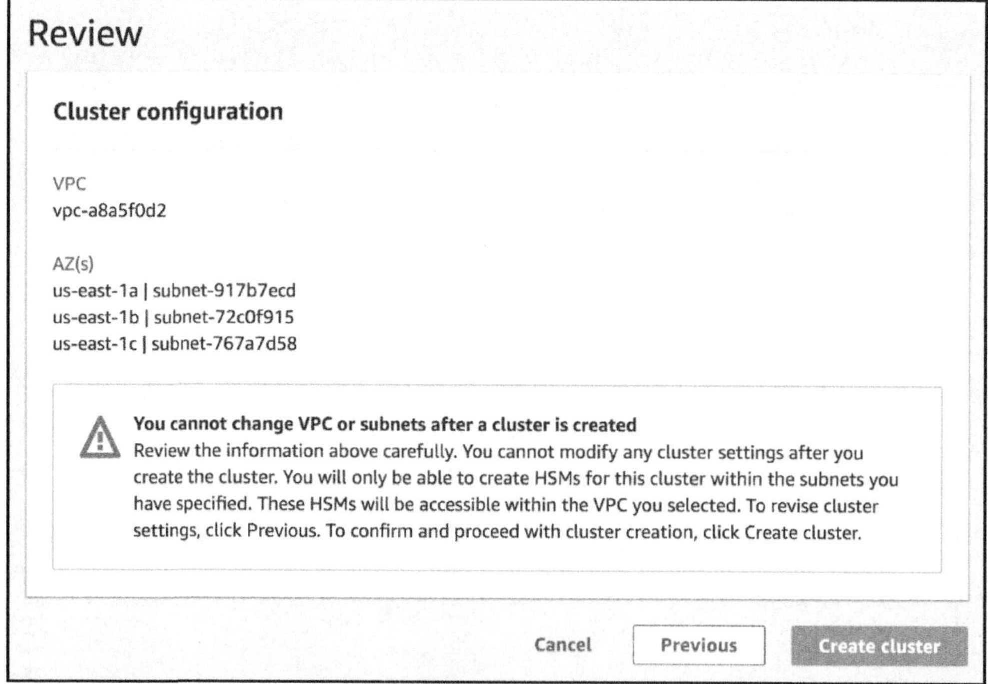

Cluster creation might take some time to complete. If the create cluster operation is successful, we should see a screen with a success message similar to the following one:

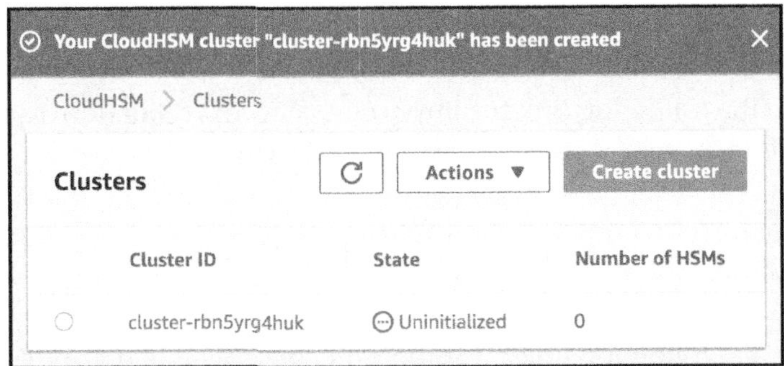

Now, we need to initialize the cluster. In the next recipe, we will initialize our cluster and create our first HSM.

How it works...

In this recipe, we created a CloudHSM cluster. I used the default VPC for convenience. You can also use it if you are experimenting with HSM for learning purposes. For practical use cases, you should install HSM into a private subnet within a custom VPC. We will look at VPCs in detail in the next chapter.

In the next recipe, we will initialize our cluster and create our first HSM. CloudHSM does not have a free tier. A provisioned HSM can cost you money for every hour it runs, so if you are following these recipes for learning or experimentation purposes, do make sure you complete the next recipe as fast as you can and clean up all the resources once you are done.

There's more...

Let's quickly go through some more important concepts related to the AWS CloudHSM service:

- An HSM is a physical computing device that's used for safeguarding and managing digital keys.
- AWS CloudHSM's HSMs provide compliance requirements such as FIPS 140-2 Level 3 validation and EAL4.

To be able to understand these recipes in greater depth, you may wish to learn about important concepts relating to cryptography. These are provided in the *See also* section.

See also

- Refer to the following link for important concepts related to asymmetric encryption: `https://heartin.tech/en/blog-entry/important-points-remember-about-asymmetric-encryption`.
- Refer to the following link for important concepts related to digital certificates and hashing: `https://heartin.tech/en/blog-entry/important-points-remember-about-digital-certificates-and-hashing`.
- Refer to the following link for important concepts related to PKI: `https://heartin.tech/en/blog-entry/important-points-remember-about-public-key-infrastructure-pki`.
- You can read more about the different types of users of CloudHSM here: `https://docs.aws.amazon.com/cloudhsm/latest/userguide/hsm-users.html`.

Initializing and activating a CloudHSM cluster

In this recipe, we will initialize and activate a CloudHSM cluster. In the previous recipe, we created a CloudHSM cluster. AWS CloudHSM is a dedicated HSM on the AWS Cloud that we can use to generate and use our own encryption keys.

Getting ready

We need a working AWS account to complete this recipe. You can create a CloudHSM cluster by following the *Creating a CloudHSM cluster* recipe in this chapter.

CloudHSM usage costs more than KMS, and CloudHSM doesn't have a free tier either. If you are following the recipes related to CloudHSM, then you should be careful while using it. After completing the steps within this recipe, you should clean up the resources that you created.

How to do it...

To initialize and activate a CloudHSM cluster, follow these steps:

1. Initialize the cluster and create our first HSM.
2. Launch an EC2 Client instance for CloudHSM and activate the cluster.

We will start by initializing the cluster.

Initializing the cluster and creating our first HSM

We can initialize our cluster by going to the CloudHSM clusters list and following these steps:

1. Select our cluster and click on **Initialize** under the **Actions** drop-down menu:

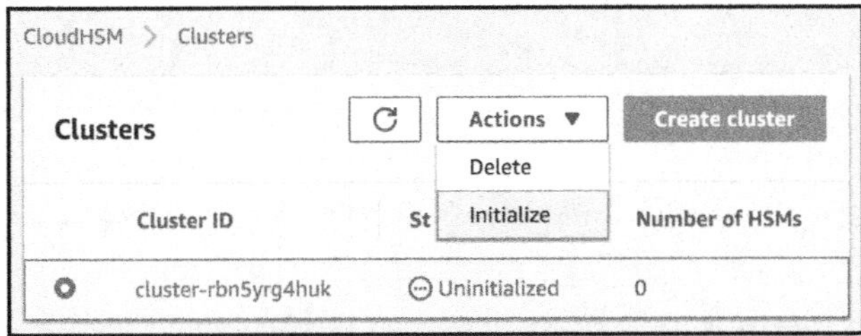

2. Create an HSM. Select one of the AZs we selected while creating the cluster and click **Create**:

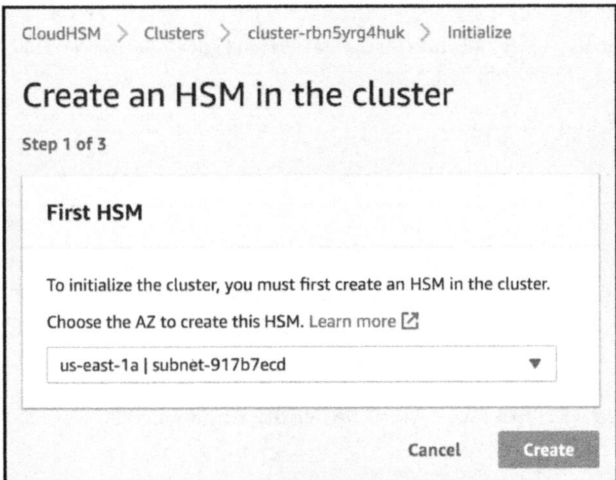

HSM creation can take some time. Once done, we should see a message similar to the one shown in the following screenshot:

Your first HSM is being created in cluster-rbn5yrg4huk
This will take a few minutes. Once the HSM has been created, you can complete the cluster initialization process.

3. Download the **certificate signing request** (**CSR**) and sign it. Optionally, we can verify the identity and authenticity of the cluster's HSM by following the *There's more...* section and the *See more* section of this recipe:

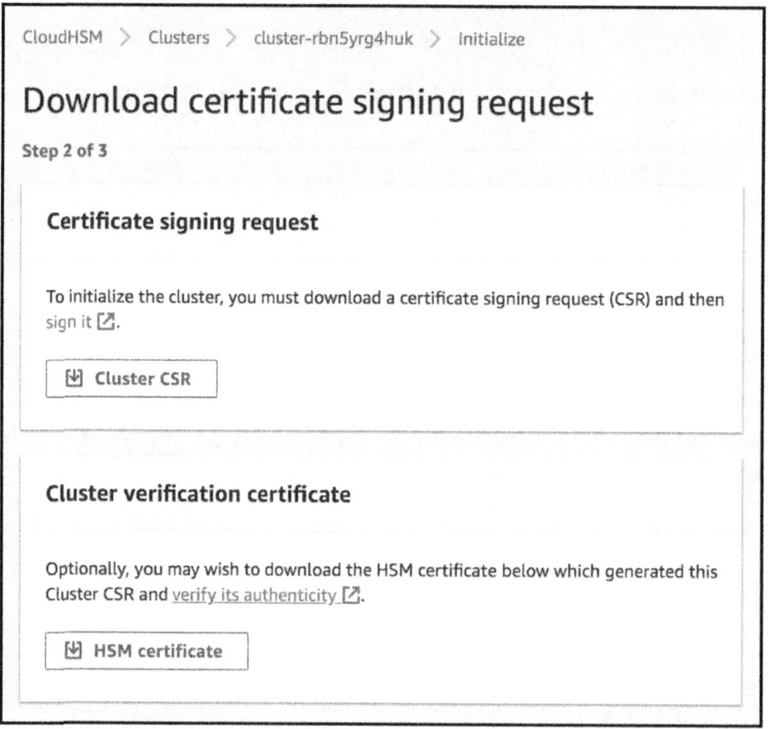

4. Generate a private key. We can generate a private key using OpenSSL for development and testing purposes. You can see any related AWS documentation by clicking on the **sign it** reference link next to the **Cluster CSR** download button:

```
openssl genrsa -aes256 -out customerCA.key 2048
```

We should get a response similar to the one shown in the following screenshot:

```
$ openssl genrsa -aes256 -out customerCA.key 2048
Generating RSA private key, 2048 bit long modulus
..........................................+++
...............................................
.......................................+++
e is 65537 (0x10001)
Enter pass phrase for customerCA.key:
Verifying - Enter pass phrase for customerCA.key:
```

5. Use our private key to create a self-signed certificate. We can use OpenSSL for development and testing purposes:

```
openssl req -new -x509 -days 3652 -key customerCA.key -out
customerCA.crt
```

Answer the questions that are received in the response output:

```
$ openssl req -new -x509 -days 3652 -key customerCA.key -out customerCA.crt
Enter pass phrase for customerCA.key:
You are about to be asked to enter information that will be incorporated
into your certificate request.
What you are about to enter is what is called a Distinguished Name or a DN.
There are quite a few fields but you can leave some blank
For some fields there will be a default value,
If you enter '.', the field will be left blank.
-----
Country Name (2 letter code) []:IN
State or Province Name (full name) []:Karnataka
Locality Name (eg, city) []:Bangalore
Organization Name (eg, company) []:Heartin Tech
Organizational Unit Name (eg, section) []:Research
Common Name (eg, fully qualified host name) []:Heartin Kanikathottu
Email Address []:awssecuritycookbook@gmail.com
```

6. Sign the cluster CSR. We can use OpenSSL with the command syntax that's available from the AWS documentation to do so:

```
openssl x509 -req -days 3652 -in cluster-
rbn5yrg4huk_ClusterCsr.csr \
                              -CA customerCA.crt \
                              -CAkey customerCA.key \
                              -CAcreateserial \
                              -out cluster-
rbn5yrg4huk_CustomerHsmCertificate.crt
```

This should create a file named `cluster-rbn5yrg4huk_CustomerHsmCertificate.crt`.

7. On the **Upload certificates** screen within the AWS console, upload the signed cluster certificate and signing certificate (issuing certificate):

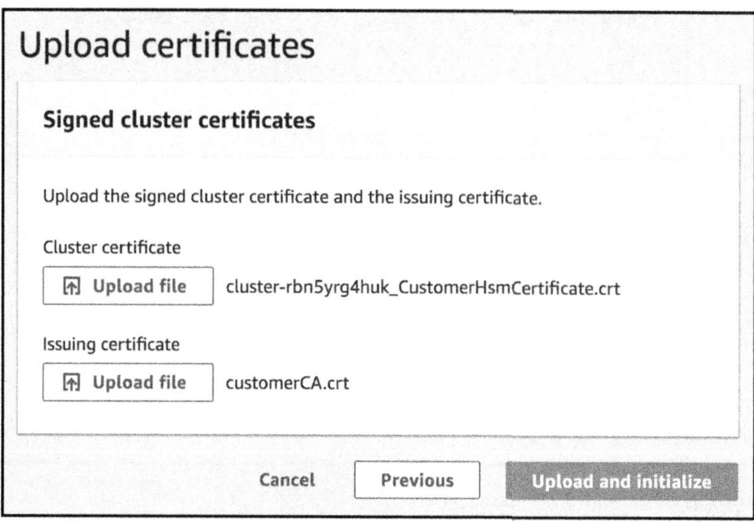

8. Click on **Upload and initialize**.

   We should immediately see a response similar to the one shown in the following screenshot:

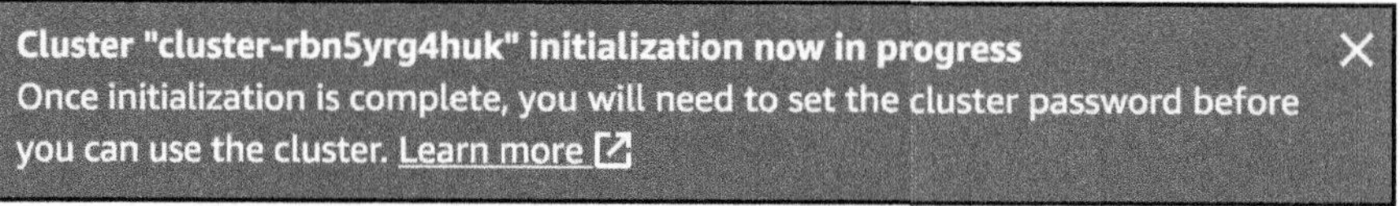

   Once the initialization is done, we should get a message similar to the one shown in the following screenshot:

9. Click on **Clusters** on the left sidebar and scroll down to select our cluster. Once you're done, take note of the IP of the HSM:

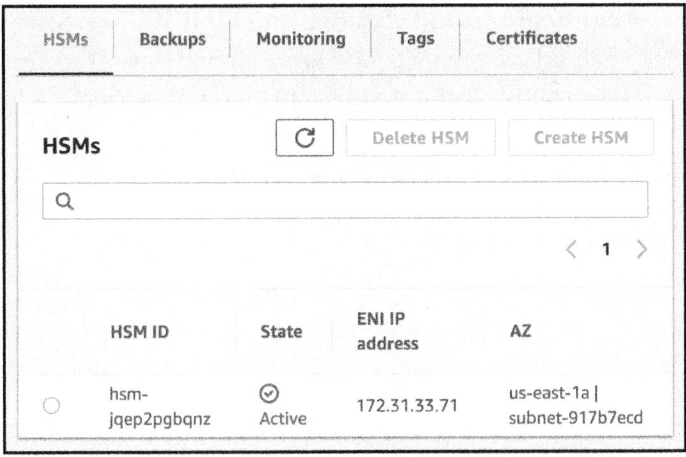

In the next section, we will launch an EC2 client instance for our HSM and activate the cluster.

Launching an EC2 client instance and activating the cluster

In this section, we will launch an EC2 client instance for our HSM and activate the cluster. Follow these steps:

1. First, we need to launch an EC2 client instance:
    1. Select the same VPC as our HSM, which is the default VPC in my case. Select a public subnet in that VPC. The **Auto-assign Public IP** option should have a value of **Enable**:

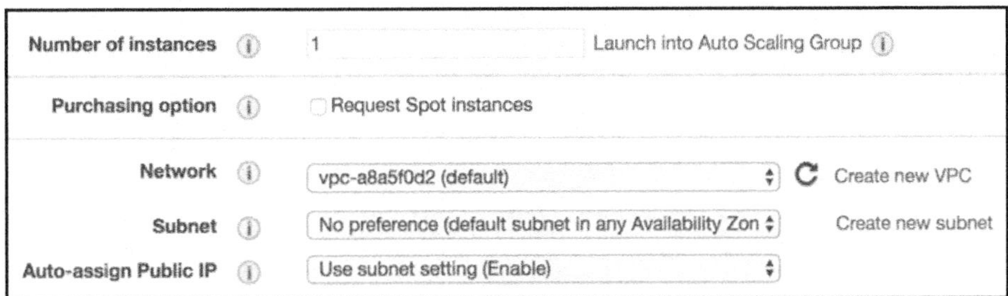

2. Leave the other options as is and click the **Next** buttons until you get to the **Configure Security Group** page.
3. On the **Configure Security Group** page, select **Select an existing security group** and choose the **default VPC security group**.
4. When asked, create a new key pair and save it securely. If you're on Mac or Linux, set a permission of `400` using `chmod` for your key file. I have saved this into a file called `aws-sec-cb-hsm-demo.pem`.

2. Post-launch, add the security group of our HSM to our EC2 instance but keep the current one too. Also, add an inbound rule in order to allow SSH traffic from your IP, if that's not present:

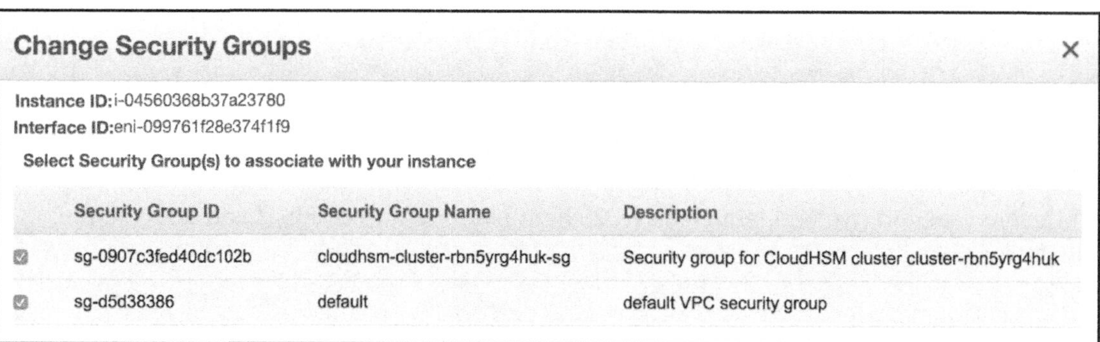

3. Copy the self-signed certificate, `customerCA.crt`, into the EC2 machine. On Mac or Linux, we can use the `scp` command to do this, as follows:

```
scp -i aws-sec-cb-hsm-demo.pem customerCA.crt ec2-
user@ec2-3-86-195-36.compute-1.amazonaws.com:/home/ec2-user
```

4. SSH into the EC2 instance. The exact command or steps may differ between operating systems. On Mac or Linux, we can use the following command:

```
ssh -i aws-sec-cb-hsm-demo.pem ec2-
user@ec2-3-86-195-36.compute-1.amazonaws.com
```

5. Run `sudo yum install`.
6. Run the following command to get the latest CloudHSM client RPM:

```
wget
https://s3.amazonaws.com/cloudhsmv2-software/cloudhsm-client-la
test.x86_64.rpm
```

7. Run the following command to install the CloudHSM client:

```
sudo yum install -y ./cloudhsm-client-latest.x86_64.rpm
```

8. Add the IP address of our HSM to the configuration. We took note of it in *step 9* of the previous section, *Initializing the cluster and creating our first HSM*:

```
sudo /opt/cloudhsm/bin/configure -a 172.31.33.71
```

9. Copy the self-signed certificate, `customerCA.crt`, into `/opt/cloudhsm/etc/`:

```
sudo cp /home/ec2-user/customerCA.crt /opt/cloudhsm/etc/
```

10. Run the following command to start the `cloudhsm_mgmt_util` utility:

```
/opt/cloudhsm/bin/cloudhsm_mgmt_util
/opt/cloudhsm/etc/cloudhsm_mgmt_util.cfg
```

    If successful, we should see the `aws-cloudhsm` Command Prompt:

```
[ec2-user@ip-172-31-93-202 ~]$ /opt/cloudhsm/bin/cloudhsm_mgmt_util /opt/cloudhsm/etc/
cloudhsm_mgmt_util.cfg

Connecting to the server(s), it may take time
depending on the server(s) load, please wait...

Connecting to server '172.31.33.71': hostname '172.31.33.71', port 2225...
Connected to server '172.31.33.71': hostname '172.31.33.71', port 2225.
aws-cloudhsm>
```

11. Enable end-to-end encryption using the `enable_e2e` command. If successful, we should get the following response:

```
aws-cloudhsm>enable_e2e
E2E enabled on server 0(172.31.33.71)

aws-cloudhsm>
```

12. List all the users using the `listUsers` command. We should get the following response:

```
aws-cloudhsm>listUsers
Users on server 0(172.31.33.71):
Number of users found:2

    User Id         User Type       User Name        MofnPubKey LoginFailureCnt  2FA
         1          PRECO           admin                  NO              0              NO
         2          AU              app_user               NO              0              NO
```

13. Log in to HSM using the `loginHSM` command as the PRECO user:

```
loginHSM PRECO admin password
```

We should get the following response:

```
aws-cloudhsm>loginHSM PRECO admin password
loginHSM success on server 0(172.31.33.71)
```

14. Change the password of the PRECO user using the `changePswd` command while providing a password that meets your requirements:

```
changePswd PRECO admin NewPassword$!
```

We should get the following response:

```
aws-cloudhsm>changePswd PRECO admin NewPassword$!
*************************CAUTION********************************
This is a CRITICAL operation, should be done on all nodes in the
cluster. Cav server does NOT synchronize these changes with the
nodes on which this operation is not executed or failed, please
ensure this operation is executed on all nodes in the cluster.
****************************************************************

Do you want to continue(y/n)?y
Changing password for admin(PRECO) on 1 nodes
```

15. List all the users using the `listUsers` command. We should get the following response:

```
aws-cloudhsm>listUsers
Users on server 0(172.31.33.71):
Number of users found:2

    User Id         User Type       User Name       MofnPubKey      LoginFailureCnt     2FA
          1         CO              admin                   NO                    0      NO
          2         AU              app_user                NO                    0      NO
```

16. We can quit the utility using the `quit` command.
17. Go back to our cluster within the console and verify that we can't see the display message that the cluster can't be used until the password is updated.

If you created this cluster for development or testing purposes, remember to delete the HSM and the cluster to avoid incurring unexpected charges.

How it works...

In this recipe, we initialized a CloudHSM cluster and created our first HSM within it. I used the default VPC for convenience. You can also use it if you are experimenting with HSM for learning purposes. For practical use cases, we should install HSM in a private subnet within a custom VPC for added security. We will look at VPCs in detail in the next chapter.

Before initializing the cluster, we need to download a CSR and sign it. For practical use cases, a certificate authority such as Verisign should sign it to create a signed certificate. For development and testing purposes, we can use a self-signed certificate to sign it using OpenSSL. To do this, follow these steps:

1. Create a private key using OpenSSL.
2. Use the private key to create a self-signed signing certificate (issuing certificate).
3. Use the self-signed signing certificate (issuing certificate) to sign the CSR we downloaded from the AWS console.
4. Finally, upload both our signed CSR certificate and the self-signed issuing certificate to AWS.

First, we logged into the system as a user with the PRECO role, which is a temporary user role that exists on the first HSM in our cluster. After we change the default password for this user, we observed that its type changed from PRECO to CO. A user of the AU type was also present.

With CloudHSM, we have four main user types:

- **Precrypto Officer** (PRECO)
- **Crypto Officer** (CO)
- **Crypto User** (CU)
- **Appliance User** (AU)

PRECO is a user role that is created by AWS that we can use until we update the password. Once updated, the user's type is changed to CO. We can create more users with the CO role. The first CO user is referred to as the Primary PCO. A Crypto Officer is responsible for managing users. CU is responsible for managing keys, including creating, deleting, sharing, importing, and exporting them. CU is also responsible for cryptographic operations such as encryption, decryption, signing, verifying, and more. AU is a limited permission user that is generally used by AWS for cloning and synchronization activities.

There's more...

In this recipe, we created, initialized, and activated a CloudHSM cluster with an HSM. We can verify the HSM's identity using the certificates that we can download from AWS. At the time of writing, the following are the six certificates that can be downloaded from CloudHSM and verified:

- Cluster CSR
- HSM certificate
- AWS hardware certificate
- Manufacturer hardware certificate
- AWS root certificate
- Manufacturer root certificate

Refer to the *See also* section for steps on how to verify the identity and authenticity of the cluster's HSM.

See also

- You can verify the identity and authenticity of the cluster's HSM by following the steps given at `https://docs.aws.amazon.com/cloudhsm/latest/userguide/verify-hsm-identity.html`.

5
Network Security with VPC

VPC stands for **Virtual Private Cloud**. VPCs can be considered virtual data centers on the cloud. With Amazon VPC, we can create our own virtual private networks isolated from the rest of the AWS public cloud infrastructure. We have complete control of our virtual private network. We can create our own IP address ranges, public or private subnets, and also configure the route tables and network gateways as per our requirements. We can launch internet-facing instances for web servers into the public subnets and launch non-internet facing instances such as database servers into the private subnets. We can also make use of multiple security mechanisms, such as security groups and **network access control lists** (**NACLs**), to secure the incoming and outgoing traffic of the instances within our VPCs.

In this chapter, we will cover the following recipes:

- Creating a VPC in AWS
- Creating subnets in a VPC
- Configuring an internet gateway and a route table for internet access
- Setting up and configuring NAT gateways
- Working with NACLs
- Using a VPC gateway endpoint to connect to S3
- Configuring and using VPC flow logs

Technical requirements

For this chapter, we'll need a working AWS account. Having a basic knowledge of the following computer networking concepts is also good to have:

- IP addresses
- Unicasting
- Broadcasting

- Subnets
- Subnet masking
- CIDR
- Routing

The code files for this chapter can be found at `https://github.com/PacktPublishing/AWS-Security-Cookbook/tree/master/Chapter05`.

Creating a VPC in AWS

In this recipe, we will create a VPC manually and explore the default configurations that are created by AWS.

Getting ready

We need a working AWS account to complete this recipe.

How to do it...

We can create a VPC in AWS as follows:

1. Log in to AWS and go to the VPC service in the console:

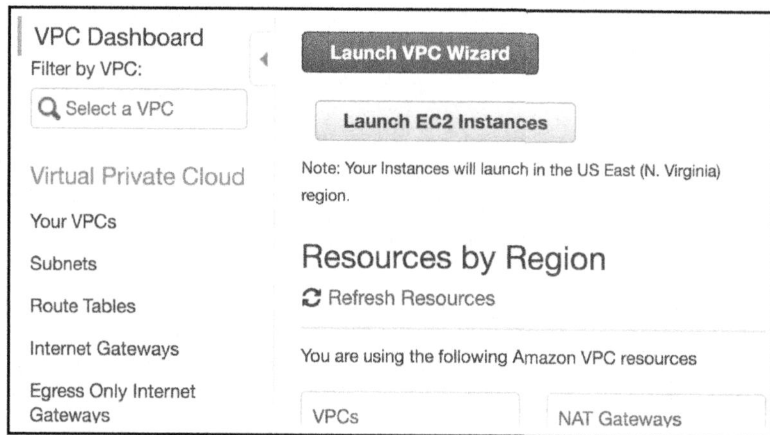

2. Click on **Your VPCs** on the left. You will be taken to the following screen:

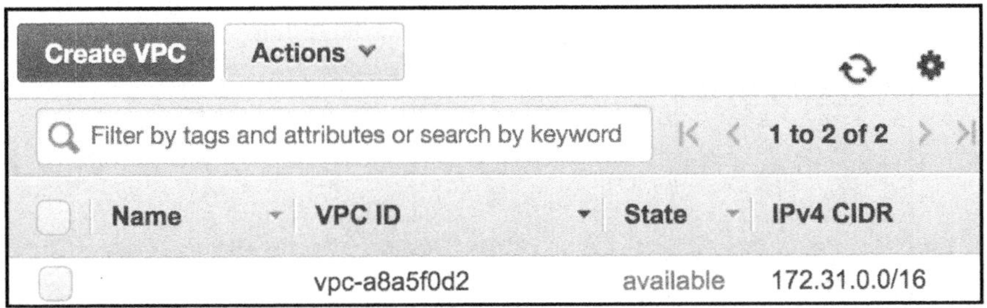

3. Click on **Create VPC**.
4. Enter the details shown in the following screenshot and click **Create**:

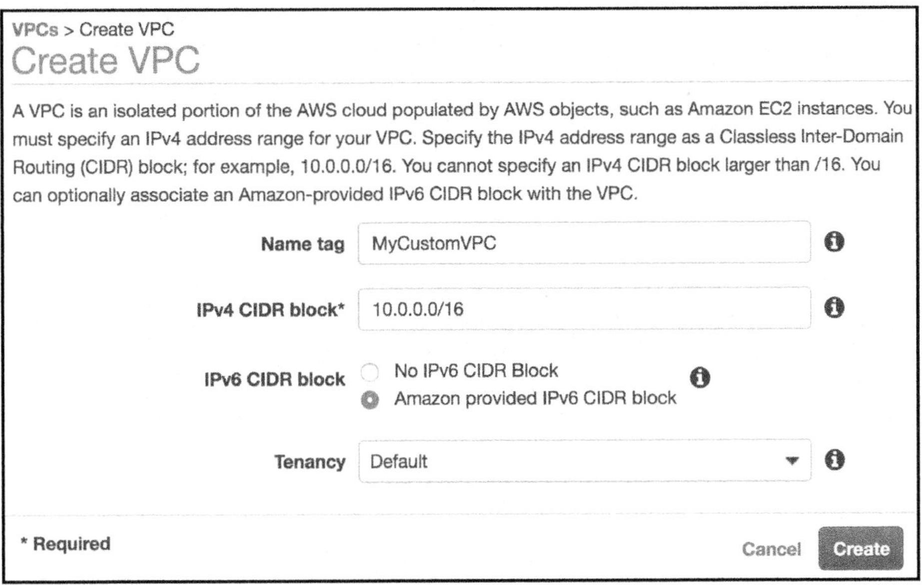

We should receive a success response similar to the one shown in the following screenshot:

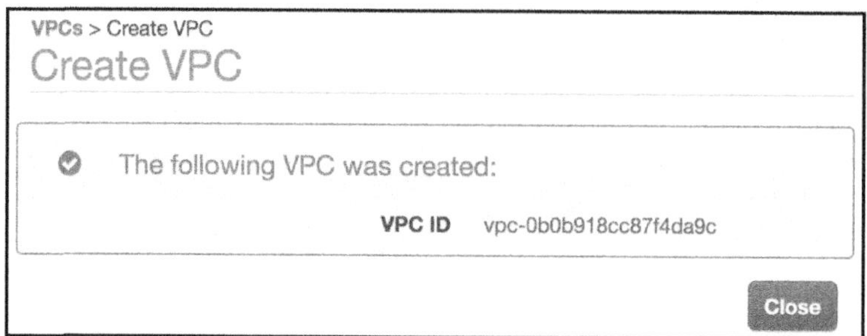

If we go to **Your VPCs** and select our VPC, we should be able to see a summary of our configuration that looks similar to the following:

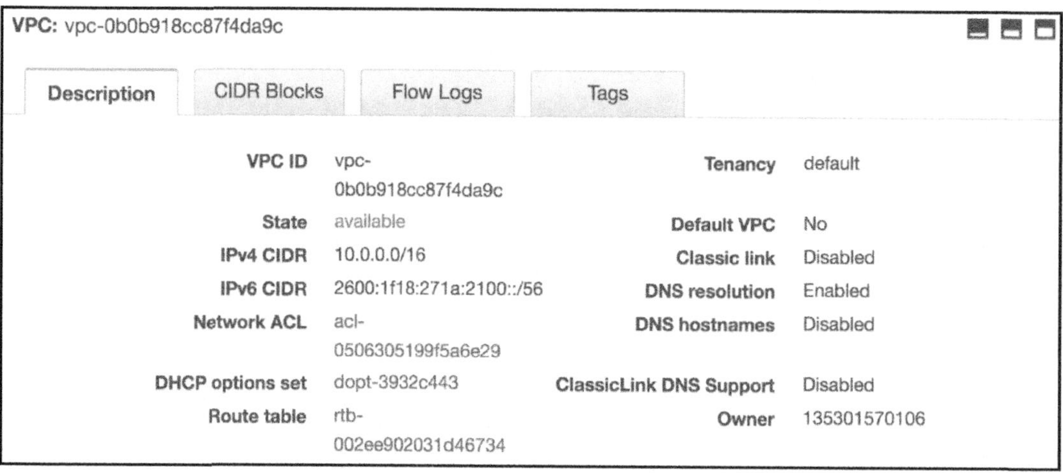

We will look at the default configurations that have been created by AWS for this VPC in the *There's more...* section.

How it works...

In this recipe, we created a VPC by providing an IPv4 CIDR block address range. AWS only supports CIDR block sizes between `/16` netmask and `/28` netmask. Therefore, `10.0.0.0/8` is not a valid CIDR block range for AWS VPCs.

We specified an IP address range of `10.0.0.0/16`, which is the largest CIDR block supported by AWS in VPCs. AWS requires us to specify the network identifier bits and leave the host identifier bits as zero. For example, `10.10.0.0/16` is a valid CIDR range since the last 16 bits are zeroes. However, `10.10.128.0/16` is not valid since there is a value in the 17th bit (128 is represented in binary as `10000000`). We can make `10.10.128.0` a valid CIDR range representation by setting the netmask to `/17`.

In theory, we can specify any IP address within a block in a CIDR block format representation. Most routers will AND it with the netmask bits to get the **network identifier** (**NID**) for that network, which is also the first IP address within that network. AWS, however, requires us to specify only the NID bits and leave the host identifier bits as zero.

We selected the **Amazon provided IPv6 CIDR block** option. Currently, AWS does not allow us to select IP address ranges for IPv6 addresses, unlike IPv4 addresses. We can only associate an Amazon-provided fixed size (`/56`) IPv6 CIDR block with our VPC by selecting this option. You can also select **No IPv6 CIDR block** as we won't be using an IPv6 CIDR block range in this chapter.

We set **Tenancy** to **Default**, which means that the instances of our VPC will use the tenancy attribute specified at their launch. An alternative is **Dedicated**, in which case the tenancy configuration that's specified at launch will be ignored and our instances will run on single-tenant dedicated hardware.

There's more...

In this recipe, we created a simple VPC without additional configuration. Some of the important default configurations that are created by AWS for our VPC are as follows:

- **DHCP Options Set** was updated with the following options: `domain-name = ec2.internal; domain-name-servers = AmazonProvidedDNS;`.
- **Main Route Table** was created with the following routes:

View: All routes

Destination	Target	Status	Propagated
10.0.0.0/16	local	active	No
2600:1f18:271a:2100::/56	local	active	No

Currently, the route table has no subnet association or route propagation configurations.

- **Network ACL** was created with inbound and outbound rules and had no subnet associations. The following were the inbound rules:

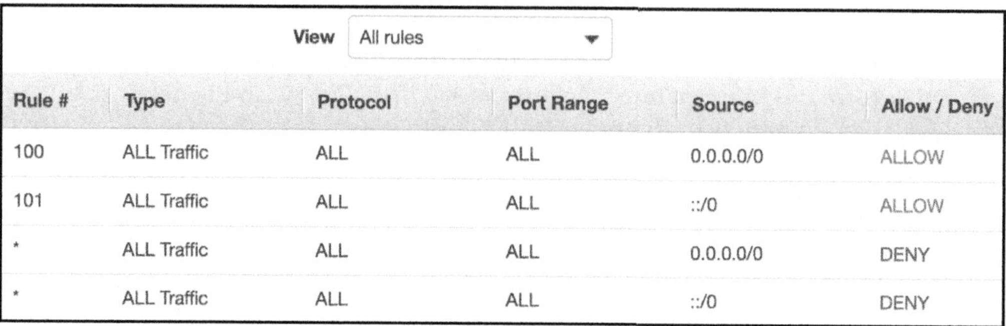

View All rules

Rule #	Type	Protocol	Port Range	Source	Allow / Deny
100	ALL Traffic	ALL	ALL	0.0.0.0/0	ALLOW
101	ALL Traffic	ALL	ALL	::/0	ALLOW
*	ALL Traffic	ALL	ALL	0.0.0.0/0	DENY
*	ALL Traffic	ALL	ALL	::/0	DENY

The following were the outbound rules:

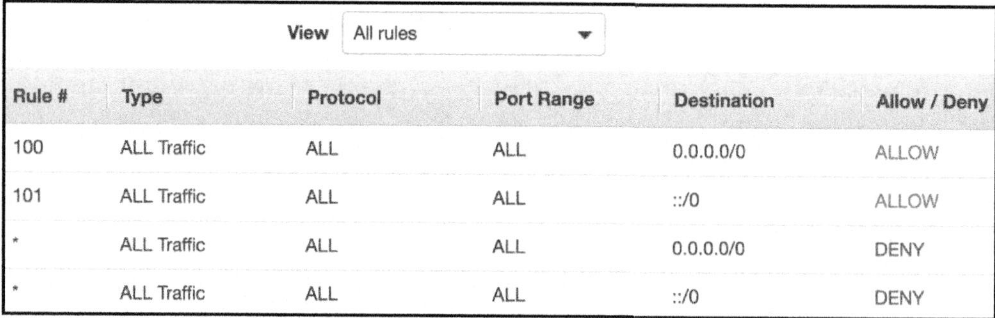

View All rules

Rule #	Type	Protocol	Port Range	Destination	Allow / Deny
100	ALL Traffic	ALL	ALL	0.0.0.0/0	ALLOW
101	ALL Traffic	ALL	ALL	::/0	ALLOW
*	ALL Traffic	ALL	ALL	0.0.0.0/0	DENY
*	ALL Traffic	ALL	ALL	::/0	DENY

- A security group was also created by AWS for our VPC. However, no subnets and internet gateways were created.

The following are some of the important settings that were created by AWS for my default VPC in the North Virginia region:

- Subnets in the default VPC have an outbound route to the internet. The following are the routes that were created for my default VPC in the North Virginia region:

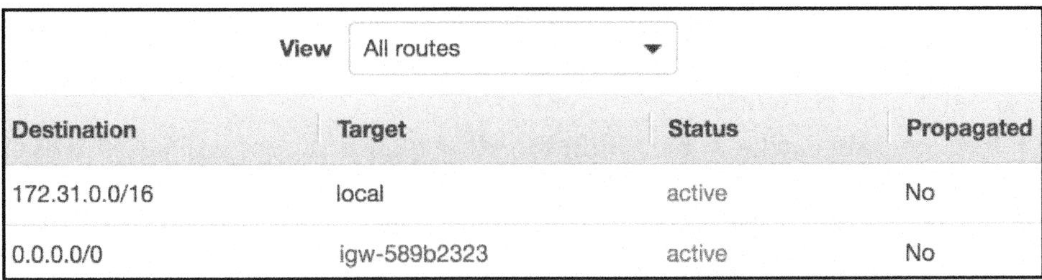

View: All routes

Destination	Target	Status	Propagated
172.31.0.0/16	local	active	No
0.0.0.0/0	igw-589b2323	active	No

- A subnet is created per availability zone. The following are the CIDR ranges for the subnets of my default VPC in the North Virginia region:

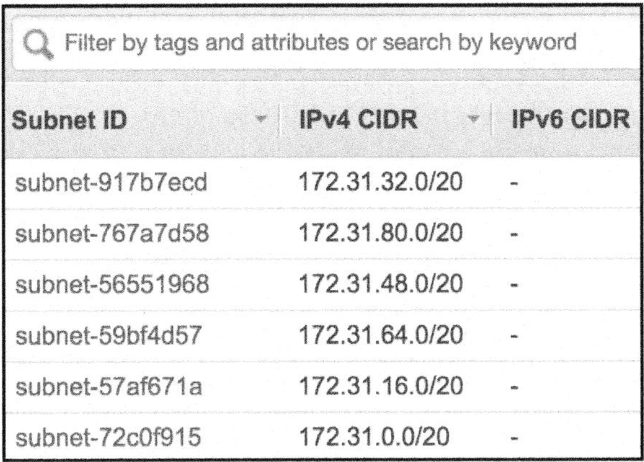

Filter by tags and attributes or search by keyword

Subnet ID	IPv4 CIDR	IPv6 CIDR
subnet-917b7ecd	172.31.32.0/20	-
subnet-767a7d58	172.31.80.0/20	-
subnet-56551968	172.31.48.0/20	-
subnet-59bf4d57	172.31.64.0/20	-
subnet-57af671a	172.31.16.0/20	-
subnet-72c0f915	172.31.0.0/20	-

- **DHCP Options Set** is updated. My default VPC has the following options set: `domain-name = ec2.internal; domain-name-servers = AmazonProvidedDNS`.

Let's quickly go through some important concepts related to AWS VPCs:

- AWS VPCs consist of subresources such as internet gateways, route tables, NACLs, subnets, and security groups.
- AWS creates a default VPC ready for us to use in every region. The following are some of its important characteristics:
    - Subnets in the default VPC have are routed to the internet.
    - A subnet is created per availability zone.
    - **DHCP Options Set** is updated.

- VPC peering can be used to connect one VPC to another through a direct route using private IP addresses, making the associated instances behave like they are on the same network.
- VPC peering can be done within the same region, across regions, and even across AWS accounts.
- Transitive peering is currently not supported for AWS VPCs. Every VPC has to be peered to every other required VPC in a star topology-like structure.
- To avoid the overhead of managing many point-to-point connections with VPC peering, we can make use of the **AWS Transit Gateway** to connect all the VPCs and even on-premise networks to a single gateway.
- Apart from the standard reserved IP addresses of network address and broadcast address, AWS also reserves three more IP addresses. So, a total of five addresses are reserved in a VPC.
- The following are the reserved IP addresses in an AWS VPC with a CIDR block range of `10.0.0.0/16`:
    - Network address: `10.0.0.0`
    - Reserved for VPC Router: `10.0.0.1`
    - Reserved for DNS: `10.0.0.2`
    - Reserved for future use: `10.0.0.3`
    - Broadcast address: `10.0.255.255`

If more CIDR blocks are configured for a VPC, the IP address of the first one will be used as a DNS server. The broadcast address is the last address of the block. If the CIDR block range is `10.0.0.0/24`, the broadcast address would be `10.0.0.255`.

- RFC 1918 recommends the use of the following ranges for private IPv4 addresses, as does AWS. However, AWS will only allow ranges with a netmask size of between `/16` and `/24`:
    - `10.0.0.0` - `10.255.255.255` (`10/8` prefix)
    - `172.16.0.0` - `172.31.255.255` (`172.16/12` prefix)
    - `192.168.0.0` - `192.168.255.255` (`192.168/16` prefix)

See also

- You can refer to the following page for resources that will help you learn the basics of computer networks that are required for this chapter, at `https://heartin.tech/en/book/computer-networks-essentials`.
- For learning essentials about IP addresses and CIDR, please refer to the following page at `https://heartin.tech/en/blog-entry/important-concepts-related-ip-addresses-and-cidr`.

Creating subnets in a VPC

In this recipe, we will add subnets to our VPC. Within our VPCs, we can create subnets with different inbound and outbound rules. For example, a web server may be launched into a public subnet and the database servers may be hosted on a private subnet, thereby only opening its database server ports for the public subnet.

Getting ready

Create a VPC with a CIDR block range of `10.0.0.0/16` by following the *Creating a VPC in AWS* recipe.

How to do it...

We can add subnets to our VPC with a netmask of `/24` each, as follows:

1. Go to VPC service in the console.
2. Click on **Subnets** in the left sidebar.
3. Click on **Create subnet**.
4. Select our VPC from the drop-down box to select the **VPC***. Now, it will display our VPC CIDRs.
5. Select **No preference** for **Availability Zone**.

6. For **IPv4 CIDR block***, provide an IP address range that is a subset of our VPC's IP address range. I will be using `10.0.1.0/24`.
7. For **IPv6 CIDR block**, select **Don't Assign Ipv6**.
8. Give the subnet a name that will help us infer the IP address range for the subnet; for example, `10.0.1.0/24`.

   Our **Create subnet** screen should now look as follows:

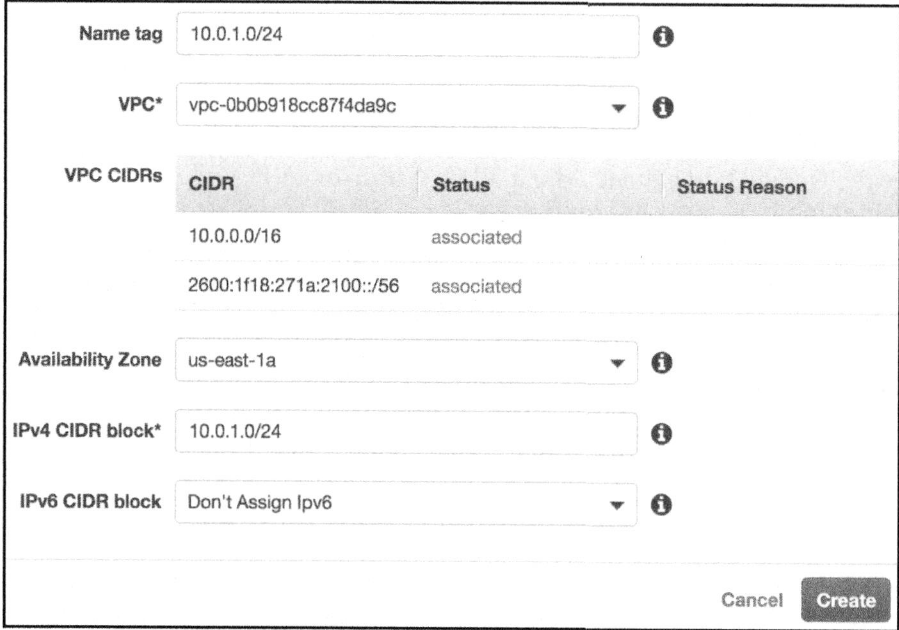

9. Click on **Create** to create a subnet.
10. Similarly, create a subnet for the IP address range `10.0.2.0/24`. The **Create subnet** screen should look as follows:

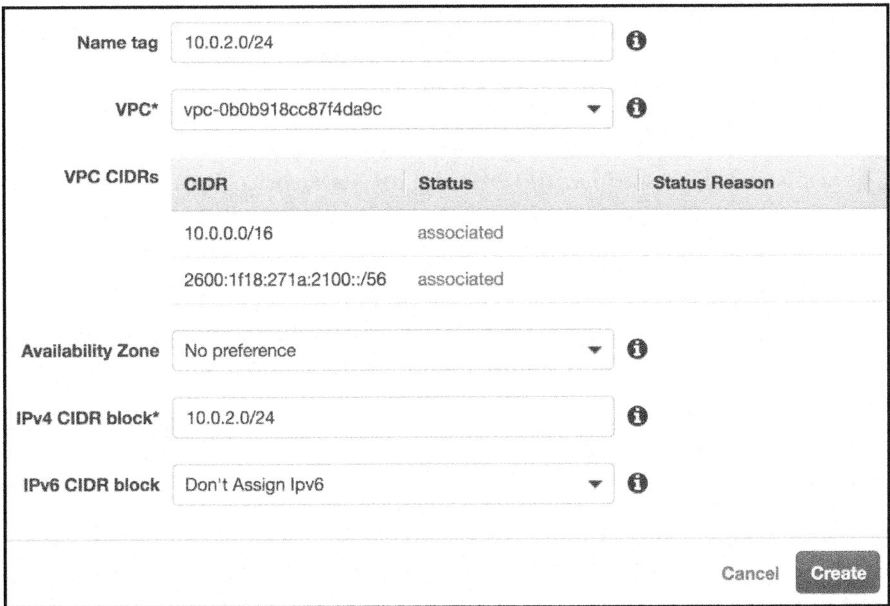

Go to the **Subnets** page from the sidebar. We should be able to see both our subnets:

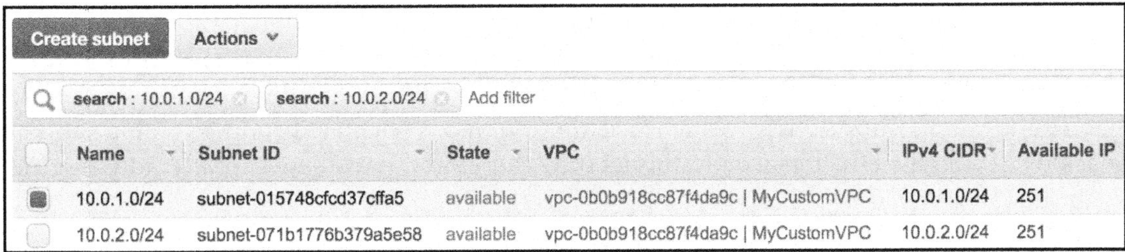

11. Select the first subnet (`10.0.1.0/24`), click on the **Actions** dropdown, and click on **Modify auto-assign IP Settings**.
12. Select **Enable auto-assign public IPv4 address** and click **Save**:

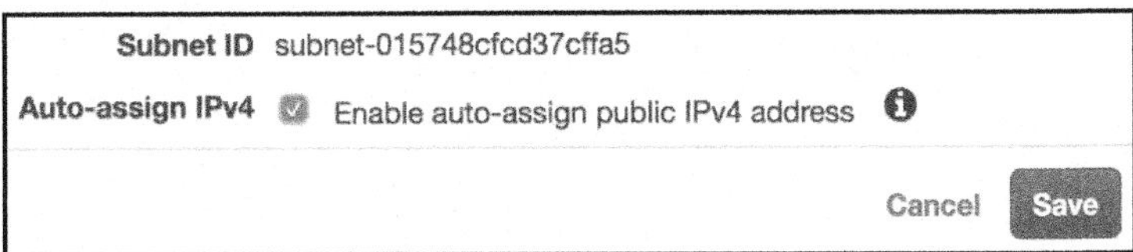

Go to the **Subnets** page from the sidebar. We should be able to see **Auto-assign public IPv4 address** set to **Yes** for our first subnet.

An auto-assigning IP address is a good-to-have feature for public EC2 instances. Selecting the **Enable auto-assign public IPv4 address** option makes it the default while creating an instance. You can override this during instance creation if you want. You can also create and attach an Elastic IP address later.

We created two subnets in this recipe, one to use as a public subnet and one to use as a private subnet. We will add further configurations to our VPC in later recipes within this chapter, including the next.

How it works...

A network can be divided into subnetworks for easy maintenance and security concerns. These subnetworks are referred to as subnets. An IP address in CIDR format is divided into NID bits and **host identifier (HID)** bits. The netmask of the IP address represents the size of the NID bits. With subnetting, additional bits from the HID part will be used for subnetting. The netmask for a subnet will, therefore, represent the combination of NID bits and subnet identifier bits, and this combined bitmask is usually called a subnet mask.

We created a VPC with a CIDR block range of `10.0.0.0/16`. Here, the netmask is `/16` and represents NID bits. HID bits can be obtained by subtracting the netmask size from the total available `32` bits for an IPv4 address. So, there will be 16 HID bits, which means we can have up to `(2^16)` hosts, out of which five are reserved. We created subnets with a subnet mask of `/24`, so the HID bits for the subnet is 8. Therefore, we can have `2^8` IP addresses in each subnet, which is 256.

The first subnet has a block address of `10.0.1.0/24` and contains IP addresses from `10.0.1.0` to `10.0.1.255`. The second subnet has an address of `10.0.2.0/24` and contains IP addresses from `10.0.2.0` to `10.0.2.255`. In the **Subnets** page, however, we saw that there are only 251 available IP addresses. This is because five of the IP addresses are reserved by AWS.

We can also create a subnet with the same IP address range as that of the VPC. We selected **Don't Assign Ipv6** for **IPv6 CIDR block**. Instead of doing this, we can provide a custom IPv6 address range here that is a subset of our VPC's IPv6 address range, or even the same as that of the VPC's IPv6 address range. We used the CIDR ranges in the subnet names. We can also add region details to the name. Since we selected **No preference** for **Availability Zone**, AWS will be selecting one for us.

There's more...

In the *Creating a VPC in AWS* recipe, we created a VPC manually. Then, in this recipe, we added subnets. We can also create a VPC using the **Launch VPC Wizard** button to create subnets based on predefined options. The wizard currently provides the following options:

- A VPC with a single public subnet:

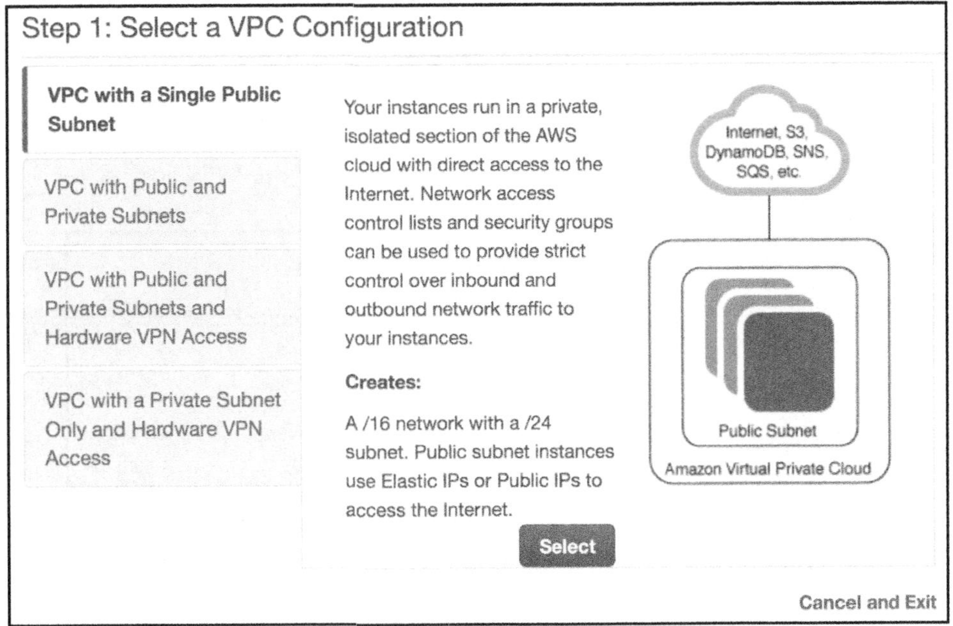

- A VPC with public and private subnets:

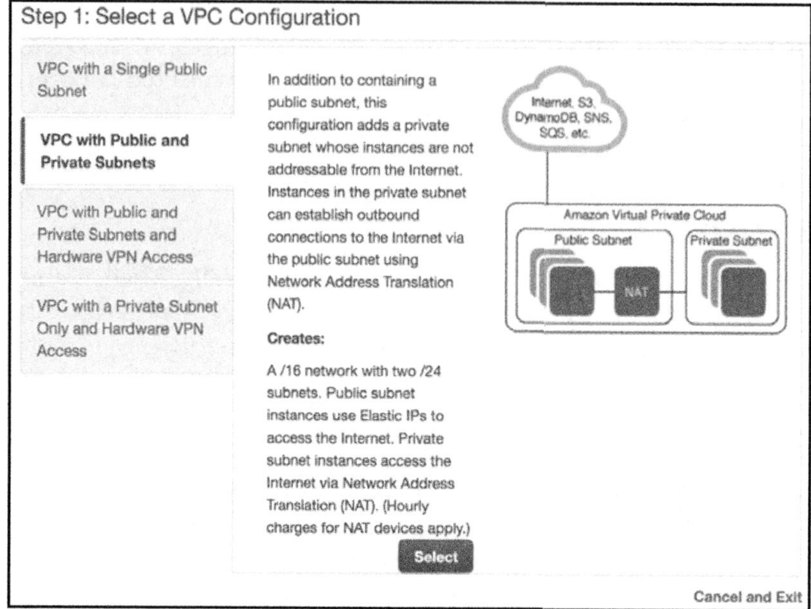

- A VPC with public and private subnets and hardware VPN access:

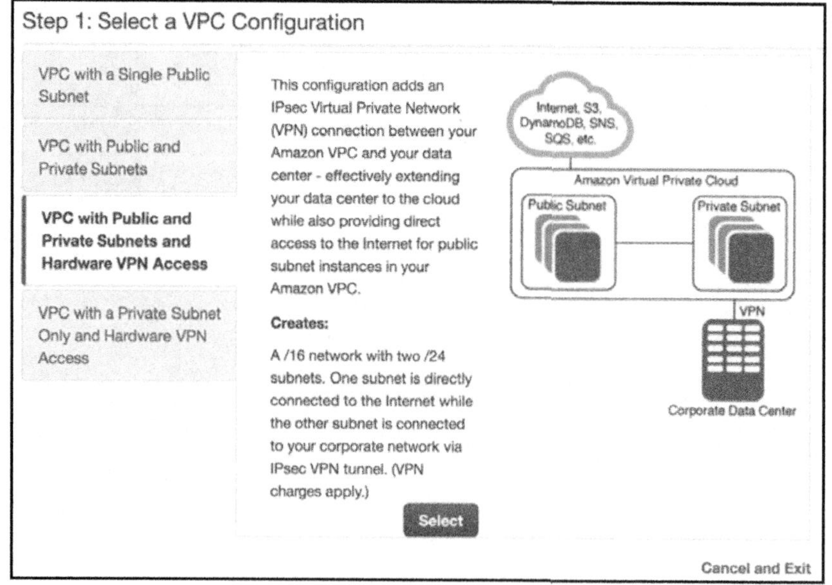

- A VPC with a private subnet only and hardware VPN access:

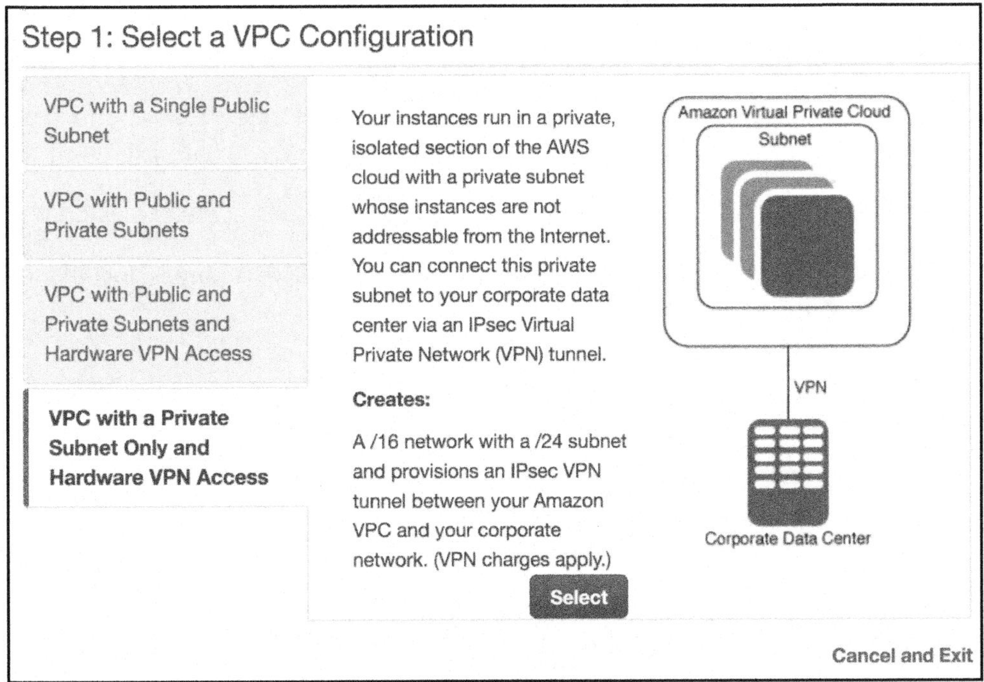

Once we select any of these options, we need to enter the corresponding details on the next page. Then, the configuration will be created accordingly.

Let's quickly go through some important concepts related to subnets in AWS:

- The first IP address of a subnet represents the subnet ID, while the last IP address represents the subnet's directed broadcast address. Therefore, we cannot use the first and last IP address of a subnet for hosts. AWS reserves additional IP addresses.
- The first IP address of the first subnet of a network represents the subnet ID, as well as the network's ID. Similarly, the last IP address of the last subnet of a network represents the subnet's and the network's directed broadcast address. When using these IP addresses from outside the network, they will be considered as the networks', and when using them within the network, they will be considered as the subnets'.
- A subnet in AWS VPC is always associated with one **Availability Zone** (**AZ**).
- While we cannot have one subnet associated with more than one AZ at a time, we can have multiple subnets associated with a single AZ.

- AWS allows us to choose a subnet without contiguous IP addresses, as shown in the following screenshot:

Name	Subnet ID	State	VPC	IPv4 CIDR
10.0.1.0/24	subnet-015748cfcd37cffa5	available	vpc-0b0b918cc87f4da9c | ...	10.0.1.0/24
10.0.2.0/24	subnet-071b1776b379a5e58	available	vpc-0b0b918cc87f4da9c | ...	10.0.2.0/24
10.0.5.0/24	subnet-02fad50229b9f62d4	available	vpc-0b0b918cc87f4da9c | ...	10.0.5.0/24

However, it is good practice to use contiguous IP address ranges, just like we did in this recipe with `10.0.1.0/24` and `10.0.2.0/24`.

See also

- You can read more about subnets at `https://heartin.tech/en/blog-entry/important-concepts-related-subnets`.

Configuring an internet gateway and a route table for internet access

In this recipe, we will create an internet gateway and configure it through a route table. We will associate the subnet we want to be public with this route table.

Getting ready

Create a VPC by following the *Creating a VPC in AWS* recipe. Create a public and private subnet by following the *Creating subnets in a VPC* recipe.

How to do it...

First, we will create and attach an internet gateway to our VPC, as follows:

1. Go to the VPC service in the console.
2. Click on **Internet Gateways** from the left sidebar.
3. Click on **Create internet gateway**.

4. Give a descriptive name for **Name tag** and click **Create**. We should get a success message that the internet gateway has been created. Click **Close** to close the message. If we go to the **Internet Gateways** screen, we will see that the **State** of our internet gateway is currently **detached**:

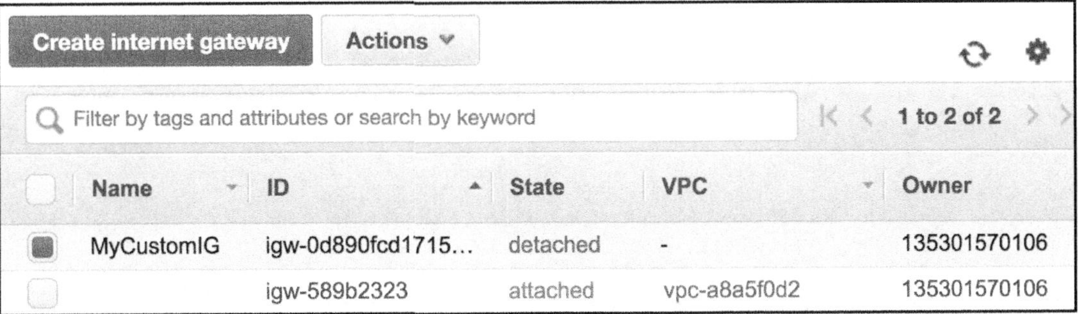

5. Select the internet gateway we created, click on the **Actions** dropdown, and click on **Attach to VPC**.
6. On the **Attach to VPC** screen, select our VPC and click on **Attach**. If we go to the **Internet Gateways** screen, we will see that the **State** of our internet gateway is now **attached**.
7. Click on **Route Tables** from the left sidebar.
8. Select the route table entry for our VPC by looking in the **VPC ID** column. This is the main route table.
9. Click on the **Routes** tab. We should see that two routes have already been created:

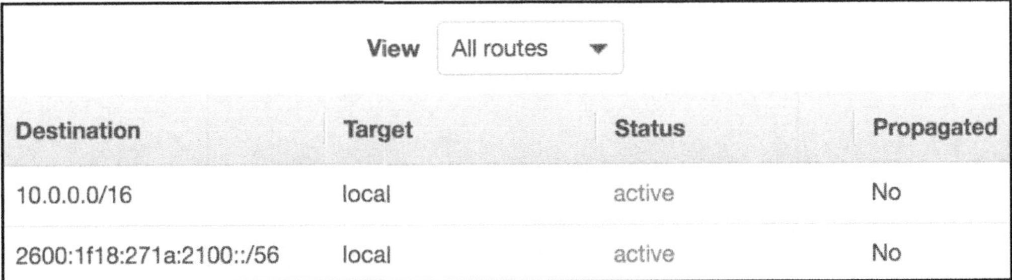

10. Click on the **Subnet Associations** tab. Here, we can see that there is no explicit association, as well as a message stating that a subnet is associated with the main route table when there is no explicit association:

Subnet ID	IPv4 CIDR	IPv6 CIDR

You do not have any subnet associations.

The following subnets have not been explicitly associated with any route tables and are therefore associated with the main route table:

1 to 2 of 2

Subnet ID	IPv4 CIDR	IPv6 CIDR
subnet-015748cfcd37cffa5 | 10.0.1.0/24	10.0.1.0/24	-
subnet-071b1776b379a5e58 | 10.0.2.0/24	10.0.2.0/24	-

By default, a subnet is associated with the main route table. If we make the main route table public, it will implicitly make all the new subnets public until we associate it with a private route table. Therefore, it is generally a good practice to create a separate route table for public access and then attach the subnets that need public access to that VPC. We will do this next.

We can attach our public subnet to a route table as follows:

1. Click on **Create route table** from the top of the page.
2. Provide a descriptive name for **Name tag**, select our VPC from the dropdown, and click **Create**:

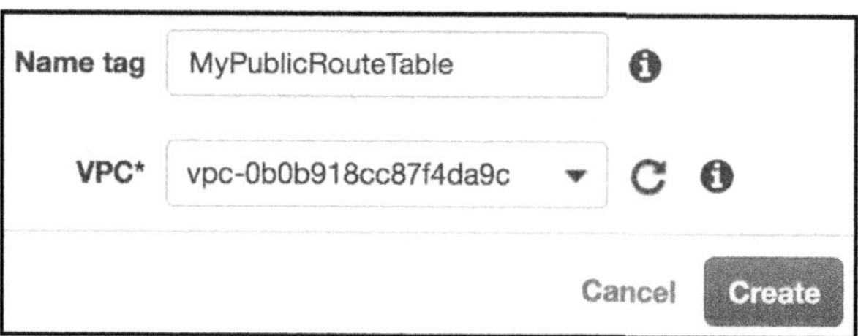

We should see a success message stating that the route table was created. If we go to the **Route Tables** page, we should see two route tables for our VPC. One is the main route table and the other is our new route table:

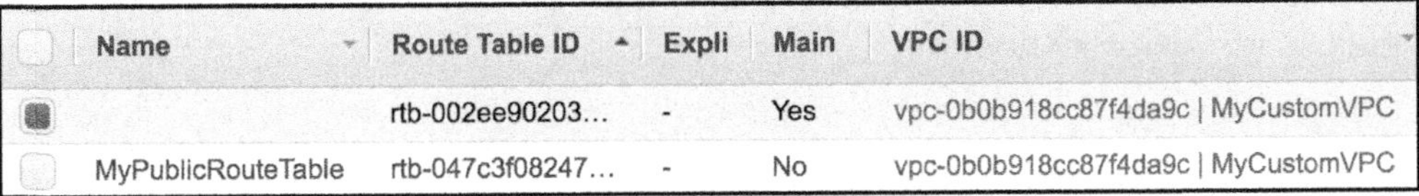

	Name	Route Table ID	Expli	Main	VPC ID
■		rtb-002ee90203...	-	Yes	vpc-0b0b918cc87f4da9c | MyCustomVPC
	MyPublicRouteTable	rtb-047c3f08247...	-	No	vpc-0b0b918cc87f4da9c | MyCustomVPC

3. Select our new route table, go to the **Routes** tab, and click on **Edit routes**.
4. On the **Edit routes** page, click on **Add route**.
5. Under the **Destination** column, add `0.0.0.0/0`. Then, under the **Target** column, expand the dropdown, click **Internet Gateway**, select the internet gateway we created, and click **Save routes**:

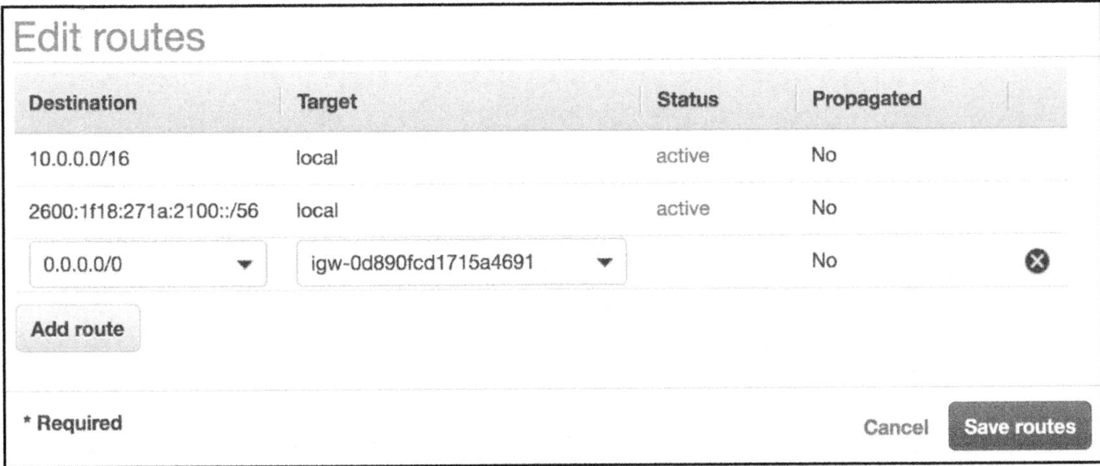

If we want to add a route for the IPv6 address, we can add a similar entry with the destination set to `::/0`.

6. Go to the **Subnet Associations** tab and click on **Edit subnet associations**.

7. Select the subnet we want to make public (the first subnet, in our case) and click **Save**:

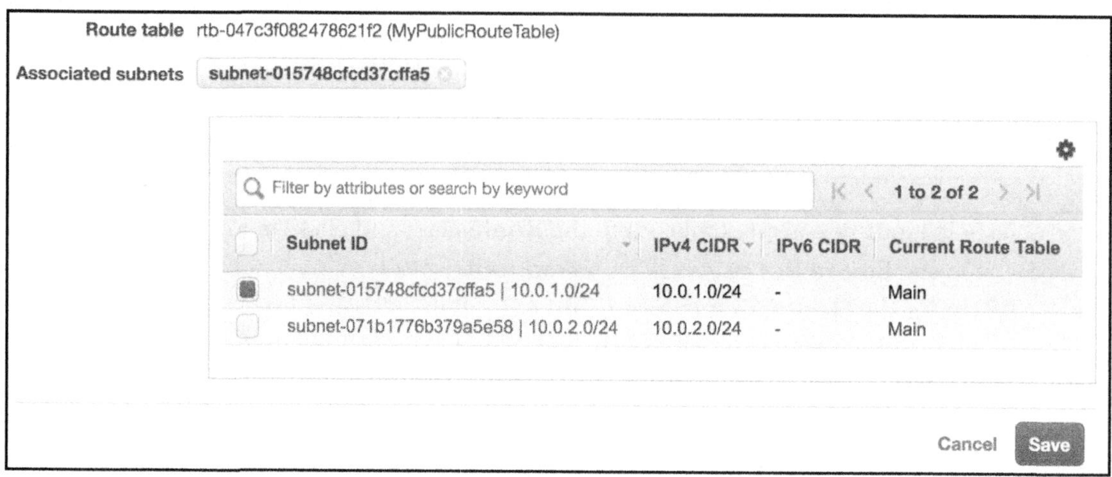

Now, we should see the subnet listed under the **Subnet Associations** tab:

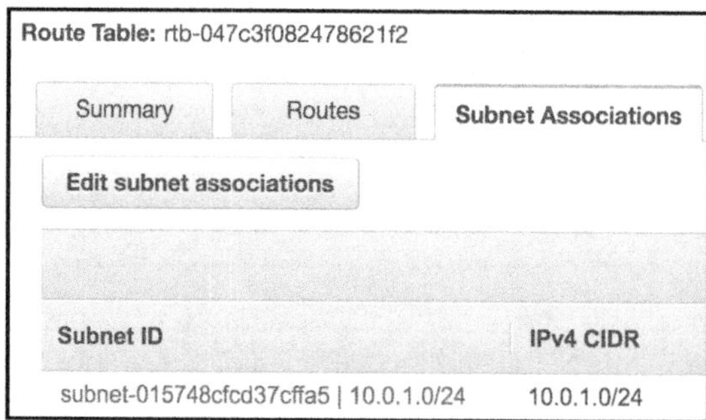

We can also launch instances into our public and private subnets with the appropriate security groups and verify these changes. We'll learn how to do this in `Chapter 6`, *Working with EC2 Instances*, in the *Launching an EC2 instance on a VPC* recipe.

How it works...

To access the internet from a VPC, or to access a VPC from the internet, we need an internet gateway. We need to attach it to our VPC and also create a route for it in a route table.

AWS created a main route table for our VPC when we created our VPC. The main route table is the primary route table that's created by AWS when we create a VPC. If a subnet is not associated explicitly with any route table, it will be associated with the main route table. A new subnet will be associated by default with the main route table until we associate it with another route table. It is good practice to not add public internet routes within the main route table. Instead, we can create another route table for public internet access and add our public subnets there.

Following the best practices, we created a new route table for public access. Then, we added a route for destination `0.0.0.0/0` and selected our internet gateway. This is to provide a route to the internet. If we want to add a route for the IPv6 address, we can add a similar entry with the destination set to `::/0`. We also associated our public subnet with this route table.

There's more...

Let's quickly go through some important concepts related to using internet gateways with AWS VPC:

- We can only attach one internet gateway per VPC.
- In the main route table, two routes are already created by AWS: one for IPv4 subnets and one for IPv6 subnets. These are provided so that our subnets can talk to each other locally. However, this is not enough for an EC2 instance in the public subnet to talk to our private subnet. We also need to allow the required protocols and ports through EC2 security groups.

See also

- You can read about internet gateways at `https://docs.aws.amazon.com/vpc/latest/userguide/VPC_Internet_Gateway.html`.
- You can read about AWS VPC route tables at `https://docs.aws.amazon.com/vpc/latest/userguide/VPC_Route_Tables.html`.

Setting up and configuring NAT gateways

In this recipe, we will learn how to create and configure NAT gateways, which is the latest and preferred option for **Network Address Translation** (**NAT**) in AWS.

Getting ready

To complete the steps within this recipe, we need a custom VPC with the following configurations:

- Create a VPC by following the *Creating a VPC in AWS* recipe. Create some subnets by following the *Creating subnets in a VPC* recipe.
- An internet gateway and a route table with a route for the internet gateway. Then, we need to associate our public subnet with that route table, as shown in the *Configuring an internet gateway and a route table for internet access* recipe.
- Launch instances in the public and private subnets with the appropriate security group configurations by following the *Configuring a security group and launching an instance into a VPC* recipe in `Chapter 6`, *Working with EC2 Instances*.

How to do it...

We can create a NAT gateway as follows:

1. Go to **VPC service** on the dashboard.
2. Click on **NAT Gateways**.
3. Click on **Create NAT Gateway**.
4. For **Subnet**, select our public subnet.
5. Click on **Create New EIP** for **Elastic IP Allocation ID**. This should populate the allocation ID for an Elastic IP. If we click inside the input box, we will see the actual Elastic IP.

The filled page should look as follows:

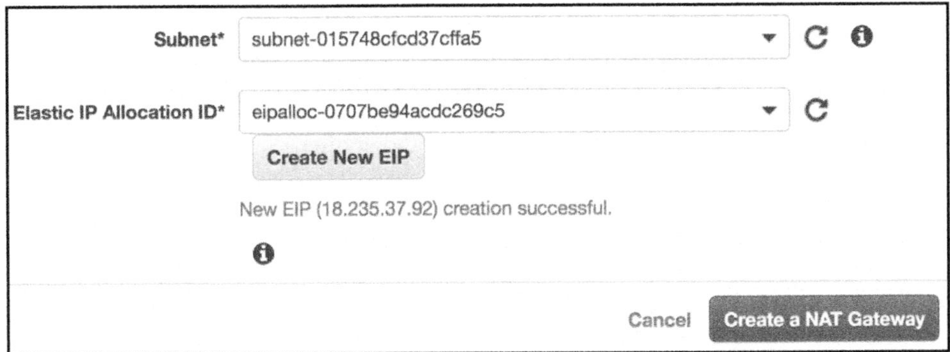

6. Click on **Create a NAT Gateway**. If successful, it will provide options for **Edit route tables** or **Close**.
7. Click on **Edit route tables**.
8. Select the main route table.
9. Go to the **Routes** tab.
10. Click on **Edit routes** and do the following:
    1. Add `0.0.0.0/0` as the **Destination**.
    2. From the dropdown for **Target**, click on **NAT Gateway** and select our NAT gateway.
    3. Click on **Save routes**:

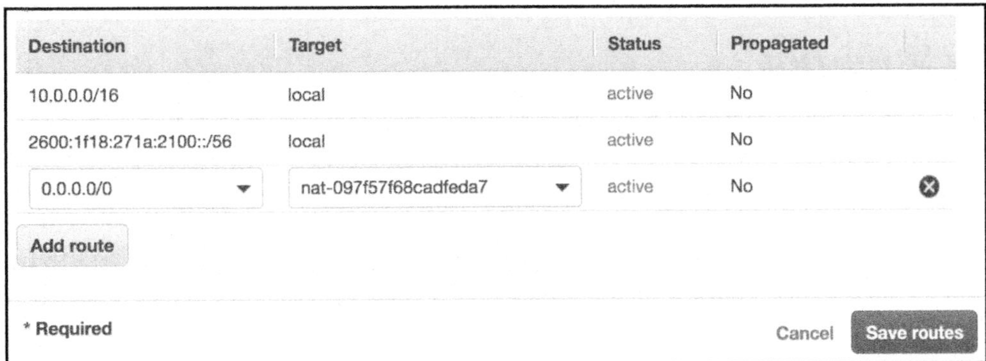

If successful, it will show a success message. Click **Close** to close the message.

11. Log in to the public EC2 instance and from there, log in to the private EC2 instance. You can refer to the *Launching an EC2 instance in a VPC* recipe in `Chapter 6`, *Working with EC2 Instances*, for the exact steps.
12. Try running any command from the Terminal that requires internet access, as follows:

```
ping.google.com
```

We should get back a successful response if there is a route to the internet; otherwise, it will timeout:

```
[ec2-user@ip-10-0-2-212 ~]$ ping google.com
PING google.com (172.217.164.142) 56(84) bytes of data.
64 bytes from iad30s24-in-f14.1e100.net (172.217.164.142): icmp_seq=1 ttl=47 time=1.92 ms
64 bytes from iad30s24-in-f14.1e100.net (172.217.164.142): icmp_seq=2 ttl=47 time=1.49 ms
64 bytes from iad30s24-in-f14.1e100.net (172.217.164.142): icmp_seq=3 ttl=47 time=1.47 ms
64 bytes from iad30s24-in-f14.1e100.net (172.217.164.142): icmp_seq=4 ttl=47 time=1.50 ms
^C
--- google.com ping statistics ---
4 packets transmitted, 4 received, 0% packet loss, time 3005ms
rtt min/avg/max/mdev = 1.472/1.597/1.921/0.187 ms
```

We can also run a `yum update` command, as follows:

```
sudo yum update
```

Follow the remaining prompts. The update will happen successfully if there is a route to the internet; otherwise, it will timeout.

How it works...

Internet access may be required for instances in our private subnets for activities such as patching, downloading software, and so on. NAT allows a private subnet in our VPC to talk to the internet. NAT is a process of remapping the IP address of a packet by modifying its IP header while in transit. AWS provides us with two ways to achieve NAT with VPCs: NAT gateways and NAT instances. We created and configured a NAT gateway in this recipe. Unlike NAT instances, NAT gateways are not associated with any security groups and hence we did not create or configure any security groups.

After creating the NAT gateway, we need to add a route for it within the route table that our private subnets are associated with. We added the route to our main route table since our private subnets are associated with the main route table. A subnet that is not associated explicitly with any route table will be associated implicitly with the main route table. If our architecture has a different route table for private subnets, we will need to add the route for the NAT gateway within that route table.

There's more...

Let's quickly go through some more important concepts related to NAT gateways:

- NAT gateways are maintained by AWS and AWS takes care of patching, availability, and scaling.
- NAT gateways are not associated with any security groups.
- NAT gateways are redundant within an AZ, but cannot span an AZ. Therefore, for better availability, we may need to create a NAT gateway per region.
- NAT is currently not supported for IPv6 traffic. We need to use an egress-only internet gateway instead of NAT for IPv6 traffic. We can create an egress-only internet gateway from the VPC dashboard.

NAT gateways are always preferred to NAT instances and we should be using NAT gateways. Still, if you want to learn or experiment with NAT instances, you can follow the *Setting up and configuring NAT instances* recipe in `Chapter 6`, *Working with EC2 Instances*.

See also

- You can read more about NAT gateways at `https://docs.aws.amazon.com/vpc/latest/userguide/vpc-nat-gateway.html`.

Working with NACLs

In this recipe, we will create a new NACL with no SSH support and associate one of our subnets with that NACL. By doing this, we'll see that we cannot SSH into EC2 instances within that subnet. After, we will add SSH support to the NACL and try to SSH again.

Getting ready

To complete the steps within this recipe, we need a custom VPC with the following configurations:

- Create a VPC by following the *Creating a VPC in AWS* recipe. Create the subnet by following the *Creating subnets in a VPC* recipe.
- Launch an instance into our public subnet with a security group configuration that allows our local machine IP to SSH into that machine. You can do this by referring to the *Launching an EC2 instance into a VPC* recipe in `Chapter 6`, *Working with EC2 Instances*.

How to do it...

We can create an NACL with no SSH permission as follows:

1. Go to **VPC service** in the console.
2. Click on **Network ACLs** on the left sidebar.
3. Click on the NACL for our custom VPC and check its subnet associations. This should contain all the subnets of our VPC that are not associated with any other VPC.
4. Click on **Create network ACL** at the top of the page.
5. Provide a name in the **Name tag** field and select our custom VPC from the dropdown for the **VPC** field:

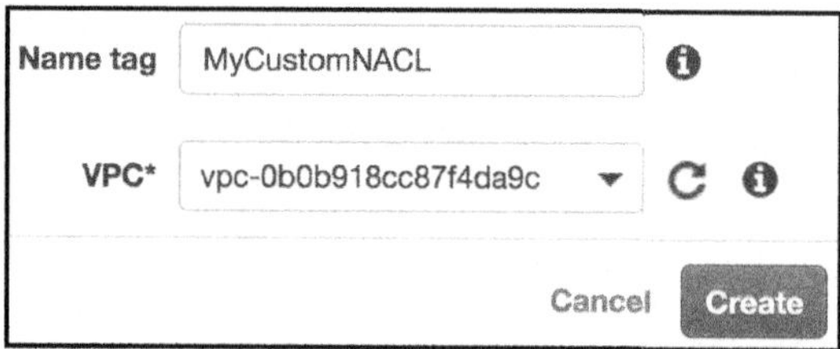

6. Click on **Create** to create the VPC. If we go to the NACL list, we will see that our new NACL doesn't have any subnets associated with it:

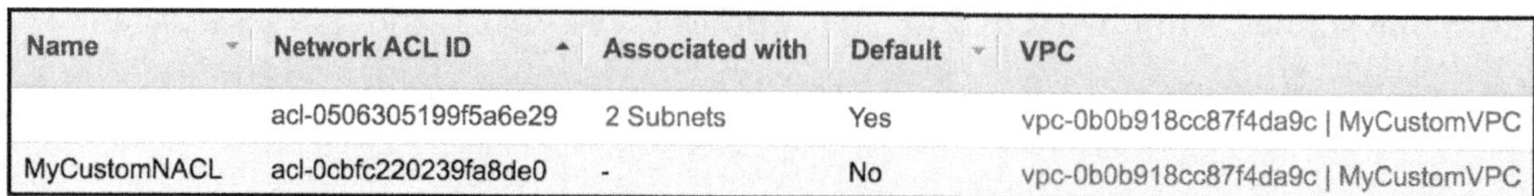

Name	Network ACL ID	Associated with	Default	VPC
	acl-0506305199f5a6e29	2 Subnets	Yes	vpc-0b0b918cc87f4da9c | MyCustomVPC
MyCustomNACL	acl-0cbfc220239fa8de0	-	No	vpc-0b0b918cc87f4da9c | MyCustomVPC

7. Select our new NACL and verify the inbound and outbound rules of the new NACL from its **Inbound Rules** and **Outbound Rules** tabs, respectively.

The inbound rules should be as follows:

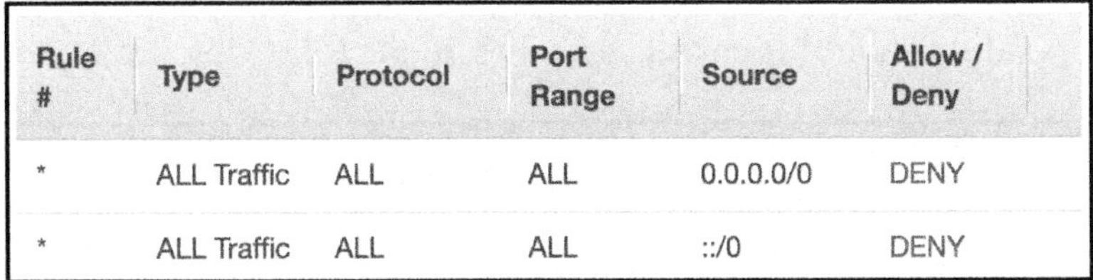

Rule #	Type	Protocol	Port Range	Source	Allow / Deny
*	ALL Traffic	ALL	ALL	0.0.0.0/0	DENY
*	ALL Traffic	ALL	ALL	::/0	DENY

The outbound rules should be as follows:

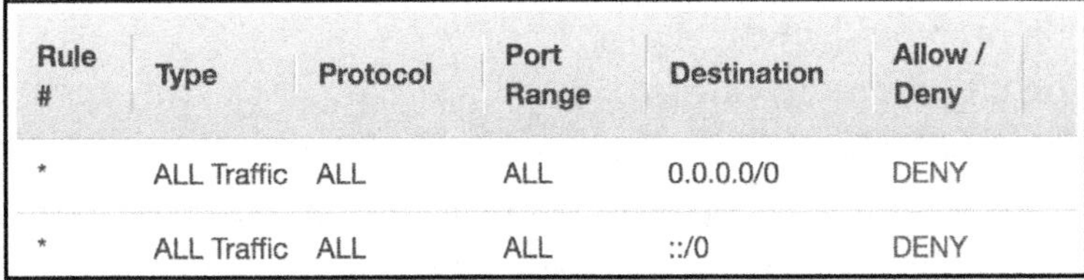

Rule #	Type	Protocol	Port Range	Destination	Allow / Deny
*	ALL Traffic	ALL	ALL	0.0.0.0/0	DENY
*	ALL Traffic	ALL	ALL	::/0	DENY

8. Click on the **Subnet associations** tab.
9. Click on **Edit subnet associations**.
10. Select our public subnet and click **Edit**. Select our new NACL and check its subnet associations. Our public subnet should now be associated with it:

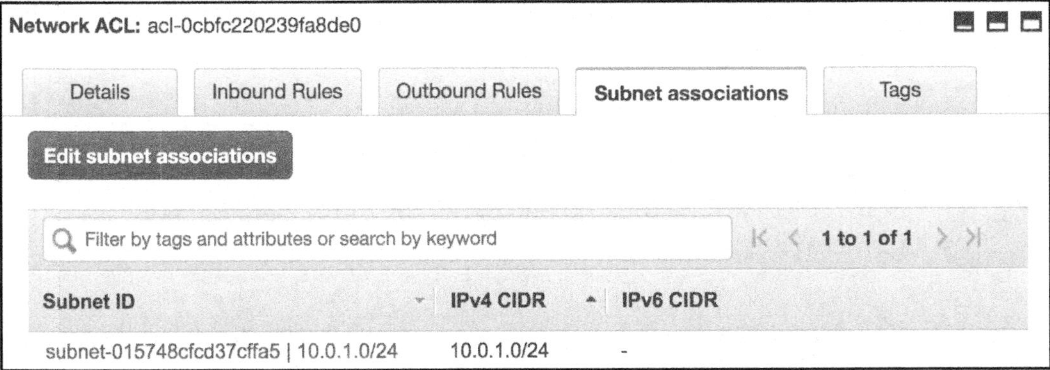

11. Try to SSH into our public EC2 instance. The exact command or steps may differ between operating systems. On macOS and most Linux systems, we can use the SSH command, as follows:

    ```
    ssh -i aws-sec-cb-demo-kp.pem ec2-user@54.145.102.218
    ```

    The operation should time out, as shown in the following screenshot:

    ```
    $ ssh -i aws-sec-cb-demo-kp.pem ec2-user@54.145.102.218
    ssh: connect to host 54.145.102.218 port 22: Operation timed out
    ```

We can add SSH support to our NACL as follows:

1. Go back to the **VPC Dashboard**, click on **Network ACLs** from the left sidebar, and select our NACL.
2. Click on **Inbound Rules**.
3. Click on **Edit inbound rules**.
4. Click on **Add Rule**.
5. Enter **Rule #** as `100`, set **Type** to **SSH(22)**, leave source as `0.0.0.0/0`, set **Allow/Deny** to **Allow**, and click on **Save**:

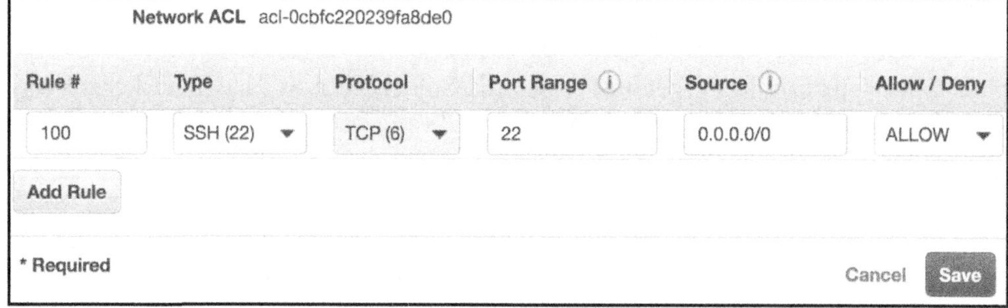

We have already restricted the security group so that it only allows SSH from our IP. You may also explicitly specify our IP here for more restricted access control.

If we try to SSH into the EC2 instance now, the SSH will fail as we have not enabled the ephemeral ports for outbound traffic.

6. Click on **Outbound Rules**.
7. Click on **Edit outbound rules**.
8. Click on **Add Rule**.
9. Enter **Rule #** as `100`, set **Type** to **Custom TCP Rule**, set **Port Range** to `1024 - 65535`, set **Allow/Deny** to **Allow**, set **Destination** to `0.0.0.0/0`, and click on **Save**:

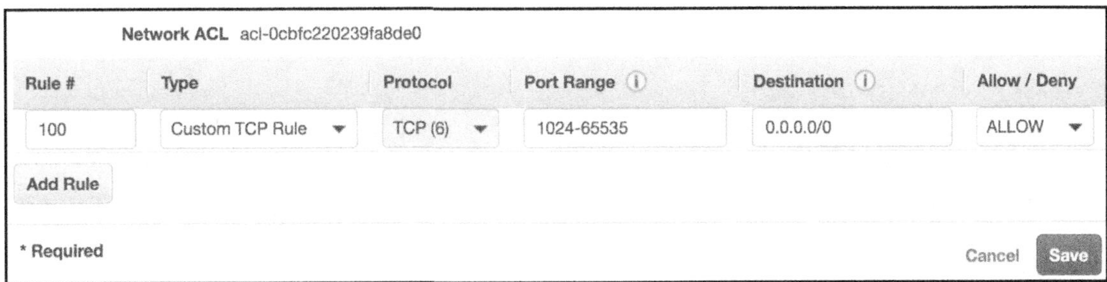

10. Try to SSH into our public EC2 instance. The exact command or steps may differ between operating systems. On macOS and most Linux systems, we can use the SSH command, as follows:

```
ssh -i aws-sec-cb-demo-kp.pem ec2-user@54.145.102.218
```

Now, we should be able to SSH successfully.

In this recipe, we only added one inbound rule and one outbound rule. You can add more rules as required.

How it works...

NACLs allow us to define inbound and outbound rules for the subnets of our VPC. We can explicitly allow or deny traffic through a port, or a range of ports. The default NACL that was created by AWS allows all inbound and outbound traffic. However, by default, a custom NACL denies all inbound and outbound traffic.

First, we created a new NACL. Then, we associated our public subnet with that NACL and verified that we cannot SSH from our local machine. A new NACL denies inbound and outbound traffic by default. To allow SSH, we added an inbound rule for SSH in our NACL and an outbound rule to allow the ephemeral port range of `1024 - 65535`.

An ephemeral port is a short-lived port for IP communications with transport protocols such as **Transmission Control Protocol** (**TCP**), **User Datagram Protocol** (**UDP**), **Stream Control Transmission Protocol** (**SCTP**), and so on. It is usually used for the return traffic from the instance or service we are connecting to. For example, the server accepts SSH traffic on port `22` and then communicates to the client through one of the ephemeral ports. In this recipe, we added outbound rules that allow the ephemeral port range as suggested by AWS for public-facing instances in order to cover various client types.

There's more...

Let's quickly go through some important concepts related to network ACLs:

- When we create a VPC, a default NACL is created by AWS. The value of the **Default** column will be **Yes** for the default NACL within the NACL list in our VPC.
- Default NACL allows all inbound and outbound traffic. However, when we create a new custom NACL, all the inbound and outbound traffic is denied by default.
- Every subnet needs to be associated with one NACL at a time. By default, a subnet is associated with the default NACL.
- One subnet can only be associated with one NACL at a time. When we associate it with a new NACL, the current association will be removed.
- A single NACL can be associated with multiple subnets.
- NACLs contain a numbered set of rules. These rules are evaluated in the order of the rule numbers. If we have an Allow rule before a Deny rule for the same port, access will be allowed for that port. Similarly, if we have a Deny rule before an Allow rule for the same port, access will be denied for that port. AWS recommends using rule numbers in multiples of 100 initially as that will let us add new rules in between if needed.
- We can block specific IP addresses with NACL, but this is not possible with security groups.
- NACLs are evaluated before security groups.

- Security groups are considered stateful, while NACLs are considered stateless. With a security group, if we send a request from the instance, the response is allowed, irrespective of the inbound rules. Similarly, if we allow an inbound request, then the corresponding outbound response is allowed to go, irrespective of the outbound rules. With NACL, we need to allow both inbound and outbound traffic explicitly for any port.

See also

- You can read more about NACLs at `https://docs.aws.amazon.com/vpc/latest/userguide/vpc-network-acls.html`.

Using a VPC gateway endpoint to connect to S3

In this recipe, we will create a VPC gateway endpoint for S3 and connect to S3 from our private subnet without any internet access.

Getting ready

To complete the steps within this recipe, we need to do the following:

1. Create a VPC by following the *Creating a VPC in AWS* recipe. Create some subnets by following the *Creating subnets in a VPC* recipe.
2. Subnets should be associated with the default NACL. Otherwise, we should define proper inbound and outbound rules so that we can log in to the private EC2 instance through the public EC2 instance.
3. We should have no internet access for the private subnet. Verify this by running `aws s3 ls --region us-east-1` from our private subnet. Our requests should fail with a timeout. If a NAT gateway or a NAT instance has been configured, remove its route from the main route table.
4. We need an S3 bucket in any region. I will be using `us-east-1`.

5. Associate an IAM role with S3 access to a private EC2 instance. To do this, refer to the *Creating and attaching an IAM Role to an EC2 instance* recipe in `Chapter 6`, *Working with EC2 Instances*:

```
[ec2-user@ip-10-0-2-212 ~]$ aws s3 ls --region us-east-1

Connect timeout on endpoint URL: "https://s3.amazonaws.com/"
```

If you have not configured an IAM role correctly, you might get an error that says **Unable to locate credentials. You can configure credentials by running aws configure. Fix the issue and test again before proceeding.**

How to do it...

We can create a VPC endpoint gateway for S3 as follows:

1. Go to **VPC service** in the console.
2. Click on **Endpoints** from the left sidebar.
3. Click on **Create Endpoint**.
4. For **Service Category**, select **AWS Service**.
5. For **Service Name**, select **com.amazonaws.us-east-1.s3**:

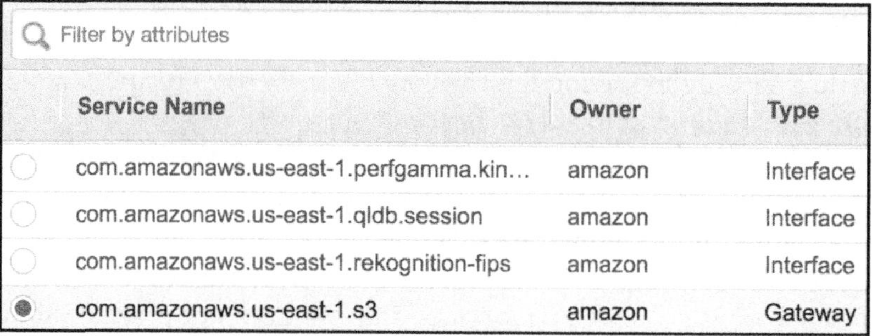

Filter by attributes
Service Name
Owner
Type
com.amazonaws.us-east-1.perfgamma.kin...
amazon
Interface
com.amazonaws.us-east-1.qldb.session
amazon
Interface
com.amazonaws.us-east-1.rekognition-fips
amazon
Interface
com.amazonaws.us-east-1.s3
amazon
Gateway

6. For **VPC**, select our custom VPC.
7. For **Route table**, select our main route table.
8. Leave the **Policy** as **Full Access**.

9. Click on **Create endpoint**. We should get a success message.
10. Try running the following S3 command from the private subnet:

```
aws s3 ls --region us-east-1
```

This should list the S3 items successfully.

To SSH into the public EC2 instance and then SSH into the private EC2 instance, you can refer to the *Launching an EC2 instance into a VPC* recipe in `Chapter 6`, *Working with EC2 Instances*.

How it works...

VPC endpoints allow us to connect to supported AWS services from our VPC privately. With VPC endpoints, instances in the VPC do not need a public IP address to communicate with supported AWS services. The traffic between our VPC and the supported AWS services does not leave AWS. VPC endpoints can be considered as highly available virtual devices.

In this recipe, we configured a VPC endpoint of the gateway endpoint type to access S3 from our subnet. We removed all public routes from our subnet and we could still connect to S3. VPC gateway endpoints are also supported by DynamoDB and work similarly to a VPC gateway. For most other services, VPC endpoints are supported through interface endpoints.

There's more...

Let's quickly go through some important concepts related to VPC endpoints:

- There are two types of VPC endpoints:
    - **Interface endpoints**: An **Elastic Network Interface** (**ENI**) with a private address that allows traffic to a supported service. There are around 20 supported services. Examples of such supported services include Amazon API Gateway, Amazon CloudWatch, AWS Config, AWS KMS, and so on.
    - **Gateway endpoints**: Like NAT gateways, they do not have private IP addresses. This is only supported for limited services such as S3 and DynamoDB.

See also

- You can read more about VPC endpoints and the supported services at `https://docs.aws.amazon.com/vpc/latest/userguide/vpc-endpoints.html`.

Configuring and using VPC flow logs

In this recipe, we will enable flow logs at the VPC level.

Getting ready

We need the following resources for completing the steps within this recipe:

- A CloudWatch log group. You can create a log group by following the *Creating a CloudWatch log group* recipe in `Chapter 8`, *Monitoring with CloudWatch, CloudTrail, and Config*.
- An IAM role with permissions to publish to the CloudWatch log group. This can be done while enabling flow logs, as we will see in this recipe.

How to do it...

We can configure VPC flow logs from the console as follows:

1. Go to **VPC service** in the console.
2. Click on **Your VPCs**.
3. Select our VPC.
4. Click on the **Flow Logs** tab.
5. Click on **Create flow log.**
6. Within the **Filter** dropdown, select **All**.
7. Set **Destination** to **Send to CloudWatch Logs**.

8. Select **Destination log group** as the log group we created in the *Getting ready* section.
9. Open the **Set Up Permissions** link against the **IAM Role** option in a new tab (or page), as follows:

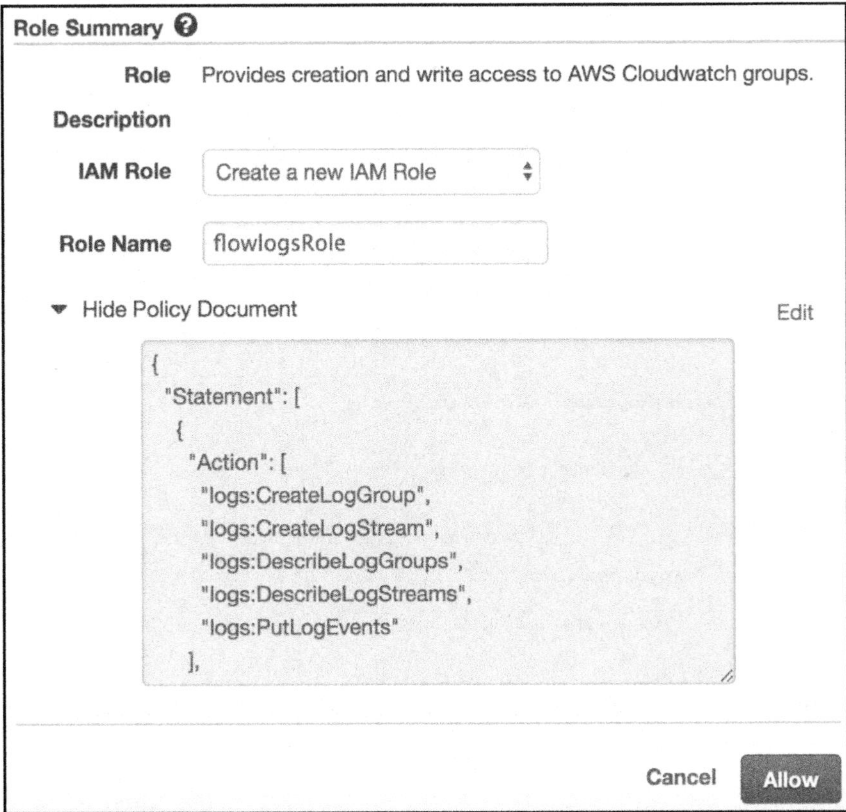

10. Click **Allow** to create the new role.

11. From the **Create flow log** tab (or page), click the refresh button against the **IAM role** and select the role that we created in the previous step. The **Create flow log** page should look as follows:

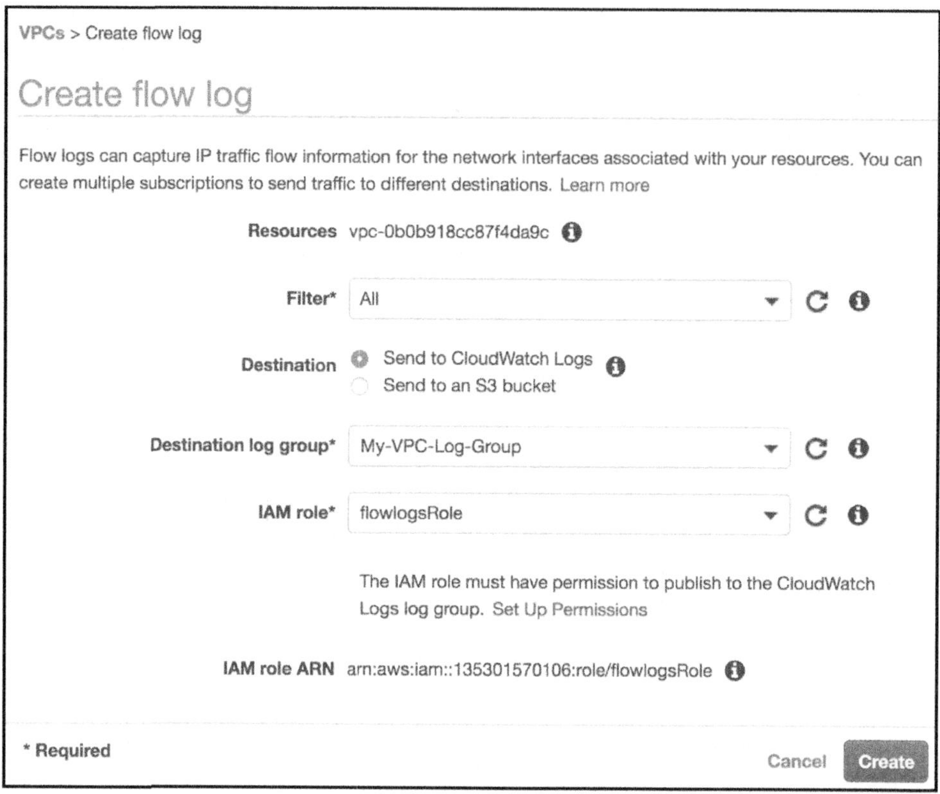

12. Click on **Create**. We should see a success message. Click **Close** to close the message. We should be able to see all further IP traffic logs within our flow logs. The following is an example of a log record from the log group for VPC logs:

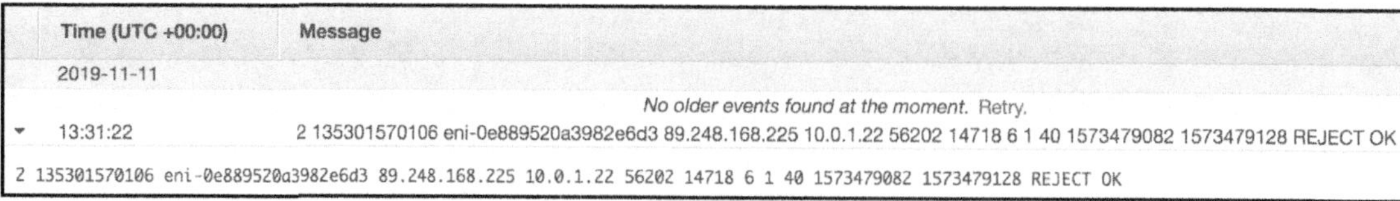

For more details on checking logs within CloudWatch, please refer to `Chapter 8`, *Monitoring with CloudWatch, CloudTrail, and Config*.

How it works...

VPC flow logs help us capture IP traffic to and from our VPCs. Data from VPC flow logs can be published to either CloudWatch logs or to an S3 bucket. We can choose to log only accepted traffic, rejected traffic, or both. VPC flow logs can be created at different levels, such as the VPC level, subnet level, and Network Interface level.

In the recipe, within the filter dropdown, we selected **All** to log all IP traffic to and from our VPCs. We can choose **Accept** to log only accepted traffic, **Reject** to log only rejected traffic, and **All** to log both accepted and rejected traffic. We needed a CloudWatch log group and an IAM role with permission to log to that log group. We created the IAM role from the console using the **Set Up Permissions** link on the **Create flow log** screen.

There's more...

Let's quickly go through some more important concepts related to flow logs:

- Currently, we cannot change a flow log configuration, such as changing the associated IAM role, once it's been created.
- Some of the IP traffic, including the ones listed here, are not monitored by flow logs:
    - Traffic to the reserved IP addresses of the default VPC router.
    - **Dynamic Host Configuration Protocol** (**DHCP**) traffic.
    - Traffic set to `169.254.169.254` for querying instance metadata.
    - Traffic while contacting Amazon DNS servers via instances. However, traffic to our own DNS server is logged.
    - Windows license activation traffic.

See also

- You can read more about flow logs at `https://docs.aws.amazon.com/vpc/latest/userguide/flow-logs.html`.
- You can find examples of log records at `https://docs.aws.amazon.com/vpc/latest/userguide/flow-logs-records-examples.html`.

6
Working with EC2 Instances

Amazon **Elastic Compute Cloud** (**EC2**) provides our virtual machines as a service. In this chapter, we will learn how to secure EC2 instances. We will learn how to launch EC2 instances into custom VPCs. We learned about VPCs in `Chapter 5`, *Network Security with VPC*, so we will carry on from where we left off. We will also learn how to configure inbound and outbound access rules with security groups. We will compare security groups against **network access control lists** (**NACLs**), which we learned about in `Chapter 5`, *Network Security with VPC*. We will use the Systems Manager Parameter Store to store and retrieve data. Then, we will learn how to bootstrap an EC2 instance with commands such as installing patches. Keeping our operating system updated with the latest patches is essential for securing our EC2 instances. We will also learn how we can encrypt data in an **Elastic Block Store** (**EBS**) attached to an EC2 instance.

In this chapter, we will cover the following recipes:

- Creating and configuring security groups
- Launching an EC2 instance into a VPC
- Setting up and configuring NAT instances
- Creating and attaching an IAM role to an EC2 instance
- Using our own private and public keys with EC2
- Using EC2 user data to launch an instance with a web server
- Storing sensitive data with the Systems Manager Parameter Store
- Using KMS to encrypt data in EBS

Technical requirements

For this chapter, we need a working AWS Account. Basic knowledge of networking, virtualization, and cryptography will be helpful for understanding some of the recipes within this chapter. Recipes related to VPCs may require knowledge or setup that was covered in `Chapter 5`, *Network Security with VPC*.

The code files for this chapter can be found at `https://github.com/PacktPublishing/AWS-Security-Cookbook/tree/master/Chapter06`.

Creating and configuring security groups

In this recipe, we will learn how to create a security group from a VPC dashboard. Similar steps can be followed for creating a security group from the EC2 dashboard. We can also create a security group while launching an EC2 instance.

Getting ready

Create a VPC by following the *Creating a VPC in AWS* recipe in `Chapter 5`, *Network Security with VPC*. You can also use the default VPC instead.

How to do it...

We can create a security group from the VPC dashboard as follows:

1. Go to the VPC dashboard.
2. Click on **Security Groups** from the left sidebar.
3. Provide values for **Security group name*** and **Description***, select our **VPC**, and click **Create**:

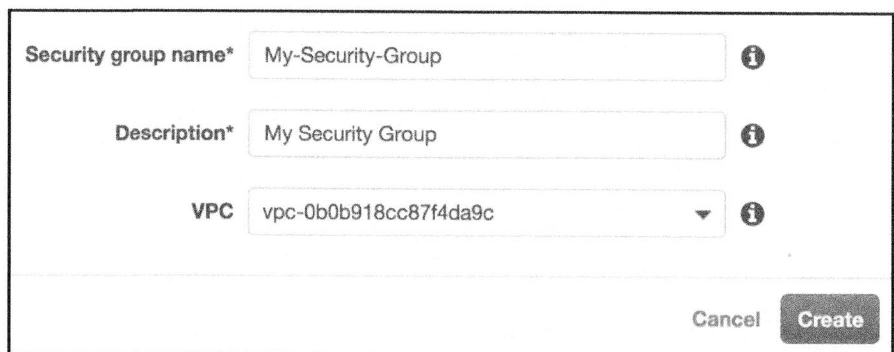

We should get a success message stating that the security group was created.

4. From the list of security groups, select our security group. We should see a **Description** tab similar to the one shown in the following screenshot:

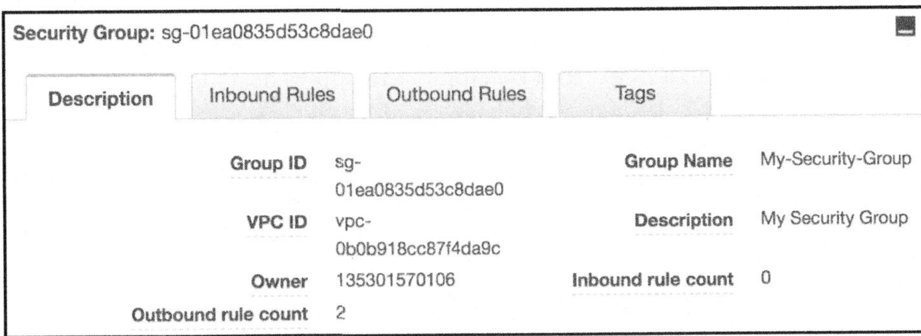

5. Click on **Inbound Rules**, and then on **Edit rules**. Add the following rules:
    1. Click on **Add Rule**, set **Type** to **HTTP, Source** to **Custom**, and set the CIDR range to `0.0.0.0/0`. Also, add a CIDR range of `::/0` if IPv6 support is needed.
    2. Click on **Add Rule**, set **Type** to **HTTPS, Source** to **Custom**, and set the CIDR range to `0.0.0.0/0`. Also, add a CIDR range of `::/0` if IPv6 support is needed.
    3. Click on **Add Rule**, set **Type** to **SSH**, and **Source** to **MY IP**. Our IP address should become populated.
    4. Click on **Save rules**:

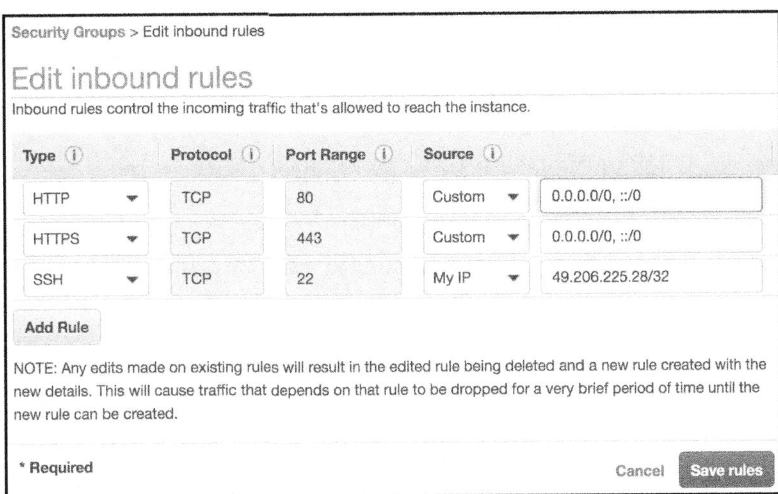

We should get a success message.

The exact rules will be different for each recipe. The preceding rules may be used for instances of a public subnet that hosts a web server. We also provided SSH access to our local IP; however, in most projects, we give SSH access to a dedicated machine, referred to as a jump host or a bastion host.

6. Click on **Outbound Rules.** We should see that the following rules have been configured:

Type	Protocol	Port Range	Destination
All traffic	All	All	0.0.0.0/0
All traffic	All	All	::/0

Default outbound rules for a security group allow all outbound traffic. For added security, we can provide outbound access to only the required protocols, such as HTTP and HTTPS.

7. If you need to change the outbound rules so that you only allow HTTP and HTTPS traffic, on the **Outbound Rules** tab, click on **Edit rules** and add the following rules:
    1. Click on **Add Rule**, set **Type** to **HTTP**, **Source** to **Custom**, and set the CIDR range to `0.0.0.0/0`.
    2. Click on **Add Rule**, set **Type** to **HTTPS**, **Source** to **Custom**, and set the CIDR range to `0.0.0.0/0`.
    3. Click on **Save rules**. We should get a success message. Click **Close** to close the message.

If IPv6 traffic is required, we can also add a CIDR range set to `::/0` to the rules.

How it works...

In this recipe, we created and configured a security group with inbound and outbound rules that are applicable for an EC2 instance in a public subnet running a web server. We will use these steps to create security groups in other recipes. The exact rules may differ based on the use case. Instead of providing the CIDR range, we can also specify another security group in a rule to say that only instances with that security group should be allowed.

In the *Working with NACLs* recipe in `Chapter 5`, *Network Security with VPC*, we explicitly allowed the ephemeral port range of `1024 - 65535` for outbound requests. This isn't needed for security groups since security groups are stateful. If an outbound port is opened, the response for a request going through that port is also allowed, irrespective of the inbound rules. Similarly, if an inbound port is opened, the response for a request coming through that port is also allowed, irrespective of the outbound rules.

There's more...

Let's quickly go through some important concepts related to security groups:

- Security groups do not span across VPCs.
- We can create security groups from the EC2 launch wizard, from the EC2 dashboard, or from the VPC dashboard.
- Security groups are stateful, unlike NACLs.
- It is good practice to have multiple security groups based on usages. For example, we can create separate security groups, one for SSH and one for application-specific ports.
- We can configure the rules for a security group to allow instances from another security group instead of providing a CIDR. We can also specify our own security group to allow only instances within the same security group to talk to each other.

See also

- You can read more about Amazon EC2 security groups here: `https://docs.aws.amazon.com/AWSEC2/latest/UserGuide/ec2-security-groups.html`.
- A rules reference for security groups can be found here: `https://docs.aws.amazon.com/AWSEC2/latest/UserGuide/security-group-rules-reference.html`.

Launching an EC2 instance into a VPC

In this recipe, we will launch EC2 instances into a public subnet and a private subnet of a VPC.

Getting ready

To complete the steps within this recipe, we need the following:

- We need to create a VPC with public and private subnets by following the *Creating a VPC in AWS* and *Creating subnets in a VPC* recipes in `Chapter 5`, *Network Security with VPC*.
- We need to add an internet gateway and configure the route table by following the *Configuring an internet gateway and a route table for internet access* recipe in `Chapter 5`, *Network Security with VPC*.
- The public subnet's security group configuration should allow internet access while the private subnet's security group configuration should only allow access from our public subnet. For creating security groups, refer to the *Creating and configuring security groups* recipe.

How to do it...

First, we will discuss the general steps regarding how to launch an EC2 instance. Then, we will discuss the specific steps for launching EC2 instances into public and private subnets.

General steps for launching an EC2 instance and doing SSH

We can launch an EC2 instance by following these steps:

1. Go to the EC2 dashboard.
2. Click on **Instances** from the left sidebar.
3. Click on the **Launch Instance** button at the top of the page.
4. Select **Amazon Linux 2 AMI (HVM), SSD Volume Type - ami-00dc79254d0461090 (64-bit x86)**.
5. On the **Choose an Instance Type** page, set **Type** to **t2.micro** and click **Next: Configure Instance Details**.

6. Within the **Configure Instance Details** page, either choose a custom VPC or the default one. You can also add user data that will be executed during the launch.
7. We can use the default configuration in the **Add Storage** page. Click **Next: Add Tags**.
8. On the **Add Tags** page, add a tag with **Key** set to `Name`. For **Value**, enter a meaningful name. Click on **Next: Configure Security Group**.

Tags are not mandatory, but a tag with **Key** set to `Name` can help us identify our EC2 instances easily from the list of EC2 instances in the EC2 dashboard.

9. On the **Configure Security Group** page, either choose an existing security group or create a new security group. Exact permission rules for the security group are provided under the respective recipes.
10. On the **Review Instance Launch** page, review the configuration and click on **Launch**.
11. We can use an existing key pair and click on **Launch Instances**, or we can create a new key pair and launch an instance, as follows:
    1. Select the **Create a new key pair** option.
    2. Click on **Download Key Pair** to download the key. Save the key safely. If you are using a Unix or Mac system, then change its file permission (`chmod`) to `400`.
    3. Click on **Launch Instances**.
12. Click on **View Instances** and wait until our instance's **Instance State** is changed to **running** and the **Status Checks** field has no errors.
13. Click on our instance and check the summary.
14. We can SSH into our EC2 instance with the following command on a Mac or Linux machine. The exact command or steps may differ between operating systems:

```
ssh -i aws-sec-cb-demo-kp.pem ec2-user@54.145.102.218
```

Here, `aws-sec-cb-demo-kp.pem` is the key pair's private key file we downloaded in *step 11*.

Launching an instance into our public subnet

In this section, we will describe the specific steps required to launch an EC2 instance into our public subnet. For general steps, refer to the *General steps for launching an EC2 instance and doing SSH* section of this recipe. Follow these steps:

1. Go to the EC2 dashboard and click on **Instances** from the left sidebar.
2. Click on the **Launch Instance** button at the top of the page, select **Amazon Linux 2 AMI**, set **Type** to **t2.micro**, and click **Next: Configure Instance Details**.
3. Within the **Configure Instance Details** page, for the **Network**, select our custom VPC. For **Subnet**, select our public subnet. Leave the option for **Auto-assign Public IP** to **Use subnet setting**, which has a value of **Enable** for our public subnet. Click **Next: Add Storage**:

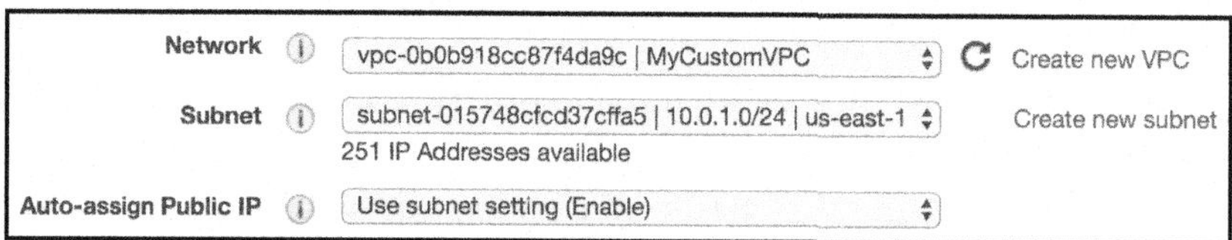

4. We will use the default configuration on the **Add Storage** page. Click **Next: Add Tags**.
5. On the **Add Tags** page, add a tag with **Key** set to `Name` and **Value** set to `MyPublicInstance`. Click on **Next: Configure Security Group**.
6. On the **Configure Security Group** page, select **Create a new security group** and provide values for **Security group name** and **Description**:

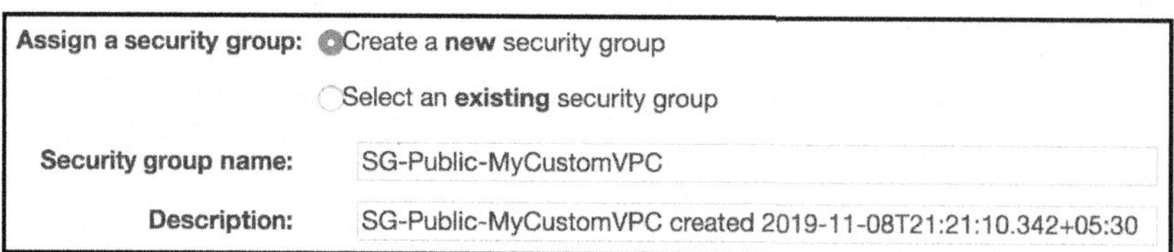

7. Add a rule for SSH (if not already present) and set **Source** to **My IP**. Our local machine IP should be automatically populated. Click on **Review and Launch**:

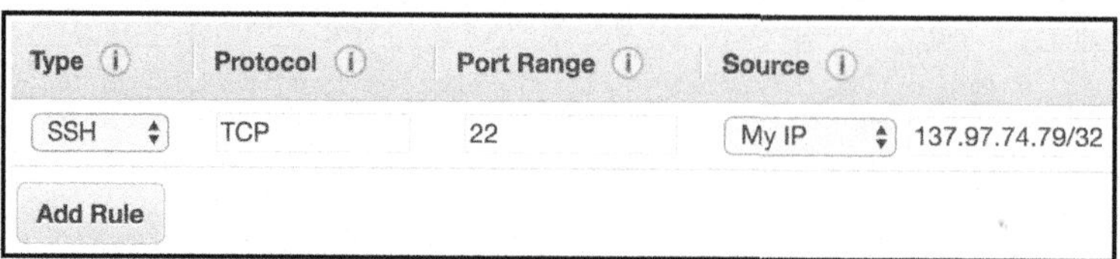

We only provided SSH access to our local IP. In the real world, you may give access to a range of IPs or to another dedicated machine referred to as a jump host or a bastion host.

8. Follow the instructions displayed on the screen to complete the EC2 launch and take note of its public IP or public DNS:

Instance ID	i-0a8b53cd37a44200c	Public DNS (IPv4)	-
Instance state	running	IPv4 Public IP	54.145.102.218
Instance type	t2.micro	IPv6 IPs	-
Elastic IPs		Private DNS	ip-10-0-1-12.ec2.internal
Availability zone	us-east-1a	Private IPs	10.0.1.12
Security groups	SG-Public-MyCustomVPC. view inbound rules. view outbound rules	Secondary private IPs	
Scheduled events	No scheduled events	VPC ID	vpc-0b0b918cc87f4da9c (MyCustomVPC)
AMI ID	amzn2-ami-hvm-2.0.20191024.3-x86_64-gp2 (ami-00dc79254d0461090)	Subnet ID	subnet-015748cfcd37cffa5 (10.0.1.0/24)

9. SSH into the EC2 instance:

```
$ ssh -i aws-sec-cb-demo-kp.pem ec2-user@54.145.102.218

       __|  __|_  )
       _|  (     /   Amazon Linux 2 AMI
      ___|\___|___|

https://aws.amazon.com/amazon-linux-2/
8 package(s) needed for security, out of 15 available
Run "sudo yum update" to apply all updates.
-bash: warning: setlocale: LC_CTYPE: cannot change locale (UTF-8): No such file or directory
[ec2-user@ip-10-0-1-12 ~]$
```

We should be able to successfully log in to the EC2 server.

In the next section, we will launch an instance into our private subnet.

Launching an instance into our private subnet

In this section, we will describe the specific steps required to launch an EC2 instance into our private subnet. For general steps, refer to the *General steps for launching an EC2 instance and doing SSH* section of this recipe. Follow these steps:

1. Go to the EC2 dashboard and click on **Instances** from the left sidebar.
2. Click on the **Launch Instance** button at the top of the page, select **Amazon Linux 2 AMI**, set **Type** to **t2.micro**, and click **Next: Configure Instance Details**.
3. Within the **Configure Instance Details** page, for the **Network** option, select our custom VPC. For **Subnet**, select our private subnet. Leave the option for **Auto-assign Public IP** to **Use subnet setting**, which has a value of **Disable** for our private subnet. Click **Next: Add Storage**:

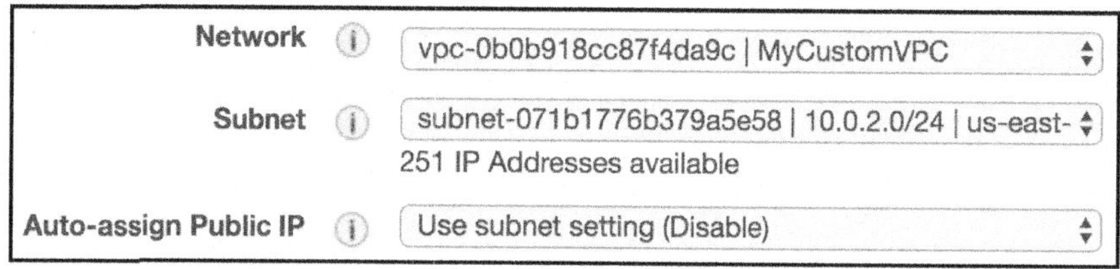

4. We will use the default configuration on the **Add Storage** page. Click **Next: Add Tags**.
5. On the **Add Tags** page, add a tag with **Key** set to `Name` and **Value** set to `MyPrivateInstance`. Click on **Next: Configure Security Group**.
6. On the **Configure Security Group** page, select **Create a new security group** and provide values for **Security group name** and **Description**.
7. Add a rule for SSH (if not already present), set **Source** to **Custom**, and enter the CIDR range for our public subnet. Also, add a rule for **All ICMP IPv4** to allow pings from our public subnet. Click on **Review and Launch**:

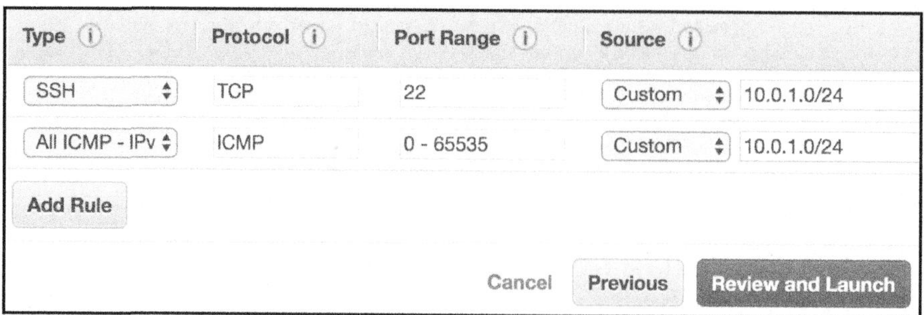

In general, public subnets host applications that are accessible from the internet, such as web servers, while private subnets host applications such as database servers, which are only accessible from public subnets. In such a case, we will only be giving the public subnets access to the application-specific ports (for example, a database port) from instances in the private subnets.

8. Follow the instructions shown on the screen to complete the EC2 launch and take note of its private IP or private DNS.
9. Copy the private key of the key pair into the EC2 instance in the public subnet. On Mac or Linux systems, we can use the `scp` command, as follows:

```
scp -i aws-sec-cb-demo-kp.pem aws-sec-cb-demo-kp.pem ec2-
user@54.145.102.218:/home/ec2-user
```

10. SSH into the EC2 instance in the public subnet.
11. Ping a private subnet IP from our public subnet instance with `ping 10.0.2.212`. We should get a successful response, as follows:

```
[ec2-user@ip-10-0-1-12 ~]$ ping 10.0.2.212
PING 10.0.2.212 (10.0.2.212) 56(84) bytes of data.
64 bytes from 10.0.2.212: icmp_seq=1 ttl=255 time=0.500 ms
64 bytes from 10.0.2.212: icmp_seq=2 ttl=255 time=0.542 ms
64 bytes from 10.0.2.212: icmp_seq=3 ttl=255 time=0.661 ms
64 bytes from 10.0.2.212: icmp_seq=4 ttl=255 time=0.606 ms
^C
--- 10.0.2.212 ping statistics ---
4 packets transmitted, 4 received, 0% packet loss, time 3048ms
rtt min/avg/max/mdev = 0.500/0.577/0.661/0.063 ms
```

12. SSH into the EC2 instance in the private subnet from the EC2 instance in the public subnet by specifying the private key that we copied in *step 8*:

```
ssh -i aws-sec-cb-demo-kp.pem ec2-user@10.0.2.212
```

We should be able to successfully log in to the EC2 server in the private subnet.

How it works...

In this recipe, we listed the general steps when it comes to launching an EC2 instance. These steps may be referred to in other recipes while launching EC2 instances. Only the specific steps will be listed in each recipe. We may also generate a key pair once and then reuse it for the rest of the recipes, as long as we have access to the private key.

First, we launched an EC2 instance into a public subnet with a security group configuration that allows us to SSH from our local machine. In real-world scenarios, we generally give access to a custom range of IPs or to another dedicated machine referred to as a jump host or a bastion host. Then, we launched an EC2 instance into a private subnet with a security group configuration that only allows access from the public subnet.

There's more...

Let's quickly go through some important concepts related to Amazon EC2:

- We can attach an Elastic IP address to our EC2 instance so that the IP address does not change when we stop and start our EC2 instances. An alternative is to register a DNS name to our public IP and change it when our IP changes. Elastic IP is free as long as it is associated with a running instance. There is also a limit of five Elastic IPs for an account, which can be increased by requesting AWS.
- We can use the EC2 placement groups cluster to have all EC2 instances provisioned within the same rack and **availability zone** (**AZ**). The instances within the placement group get up to 10 Gbps bandwidth between them. However, a failure to the rack or AZ will affect all those instances.
- We can use EC2 placement groups to have the instances within a placement group spread across different AZs. However, there is a limit on the number of instances per placement group, per AZ. This option of placement groups may be used when high availability is needed.
- We can choose an EC2 instance type that matches our requirements based on the following parameters: **random access memory** (**RAM**), **central processing unit** (**CPU**), **input and output** (**I/O**), network, and **graphical processing unit** (**GPU**).
- We can check the memory status of our Linux-based EC2 instance using `free -m`. We can use the `top` command to see more details, including memory and CPU.
- Each core within the CPU can work up to 100%. So, with four cores, it will work at 400%. However, adding more cores will not help performance if the application is single-threaded as single-threaded applications only work with one core.

See also

- For more details on EC2 instance types and selecting the right instance type, you can refer to `https://aws.amazon.com/ec2/instance-types`.
- You can read and learn more about EC2 instances here: `https://cloudmaterials.com/en/book/amazon-ec2-and-other-compute-services`.

Setting up and configuring NAT instances

Internet access may be required for instances in a private subnet for activities such as patching, downloading software, and more. **Network address translation** (**NAT**) allows an instance in a private subnet to connect to the internet. AWS provides two ways to achieve NAT with VPCs: the newer NAT gateways and the older NAT instances. In this recipe, we will learn how to create and configure NAT instances. We learned about NAT gateways in the *Setting up and configuring NAT gateways* recipe in `Chapter 5`, *Network Security with VPC*.

Getting ready

To complete the steps within this recipe, we need the following:

1. We need to create a VPC with public and private subnets by following the *Creating a VPC in AWS* and *Creating subnets in VPC* recipes in `Chapter 5`, *Network Security with VPC*.
2. We need to add an internet gateway and configure the route table by following the *Configuring an internet gateway and a route table for internet access* recipe in `Chapter 5`, *Network Security with VPC*.
3. We need to create a security group for our NAT instance. Inbound rules should allow HTTP and HTTPS from the CIDR range of our private subnet. We have allowed ICMP from private subnet instances so that we can ping the instance and our local IP for SSH access:

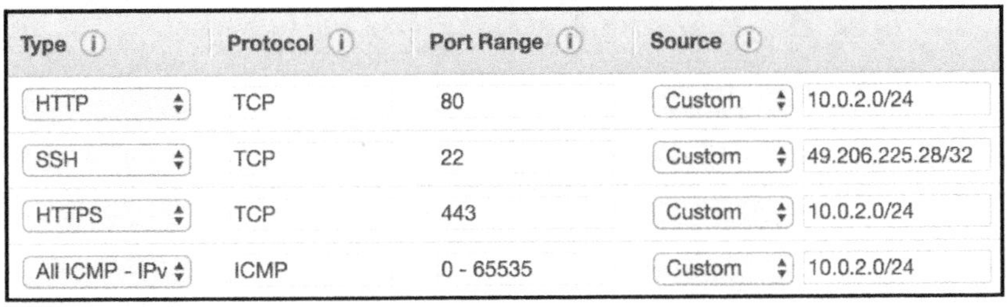

Type	Protocol	Port Range	Source	
HTTP	TCP	80	Custom	10.0.2.0/24
SSH	TCP	22	Custom	49.206.225.28/32
HTTPS	TCP	443	Custom	10.0.2.0/24
All ICMP - IPv	ICMP	0 - 65535	Custom	10.0.2.0/24

Provide outbound access to ports for HTTP, HTTPS, and ICMP, like so:

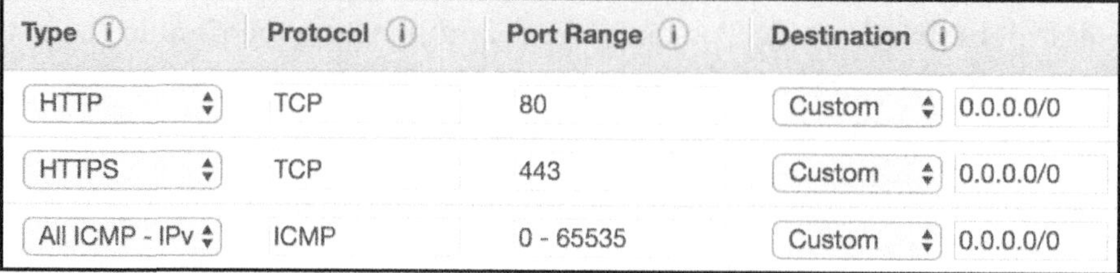

Type	Protocol	Port Range	Destination	
HTTP	TCP	80	Custom	0.0.0.0/0
HTTPS	TCP	443	Custom	0.0.0.0/0
All ICMP - IPv	ICMP	0 - 65535	Custom	0.0.0.0/0

The default outbound rules for a security group allow all outbound traffic, and our NAT instances will work fine with those set of rules. However, for added security, we have only provided outbound access to the required ports.

If you have already created a route for a NAT gateway in the main route table, please remove that route and make sure the `ping google.com` command fails (due to lack of internet access).

How to do it...

We can create a NAT instance as follows:

1. Go to the EC2 dashboard, click on **Instances** from the left sidebar, and click on the **Launch Instance** button at the top of the page.
2. Click on **Community AMIs**, search for `NAT`, and select the latest NAT instance that's available:

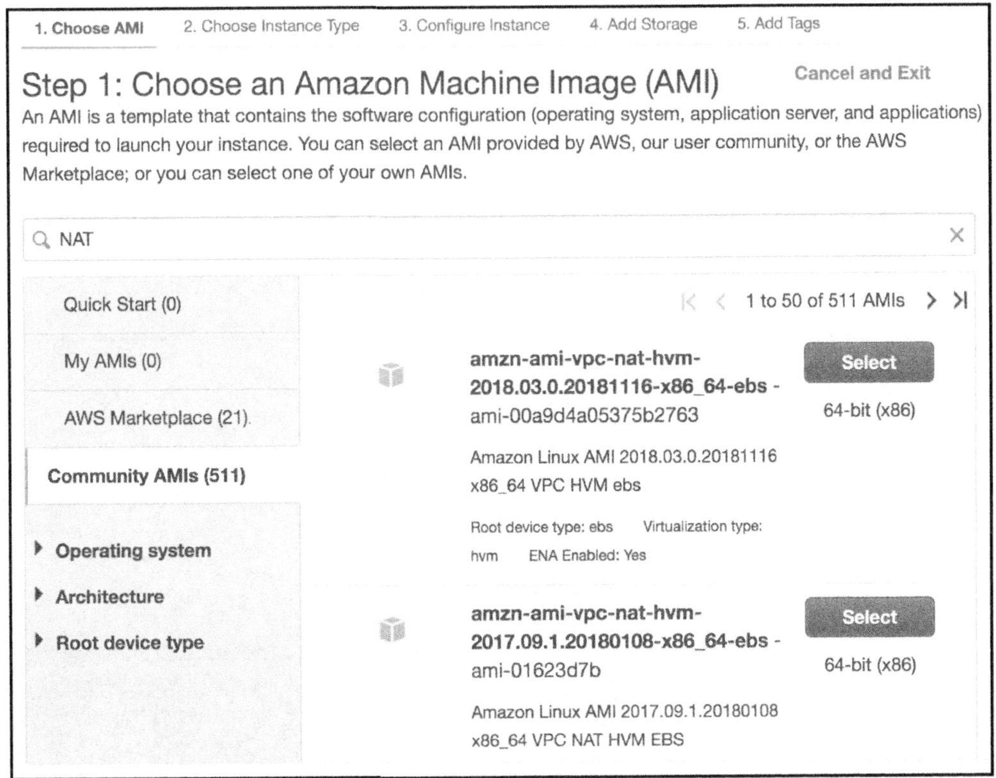

3. On the **Choose an Instance Type** page, set **Type** to **t2.micro** and click **Next: Configure Instance Details**.
4. Within the **Configure Instance Details** page, set our custom VPC to **Network**, set our public subnet to **Subnet**, leave the option for **Auto-assign Public IP** as is, and click **Next: Add Storage**:

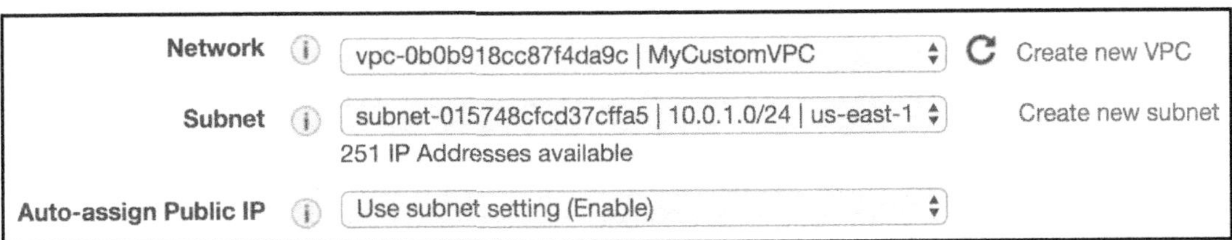

5. We can use the default configuration on the **Add Storage** page. Click **Next: Add Tags**.

6. Add a tag in the **Add Tags** page with **Key** set to `Name` and **Value** set to `My-NAT-Instance`. Click on **Next: Configure Security Group**.
7. On the **Configure Security Group** page, select **Select an existing security group**, select the security group that we created in the *Getting ready* section, and click on **Review and Launch**.
8. Follow the instructions shown on the screen to complete the EC2 launch.
9. Once the launch has completed, select our instance, click on **Actions**, click on **Networking**, and click on **Change Source/Dest. Check**:

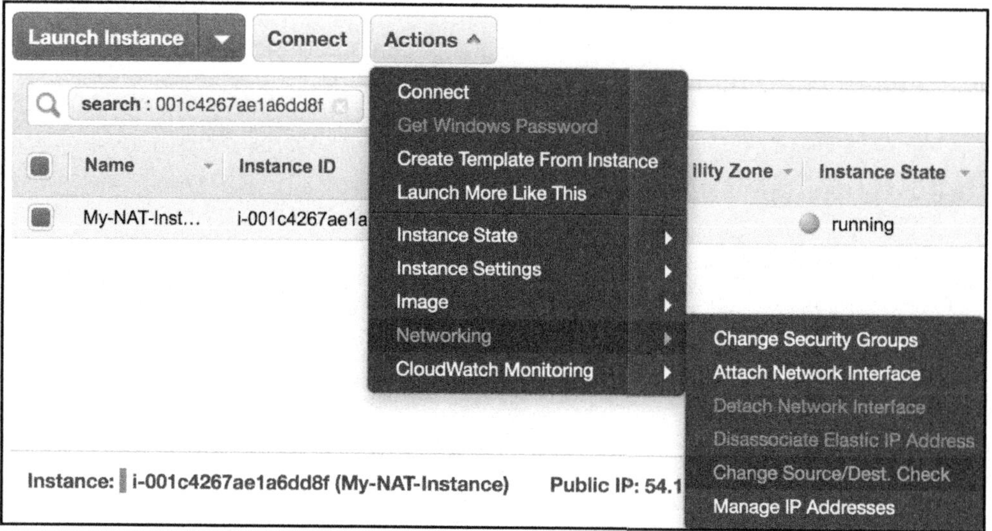

We should see the following pop-up screen:

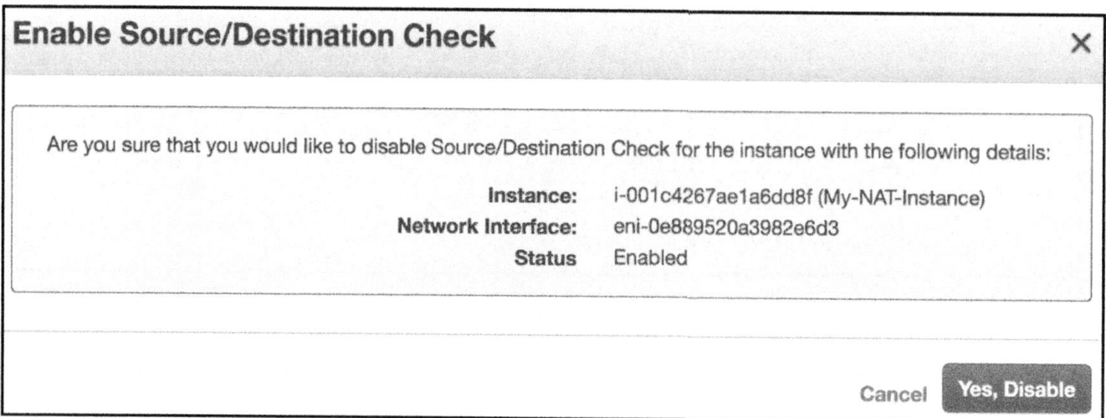

10. Click on **Yes, Disable** on the **Enable Source/Destination Check** pop-up screen.

In the next section, we will create a route to this NAT instance in our main route table.

Adding a route for the NAT instance

We can add a route for our NAT instance as follows:

1. Go to the VPC dashboard.
2. Click on **Route Tables**.
3. Select the main route table for our VPC.
4. Click on the **Routes** tab.
5. Click on **Edit routes**.
6. Click on **Add route** and do the following:
    1. **Set Destination** to `0.0.0.0/0`.
    2. From the drop-down menu for **Target**, click on **Instance** and then select our NAT instance.
    3. Click on **Save routes**:

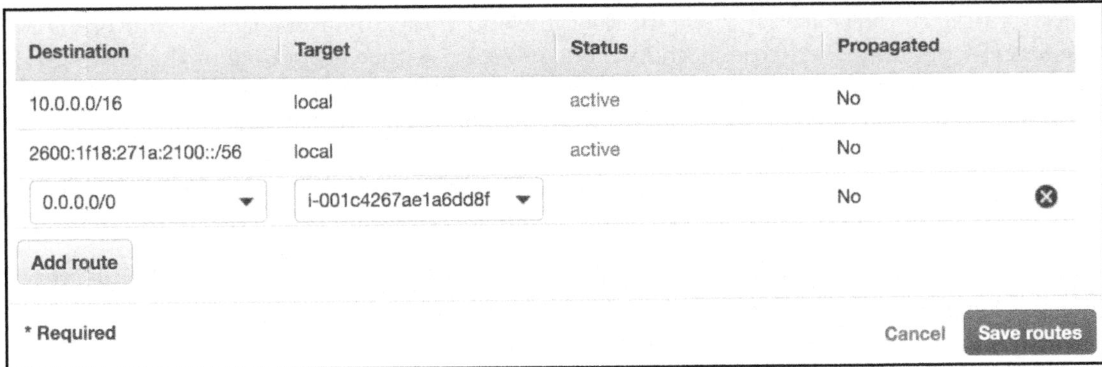

We should get a success message.

7. Log in to the EC2 instance in the public subnet. From there, log in to the private EC2 instance. You can refer to the *Launching an EC2 instance into a VPC* recipe for the exact steps.

8. Try running any command from Terminal that requires internet access, such as `ping google.com`. We should get a response if there is a route to the internet; otherwise, it will timeout. We can also run a `yum update` command and follow the prompts to update the operating system.

The effort to set up, maintain, and scale a NAT instance is more than what's required for a NAT gateway. Therefore, it is always advised to use NAT gateways instead of NAT instances.

How it works...

NAT allows instances in private subnets to talk to the internet and perform activities such as patching, downloading software, and more. NAT is the process of remapping the IP address of a packet by modifying its IP header while it's in transit. AWS provides two ways to achieve NAT with VPCs: NAT gateways and NAT instances. In this recipe, we learned how to create and configure NAT instances. We launched our NAT instance from a community AMI. Then, we searched for `NAT` in the **Community AMIs** tab to list all the NAT instance AMIs. AWS recommends using the latest one that's available.

After creating the NAT instance, we disabled the source/destination check for our NAT instance. By default, AWS expects an EC2 instance to be either the source or the destination of IP traffic. However, a NAT instance forwards requests between our private subnet and the internet, so it acts as both the source and destination. We also created a route to our NAT instance in our main route table. We added the route to our main route table since our private subnets are associated with the main route table. If our architecture has a different route table for private subnets, we need to add our route there.

NAT gateways are not associated with any security groups, while NAT instances are. For our NAT instance, we created a security group with inbound rules that allow **HTTP**, **HTTPS**, and **All ICMP - IPv4** from our private subnet. An ICMP protocol was added to help in debugging. The ICMP protocol is used for pings. For outbound rules, we enabled HTTP, HTTPS, and ICMP for the internet by specifying the CIDR range as `0.0.0.0/0`.

There's more...

Let's quickly go through some important concepts related to NAT instances:

- NAT instances are individual EC2 instances and we need to take care of patching, availability, and scaling. NAT gateways are maintained by AWS and AWS takes care of patching, availability, and scaling.
- NAT instances can create bottlenecks if many EC2 instances are using them at the same time; that is, unless we spend extra effort to improve scaling manually.
- NAT instances are individual EC2 instances and are associated with security groups. NAT gateways are not associated with any security groups.
- It is a common practice to allocate Elastic IPs to the NAT instances.

See also

- You can read more about NAT instances here: `https://docs.aws.amazon.com/vpc/latest/userguide/VPC_NAT_Instance.html`.

Creating and attaching an IAM role to an EC2 instance

In this recipe, we will create a role that allows an EC2 instance to access S3 APIs and then attach it to an EC2 instance. IAM roles provide temporary permissions for an AWS service or user to access another AWS service. A service or user assume a role, and then they are provided with temporary credentials for that session.

Getting ready

We need a working AWS account to complete this recipe. It would be good if you had a working knowledge of IAM and S3 services.

How to do it...

We can create an IAM role with access to S3 APIs as follows:

1. Go to the IAM dashboard.
2. Click on **Roles** from the left sidebar.
3. Click on **Create role**.
4. Select **EC2** as the service that will use this role and click **Next: Permissions**.
5. Select **AmazonS3FullAccess** and click **Next: Tags**.
6. Optionally, add any tags and click **Next: Review**.
7. Give the role a name (for example, `MyS3AccessRole`) and click **Create role**.

We can associate the role with an EC2 instance as follows:

1. Go to the EC2 dashboard.
2. Click on **Instances** from the left sidebar.
3. Select our private instance, click on **Actions**, click on **Instance Settings**, and click on **Attach/Replace IAM Role**:

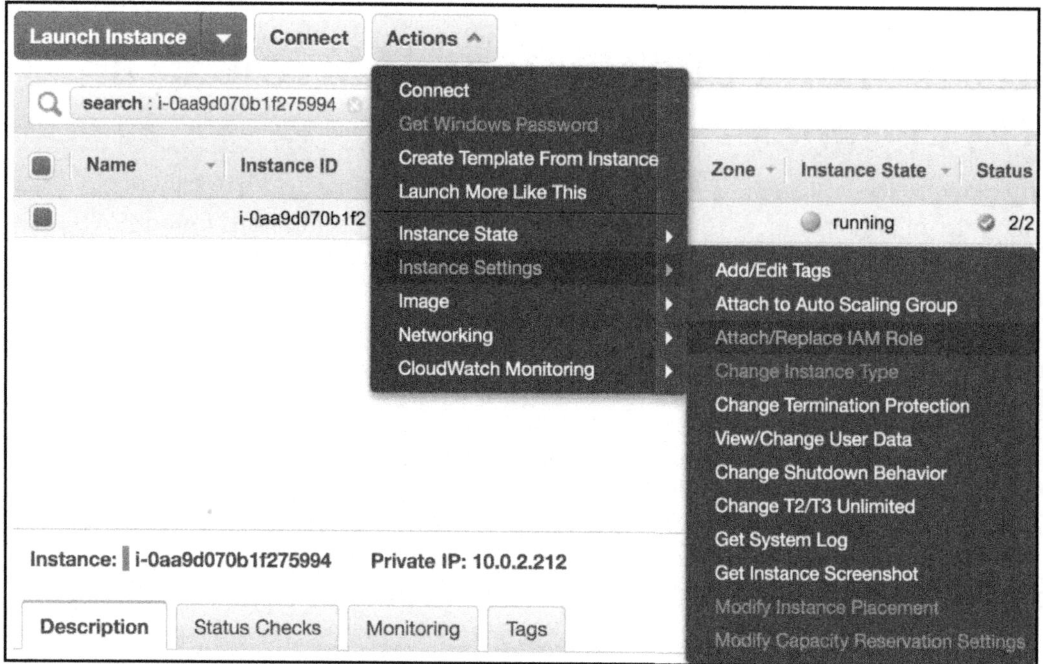

4. Select our new IAM role and click **Apply**:

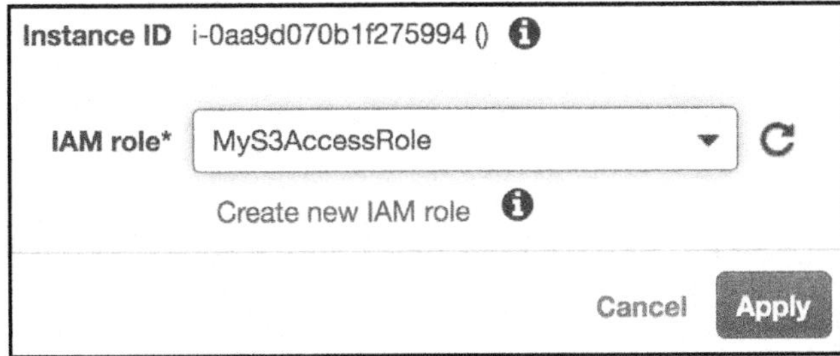

We should get a success message.

How it works...

IAM roles provide temporary permissions for an AWS service or user so that they can access another AWS service. An IAM role is an AWS identity with permissions policies. A service or user assumes a role, and then they are provided with temporary credentials for that session. We can use IAM roles to give permissions to users, services, and applications.

In this recipe, we gave S3 access permissions to our EC2 instance. Now, we can execute supported S3 operations (for example, run the `s3 ls` command from a Terminal) from our EC2 instance without configuring the credentials. An alternative is to configure the AWS credentials inside the EC2 machine, but if anyone breaks into the machine, these credentials will be exposed.

There's more...

A role that a service assumes to perform actions on our behalf is referred to as an AWS service role. An AWS service role for an EC2 instance is one such example. With an AWS service role for an EC2 instance, the applications running on an EC2 instance can get temporary credentials to perform actions that are allowed for that role.

This was a simple recipe. Note that we will be using the steps outlined within this recipe in other recipes.

See also

- You can read more about IAM roles here: https://docs.aws.amazon.com/IAM/latest/UserGuide/id_roles_terms-and-concepts.html.

Using our own private and public keys with EC2

In this recipe, we will generate a key pair in our local machine using OpenSSL and upload our public key into AWS. In the previous recipes, we generated key pairs in AWS and downloaded the private key.

Getting ready

We need a working AWS account to complete this recipe. We also need OpenSSL or a similar tool to generate the keys.

How to do it...

First, we will generate a private key and a public key on our local machine using OpenSSL. Then, we will upload our public key into AWS. After that, we will specify the key pair while launching an EC2 instance. Finally, we will SSH into the instance using our private key.

Generating the keys

Follow these steps on Mac and Linux systems in order to generate private and public keys using OpenSSL:

1. Generate a private key using OpenSSL with the following command:

```
openssl genpkey -algorithm RSA -out my_private_key.pem -pkeyopt
rsa_keygen_bits:2048
```

2. Generate a public key by providing our private key with the following command:

```
openssl rsa -pubout -in my_private_key.pem  -out
my_public_key.pem
```

3. We need to restrict the permissions for the private key file to `600` or `400` before we can use it for SSH:

```
chmod 400 my_private_key.pem
```

In the next section, we will upload our keys to AWS.

Uploading a key to EC2

We can upload our key pair's public key to EC2 as follows:

1. Go to the EC2 dashboard.
2. Click on **Key Pairs** from the left sidebar:

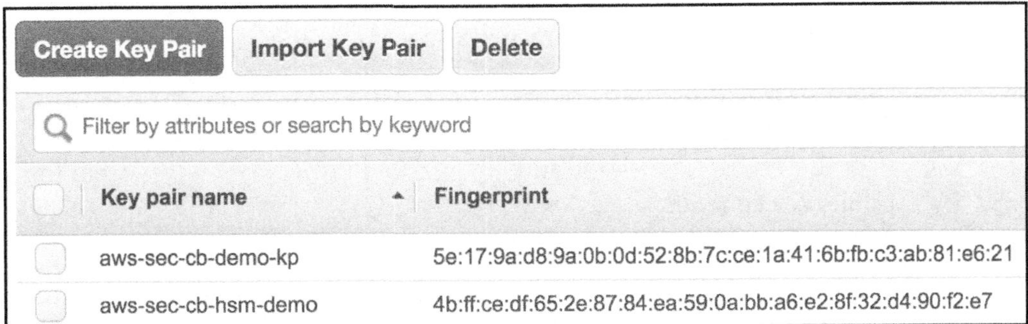

We should be able to see the keys that we have already created.

3. Click on **Import Key Pair** from the top of the page.

4. On the **Import Key Pair** page, click **Choose file** and select our public key:

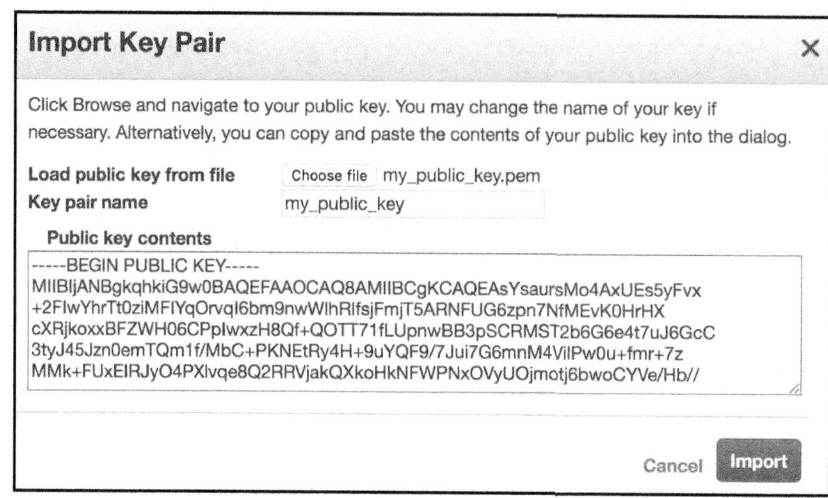

5. Remove `-----BEGIN PUBLIC KEY-----` from the beginning of the key and `-----END PUBLIC KEY-----` from the end of the key inside the textbox for **Public key contents**. You can remove any extra space from the beginning or end, but this is optional.

The AWS console currently throws an error if we don't remove `-----BEGIN PUBLIC KEY-----` and `-----END PUBLIC KEY-----` from the public key contents.

6. Click on **Import**. You will be taken to a screen similar to the following screenshot:

We should be able to see our new key under the **Key Pairs** page.

7. Launch an EC2 instance by following the standard steps. Then, on the **Select an existing key pair or create a new key pair** screen, select our newly created key pair:

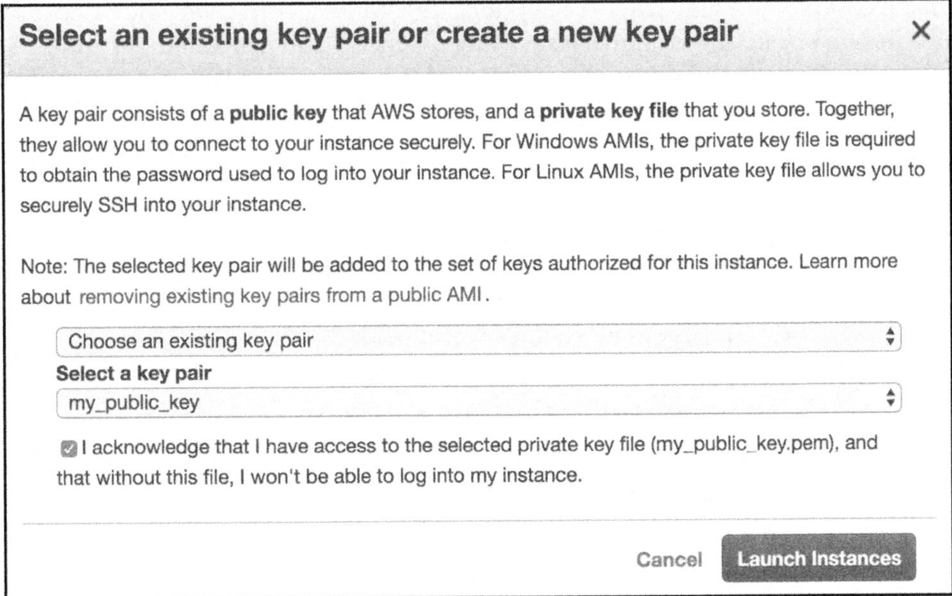

8. Click on **Launch Instances** and follow the onscreen instructions to complete the EC2 instance launch. Select the instance and take note of the public IP of our EC2 machine.
9. SSH into the EC2 machine using our private key file:

```
ssh -i my_private_key.pem ec2-user@54.174.247.166
```

We should be able to SSH into the EC2 machine successfully.

For detailed steps on how to launch an instance, refer to the *Launching an EC2 instance into a VPC* recipe.

How it works...

AWS allows us to generate a key pair from within the EC2 dashboard, from the **Key Pairs** page or from within the EC2 instance launch wizard. AWS also allows us to generate a key pair outside of AWS and then import the public key. In this recipe, we generated a private key and a public key in our local machine using OpenSSL and uploaded our public key alone into AWS. Thus, AWS never got a chance to see our private key.

There's more...

Windows users may follow these steps to generate a private key and a public key:

1. Download and install PuTTY from `https://www.putty.org`.
2. Use PuTTYgen to generate a key, as follows:
    1. Set **Type of key to generate** to RSA.
    2. Set **Number of bits in a generated key** to `2048`.
    3. Click **Generate**. You can also generate randomness by moving the mouse, as suggested.
3. Click on **Save private key** to save the private key.
4. Click on **Save public key** to save the public key.

Now, we can upload the public key by following the *Uploading a key to EC2* section of this recipe. After the key has been imported and associated with our EC2 instance, we can use PuTTY to log in to our machine.

Let's quickly go through some more important concepts related to EC2 and keys:

- EC2 key pairs are asymmetric keys.
- KMS keys are symmetric keys and cannot be used for SSHing into an EC2 instance.
- CloudHSM supports both symmetric and asymmetric keys. We can use asymmetric keys from CloudHSM to SSH into an EC2 instance.
- We cannot import a public key and create a key pair with KMS. We import a key material with KMS.
- We can use KMS keys to encrypt data in S3 or encrypt an EBS volume.
- We can see the public keys associated with an EC2 instance from an instance's Terminal by going to `/home/ec2-user/.ssh/authorized_keys`.

- We can add more key pairs to an EC2 instance by appending the public keys for those key pairs to the `/home/ec2-user/.ssh/authorized_keys` file.
- We can also see our public key by querying EC2 instance metadata; for example, `curl http://169.254.169.254/latest/meta-data/public-keys/0/openssh-key`.

With symmetric keys, the same key is used for encryption and decryption. With asymmetric keys, a key pair is used: one key is used to encrypt and the other is used to decrypt. KMS only supports symmetric keys. CloudHSM supports both symmetric and asymmetric keys.

See also

- You can read more about OpenSSL and download it from `https://www.openssl.org`.
- You can read more about PuTTY and download it from `https://www.putty.org`.

Using EC2 user data to launch an instance with a web server

We can run commands at the launch of an EC2 machine using EC2 user data. In this recipe, we will make use of EC2 user data to update our operating system and set up a simple Apache web server. Keeping the operating system updated is an important step for securing our EC2 instances. We will be using this Apache web server in future recipes.

Getting ready

We need a working AWS account to complete this recipe.

How to do it...

We can set up a simple Apache web server on an EC2 instance at launch using EC2 user data as follows:

1. Go to the EC2 dashboard and click on **Instances** from the left sidebar. Click on the **Launch Instance** button at the top of the page, select **Amazon Linux 2 AMI**, set **Type** to **t2.micro**, and click **Next: Configure Instance Details**.
2. On the **Configure Instance Details** page, leave the **Network**, **Subnet**, and **Auto-assign Public IP** settings with their default values and scroll down to the **Advanced Details** section.
3. In the **User data** textbox under the **Advanced Details** section, enter the following text:

```
#!/bin/bash
sudo su
yum update -y
yum install -y httpd
systemctl start httpd.service
systemctl enable httpd.service
```

The **Advanced Details** section should look as follows:

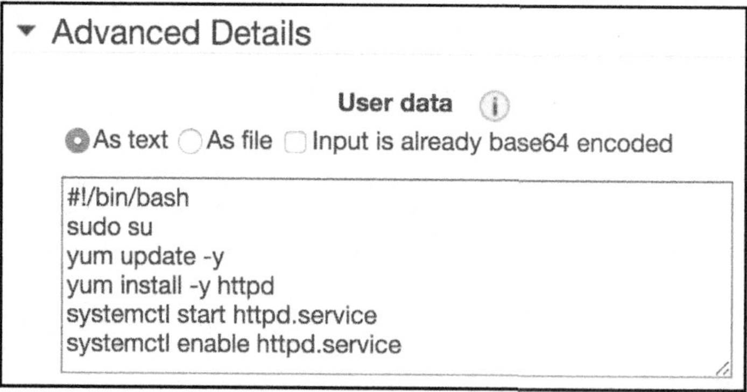

4. Click **Next: Add Storage**, leave the defaults as is, and click **Next: Add Tags**.
5. Add a tag with **Key** set to `Name` and **Value** set to `UserDataDemo`. Click **Next: Configure Security Group**.
6. Create a new security group with HTTP rules for everyone, and then SSH from our local IP.
7. Click on **Review and Launch** and follow the onscreen instructions to complete the EC2 launch.

8. Run the instance's public DNS name or public IP from a browser. We should get the default **Test Page** response from the Apache server:

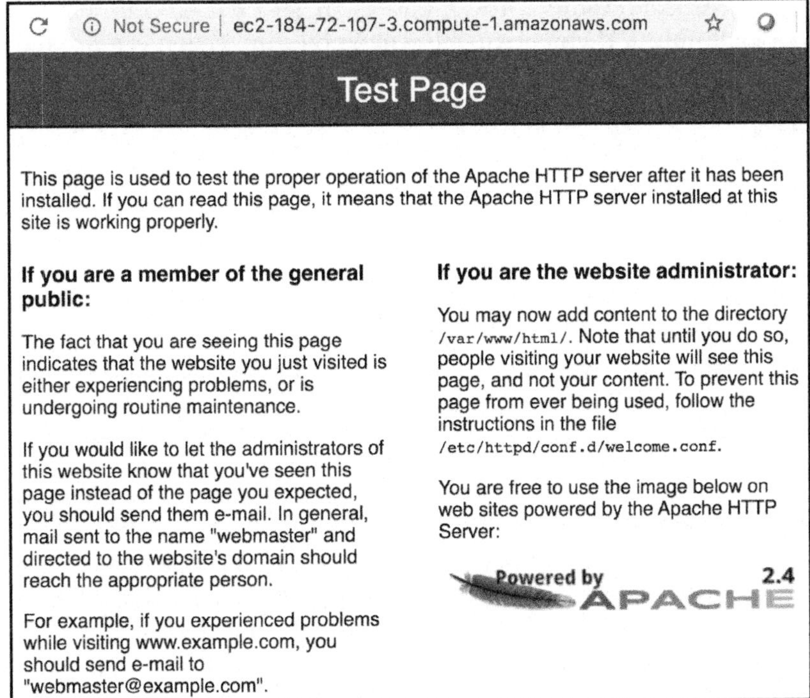

We can SSH into the EC2 machine and run the following commands in order to set up a custom `index.html` file instead of the default landing page:

```
sudo su
cd /var/www/html
echo "<html><h1>My Web Server</h1></html>" > index.html
```

If we go back to the browser and refresh the page after making the preceding change, we should see the following output:

We can also create the `index.html` file with the EC2 user data itself.

How it works...

In this recipe, we updated our instance and set up a simple Apache web server using EC2 user data. We used Amazon Linux 2 as our base AMI, so we used commands that are specific to Amazon Linux 2. If you are using Amazon Linux 1, you can use the following set of commands instead:

```
#!/bin/bash
yum update -y
yum install -y httpd
service httpd start
chkconfig httpd on
```

For the instance that hosts the web server, we allowed HTTP through our security group. We also added a rule to allow SSH from our local IP for configuring and troubleshooting. In most real-world projects, this would be done through another dedicated machine, known as a bastion host or a jump host.

There's more...

In this recipe, we updated our OS and set up a simple Apache web server. Updating the OS is always key to ensuring the security of our instances. The web server we set up in this recipe will be used in later recipes in this book, including the recipes that discuss **AWS Certificate Manager** (**ACM**), Amazon **Elastic Load Balancers** (**ELBs**), and more.

See also

- You can read more about running commands on a Linux instance at launch here: `https://docs.aws.amazon.com/AWSEC2/latest/UserGuide/user-data.html`

Storing sensitive data with the Systems Manager Parameter Store

We can store data using the Systems Manager Parameter Store with and without encryption, and then reference it from various services without having to hardcode the data in any place. In this recipe, we will learn how to store data with encryption in an AWS Systems Manager Parameter Store and then retrieve it from an EC2 instance.

Getting ready

We need a working AWS account to complete this recipe. You would benefit from being familiar with EC2 and KMS.

How to do it...

First, we will create a parameter in the AWS Systems Manager Parameter Store. Then, we will attach a role that's necessary for accessing the AWS Systems Manager from an EC2 instance. Finally, we will retrieve the parameter's information from that EC2 instance.

Creating a parameter in the AWS Systems Manager Parameter Store

We can create a Systems Manager Parameter Store parameter as follows:

1. Go to the AWS Systems Manager dashboard.
2. Click on **Parameter Store** from the left sidebar.
3. Click on **Create parameter**.
4. Set **Name** to `MySecureParameter` and set **Tier** to **Standard**:

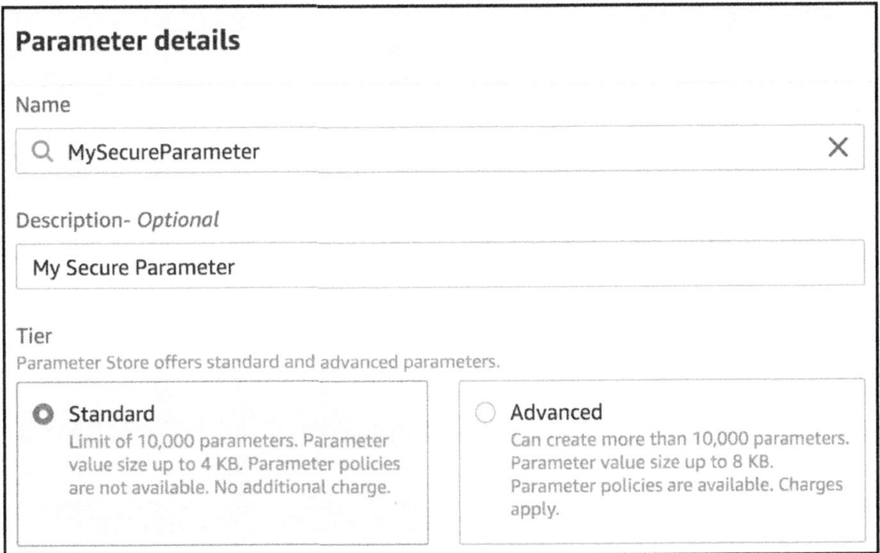

5. **Set Type** to **SecureString**, **KMS Key ID** to **alias/aws/ssm**, and **Value** to `MySecureValue`:

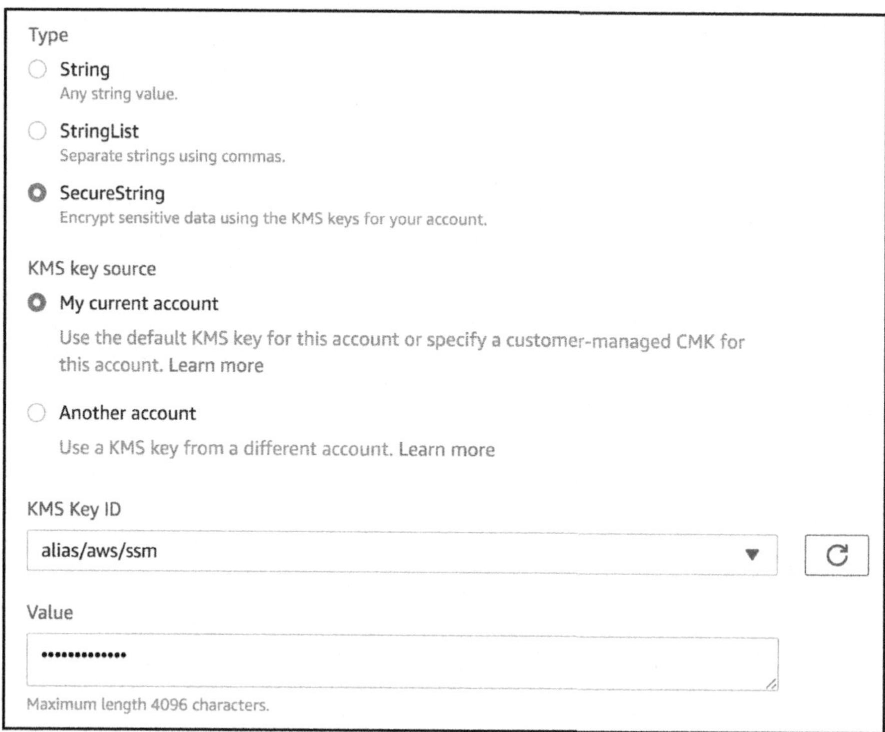

6. Scroll down and click on **Create parameter**. We should get a message stating that the create parameter request succeeded.

Next, we will create and attach a role to our EC2 instance in order to access the AWS Systems Manager.

Creating and attaching role for the AWS Systems Manager

To use the AWS Systems Manager from an EC2 instance, we need to attach a role to an EC2 instance, as follows:

1. Go to the IAM dashboard, click on **Roles**, and click on **Create role**.
2. Select **EC2** from the list of services.

You shouldn't choose the EC2 option mentioned separately at the top; instead, choose EC2 from the following bigger list of services.

3. Scroll down and select **EC2 Role for AWS Systems Manager**.
4. Click **Next:Permissions**.
5. Verify that the **AmazonEC2RoleforSSM** role is attached. Click **Next: Tags**.
6. Optionally, provide any tags. Click **Next: Review**.
7. Give the role a name and click **Create role**:

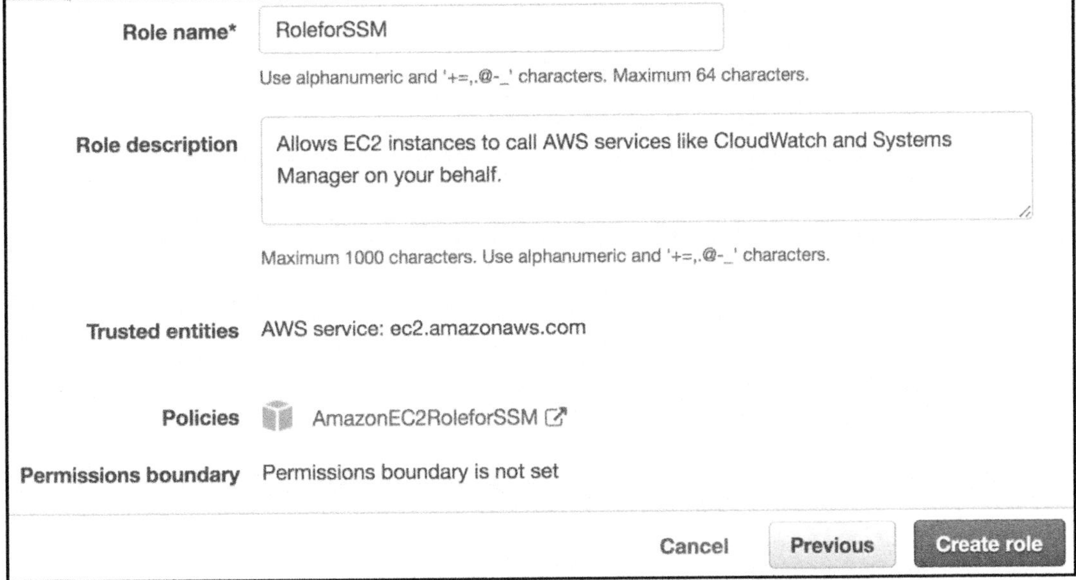

We should see a message that says **Role created successfully**.

8. Attach this role to our EC2 instance.

Follow the *Creating and attaching an IAM role to an EC2 instance* recipe for detailed steps on how to create and attach a role to an EC2 instance.

Retrieving parameters from the AWS Systems Manager Parameter Store

SSH into the EC2 instance and run the following command:

```
aws ssm get-parameters --names MySecureParameter --with-decryption --region us-east-1
```

We should get the following response:

```
{
    "InvalidParameters": [],
    "Parameters": [
        {
            "Name": "MySecureParameter",
            "LastModifiedDate": 1574254587.102,
            "Value": "MySecureValue",
            "Version": 1,
            "Type": "SecureString",
            "ARN": "arn:aws:ssm:us-east-1:135301570106:parameter/MySecureParameter"
        }
    ]
}
```

The parameter value should be decrypted.

We also have a `get-parameter` subcommand for the `aws ssm` CLI command; however, currently, the AWS-provided **AmazonEC2RoleForEC2** role does not include it. You can add the permission manually and then use `get-parameter`.

How it works...

In this recipe, we created a parameter in the AWS Systems Manager Parameter Store and retrieved it. We can use the parameter from any service without needing to hardcode its values. Now, we can update the value for that parameter from one place.

For retrieving and decrypting the parameter value that was encrypted, we used the `get-parameters` subcommand of the `aws ssm` CLI command with the `--with-decryption` option. The default is `--no-with-decryption` if none is specified and does not decrypt the value.

We can also create parameters without encryption by setting **Type** to **String** instead of **SecureString**.

There's more...

In this recipe, we only used one of the features of the AWS Systems Manager, namely the Parameter Store. Let's quickly go through some more important features of the AWS Systems Manager:

- AWS Systems Manager allows us to group resources such as EC2 instances, S3 buckets, RDS instances, and more. After we've done this, we can perform actions, such as installing a patch across a group.
- We can use the parameter in the AWS Systems Manager Parameter Store from various services, such as EC2, Lambda, CloudFormaton, and more. We can also use the parameter in a systems manager run command.
- The EC2 run command can be used to automate admin tasks and configuration changes across a group of EC2 machines.
- The EC2 role for a simple systems manager gives us permission to use the EC2 run command from our EC2 instances.
- We can specify EC2 target instances manually or based on a tag attached to the EC2 instances.
- When we configure an EC2 run command from the console, AWS provides us with the corresponding CLI command that we can run.
- For working with the EC2 run command, the SSM agent needs to be installed on the instances.
- We can use the run command to execute actions on on-premises systems as well.

See also

- You can read all about the AWS Systems Manager at `https://docs.aws.amazon.com/systems-manager/latest/userguide/what-is-systems-manager.html`.
- You can read all about the AWS Systems Manager Parameter Store at `https://docs.aws.amazon.com/systems-manager/latest/userguide/systems-manager-parameter-store.html`.

Using KMS to encrypt data in EBS

In this recipe, we will use KMS keys to encrypt EBS volumes. EBS is a block storage service designed to be used as the storage system for EC2 instances.

Getting ready

We need a working AWS account to complete this recipe.

How to do it...

We can encrypt an EBS storage volume while creating an EC2 instance as follows:

1. Go to the EC2 dashboard and click on **Instances** from the left sidebar. Click on the **Launch Instance** button at the top of the page, select **Amazon Linux 2 AMI**, set **Type** to **t2.micro**, and click **Next: Configure Instance Details**.
2. Leave the default values as they are in the **Configure Instance Details** page and click **Next: Add Storage**.

   Now, we should see the **Add Storage** page with the **Root** volume:

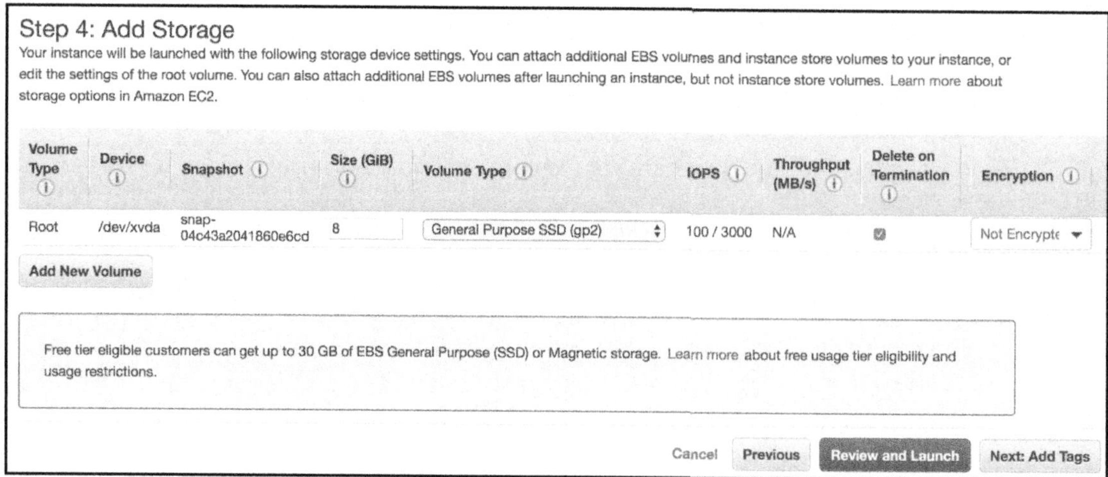

3. Click on the drop-down menu for **Encryption** and select our **customer master key (CMK)**. I will select the default AWS-managed KMS key for EBS:

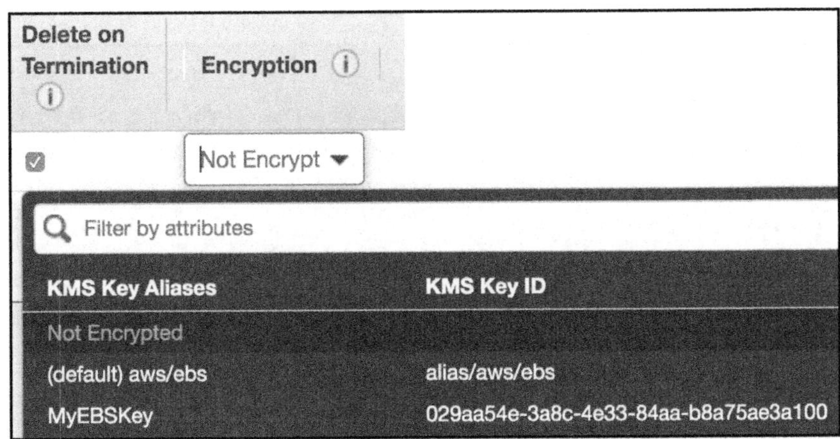

Optionally, we can click on **Add New Volume** to add new EBS volumes and enable encryption the same way.

To use our own CMK to encrypt an EBS volume, we need to create a CMK from KMS. We can create a key by following the *Creating keys in KMS* recipe in `Chapter 4`, *Key Management with KMS and CloudHSM*. We also need to add the appropriate users for administering and using the key and use a user with key usage permission. I added a key called `MyEBSKey` in the `us-east-1` region.

4. Click **Next: Add Tags** and add a tag with **Key** set to `Name` and **Value** set to `MyEC2WithEncryptedEBS`:

5. Follow the onscreen instructions to complete the EC2 launch. We can go to the EC2 dashboard home page, click on **Volumes** from the left sidebar, select our volume, and verify our new volume's details:

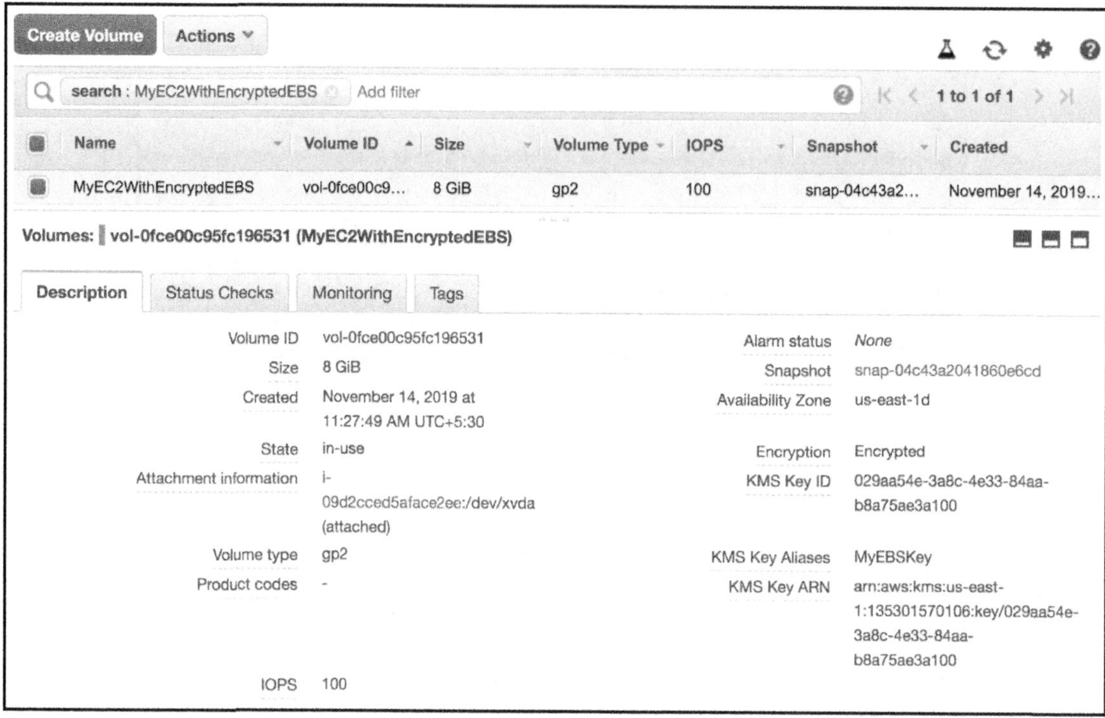

Note that we can apply the same tag to both instance and volume.

How it works...

Since KMS is a region-specific service, we need to create the KMS key within the same AWS region where we need to use the key for encryption or decryption. We can either use the AWS-managed default key for EBS, as we saw in this recipe, or use our own CMK.

To use our CMK to encrypt an EBS volume, we need to create a CMK from the KMS service dashboard. However, to use the AWS-managed default key for EBS, the additional steps are not required. The AWS-managed default key for EBS has an **Alias Name** of `(default) aws/kms` and a **KMS Key ID** of `alias/aws/ebs`.

It is important to note that we cannot use EC2 key pairs to encrypt our EBS volumes. EC2 key pairs are asymmetric keys and can be used for SSH. KMS keys are symmetric keys and can be used for encrypting data in EBS volumes, S3, and more.

There's more...

Previously, encrypting a root volume was not supported while launching an EC2 instance, so we had to do the following workaround to encrypt a root volume:

1. Create a snapshot of our volume.
2. Create an AMI from the snapshot.
3. Create a copy of the AMI. While creating the copy, we can select the **Encrypt target EBS snapshots** option.

Currently, we do not have to go through these extra steps.

See also

- You can read more about AWS EBS here: `https://aws.amazon.com/ebs`.

7
Web Security Using ELBs, CloudFront, and WAF

Load balancers distribute the load across different systems. They help us handle loads effectively to achieve reliability and high availability. Load balancers can terminate TLS at the load balancer level and provide us with a single place to manage the X.509 certificates that are required. They can also perform TCP passthrough for the TLS traffic and let TLS terminate at the instance level. Firewalls are important security mechanisms that protect networks and systems by monitoring and controlling incoming and outgoing traffic. In this chapter, we will learn about various ways in which we can implement load balancers and firewalls within AWS.

This chapter will cover the following recipes:

- Enabling HTTPS on an EC2 instance
- Creating an SSL/TLS certificate with ACM
- Creating a classic load balancer
- Creating ELB target groups
- Using an application load balancer with TLS termination at the ELB
- Using a network load balancer with TLS termination at EC2
- Securing S3 using CloudFront and TLS
- Configuring and using the AWS **web application firewall** (**WAF**)

Technical requirements

We'll need a working AWS account for this chapter. Basic knowledge of S3 and CloudFront will be helpful for understanding some of the recipes within this chapter.

The code files for this chapter are available at `https://github.com/PacktPublishing/AWS-Security-Cookbook/tree/master/Chapter07`.

Enabling HTTPS on an EC2 instance

In this recipe, we will configure TLS on an Amazon Linux 2 EC2 instance to enable HTTPS access to our web server.

Getting ready

We need to follow the *Using EC2 user data to launch an instance with a web server* recipe in `Chapter 6`, *Working with EC2 Instances*, in order to set up an EC2 instance. You will also need the following:

- The security group should allow HTTP (80) and HTTPS (443) for everyone, and SSH (22) for our local IP.
- Apache web server should be installed and configured to start on system reboot. You can verify that your Apache server is enabled by SSHing into the EC2 instance and running the `sudo systemctl is-enabled httpd` command. This should return `enabled`.

How to do it...

We can enable HTTPS on an Amazon Linux 2 EC2 instance as follows:

1. Install the Apache `mod_ssl` module:

   ```
   sudo yum install -y mod_ssl
   ```

   If the installation is successful, then the `/etc/httpd/conf.d/ssl.conf` and `/etc/pki/tls/certs/make-dummy-cert` files will be created in our EC2 instance.

   We should be able to see entries for **Server Certificate** and **Server Private Key** in the `ssl.conf` file:

```
#   Server Certificate:
# Point SSLCertificateFile at a PEM encoded certificate.  If
# the certificate is encrypted, then you will be prompted for a
# pass phrase.  Note that a kill -HUP will prompt again.  A new
# certificate can be generated using the genkey(1) command.
SSLCertificateFile /etc/pki/tls/certs/localhost.crt

#   Server Private Key:
#   If the key is not combined with the certificate, use this
#   directive to point at the key file.  Keep in mind that if
#   you've both a RSA and a DSA private key you can configure
#   both in parallel (to also allow the use of DSA ciphers, etc.)
SSLCertificateKeyFile /etc/pki/tls/private/localhost.key
```

Take note of the name and location of the server certificate, which is `/etc/pki/tls/certs/localhost.crt`.

2. Edit the `ssl.conf` file and comment out the entry for `Server Private Key` (`localhost.key`), as follows:

```
#   Server Private Key:
#   If the key is not combined with the certificate, use this
#   directive to point at the key file.  Keep in mind that if
#   you've both a RSA and a DSA private key you can configure
#   both in parallel (to also allow the use of DSA ciphers, etc.)
#SSLCertificateKeyFile /etc/pki/tls/private/localhost.key
```

3. Run `make-dummy-cert` to generate a self-signed dummy certificate and private key onto a file with the same name and location of the **Server Certificate** file that was provided in the `ssl.conf` file:

```
sudo /etc/pki/tls/certs/make-dummy-cert
/etc/pki/tls/certs/localhost.crt
```

If we check the contents of the `localhost.crt` file, we'll see that it contains both the certificate and the key in the PEM format, as required by the Apache server. When we replace this dummy certificate and the key with our actual certificate and key, we should make sure they are also in the PEM format.

4. Restart the Apache server with the following command:

```
sudo systemctl restart httpd
```

5. Enter our EC2 instance's public IP from a browser with the `https://` prefix (for example, `https://54.172.73.194`).

We may see a warning that the connection is not private since we have used a self-signed certificate. Click on **Advanced** and then click on the proceed button/link. We should see that our sample web page has been loaded with the `https` prefix:

If we haven't added the custom `index.html` file, we will see the default Apache server landing page.

How it works...

First, we installed the Apache `mod_ssl` module. This module adds TLS v1.2 support to our Apache server. The current version of the module also supports SSL v3 and all versions of TLS. When we installed the `mod_ssl` module, two new files were created in our EC2 instance: `ssl.conf`, which is the configuration file for `mod_ssl`, and `make-dummy-cert`, which is a helper script for generating a dummy certificate and a private key for testing purposes.

The certificate file that was generated contained both the certificate and the private key. Therefore, we commented out the **Server Private Key** file entry from the `ssl.conf` file. The certificate and the key are generated in PEM format, as required by the Apache server. If we are adding our own certificate and key, we need to make sure they are in PEM format.

Also, since we were using a self-signed certificate, we received a warning when we used the `https` prefix. In production, we should use a certificate signed by a trusted **certificate authority** (**CA**) so that this warning doesn't occur.

There's more...

Historically, the protocol for HTTPS is referred to as SSL, even though the actual protocol that's used today is mostly TLS. SSL is considered not safe to use anymore. Even the earlier versions of TLS, namely TLS 1.0 and TLS 1.1, are currently not recommended for use. Amazon Linux 2 supports TLS 1.2, which is why we used it within this recipe.

See also

- You can find detailed steps for configuring SSL/TLS on an EC2 instance at the following link: `https://docs.aws.amazon.com/AWSEC2/latest/UserGuide/SSL-on-amazon-linux-2.html`.

Creating an SSL/TLS certificate with ACM

In this recipe, we will create an X.509 certificate for a public domain that we own using **AWS Certificate Manager** (**ACM**). ACM public certificates are used with AWS services such as **elastic load balancing** (**ELB**), Amazon CloudFront, AWS Elastic Beanstalk, Amazon API Gateway, and AWS CloudFormation.

Getting ready

We need a domain name to complete the steps within this recipe. We can use a domain registered with Route 53 or an outside registrar.

How to do it...

We can create a TLS certificate in ACM as follows:

1. Go to the **AWS Certificate Manager** dashboard. If you are using ACM for the first time, you should see the **Get started** options. Currently, AWS provides options so that you can **Provision certificates** and creates a **Private certificate Authority**.
2. Click on **Get started** under **Provision certificates**. We should see options to **Import a certificate**, **Request a public certificate**, and **Request a private certificate**.

The option to request a private certificate will only be active if no private CAs are available.

3. Select **Request a public certificate** and click on **Request a certificate**.
4. Enter your fully qualified domain name in the text box for **Domain name** and click **Next**. I will be using the domain name with a wildcard of `*.heartin.cloud`.
5. On the **Select validation method** screen, set the validation method to **DNS validation** and click **Next**.
6. On the **Add Tags** screen, you can add tags as required (this is optional), and click on **Review**.
7. Review the details and click on **Confirm and request**. We can expand our domain's name from the list to get details of a CNAME record that needs to be updated at the domain's DNS server for validation:

Domain	Validation status
▾ ***.heartin.cloud**	Pending validation

Add the following CNAME record to the DNS configuration for your domain. The procedure for adding CNAME records depends on your DNS service Provider. Learn more.

Name	Type	Value
_d7421f63455c6f73b992687241108676.heartin.cloud.	CNAME	_688023dab66a33bb19296867b887a712.kirrbxfjtw.acm-validations.aws.

Note: Changing the DNS configuration allows ACM to issue certificates for this domain name for as long as the DNS record exists. You can revoke permission at any time by removing the record. Learn more.

We can also click on the **Export DNS configuration to a file** link to get the CNAME details of all the domains for DNS validation.

8. Take note of the CNAME details and click on **Continue**. The **Status** of our certificate will be **Pending validation** initially.
9. Add a CNAME record with the CNAME details in the domain's DNS management service.

AWS-provided CNAME record names contain the domain name part, such as `_d7421f63455c6f73b992687241108676.heartin.cloud.`. Certain DNS management services auto append the domain name to your CNAME record name. In such cases, enter the host part without the domain name part (for example, `_d7421f63455c6f73b992687241108676`). Most DNS management services set the **Name** to **Host** and **Value** to **Points to**.

10. Go to the **Certificates** screen and check the **Status**. Once successful, the **Status** of our certificate will be **Issued**. If the **Status** is **Pending validation**, check back again after some time, or refresh the page using the refresh button, until the **Status** has changed to **Issued**.

How it works...

In this recipe, we created a certificate using ACM. We can request a certificate for one or more domain names. We need to specify a fully qualified domain name such as `www.heartin.cloud` or one that uses a wildcard, such as `*.heartin.cloud`, that represents all the subdomains of heartin.cloud.

Before issuing the certificate, we need to validate the ownership of the domain. We can do this either through DNS validation or through email validation. We performed DNS validation in this recipe. AWS will provide a CNAME record per domain for DNS validation. We need to update this CNAME record on our domain's DNS management service. Route 53 is Amazon's DNS management service.

There's more...

ACM public certificates are supported for AWS services such as ELB, Amazon CloudFront, AWS Elastic Beanstalk, Amazon API Gateway, and AWS CloudFormation. AWS does not allow us to use the ACM public certificates to enable SSL/TLS on our EC2 instances. ACM private CA issued certificates can, however, be used with EC2 instances, containers, and even our own servers.

AWS does not charge us for the public TLS certificates that are provisioned through ACM. We only need to pay for the AWS resources we create to run our application. However, creating an ACM private **certificate authority** (**CA**) is not free. For a private CA, we are charged a monthly fee, as well as for the private certificates we issue. We are not charged once we delete a private CA; however, if we restore a private CA, we will be charged for the time when it was deleted.

See also

- You can read more about ACM service integrations and view the current list of supported services here: `https://docs.aws.amazon.com/acm/latest/userguide/acm-services.html`.

Creating a classic load balancer

Classic load balancers are previous generation load balancers. AWS's recommendation is to use one of the newer load balancers, namely, an application load balancer or a network load balancer. However, you may still want to know about classic load balancers for older projects and when we need to use the EC2-classic model.

Getting ready

We need to create two EC2 instances to complete this recipe. We can do this by following the *Using EC2 user data to launch an instance with a web server* recipe in Chapter 6, *Working with EC2 Instances*, but using the following EC2 user data commands:

```
#!/bin/bash
sudo su
yum update -y
yum install -y httpd
systemctl start httpd.service
systemctl enable httpd.service
cd /var/www/html
echo "<html><h1>My Web Server 1</h1></html>" > index.html
```

Replace `My Web Server 1` with `My Web Server 2` for the second instance.

Add **Name** tags (tags with **Key** as `Name`) for the instances to identify them from the instances list. For the first instance, set **Value** to `WebServer1`. For the second instance, set **Value** to `WebServer2`.

Before proceeding, make sure that our instances are running and accessible directly from a browser. The first server should give a response similar to the following:

The second server should give a response similar to the following:

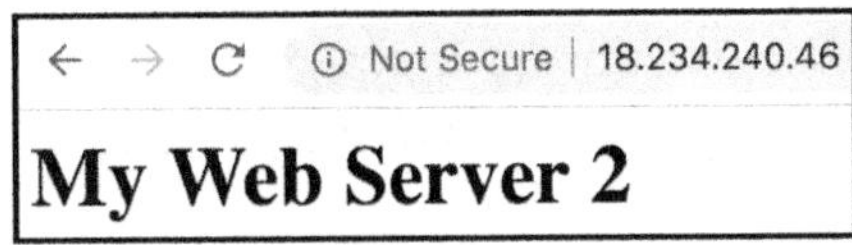

Currently, we have given HTTP access to everyone. For additional security, after the ELB has been configured and tested, we may restrict access to the instances from only our ELB's security group.

How to do it...

We can create and test a classic load balancer as follows:

1. Go to the EC2 service in the console.
2. Click on **Load Balancers** from the left sidebar.
3. Click on **Create Load Balancer**. We should see the options to create the three types of load balancers, namely application load balancer, network load balancer, and classic load balancer. Classic load balancer is currently marked as a previous generation and is grayed out.
4. Under **Classic Load Balancer**, click on **Create**.
5. For **Load Balancer name**, provide a meaningful name. Leave the other options with their defaults:

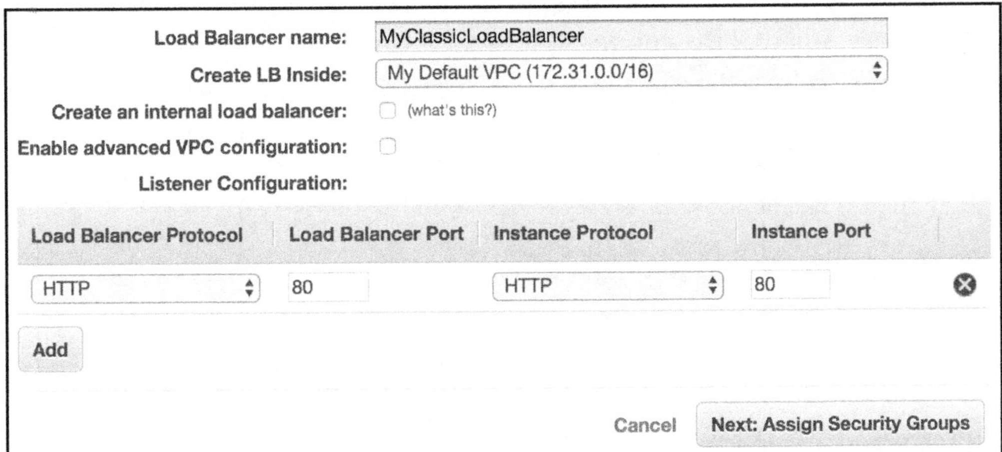

6. Click **Next: Assign Security Groups**.
7. Select a security group that allows HTTP from `0.0.0.0/0`. You may use the **MyWebServerSG** security group that we created in the *Using EC2 user data to launch an instance with a web server* recipe in `Chapter 6`, *Working with EC2 Instances*.
8. Click **Next: Configure Security Settings**.

On the **Configure Security Settings** page, we will get a warning that our instance does not use an HTTPS or SSL protocol for frontend encryption. We will learn how to use HTTPS with ELB in the *Using an application load balancer with TLS termination at the ELB* recipe of this chapter.

9. Click **Next: Configure Health Check**.
10. On the **Configure Health Check** screen, we will use the defaults:

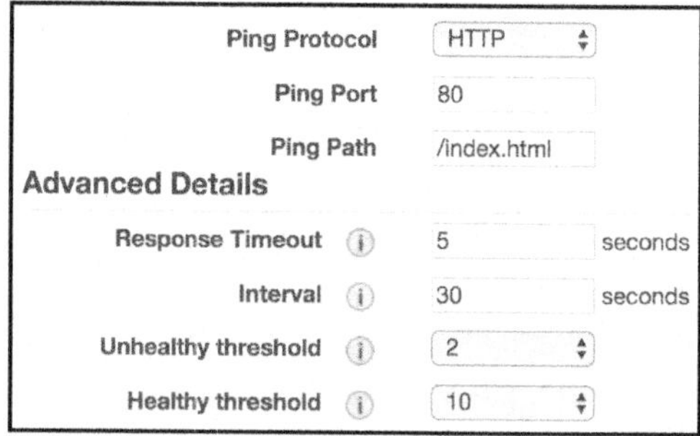

11. Click **Next: Add EC2 Instances**.
12. On the **Add EC2 Instances** screen, add the two instances and for other options, use the defaults:

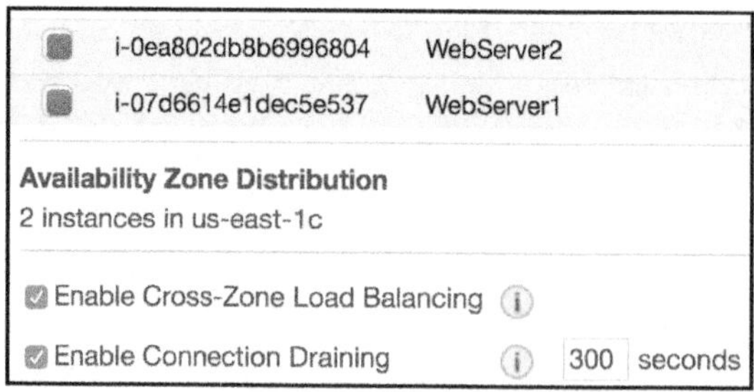

13. Click **Next: Add Tags** and add any tags for the ELB (this is optional).
14. Click on **Review and Create**.

15. Review and then click on **Create**. Initially, we will see the **Status** set to **OutOfService** while the instances are being registered:

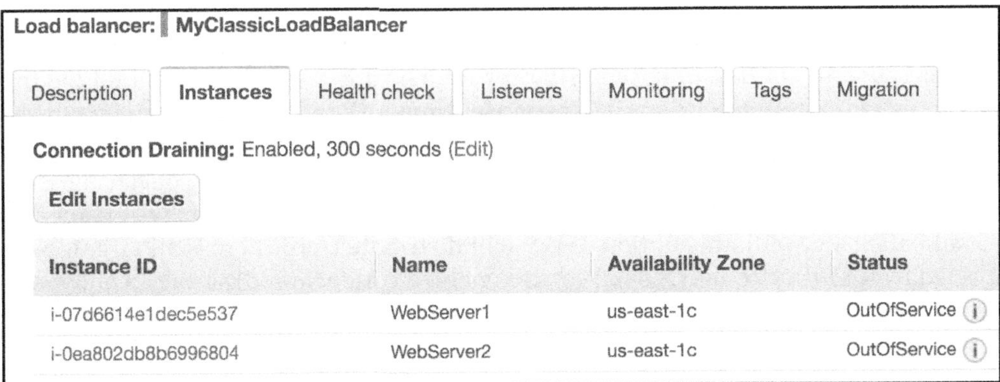

After the instances have been registered, the **Status** will change to **InService**.

16. Copy the **DNS name** from the ELB's **Description** tab and run it from a browser:

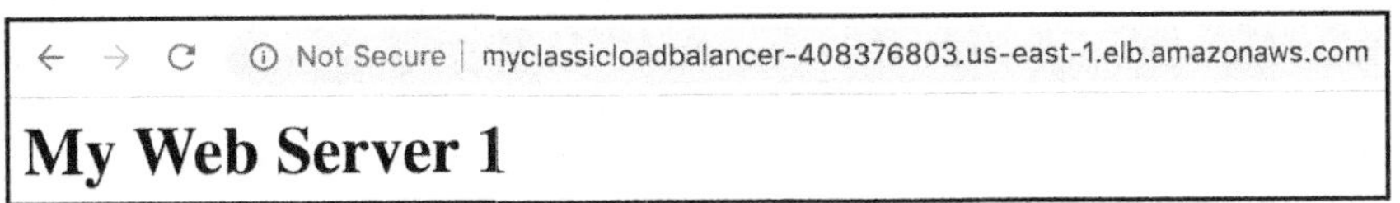

Every time we run the URL, we will get a response either from web server 1 or web server 2.

How it works...

First, we created a classic load balancer by selecting the default VPC. We can also choose a custom VPC. We did not choose the **Create an internal load balancer** option since that will make our load balancer internal. An internal load balancer is only accessible from our VPC through private IP addresses. Internet-facing load balancers have public DNS and are reachable from the internet. We did not select the **Enable advanced VPC configuration** option. These options will allow us to select the subnets for our VPC.

We used the default listener configuration: **Load Balancer Protocol** set to `HTTP`, **Load Balancer Port** set to `80`, **Instance Protocol** set to `HTTP`, and **Instance Port** set to `80`. **Load Balancer Protocol** and **Load Balancer Port** are the protocol and port that the ELB listens from. **Instance Protocol** and **Instance Port** are the protocol and port of the EC2 instances.

The following protocols are supported by the classic load balancer for the **Load Balancer Protocol** and **Instance Protocol**: **HTTP**, **HTTPS (Secure HTTP)**, **TCP**, and **SSL (Secure TCP)**.

On the **Configure Health Check** screen, we configured the **Ping Protocol**, **Ping Port**, and **Ping Path**. These are used to ping the instances for a health check. We provided the time to wait for a response from the instance (**Response Timeout**), the time between health checks (**Interval**), the number of consecutive failures before declaring an instance unhealthy (**Unhealthy threshold**), and the number of consecutive successes before declaring an instance healthy (**Healthy threshold**). On the **Add EC2 Instances** screen, we enabled cross-zone load balancing. With this option, AWS will distribute traffic across all targets across all selected **availability zones** (**AZs**). We also enabled connection draining to allow existing traffic to continue flowing when an instance is deregistered.

There's more...

AWS supports three types of **elastic load balancers** (**ELBs**), namely, application load balancer, network load balancer, and classic load balancer. When we need a flexible set of features at the application layer, it is recommended to use the application load balancer. The application load balancer only supports HTTP or HTTPS protocols. Therefore, when using other protocols, such as TCP, and for TLS termination at the EC2 instance, we should use a network load balancer, even if a classic load balancer can be used. Also, when extreme performance is required, it is recommended to use a network load balancer.

Let's quickly go through some more important concepts related to classic load balancers:

- With classic load balancers, we can use application layer (application layer of the OSI model) features such as X-forwarded and sticky sessions.
- With classic load balancers, we can also use strict layer 4 load balancing for TCP traffic.
- With classic load balancers, a 504 gateway timeout error means that there is a timeout from the application running on the EC2 instance and does not mean a timeout from the load balancer.
- When you create a classic load balancer within a VPC, we can choose whether to make it a private (internal) load balancer or an internet-facing load balancer.
- A classic load balancer is a previous generation load balancer, which means we can only use it if we are working with the legacy EC2-classic network. AWS provides a migration wizard for migrating from a classic load balancer to an application load balancer in the **Migration** tab of the classic load balancer in the console.

Let's quickly go through some more important general concepts related to load balancers in AWS:

- Subnets associated with an ELB should belong to different availability zones.
- A sticky session binds a user's session to one EC2 instance.
- The following headers are provided to get information about the requester from an EC2 instance:
    - `X-Forwarded-For`, to get the original IP address of the requester
    - `X-Forwarded-Protocol`, to get the protocol used by the requester
    - `X-Forwarded-Port`, to get the port used by the requester
- Internet-facing load balancers need to be associated with public subnets.
- Internal load balancers are associated with internal (private) subnets and can only be reached through instances that have access to the VPC's private IP addresses.

See also

- You can read more about classic internal load balancers here: `https://docs.aws.amazon.com/elasticloadbalancing/latest/classic/elb-internal-load-balancers.html`.

Creating ELB target groups

In this recipe, we will learn how to create a target group. The application load balancer and network load balancer route traffic to target groups, unlike classic load balancers, which route traffic to individual EC2 instances.

Getting ready

We need to create two EC2 instances to complete this recipe. We can do this by following the *Using EC2 user data to launch an instance with a web server* recipe in `Chapter 6`, *Working with EC2 Instances*, but using EC2 user data, as we used in the *Getting ready* section of the *Creating a classic load balancer* recipe of this chapter.

Add name tags (tags with **Key** set to `Name`) for the instances to identify them from the instances list. For the first instance, set **Value** to `WebServer1`. For the second instance, set **Value** to `WebServer2`.

Before proceeding, make sure that our instances are running and accessible directly from a browser. For additional security, after the ELB has been configured and tested, we can restrict access to these instances from our ELB's security group.

How to do it...

We can create a target group as follows:

1. Go to the EC2 service in the console.
2. Click on **Target Groups** from the left sidebar.
3. Click **Create target group**.
4. On the **Create target group** page, enter a meaningful name for the **Target group name**. For **Target type**, select **Instance**. For **Protocol**, select **HTTP**. For **Port**, enter `80`. Finally, for **VPC**, select our default VPC:

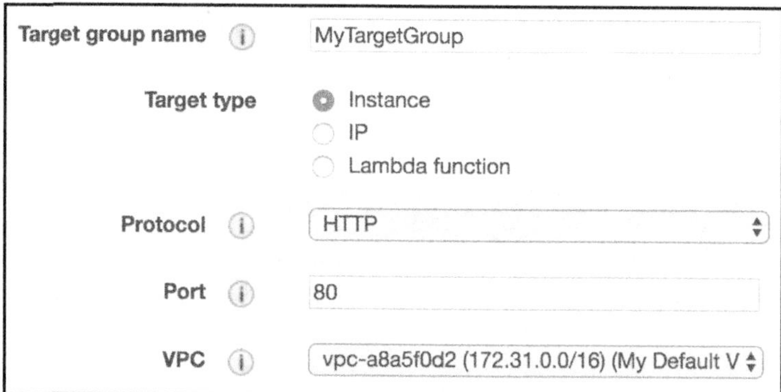

5. Configure the health check settings, as follows:

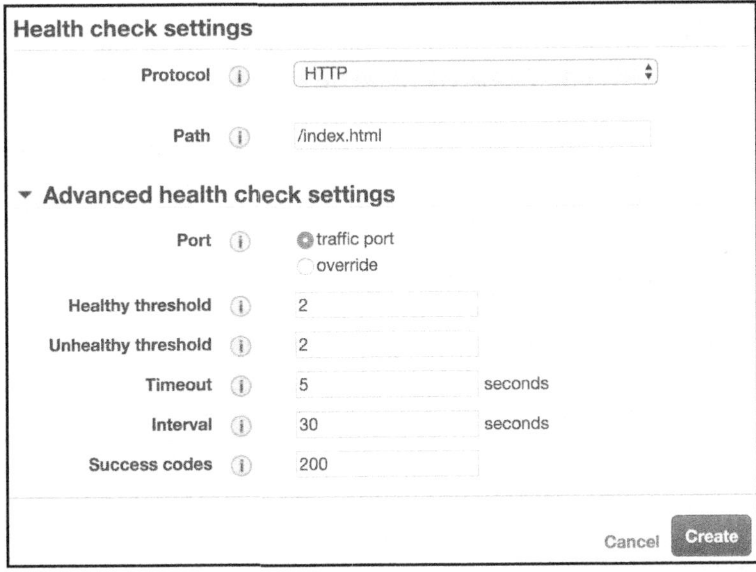

6. Click **Create**. If we go to the **Targets** tab of our target group, no targets will be attached.
7. Click on **Edit** from the **Targets** tab.
8. Select our instances and click on **Add to register**. Instances should now appear under **Registered targets**. Click **Save** at the bottom of the page. On the **Targets** tab, the **Status** of our instances will now be **unused**:

Registered targets

Instance ID	Name	Port	Availability Zone	Status	Description
i-07d6614e1dec5e537	WebServer1	80	us-east-1c	unused	Target group is not configured to receive traffic from the load balancer
i-0ea802db8b6996804	WebServer2	80	us-east-1c	unused	Target group is not configured to receive traffic from the load balancer

Availability Zones

Availability Zone	Target count	Healthy?
us-east-1c	2	No (Availability Zone contains no healthy targets)

The state of the targets will change after they have been attached to an ELB.

How it works...

In this recipe, we created a target group for EC2 instances with the HTTP protocol. We can create an application load balancer with a target group with the HTTP or HTTPS protocol. A network load balancer needs a target group with a TCP or TLS protocol. We can also create target groups for IP addresses and AWS Lambda functions. By selecting the IP address option, we can even select public IP addresses that are outside of AWS.

For the health check, we set the protocol to HTTP and the path to `/index.html`. We can override the port for a health check if needed by selecting the **Override** option for the port under the **Advanced health check** settings. We can set the time to wait for a response from instance (timeout), time between health checks (interval), number of consecutive failures before declaring an instance unhealthy (unhealthy threshold), number of consecutive successes before declaring an instance healthy (healthy threshold), and the HTTP response codes to check for success (success codes).

The target group instances will have an initial state of unused when they are created. When the target group is attached to an ELB, the status will change to initial. If the health checks pass, then the status changes to healthy. Other supported statuses include unhealthy if the health check fails, or draining if the target is being unregistered and connection draining is going on.

There's more...

In this recipe, we created a target group with the HTTP protocol. Target groups can be created with the following protocols: HTTP, HTTPS, TCP, TLS, UDP, and TCP_UDP. We can follow the steps in this recipe to create target groups with other protocols. For example, we can add a target group with the protocol as HTTPS with the port set to `443`, and then add EC2 instances with SSL/TLS enabled to the target group. For TCP passthrough of an HTTPS request with a network load balancer, which is needed for TLS termination at EC2, we should set the protocol to TCP, but with the port set to `443`.

See also

- You can read more about target groups here: `https://docs.aws.amazon.com/elasticloadbalancing/latest/application/load-balancer-target-groups.html`.

Using an application load balancer with TLS termination at the ELB

Application load balancers work at the request layer (application layer of the OSI model) and are used for HTTP and HTTPS requests. Application load balancers provide advanced routing capabilities at the application layer for requesting and path parameter-based routing. Architecture patterns such as the microservices architecture can make use of application load balancers to route requests to different web servers while making use of request parameters.

Getting ready

We need to create a target group to complete this recipe. We can do this by following the *Creating ELB target groups* recipe of this chapter and adding two EC2 instances that have Apache web server set up and have a security group that allows HTTP and SSH.

When selecting **HTTPS (Secure HTTP)** as the ELB listening protocol, we need an ACM certificate. We can create an ACM certificate by following the *Creating an SSL/TLS certificate with ACM* recipe of this chapter. If you are using the HTTP protocol, then you won't need a certificate.

How to do it...

We can create and test an application load balancer as follows:

1. Go to the EC2 service in the console.
2. Click on **Load Balancers** from the left sidebar.
3. Click on **Create Load Balancer**. We should see the options to create the three types of load balancers: **Application Load Balancer**, **Network Load Balancer**, and **Classic Load Balancer**.
4. Under **Application Load Balancer**, click on **Create**.

5. On the **Configure Load Balancer** screen, enter a meaningful name in the **Name** field. For **Scheme**, select **internet-facing**. Finally, for **IP address type**, select **IPv4**:

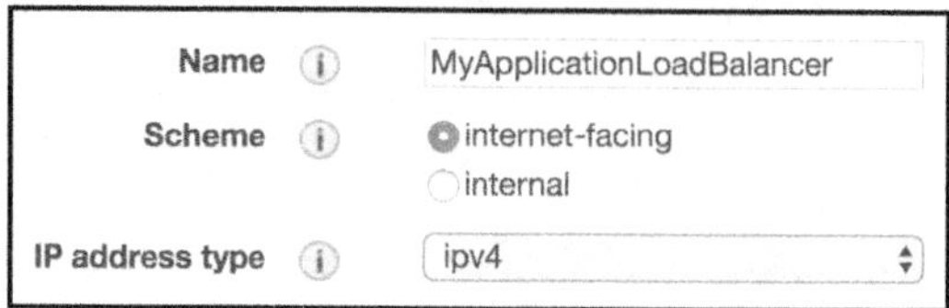

6. Under **Listeners**, set **Load Balancer Protocol** to **HTTPS (Secure HTTP)** and set **Load Balancer Port** to `443`:

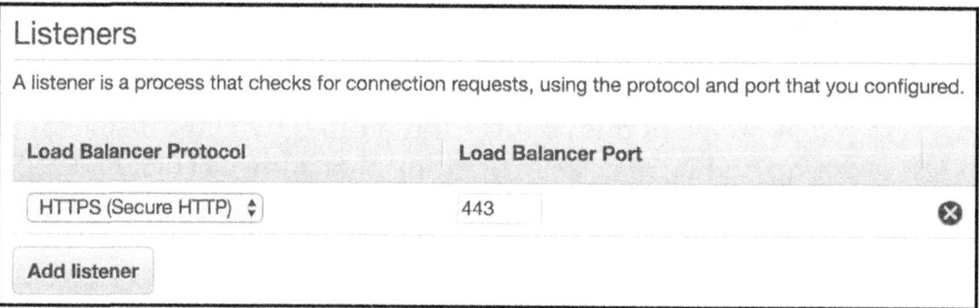

7. Under **Availability Zones**, select the default VPC and select the availability zones that contain our instances:

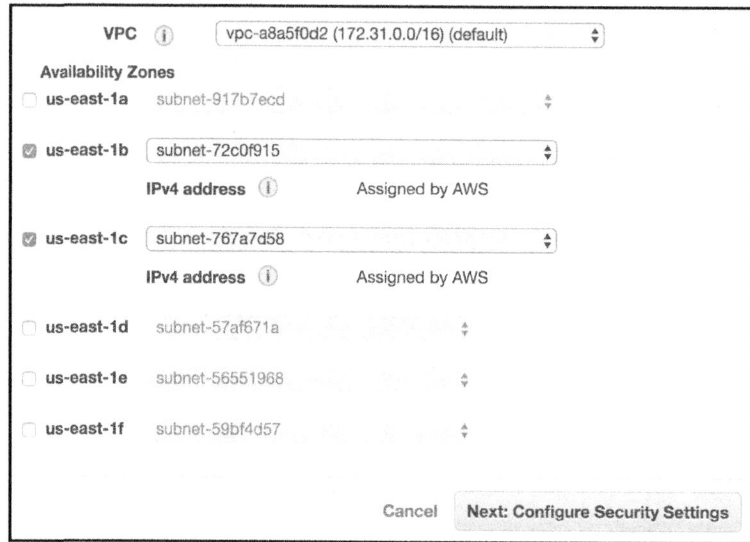

8. Click **Next: Configure Security Settings**.
9. On the **Configure Security Settings** page, for **Certificate type**, select **Choose a certificate from ACM (recommended)**, and for **Certificate name**, select the ACM certificate we created for this recipe. See the *Getting ready* section for more details:

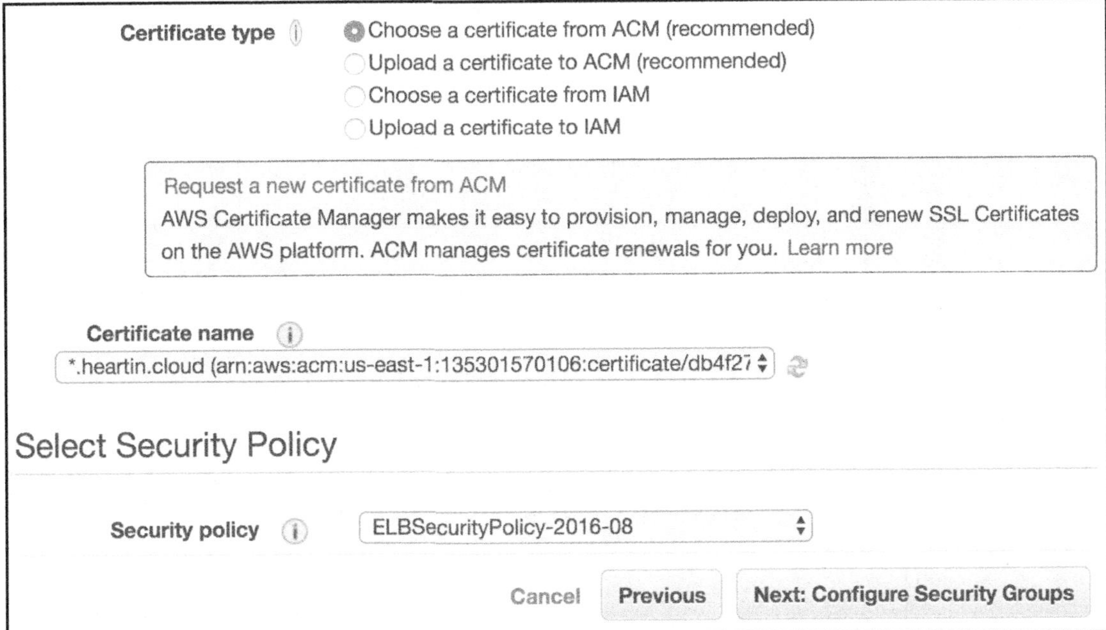

10. Click **Next: Configure Security Groups**.
11. Select a security group that allows HTTP and HTTPS from `0.0.0.0/0`. You may use the **MyWebServerSG** security group that we created in the *Using EC2 user data to launch an instance with a web server* recipe in `Chapter 6`, *Working with EC2 Instances*.
12. Click **Next: Configure Routing**.

13. On the **Configure Routing** page, select our target group in the **Target group** section:

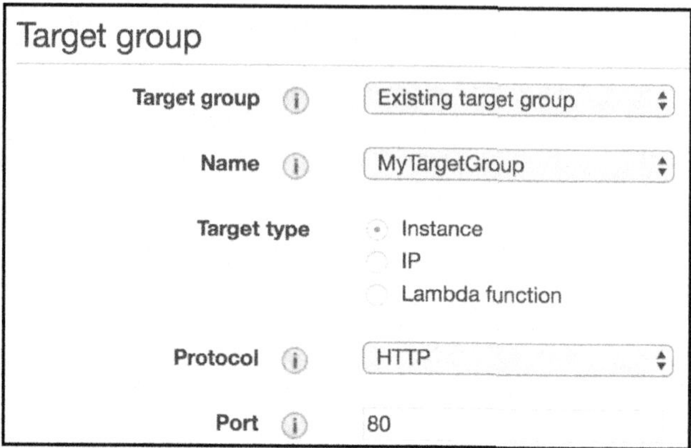

14. Verify the health checks settings and click on **Next: Register Targets**:

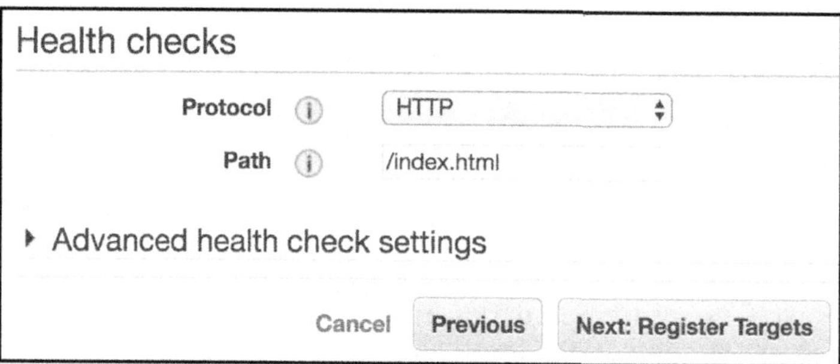

15. On the **Register Targets** page, verify our registered targets and click **Next: Review**.
16. On the **Review** page, review the load balancer settings and click **Create**. If we go to the target group, the **Status** of our instances will be the first **initial**. After some time, the **Status** should change to **healthy**.
17. Copy the **DNS name** from the ELB's **Description** tab and run this from a browser with an `https://` prefix. If we get a warning that the connection is not secure, click on **Advanced** and click on the proceed button/link. We should see that our web page loaded from either web server 1 or web server 2:

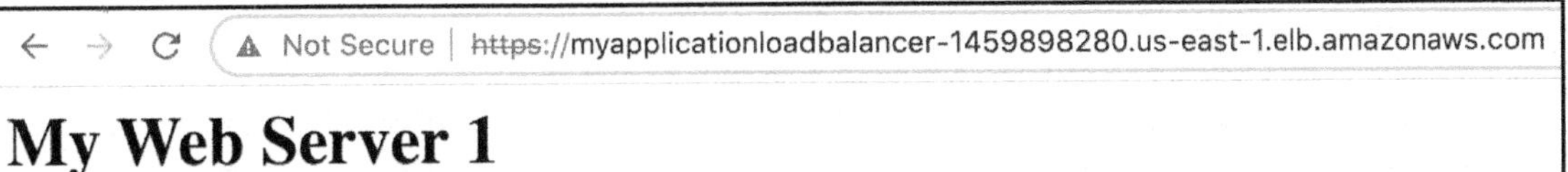

We are getting a warning since our URL (ELB DNS) is not matching with the certificate's domain, which is `*.heartin.cloud` in my case.

18. Optionally, create a **CNAME** record for the domain with **Name** (or **Host**) set to `mywebserver.heartin.cloud` (only `mywebserver` if the DNS service provider automatically appends domain name) and **Value** (or **Points to**) as our DNS name, which in my case is `myapplicationloadbalancer-1459898280.us-east-1.elb.amazonaws.com`. Now, I can run `https://mywebserver.heartin.cloud` and get a successful response:

Updating the DNS and any related changes may have a propagation delay, which is dependent on the DNS service provider.

There are multiple ways to point our domain with ELB, including creating a Route 53 account and changing the names of the servers of our domain, adding a CNAME record for a subdomain, and so on.

How it works...

In this recipe, we created an internet-facing load balancer. We set the listening protocol to **HTTPS (Secure HTTP)** and on the **Configure Security Settings** page, we selected an ACM certificate. We set the **Security policy** to **ELBSecurityPolicy-2016-08**. The security policy is an SSL negotiation configuration that's used to negotiate SSL connections with clients.

We terminated TLS at the ELB level. Note that the connection to the instance from the ELB is without TLS. The application load balancer only supports TLS/SSL termination at the ELB level. The network load balancer and classic load balancer can be used for terminating TLS/SSL at the EC2 instance level by using the TCP protocol on port `443`.

When we terminate TLS at the ELB for an HTTPS request, the request is decrypted at the ELB and is sent unencrypted to the EC2 instances over the private network within our VPC. When we terminate an HTTPS request's TLS at the EC2 instance, the request is not decrypted at the ELB and is only decrypted at the EC2 instance.

Terminating TLS at the ELB level avoids the overhead of TLS termination at EC2 instances and is more efficient. However, if there is a compliance requirement for end-to-end encryption, we should terminate at the EC2 instance level.

There's more...

Let's quickly go through some more important concepts related to application load balancers:

- Application load balancers only support HTTP or HTTPS protocols. For other protocols, such as TCP, we need to use a network load balancer or classic load balancer.
- Application load balancers only support TLS/SSL termination at the ELB level.
- We can enable sticky sessions for application load balancers at the target group level. We cannot, however, enable sticky sessions at individual EC2 instances with application load balancers.
- We can do path-based routing with application load balancers if path patterns are enabled.

- We set the **Security policy** for SSL/TLS negotiation to **ELBSecurityPolicy-2016-08**, which is the default. The following are the current list of policies that are available: **ELBSecurityPolicy-2016-08**, **ELBSecurityPolicy-TLS-1-2-2017-01**, **ELBSecurityPolicy-TLS-1-1-2017-01**, **ELBSecurityPolicy-TLS-1-2-Ext-2018-06**, **ELBSecurityPolicy-FS-2018-06**, **ELBSecurityPolicy-2015-05**, **ELBSecurityPolicy-TLS-1-0-2015-04**, **ELBSecurityPolicy-FS-1-2-Res-2019-08**, **ELBSecurityPolicy-FS-1-1-2019-08**, and **ELBSecurityPolicy-FS-1-2-2019-08**.

See also

- You can read more about creating a listener for our application load balancer at `https://docs.aws.amazon.com/elasticloadbalancing/latest/application/create-https-listener.html`.

Using a network load balancer with TLS termination at EC2

Network load balancers are used for load balancing TCP traffic and work at layer 4 of the OSI model. They provide very high performance compared to other load balancer types and can support millions of requests per second with very low latencies.

Getting ready

We need to create a target group to complete this recipe. We can do this by following the *Creating ELB target groups* recipe of this chapter but with two EC2 instances that have Apache web server set up and a security group that allows HTTP, HTTPS, and SSH, but with the following exceptions:

- Enable HTTPS on the EC2 instances by following the *Enabling HTTPS on an EC2 instance* recipe.
- Select `TCP` instead of HTTP as the protocol for the target group and set `443` as the port.

The description tab of the target group should look as follows:

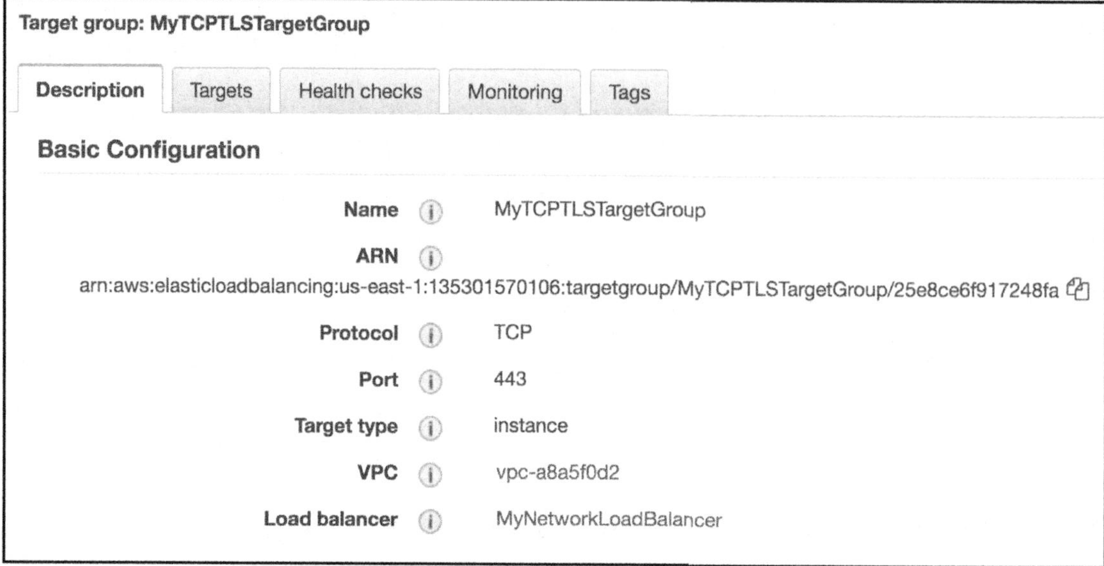

Make sure that our instances can be reached using the `https://` prefix.

How to do it...

We can create and test a network load balancer with TLS termination at an EC2 instance as follows:

1. Go to the EC2 service in the console.
2. Click on **Load Balancers** from the left sidebar.
3. Click on **Create Load Balancer**. We should see the options to create the three types of load balancers: **Application Load Balancer**, **Network Load Balancer**, and **Classic Load Balancer**.
4. Under **Network Load Balancer**, click on **Create**.
5. On the **Configure Load Balancer** screen, enter a meaningful name in the **Name** field, and for **Scheme**, select **internet-facing**.

6. Under **Listeners**, for **Load Balancer Protocol**, select **TCP** and set the value for **Load Balancer Port** to `443`.
7. Under **Availability Zones**, select the default VPC and two availability zones. I have selected **us-east-1b** and **us-east-1c**.
8. Click on **Next: Configure Security Settings**.
9. Click on **Next: Configure Routing**.
10. On the **Configure Routing** page, for **Target group**, select **Existing target group**. For **Name**, select the target group we created in the *Getting ready* section with the protocol set to **TCP** and the port set to `443`:

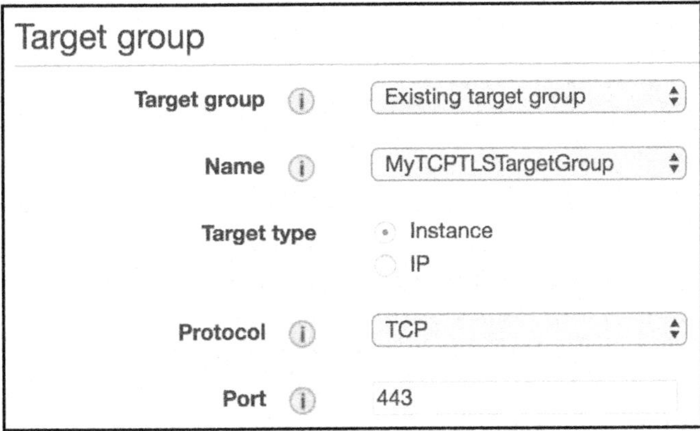

11. Verify the health checks settings and click on **Next: Register Targets**.
12. On the **Register Targets** page, verify our registered targets and click **Next: Review**.
13. On the **Review** page, review the load balancer settings and click **Create**. Initially, the **State** of our NLB will be **provisioning**. If we go to the target group, the **Status** of our instances will be **initial**. After some time, the **State** of the NLB should change to **active**. The **Status** of instances within the target group should be **healthy**.

14. Go to the URL from the browser with an `https://` prefix. If we get a warning stating that the connection is not secure, click on **Advanced** and click on the proceed button/link to see our web page being loaded from either web server 1 or web server 2:

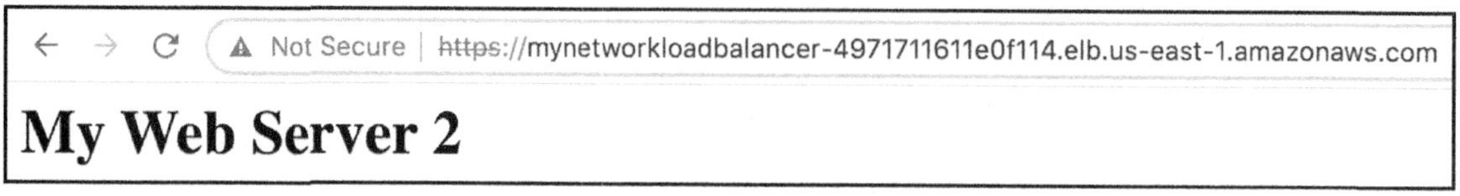

Not Secure | https://mynetworkloadbalancer-4971711611e0f114.elb.us-east-1.amazonaws.com

My Web Server 2

We are getting a warning since we are using a self-signed certificate. If we use a certificate signed by a CA, we won't receive a warning.

How it works...

In this recipe, we created a **network load balancer** (**NLB**) with TLS termination at EC2. Most of the options were the same as what we had seen in the *Using an application load balancer with TLS termination at the ELB* recipe of this chapter. In this recipe, we are using the **TCP** protocol and port `443`. This was done to allow the NLB to simply pass the HTTPS request to the EC2 instance without decrypting it at the ELB level. The target group should also be configured with the **TCP** protocol and with port `443` to allow TCP passthrough. If we select TLS (secure TCP) instead of TCP, NLB will decrypt the request at ELB itself.

There's more...

In this recipe, we did TCP passthrough for an HTTPS request and did TLS termination at the EC2 instance. TLS termination at the EC2 instance will consume more EC2 resources and will provide an extra load for the EC2 instance. We will also need to manage the certificate across all the EC2 instances. However, if we have a requirement for end-to-end encryption due to compliance or government policies, this is the preferred way. Otherwise, the preferred approach is to do SSL/TLS termination at the ELB level, as we saw in the *Using an application load balancer with TLS termination at the ELB* recipe of this chapter. For terminating SSL/TLS at the NLB, we need to set the protocol to **TLS (Secure TCP)** and select an ACM certificate.

See also

- You can read more about TLS termination for network load balancers here: `https://aws.amazon.com/blogs/aws/new-tls-termination-for-network-load-balancers`.

Securing S3 using CloudFront and TLS

In this recipe, we'll learn how to secure an S3 bucket by adding a CloudFront distribution layer. We will enable SSL/TLS on the CloudFront distribution to allow only HTTPS traffic. We will configure this so that we can redirect HTTP requests to HTTPS requests. We will use the default CloudFront certificate (`*.cloudfront.net`) for this recipe.

Getting ready

We need an S3 bucket to practice the steps within this recipe. To set up an S3 bucket, follow these steps:

1. Go to the S3 service in the console.
2. Create an S3 bucket.
3. Upload an `index.html` file into the bucket.

For the *CloudFront distribution with a custom domain and ACM certificate* section of this recipe, we need an ACM certificate. We can create an ACM certificate by following the *Creating an SSL/TLS certificate with an ACM* recipe of this chapter.

How to do it...

We can add a CloudFront distribution to an S3 bucket with or without a custom domain.

CloudFront distribution with CloudFront default domain

We can add a CloudFront distribution to an S3 bucket with a default CloudFront domain and certificate as follows:

1. Go to the CloudFront service in the console.
2. Click on **Create Distribution**. We should see options for creating both **Web** and **RTMP** distributions:

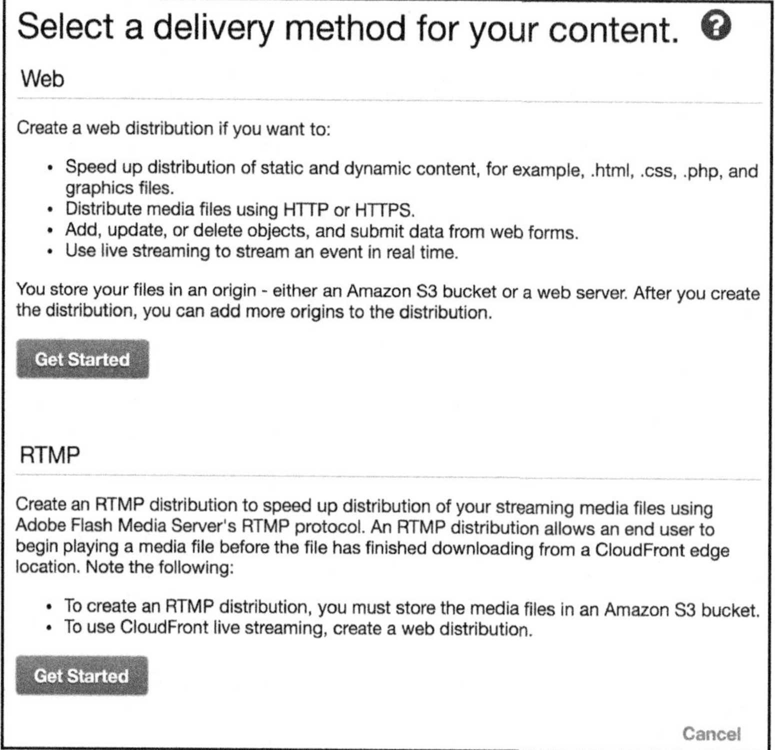

3. Click **Get Started** under **Web** distribution.
4. Set up the **Origin Settings** as follows: For **Origin Domain Name**, select the S3 bucket we created for this recipe in the *Getting ready* section. Leave **Origin Path** empty. Use the auto-populated value for **Origin ID**. For **Restrict Bucket Access**, select **Yes**. For **Origin Access Identity**, select **Create a New Identity**. Set **Comment** to `access-identity-mycfdemo`. For **Grant Read Permissions on Bucket**, select **Yes, Update Bucket Policy**:

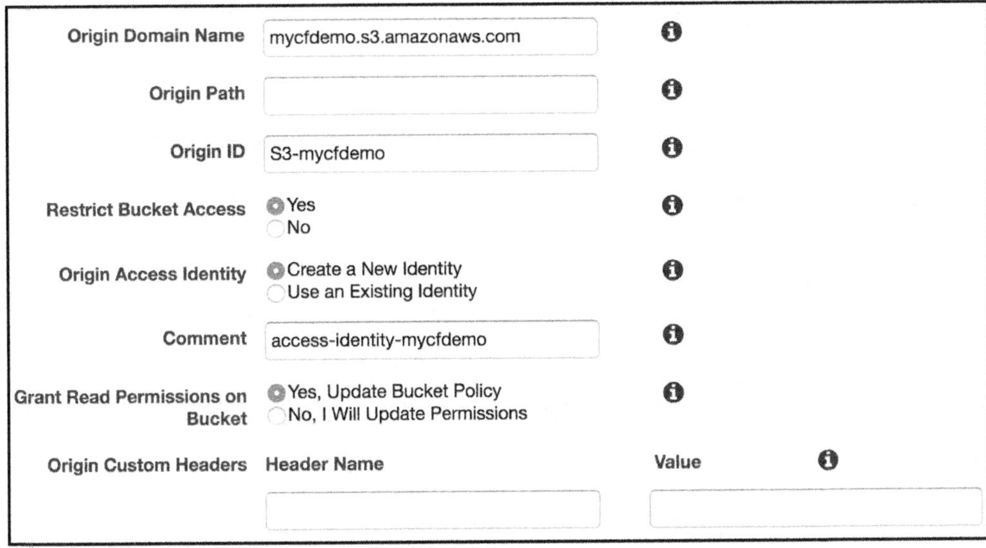

5. Under **Default Cache Behavior Settings**, for **Viewer Protocol Policy**, select **Redirect HTTP to HTTPS**.
6. Under **Distribution Settings**, for **SSL Certificate**, select **Default CloudFront Certificate (*.cloudfront.net)**. For the **Default Root Object**, enter `index.html`.
7. For the other options, use their default values and click **Create Distribution**. Click on **Distributions** from the left sidebar. Initially, the **Status** of our distribution will be **In Progress**. After some time, **Status** will become **Deployed**:

8. Once the **Status** becomes **Deployed**, run the domain name from the browser. We should see that our web page has been loaded:

Next, we will learn how to use a custom domain with our own ACM certificate.

CloudFront distribution with a custom domain and ACM certificate

We can add a CloudFront distribution to an S3 bucket with a custom domain and ACM certificate as follows:

1. Follow *steps 1* to *5* of the *CloudFront distribution with a CloudFront default domain* section of this recipe.
2. Under **Distribution Settings**, for **Alternate Domain Names (CNAMEs)**, enter `*.heartin.cloud`. For **SSL Certificate**, select **Custom SSL Certificate (example.com)** and select the ACM certificate we created in the *Getting ready* section:

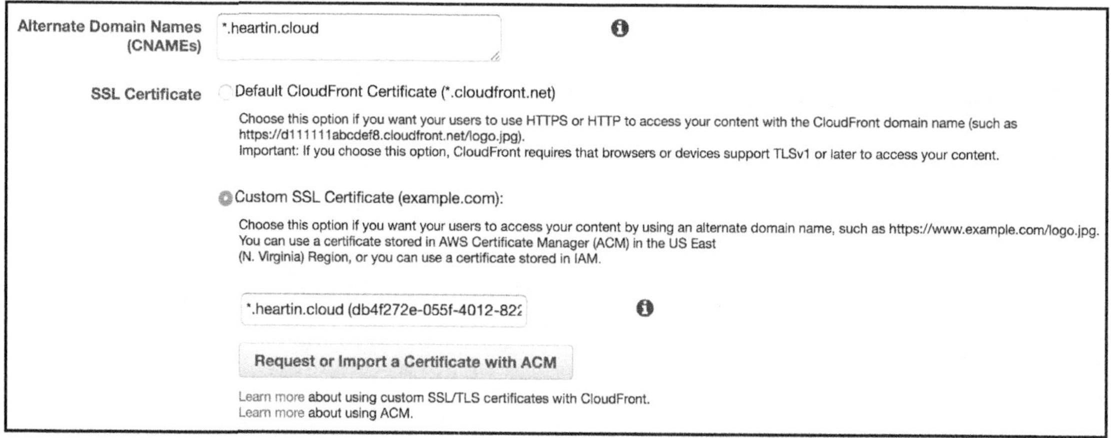

3. For the **Default Root Object**, enter `index.html`. For the other options, use their defaults and click **Create Distribution**. Click on **Distributions** from the left sidebar. Initially, the **Status** will be **In Progress**. After some time, **Status** will become **Deployed**.
4. Create a **CNAME** record for the domain with **Name** (or **Host**) set to `mywebserver.heartin.cloud` (only `mywebserver` if the DNS service provider automatically appends the domain name) and **Value** (or **Points to**) as our CloudFront **Domain Name**, which in my case is `d1wdr2pvinttjd.cloudfront.net`.
5. Run `https://mywebserver.heartin.cloud`; you will get a successful response:

Instead of the preceding URL, we can also reach the web page using a URL composed of the CloudFront domain name, which in my case is `d1wdr2pvinttjd.cloudfront.net`.

How it works...

In this recipe, we created a CloudFront distribution layer over a private S3 bucket to access the S3 bucket securely using HTTPS. We configured this to redirect all HTTP requests into HTTPS requests. If we choose **HTTP and HTTPS**, both HTTP and HTTPS requests are allowed. If we choose **Only HTTPS**, all HTTP requests will be discarded.

In the *CloudFront distribution with a CloudFront default domain* section of this recipe, we used the default certificate provided by CloudFront (`*.cloudfront.com`) for SSL. This certificate allows us to use HTTPS without the need for creating a certificate. In the *CloudFront distribution with a custom domain and ACM certificate* section of this recipe, we specified a wildcard domain name (`*.heartin.cloud`) for **Alternate Domain Names (CNAMEs)**. This will allow any subdomain to be entered as a CNAME record at the DNS service provider side and be forwarded to our web page.

We selected an ACM certificate that was created for a custom domain. We entered a CNAME record on our DNS service provider that points to our CloudFront domain name. The exact steps for adding the CNAME record at the DNS service provider server may be specific to a DNS service provider. You can look at the DNS service provider documentation (`https://aws.amazon.com/route53/what-is-dns/`) for more details.

There's more...

In this recipe, we used our own ACM certificate and used it as a CNAME that was configured at an outside DNS provider so that it could use a subdomain to access our web page in the S3 bucket. Instead, we can use Route 53 to manage the DNS for our domain and point a top-level domain to our CloudFront distribution.

See also

- You can read more about routing traffic to a CloudFront distribution using Route 53 here: `https://docs.aws.amazon.com/Route53/latest/DeveloperGuide/routing-to-cloudfront-distribution.html`.

Configuring and using the AWS web application firewall (WAF)

AWS WAF is a firewall service for monitoring our web traffic. Unlike security groups and NACLs, which only check for ports and IP addresses, AWS WAF can find malicious content that can lead to common attacks such as SQL injection and cross-site scripting. Currently, we can only use WAF with API Gateway, CloudFront, and application load balancers. This cannot be used directly with services such as EC2 or Route 53.

Getting ready

To create a WAF with a CloudFront distribution, we need to create a CloudFront distribution over an S3 bucket by following the *Securing S3 using CloudFront and TLS* recipe of this chapter.

We can use WAF with CloudFront distributions, application load balancers, and the API Gateway. With minor tweaks to the steps in this recipe, we can use WAF over an application load balancer or an API gateway. However, it is worth noting that CloudFront distributions are global, but application load balancers and the API Gateway are regional resources.

How to do it...

We can create and configure an AWS WAF for a CloudFront distribution as follows:

1. Log in to **AWS WAF and AWS Shield** dashboard. We should see **Go to** links for AWS WAF, AWS Shield, and AWS Firewall Manager.

Currently, AWS WAF, AWS Shield, and AWS Firewall Manager are accessible from the same dashboard. If AWS decides to separate them, go to the dashboard for AWS WAF and continue with this recipe.

2. Click on **Go to AWS WAF**. We should see the new AWS WAF landing page:

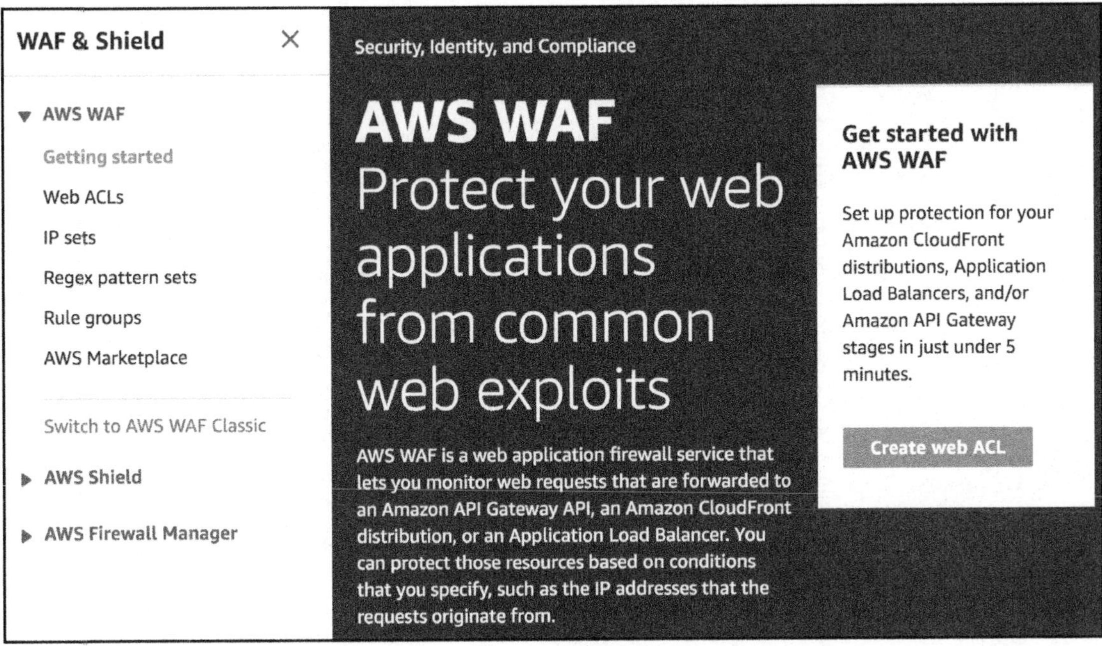

AWS currently provides an option to **Switch to AWS WAF Classic**. We will be using **New AWS WAF**, which is more flexible than **AWS WAF Classic**. AWS managed rule groups are only supported by the new WAF. Classic WAF also has a limit of 10 rules and 2 rule groups per web ACL. Exact UI options for the new WAF and the classic WAF may differ a bit. However, the core concept will remain the same.

3. Click on **Create web ACL**.
4. In the **Web ACL details** section, provide a name in the **Name** field. Optionally, provide a description in the **Description** field. We will use the auto-populated value for the **CloudWatch metric name** field. For **Resource type**, select **CloudFront distributions**:

Web ACL details

Name

MyQueryStringFilterACL

The name must have 1-128 characters. Valid characters: A-Z, a-z, 0-9, - (hyphen), and _ (underscore).

Description - *optional*

My Query String Filter ACL

The description can have 1-256 characters.

CloudWatch metric name

MyQueryStringFilterACL

The name must have 1-128 characters. Valid characters: A-Z, a-z, 0-9, - (hyphen), and _ (underscore).

Resource type

Choose the type of resource to associate with this web ACL.

CloudFront distributions

Regional resources (Application Load Balancer and API Gateway)

Region

Choose the AWS region to create this web ACL in.

Global (CloudFront)

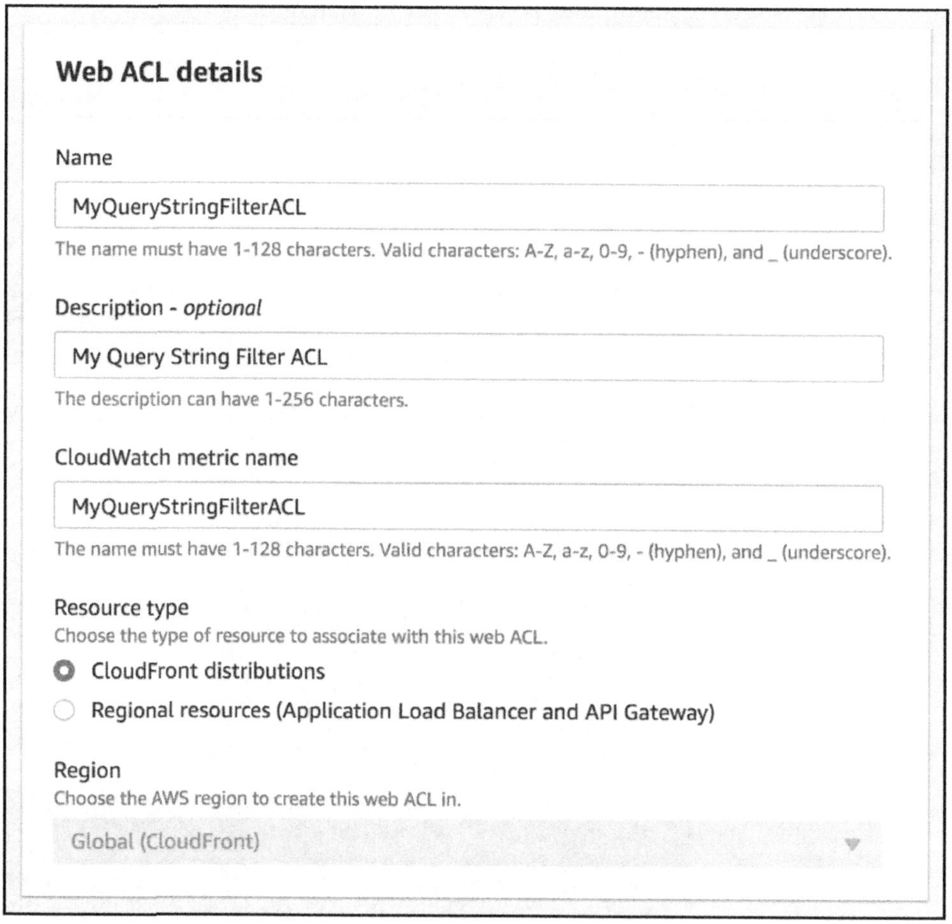

5. Under the **Associated AWS resources** section, click on **Add AWS Resources**.
6. On the **Add AWS resources** screen, select one of the CloudFront distributions that we created for this recipe, as we mentioned in the *Getting ready* section, and click **Add**.
7. Once you're back at the **Associated AWS resources** section, select our CloudFront distribution and click **Next**.
8. On the **Add rules and rule groups** page, expand the **Add rules** dropdown and select **Add my own rules and rule groups**:

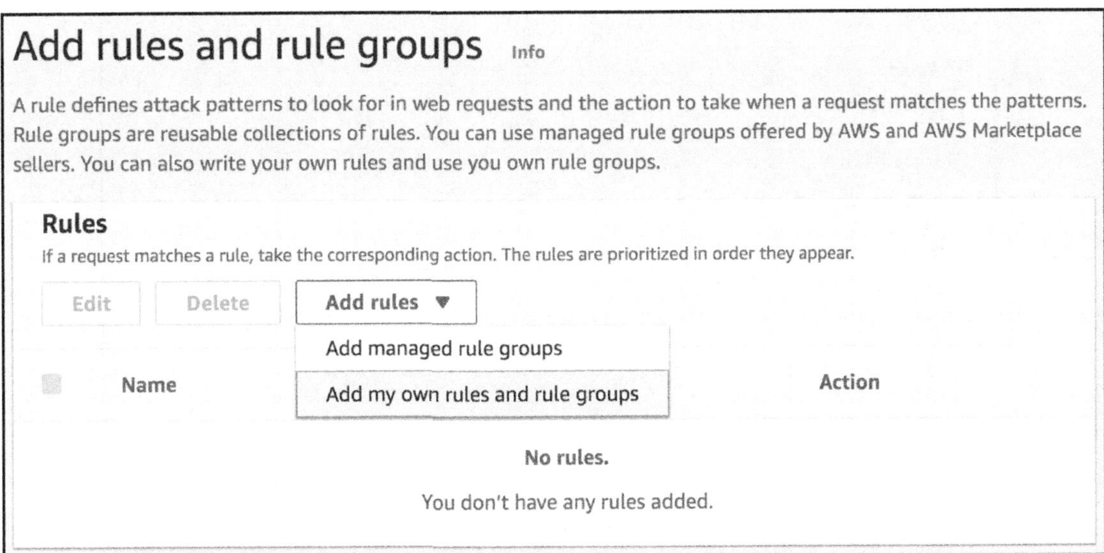

9. On the **Add my own rules and rule groups** page, select **Rule builder**.

Apart from **Rule builder**, you also have the **IP set** and **Rule group** rule types available to choose from.

10. Under **Rule builder**, in the **Rule** section, put a name in the **Name** field and set **Type** to **Regular rule**.

11. Under the **If** section, add a **Statement** to check if the query string contains the word `badstring`:

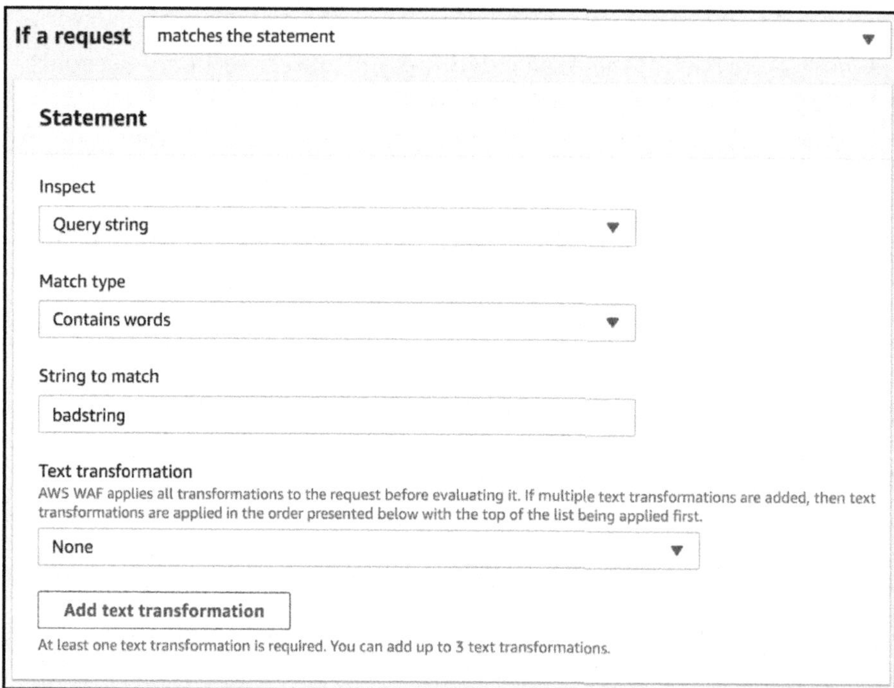

12. Under the **Then** section, add an **Action** to **Block** and click **Add rule**:

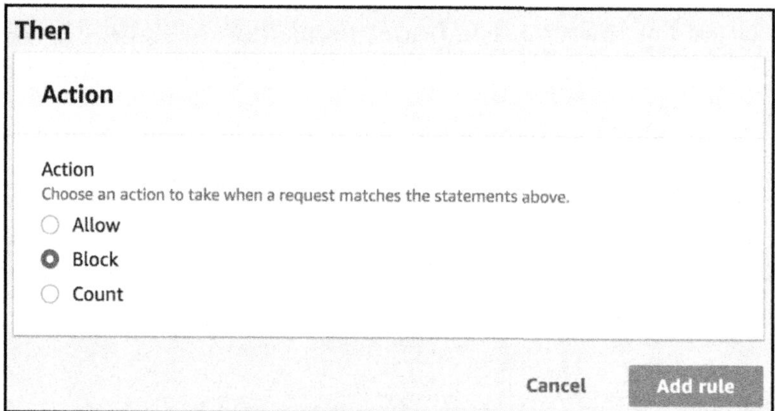

13. On the **Add rules and rule groups** page, for **Default web ACL action for requests that don't match any rules**, select **Allow** and click **Next**.
14. On the **Set rule priority** page, select our rule as the first one and click **Next**.
15. On the **Configure metrics** page, select our rule. We will use the auto-populated value for **CloudWatch metric name**. Click **Next**.
16. On the **Review and create web ACL** page, review the changes and click **Create web ACL**. If we go to the CloudFront distribution, its **Status** will be **In Progress**. Wait until the **Status** changes to **Deployed**.
17. Once the **Status** changes to **Deployed**, go to the URL from the browser with a query string that contains `badstring`; for example, `https://d39dz0ed00e5vl.cloudfront.net/?name=badstring`.

   We should get a 403 error, as follows:

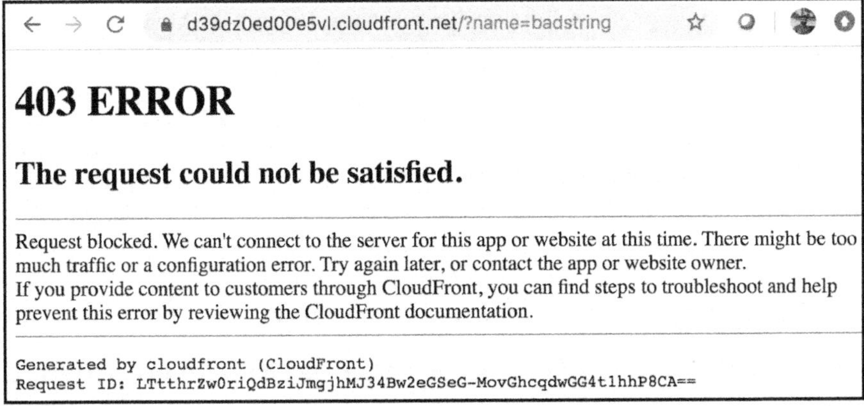

   There will be no error if we do not use the word `badstring` anywhere within our URL.

18. Dissociate the web ACL from our CloudFront distribution, wait until **Status** changes to **Deployed**, and run the URL again from a browser with a query string that contains `badstring`. The page should load successfully this time, without any errors.
19. Alternatively, we can dissociate the web ACL from the CloudFront distribution from the CloudFront dashboard as follows:
    1. Select the CloudFront distribution.
    2. Click on **Distribution Settings**. Click **Edit**.
    3. For **AWS WAF Web ACL**, select **None**.

20. We can also dissociate a CloudFront distribution and a web ACL from the WAF dashboard as follows:
    1. Click on our web ACL.
    2. Go to the **Associated AWS resources** tab.
    3. Select our CloudFront distribution.
    4. Click on **Remove**.

How it works...

A web ACL is the primary component within AWS WAF. A web ACL contains one or more rules. Rules contain conditional statements (for example, block access from a range of IP addresses). We added our own rule using the rule builder. The rule builder has an **IF** part and a **THEN** part. The **IF** part contains the condition, while the **THEN** part contains the action that needs to be taken when the condition in the **IF** part is satisfied. In this recipe, we added a simple rule that checks if the query string contains a string, `badstring`, and blocks such requests.

In the **IF** part, we can currently inspect the following request components: **Header**, **Single query parameter**, **All query parameters**, **URI path**, **Query string**, **Body**, and **HTTP method**. We can also check if an IP address is part of an IP set or if a request originated from a particular country. We created a regular rule in this recipe. We can also create a **Rate-based rule** to set a rate limit for requests from a single user. For example, WAF can block users based on the number of bad requests (4xx errors) they make.

We can create supporting resources such as **IP sets**, **Regex pattern sets**, and **Rule groups**, which are used by some of the conditions, from the left sidebar of the WAF dashboard. We can find the AWS Marketplace rule groups using the **AWS Marketplace** link, which can be found in the left sidebar of the WAF dashboard. Instead of creating our own rules, we can also add an AWS managed rule group. Currently, there are three categories of managed rule groups in the console: **AWS managed rule groups**, **Cyber Security Cloud Inc. managed security groups**, and **Fortinet managed rule groups**.

The following are the rule groups that are currently available under **AWS managed rule groups**: **Admin protection** for admin pages:

- **Amazon IP reputation list**, which is based on Amazon threat intelligence.
- **Core rule set** with general rules for web applications.
- **Known bad inputs** with request patterns that are known to be invalid and associated with vulnerabilities.

- **Linux operating system** with rules specific to Linux vulnerabilities.
- **PHP application** with rules specific to PHP vulnerabilities.
- **POSIX operating system** with rules for vulnerabilities specific to POSIX/POSIX-like OS, such as LFI attacks.
- **SQL database** with rules related to SQL database vulnerabilities, such as SQL injection attacks.
- **Windows operating system** with rules specific to Windows vulnerabilities.
- **WordPress application** with rules specific to WordPress site vulnerabilities.

The following are the rule groups currently available under **Cyber Security Cloud Inc. managed security groups**: **Cyber Security Cloud Managed Rules for AWS WAF -API Gateway/Serverless**, which is designed to mitigate and minimize the OWASP API Security/Serverless Top 10 Threats, and **Cyber Security Cloud Managed Rules for AWS WAF -HighSecurity OWASP Set**, which is designed to mitigate and minimize OWASP Top 10 Web Application Threats. Under **Fortinet managed rule groups**, we have **OWASP Top 10 - The Complete Ruleset**, which is designed to address threats as described in OWASP Top 10.

OWASP stands for **Open Web Application Security Project**. You can read more about OWASP at `https://www.owasp.org`.

There's more...

At the time of writing, the AWS WAF and AWS Shield services have the same service home page, as we saw in the *How to do it...* section. We saw AWS WAF in detail in this recipe. We will quickly go through some important concepts related to AWS Shield in this section.

AWS Shield is a managed **Distributed Denial of Service (DDoS)** protection service that provides always-on detection and automatic inline mitigations to minimize application downtime and latency without engaging AWS Support to benefit from DDoS protection.

There are two tiers of AWS Shield: Standard and Advanced. Shield Standard defends against known infrastructure attacks in the network (layer 3) and transport layer (layer 4) that target our website or applications and is most effective when used with Amazon CloudFront and Amazon Route 53. AWS Shield Advanced provides higher levels of protection against attacks targeting our applications running on EC2, ELB, CloudFront, AWS Global Accelerator, and Route 53 resources.

See also

- You can read more about AWS WAF, AWS Shield, and AWS Firewall Manager here: `https://docs.aws.amazon.com/waf/latest/developerguide/what-is-aws-waf.html`
- You can read more about AWS Shield here: `https://aws.amazon.com/shield`

8
Monitoring with CloudWatch, CloudTrail, and Config

We've already looked at many aspects of security, such as confidentiality, integrity, authentication, authorization, and availability. **Accountability**, the **A** in the **CIA** model, can be achieved through continuous monitoring, alerting, and regular auditing. Proper monitoring and alerting can also help in better availability through auto-remediation. In this chapter, we will look into Amazon CloudWatch, AWS CloudTrail, and AWS Config. CloudWatch is the primary service within AWS for application logging, monitoring, and alerting. CloudTrail can log the API calls within AWS. AWS Config can record and evaluate configurations. We will also learn about the **Simple Notification Service** (**SNS**), which will allow us to send notifications.

In this chapter, we will cover the following recipes:

- Creating an SNS topic to send emails
- Working with CloudWatch alarms and metrics
- Creating a dashboard in CloudWatch
- Creating a CloudWatch log group
- Working with CloudWatch events
- Reading and filtering logs in CloudTrail
- Creating a trail in CloudTrail
- Using Athena to query CloudTrail logs in S3
- Cross-account CloudTrail logging
- Integrating CloudWatch and CloudTrail
- Setting up and using AWS Config

Technical requirements

We need a working AWS account to complete this chapter.

The code files for this chapter are available at `https://github.com/PacktPublishing/AWS-Security-Cookbook/tree/master/Chapter08`.

Creating an SNS topic to send emails

In this recipe, we will learn how to create an SNS topic for sending emails. SNS is a managed publish/subscribe messaging service and can be used with many endpoints, such as email, SMS, Lambda, SQS, and more.

Getting ready

We need a working AWS account and a working email address to complete this recipe.

How to do it...

We can configure an SNS topic to send emails as follows:

1. Go to the SNS service in the console.
2. Click on **Topics**.
3. Click on **Create topic**.
4. For the **Name** and **Display name** fields, give meaningful values. I have set the **Name** to `MyEmailTopic` and the **Display name** to `My Email Topic`.
5. Leave the other options as is and scroll down to the bottom of the page. Click on **Create topic**.
6. Go to our topic and select the **Subscriptions** tab.
7. Click on **Create subscription**.
8. Set the **Protocol** to **Email** and provide an email address for **Endpoint**:

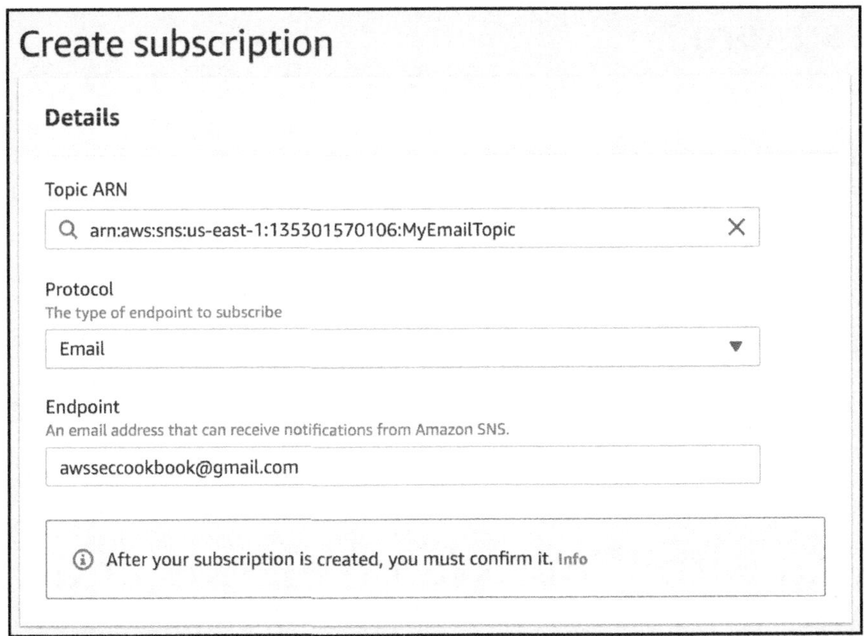

9. Scroll down and click **Create subscription**. The **Status** of our subscription will be **Pending confirmation**.
10. Log in to your email and click on the **Confirm subscription** hyperlink. We should get a success message. If we go back to our subscription in AWS console, our **Status** should be **Confirmed**.

How it works...

In this recipe, we created an SNS topic with an email subscription. To avoid spam, AWS requires us to manually confirm the ownership of the email address by clicking on the confirmation link that was sent to the specified email address. This SNS topic will be used within other recipes in this chapter and later chapters for sending email notifications.

In this recipe, we selected the **Protocol** as **Email**. The following are the protocols that are currently supported: **HTTP**, **HTTPS**, **Email**, **Email-JSON**, **Amazon SQS**, **AWS Lambda**, **Platform application endpoint**, and **SMS**. **Email-JSON** is different from the **Email** protocol. The **Email-JSON** protocol structures the output as a JSON and is useful for services that read emails and process them automatically.

There's more...

We can also use a **Simple Email Service** (**SES**) to send email notifications instead of using SNS. SES is a cloud-based email service for sending and receiving emails. It uses the SMTP interface and can be accessed through APIs as well. All connections to the SMTP endpoint should be encrypted using TLS. The default port for SES is `25`, but to avoid EC2 throttling email traffic, we can also use port `587` or `2587`.

See also

- You can read more about SNS at `https://aws.amazon.com/sns`.
- You can read more about SES at `https://aws.amazon.com/ses`.

Working with CloudWatch alarms and metrics

In this recipe, we will create a CloudWatch alarm using one of the metrics already available. Being the first recipe about CloudWatch, we will also learn about some of the important features of CloudWatch.

Getting ready

Create an SNS topic with an email subscription by following the *Creating an SNS topic to send emails* recipe.

How to do it...

We can create a CloudWatch alarm using existing metrics as follows:

1. Go to the CloudWatch service in the console.
2. Click on **Alarms** from the left sidebar.
3. Click on **Create alarm**.
4. Click on **Select metric**. This should show us all the metrics that are available to us based on the services we use:

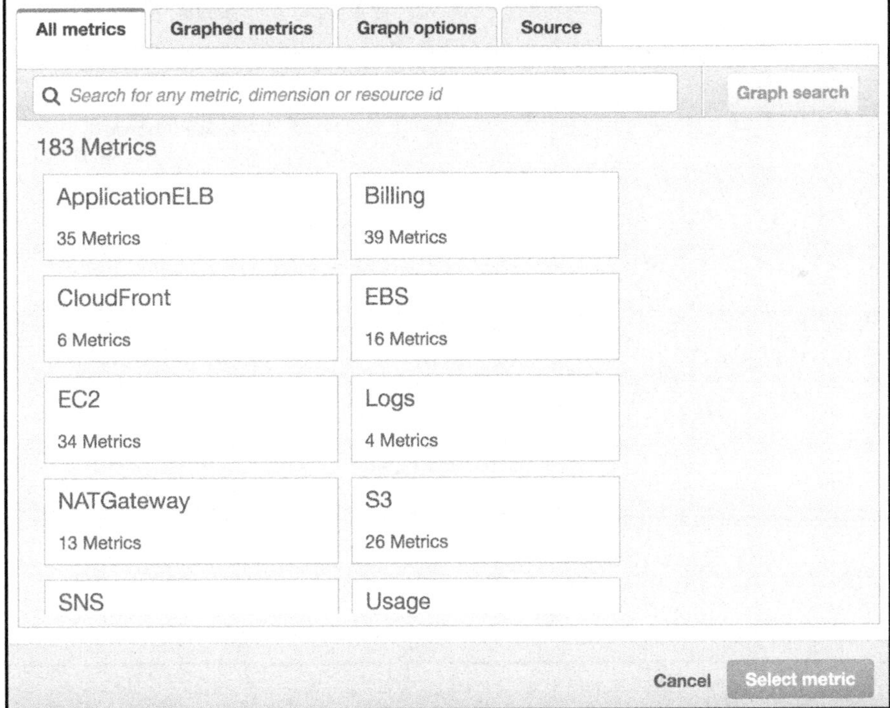

5. Click on **Billing**.
6. Click on **By Service**.
7. Click on **Amazon EC2**.
8. Click on **Select metric**. This will take us to the **Specify metric and conditions** screen.

9. In the **Metric** section of the **Specify metric and conditions** screen, use the defaults shown in the following screenshot:

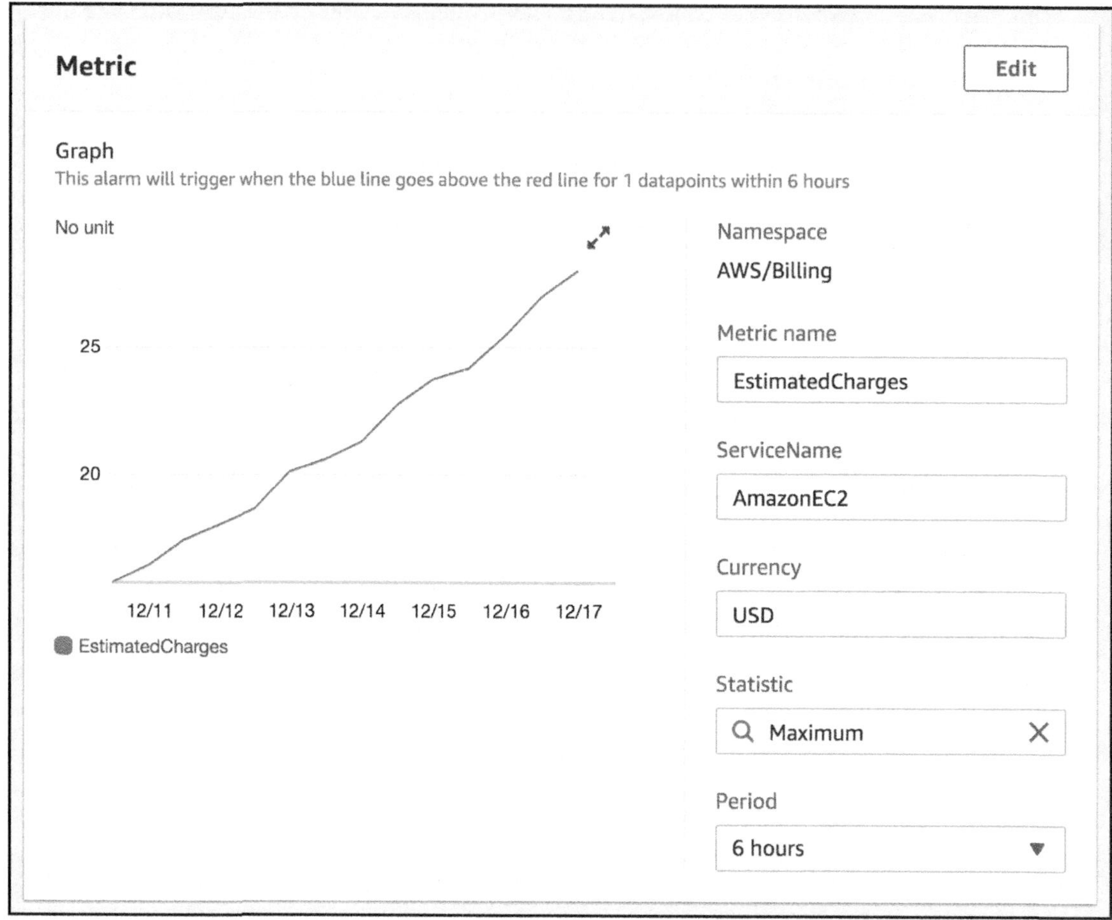

10. In the **Condition** section of the **Specify metric and conditions** screen, provide a threshold value of `1` and use the defaults for the other fields:

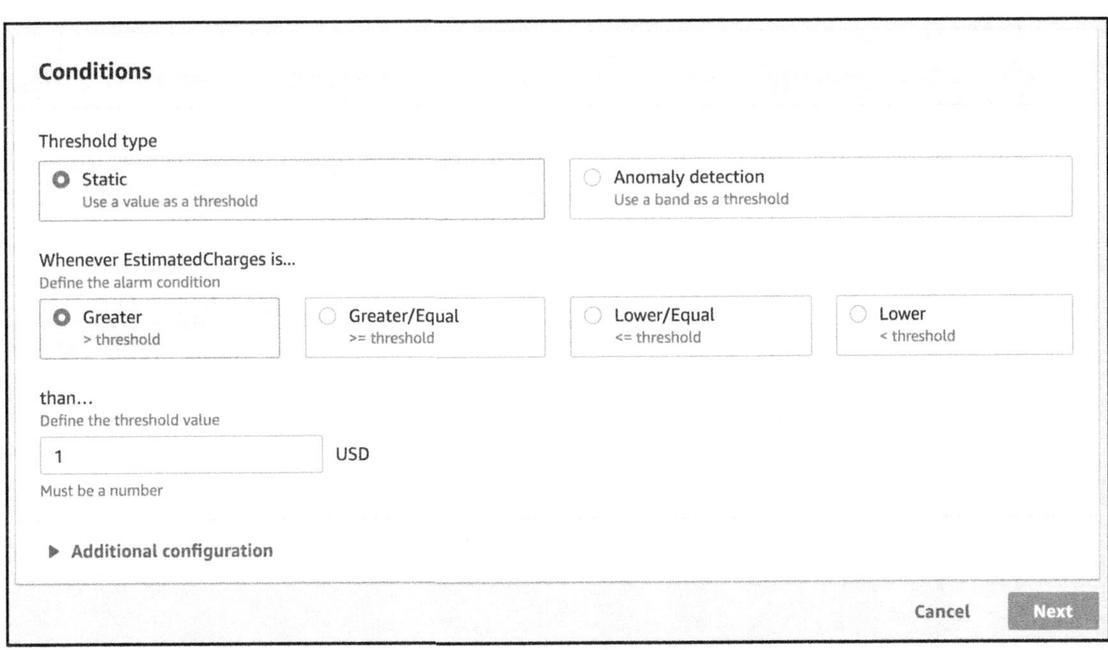

11. Optionally, expand **Additional configuration** and configure **Datapoints to alarm** and **Missing data treatment**:

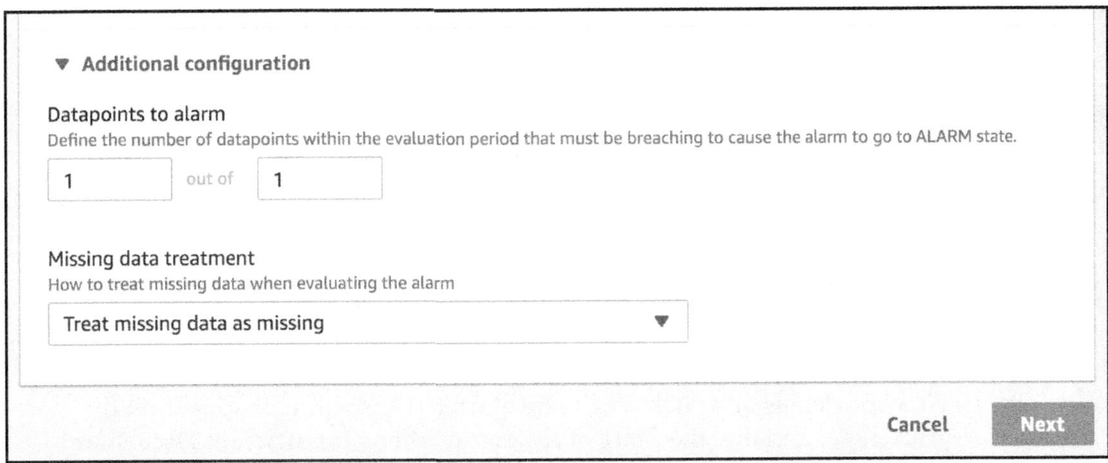

12. Click **Next**.
13. On the **Configure actions** page, under **Notification**, select the **Select an existing SNS topic** option and select the SNS topic we created in the *Getting ready* section. Leave the other options as is, as shown in the following screenshot:

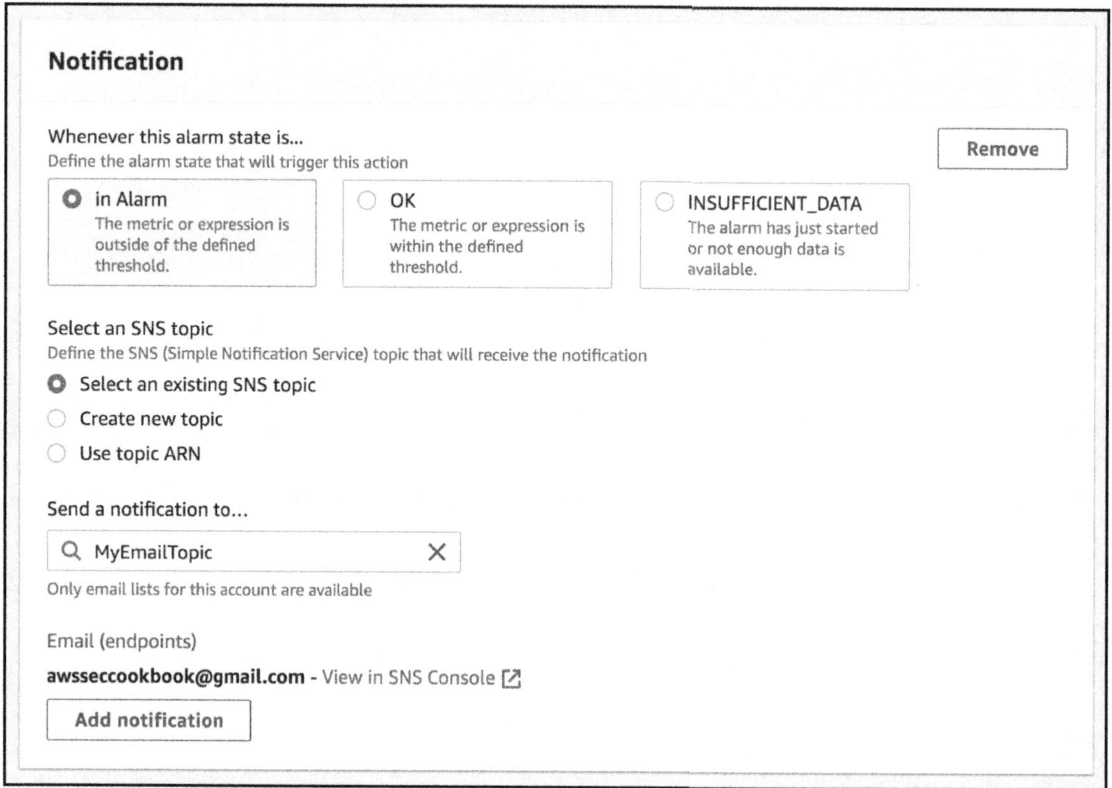

14. Click **Next**.
15. Provide a **Name** and **Description** for our alarm. I have set the **Name** to `MyEC2BillingAlarm` and the **Description** to `My EC2 Billing Alarm`. Click **Next**.
16. Review the details and click on **Create alarm**. The alarm will appear on the **Alarms** page. Initially, the **State** of the alarm will be **Insufficient Data**. In my case, the alarm **State** has changed to **in alarm** and I received the following email:

ALARM: "MyEC2BillingAlarm" in US East (N. Virginia) Inbox ×

My Email Topic <no-reply@sns.amazonaws.com> 1:08 PM (4 minutes ago)

to me

You are receiving this email because your AmazonEC2 estimated charges are greater than the limit you set for the alarm "MyEC2BillingAlarm" in AWS Account 135301570106.

The alarm limit you set was $ 1.00 USD. Your total estimated charges accrued for this billing period are currently $ 28.04 USD as of Wednesday 18 December, 2019 07:38:22 UTC. The actual charges you will be billed in this statement period may differ from the charges shown on this notification. For more information, view your estimated bill at: https://us-east-1.console.aws.amazon.com/billing/home#/bill?year=2019&month=12

More details about this alarm are provided below:

I have used a considerably lower value for the threshold and used the EC2 service enough to trigger an alarm. You may use a threshold value as per your requirements.

How it works...

A CloudWatch alarm can monitor a metric. We specify the metric while creating the alarm. We can also specify the time period to evaluate the metric, the number of such periods to evaluate before raising an alarm, and the number of data points within the evaluation period, during which the threshold should be crossed, for an alarm to trigger. An alarm's trigger can further trigger additional actions, such as sending a notification through an email, configuring Auto Scaling actions, as well as EC2 actions such as rebooting a failed instance.

A CloudWatch alarm has three states, namely **INSUFFICIENT DATA**, **OK**, and **ALARM**. Until it gets enough data to do the analysis, the state will be **INSUFFICIENT DATA**. After it has enough data points to evaluate and if the result does not cross the threshold over the specified time periods, the state will be **OK**. If the result crosses the threshold in the specified time periods, the alarm is triggered and the CloudWatch alarm goes to the **ALARM** state.

There's more...

Let's go through some important concepts related to CloudWatch:

- The CloudWatch service consists of three components, namely the CloudWatch component, the CloudWatch logs component, and the CloudWatch events component, all of which can be accessed from the console and using APIs and the CLI. Let's go over what these components do:
    - The CloudWatch component support alarms, metrics, and dashboards.
    - The logs component provides log streams and log groups so that we can log data from our applications.
    - The events component support notifications and also auto-remediation using AWS Lambda.
- AWS provides us with some metrics out of the box and also allows us to create custom metrics for our applications.
- We can see the metrics that are available by clicking on **Metrics** from the left sidebar of the CloudWatch console.
- CloudWatch integrates with other services such as SNS, **Simple Queue Service** (**SQS**), AWS Lambda, AWS Auto Scaling, and more for notifications and auto-remediation.
- Under **Alarms** in the left sidebar, we have a dedicated option to set up a **Billing** alarm.
- Important operations that are supported by the default EC2 metrics include CPU utilization, disk read and write operations, network in and out operations, and status check failures.

See also

- You can read about publishing custom metrics here: `https://docs.aws.amazon.com/AmazonCloudWatch/latest/monitoring/publishingMetrics.html`.

Creating a dashboard in CloudWatch

In this recipe, we will create a dashboard in the CloudWatch console. Dashboards provide us with a single place to look into related metrics. We can create dashboards to group metrics based on their relevance, such as performance, security, networking, cost optimizations, and so on.

Getting ready

We'll need a working AWS account to complete this recipe.

How to do it...

We can create a CloudWatch dashboard as follows:

1. Go to the CloudWatch service in the console.
2. Click on **Dashboards** from the left sidebar.
3. Click on **Create dashboard**.
4. In the pop-up screen, give the dashboard a **Name** and click **Create dashboard**. I have set the **Name** to `MySecurityDashboard`.
5. On the screen for selecting a widget type, select **Line** and click **Configure**:

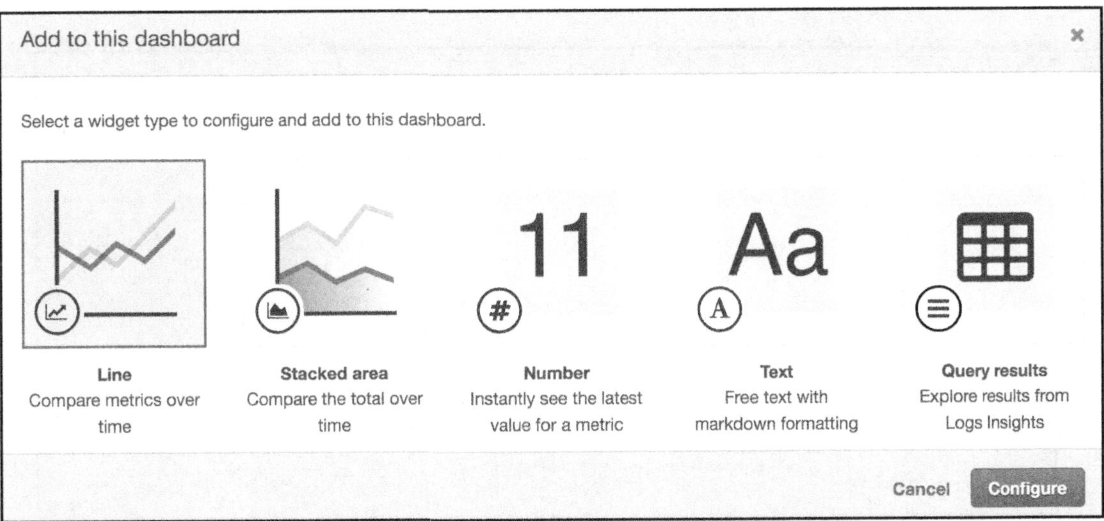

6. From the list of metric categories, click on **Billing**.
7. Select **By Service**.
8. Select all the services you need to monitor. Change the duration and type if needed. Here, I have selected a duration of 1 week, denoted as **1w**, and set the type to **Line**:

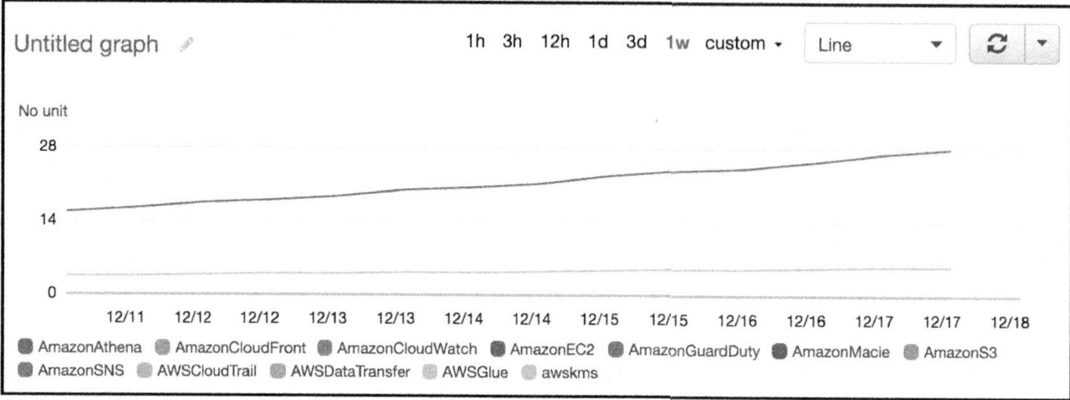

9. Scroll down and click **Create widget**. The widget should now appear on our dashboard.
10. Click on **Save dashboard**. The link to the new dashboard should now appear on the left sidebar. Once we click on it, we should see our dashboard with widgets on the right-hand side:

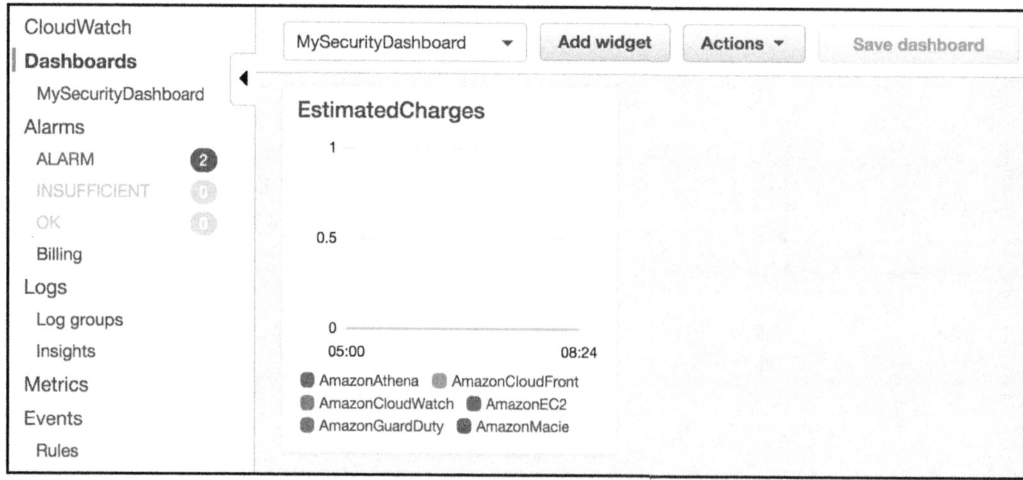

You can add additional widgets by clicking on the **Add widget** button. Save the dashboard by clicking on the **Save dashboard** button after adding the widgets.

How it works...

In this recipe, we created a dashboard in CloudWatch. We created a widget for the dashboard by selecting metrics from multiple services. When we created an alarm, we could only select one metric. We can also create more widgets and add them to the dashboard.

AWS currently supports the following types of visualizations for the widgets in a dashboard: line, stacked area, number, text, and query results. We selected line visualization in this recipe. We set the time period to 1 week. We can also add a custom time period.

There's more...

Let's go through some important concepts related to CloudWatch dashboards:

- We can add metrics from different services in the same dashboard widget and then correlate their usages.
- Within the widget configuration, we can set the refresh intervals in order to update data in the widget UI:

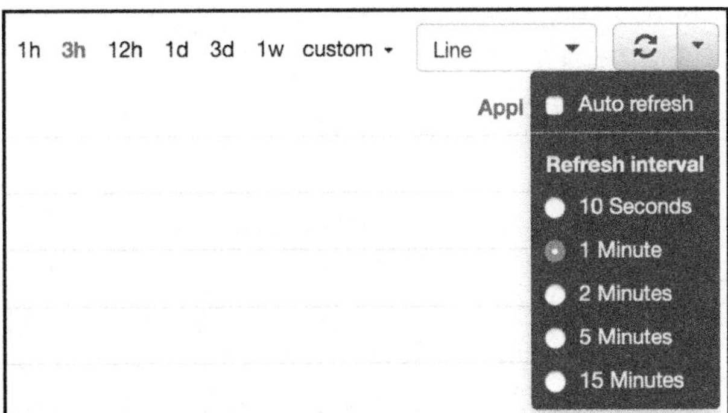

The preceding screenshot shows the duration and the type dropdown.

See also

- You can read more about CloudWatch dashboards here: `https://docs.aws.amazon.com/AmazonCloudWatch/latest/monitoring/CloudWatch_Dashboards.html`.

Creating a CloudWatch log group

In this recipe, we will create a CloudWatch log group that will be used in other recipes in this book.

Getting ready

We'll need a working AWS account to complete this recipe.

How to do it...

We can create a CloudWatch log group as follows:

1. Go to the CloudWatch service in the console.
2. Click on **Logs** from the left sidebar.
3. Click on **Actions** and click on **Create log group**:

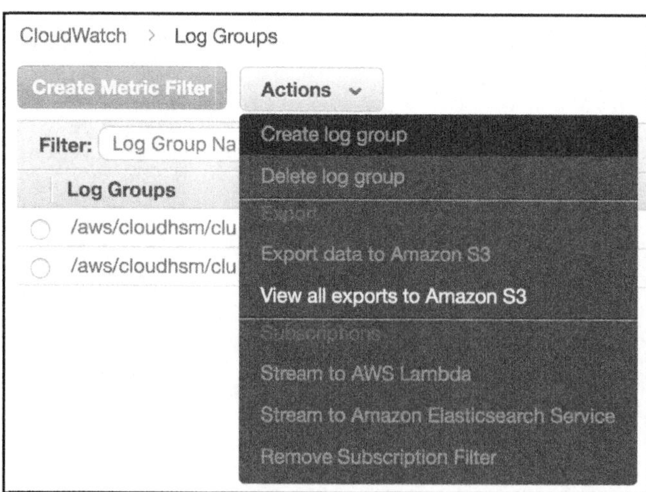

4. Give the log group a name that describes its purpose and click on **Create log group**:

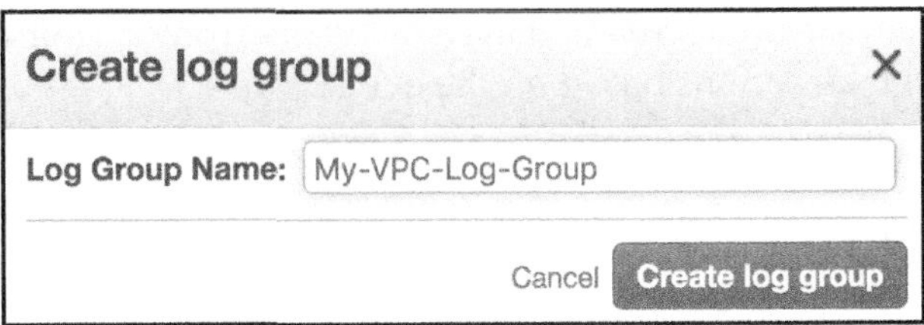

This will create a new log group for us.

How it works...

There are not many settings that need to be provided while creating a log group. We can use this log group within other recipes where we log into CloudWatch. A log group is a group of log streams. A log stream is a sequence of log events from the same source. Log streams within a log group share the same retention, monitoring, and access control settings. We can specify which streams to put into each log group. There is no limit on the number of log streams in a log group.

There's more...

Log groups may be used from other services and features, such as VPC Flow Logs, as we've seen in the book. Log groups can also be used for our custom-built applications and microservices.

See also

- You can learn more about CloudWatch logs here: `https://cloudmaterials.com/en/book/amazon-cloudwatch-essentials`.

Working with CloudWatch events

In this recipe, we will learn how to create and use CloudWatch events. CloudWatch events provide us with a near real-time stream of system events from various AWS resources and we can create rules to take actions based on the event data.

Getting ready

We'll need to create an SNS topic with an email subscription to complete this recipe. We can do this by following the *Creating an SNS topic to send emails* recipe of this chapter.

How to do it...

We can create a CloudWatch event as follows:

1. Go to the CloudWatch service in the console.
2. If we are using CloudWatch events for the first time, we should see a **Getting started** page. Click on **Get started**. We should be taken to the **Create rule** page.

We can also reach the **Create rule** page as follows: click on **Rules** from the left sidebar and click on **Create rule** on the **Rules** page.

3. Under the **Event Source** section, do the following:
    1. Select **Event Pattern**.
    2. Set **Service Name** to **EC2**.
    3. Set **Event Type** to **EC2 Instance State-change Notification**.
    4. Select **Any state** and **Any instance**:

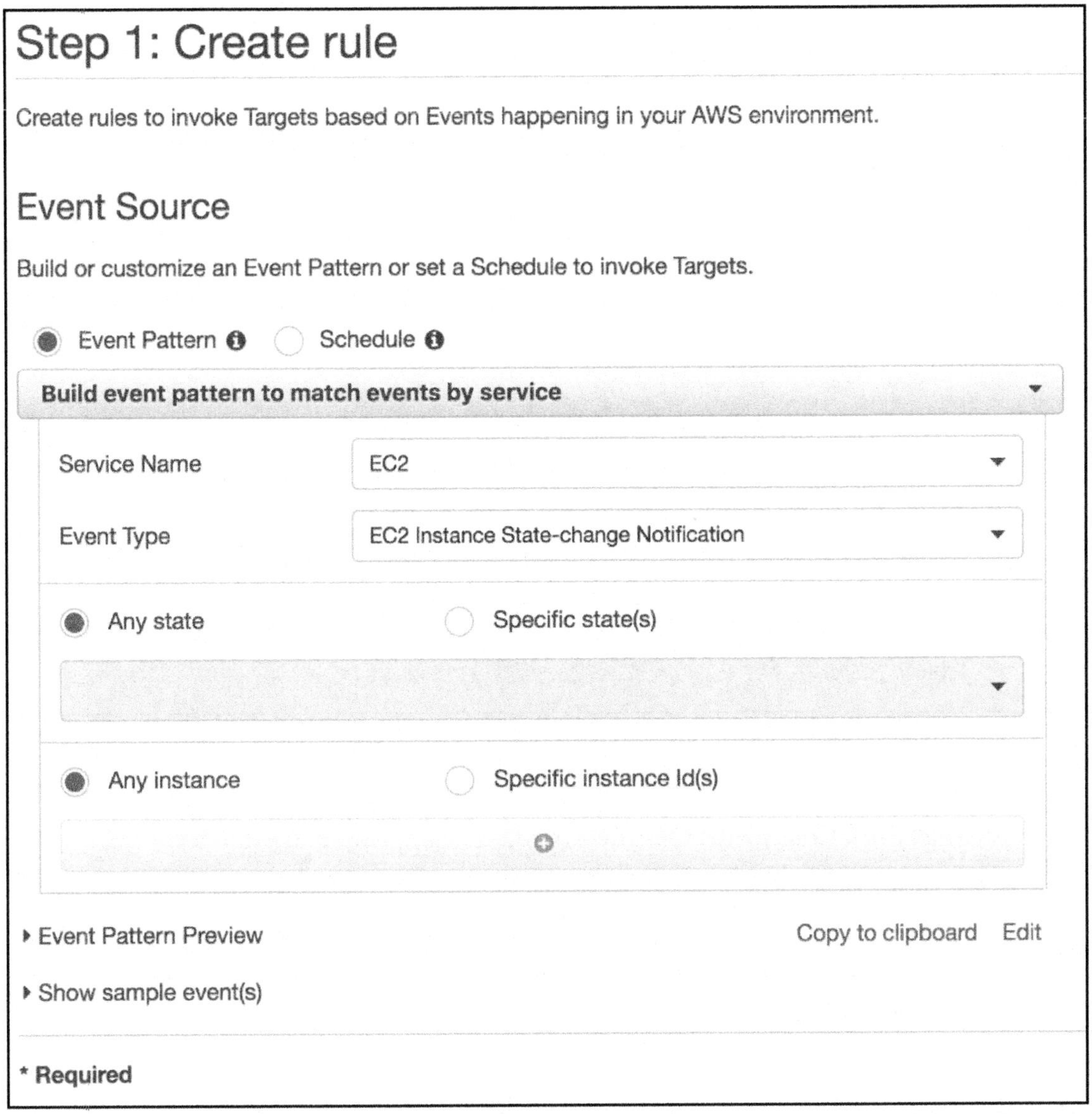

Step 1: Create rule

Create rules to invoke Targets based on Events happening in your AWS environment.

Event Source

Build or customize an Event Pattern or set a Schedule to invoke Targets.

Event Pattern   Schedule

Build event pattern to match events by service

Service Name   EC2

Event Type   EC2 Instance State-change Notification

Any state   Specific state(s)

Any instance   Specific instance Id(s)

Event Pattern Preview   Copy to clipboard   Edit

Show sample event(s)

*** Required**

4. Under **Targets**, do the following:
    1. Click on **Add target**.
    2. Select **SNS topic** from the dropdown.
    3. Select the SNS topic we created in the *Getting ready* section:

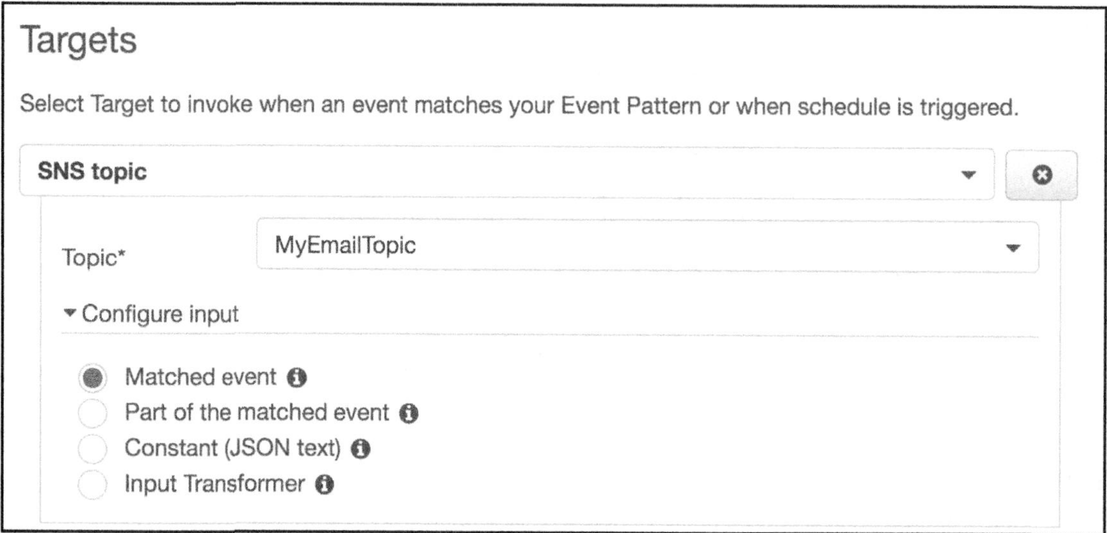

5. Scroll down and click on **Configure details**.
6. On the **Configure rule details** page, provide a **Name** and **Description** for our rule. Click **Create rule**. Our rule should now appear on the **Rules** page.
7. Go to the EC2 dashboard. Create an instance. We should get a notification email with the **state** as **pending**. After that, we will get a notification with the **state** as **running**. If we terminate the instance, we will get a notification with the **state** as **shutting-down**. After that, we will get a notification with the **state** as **terminated**.

How it works...

In this recipe, we selected **Event Pattern** and set the **Service Name** to **EC2** and **Event Type** to **EC2 Instance State-change Notification** to match EC2 events whose state gets changed. Instead of an event pattern, we can select **Schedule** to invoke our targets on a schedule, just like we can with cron jobs.

We configured to notify any state change. We can also select a specific state, such as **pending**, **running**, **shutting-down**, **stopped**, **stopping**, or **terminated**. We also configured to apply this rule to all the instances within our account. Instead of doing this, we can select a specific EC2 instance. We selected our SNS topic as the target. When we configure a target, CloudWatch Events will provide necessary permissions for targets so that they can be invoked when the rules are triggered.

There's more...

While configuring the event, we selected an SNS topic as our target. The following are the current list of target types available for us to select: **Batch job queue**, **CloudWatch log group**, **CodeBuild project**, **CodePipeline**, **EC2 CreateSnapshot API call**, **EC2 RebootInstances API call**, **EC2 StopInstances API call**, **EC2 TerminateInstances API call**, **ECS task**, **Event bus in another AWS account**, **Firehose delivery stream**, **Inspector assessment template**, **Kinesis stream**, **Lambda function**, **SNS topic**, **SQS queue**, **SSM Automation**, **SSM OpsItem**, **SSM Run Command**, and **Step Functions state machine**.

See also

- You can read more about CloudWatch events here: `https://docs.aws.amazon.com/AmazonCloudWatch/latest/events/WhatIsCloudWatchEvents.html`.

Reading and filtering logs in CloudTrail

In this recipe, we will learn how to read and filter the CloudTrail log events that are automatically generated and made available through the CloudTrail dashboard.

Getting ready

We'll need a working AWS account to complete this recipe.

How to do it...

We can check the automatically populated event logs in CloudTrail as follows:

1. Log in to the CloudTrail service in the console. We should see a list of recent events on the dashboard:

Recent events

These are the most recent events recorded by CloudTrail. To view all events for the last 90 days, go to Event history.

	Event time	User name	Event name
▶	2019-12-10, 08:27:23 AM	i-07d6614e1dec5e537	UpdateInstanceInformation
▶	2019-12-10, 08:22:23 AM	i-07d6614e1dec5e537	UpdateInstanceInformation
▶	2019-12-10, 08:17:23 AM	i-07d6614e1dec5e537	UpdateInstanceInformation
▶	2019-12-10, 08:12:23 AM	i-07d6614e1dec5e537	UpdateInstanceInformation
▶	2019-12-10, 08:07:23 AM	i-07d6614e1dec5e537	UpdateInstanceInformation

View all events

2. Click on **Event history** from the left sidebar. This will take us to the **Event history** page.

We can also go to the **Event history** page by clicking on the **View all events** link below the list of recent events.

3. Select the **User name** from the dropdown. Copy and paste one of the usernames from the preceding list and search for all activity from that user for a period of 10 days. I have used a time range of `December 1, 2019` to `December 10, 2019`:

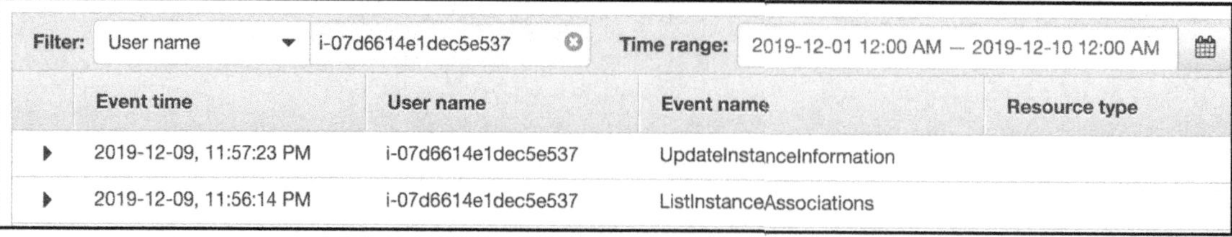

Filter: User name | i-07d6614e1dec5e537 | Time range: 2019-12-01 12:00 AM – 2019-12-10 12:00 AM

	Event time	User name	Event name	Resource type
▶	2019-12-09, 11:57:23 PM	i-07d6614e1dec5e537	UpdateInstanceInformation	
▶	2019-12-09, 11:56:14 PM	i-07d6614e1dec5e537	ListInstanceAssociations	

4. Click on the download icon at the top right corner and then click on **Download CSV** to download the result as a CSV file:

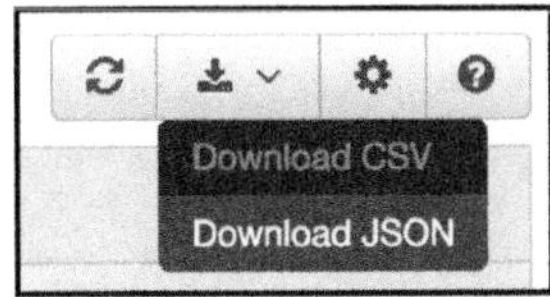

We can also download the result as a JSON file.

How it works...

AWS CloudTrail is a service from Amazon that can continuously monitor and log API activities within an AWS account. Without any additional configuration, CloudTrail will log API activity events in our account and is made available for 90 days through the CloudTrail console. After going to the **Events history** page, we can filter based on various criteria and time ranges. We filtered based on **User name** in this recipe. Apart from **User name**, we can also filter based on the following parameters: **Event name**, **Resource type**, **Resource name**, **Event source**, **Event ID**, **AWS access key**, and **Read only**.

There's more...

In this recipe, we queried our logs from the console. We can also query logs from the CLI. The following are some of the important CLI commands for querying CloudTrail logs:

- The `aws cloudtrail lookup-events` command can be used to query the last 90 days of automatically generated event logs. A pagination token is returned if there are more results.
- We can limit the number of items that are returned by the `aws cloudtrail lookup-events` command by specifying the `max-items` option; for example, `aws cloudtrail lookup-events --max-items 10`.
- We can specify a date range using the `start-time` and `end-time` parameters; for example, `aws cloudtrail lookup-events --start-time 2019-01-12 --end-time 2019-10-12`. We can also specify hours, minutes, and seconds with one of these parameters; for example, `--start-time 2019-01-12T00:30:45`.

- We can use the `lookup-attributes` parameter to specify the values of any parameter; for example, `aws cloudtrail lookup-events --lookup-attributes "AttributeKey=Username,AttributeValue=i-07d6614e1dec5e537"`.

Let's go through some more important concepts related to CloudTrail logs:

- The CloudTrail service helps us achieve event-driven security by analyzing events and responding to them.
- CloudTrail only records events that involve AWS API calls. Therefore, if an application running on an EC2 instance throws an error, it won't be captured. CloudWatch can be used for logging from applications on EC2 or from Lambda functions.
- By default, a trail will record events in one region. However, we can configure a trail as a multi-region trail.
- CloudTrail can integrate with other AWS services to provide additional security and compliance. These integrations include CloudWatch for raising alarms, GuardDuty for analyzing patterns, Macie to discover, classify, and protect sensitive data, and so on.
- The current CloudTrail pricing model is as follows: the first tier in each region is free (except S3 and Lambda data events). After the free tier, CloudTrail charges us for management events and data events.

See also

- You can read about CloudTrail's pricing, along with examples, at `https://aws.amazon.com/cloudtrail/pricing`.

Creating a trail in CloudTrail

In this recipe, we will learn how to create a trail in CloudTrail and how to read logs from the associated S3 bucket. By default, CloudTrail API event logs are made available for 90 days. The data events, such as S3 bucket operations and Lambda invocations are also not logged by default. To store our logs for more than 90 days, to enable logging data events from S3 or Lambda, and for additional flexibility in searching the logs, we can create a trail to log data in an S3 bucket.

Getting ready

We'll need a working AWS account to complete this recipe.

How to do it...

We can create a trail in CloudTrail as follows:

1. Log in to the CloudTrail service in the console.
2. Click on **Trails** from the left sidebar.
3. Click on **Create trail**.
4. Set a meaningful name for the **Trail name**. For **Apply trail to all regions**, select **Yes**:

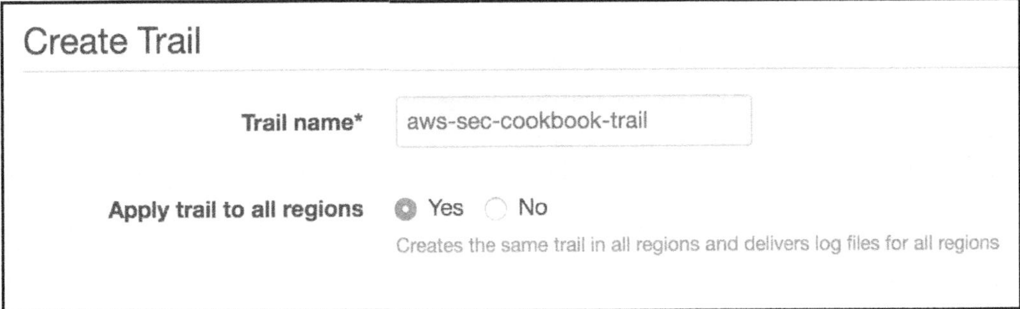

If you are following this recipe from an AWS Organizations master account, you will also see the option to **Apply trail to my organization.** If you want to enable CloudTrail for all accounts within an Organization and use the current account as the master log account, set the option to **Yes**. For more details on cross-account CloudTrail logging, refer to the *Cross-account CloudTrail logging* recipe of this chapter.

5. Under **Management events**, for **Read/Write events**, select **All**. For **Log AWS KMS events**, select **Yes**:

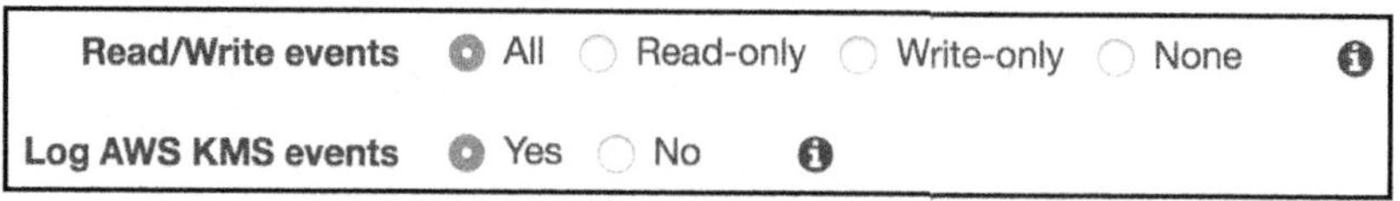

6. Under **Insights events**, set **Log Insights events** to **No**.
7. Under **Data events**, leave the selections for the S3 and Lambda data events unchecked.
8. Under **Storage location**, select **Yes** for **Create a new S3 bucket** and provide a unique name for our bucket:

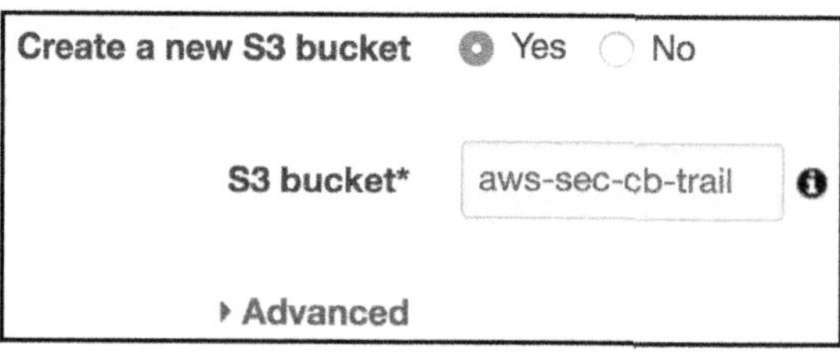

9. Expand the **Advanced** option to verify the additional settings. Leave them with their default values, as follows:

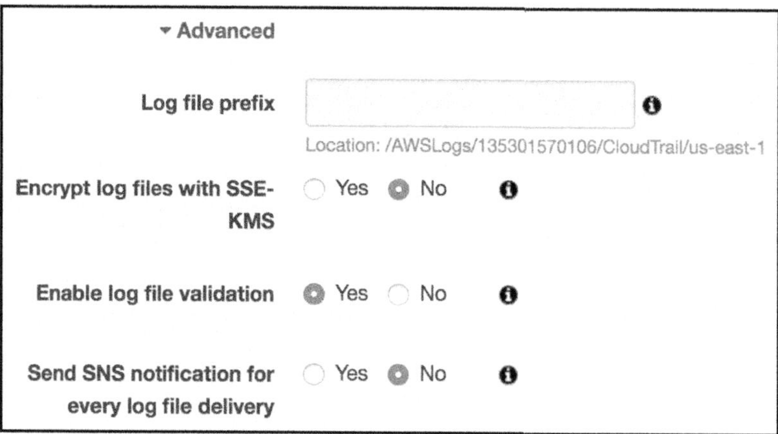

10. Scroll to the bottom of the page and click **Create**. We can click on **Trails** from the left sidebar of the CloudTrail dashboard and verify that our trail's **Status** is a success.
11. Click on our trail's name to go to the trail's **Configuration** page. We can change any configuration from this page. We can also stop logging for this trail using the **Logging** button. Currently, its value should be **ON**:

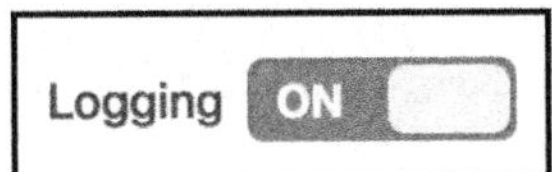

We can view our CloudTrail logs from the S3 bucket as follows:

1. Go to the **Trails** list and click on our trail's S3 bucket name to go to our trail's S3 bucket's log folder. We can also manually go to the S3 dashboard and access this folder. We should see that a folder has been created per region where we have activities since we created a multi-region trail.
2. Go inside the folders until we see the actual log files. The log file name contains the account number, region, and timestamp; for example, `135301570106_CloudTrail_us-east-1_20191210T0415Z_1sv2LnhPyOY5ioQi.json.gz`. This should be present inside a folder structure similar to `Amazon S3` | `aws-sec-cb-trail` | `AWSLogs` | `135301570106` | `CloudTrail` | `us-east-1` | `2019` | `12` | `10`.
3. View the file in S3. To do this, select the file, and in the popup, click on **Select from**. Set **File format** to **JSON**, **JSON type** to **JSON lines**, **Compression** to **GZip**, and click on **Show file preview**. This will show a preview of our log file:


```
{
    "Records": [
        {
            "eventVersion": "1.05",
            "userIdentity": {
                "type": "AWSService",
                "invokedBy": "vpc-flow-logs.amazonaws.com"
            },
            "eventTime": "2019-12-10T04:14:21Z",
            "eventSource": "sts.amazonaws.com",
```


Next

4. Click **Next**. We should now see the SQL query run so that we can get the actual result:

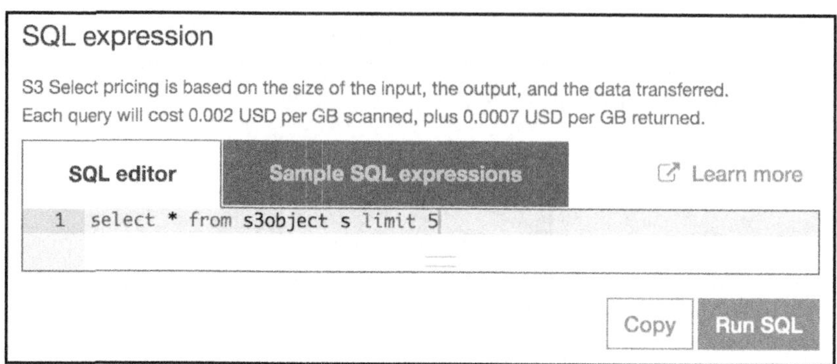

5. Modify the SQL as required and click on **Run SQL**. We should see the actual result in another text box, as shown in the following screenshot:

Result


```
{
    "Records": [
        {
            "eventVersion": "1.05",
            "userIdentity": {
                "type": "AWSService",
                "invokedBy": "vpc-flow-logs.amazonaws.com"
            },
```


6. Scroll down and click **Download** to download the result. We should get a file with a name similar to `select_result_135301570106_CloudTrail_us-east-1_20191210T0415Z_1sv2LnhPyOY5ioQi_json.gz_1575968762090`. We can open this file using any compatible applications, such as Microsoft Word.

How it works...

For storing logs for more than 90 days, we need to create a trail and trails will send logs into an S3 bucket. In this recipe, we created a multi-region trail. We configured the options to log all events. We can also select from one of the following options: **Read-only**, **Write-only**, and **None**. We configured to log AWS KMS events. We did not enable log insights.

Insights events capture any unusual call volumes of write management APIs. Insights events have additional charges.

We did not enable S3 and Lambda data events. Enabling these will log resource operations (data events) that are performed on or within an S3 bucket or a Lambda function. These operations may also be called data plane operations. There is an additional cost for data events.

We asked AWS to create a new S3 bucket. Under the **Advanced** link, we used the defaults for the following parameters:

- **Log file prefix** to make log files easier to browse.
- **Encrypt log files with SSE-KMS** instead of the default SSE-S3 encryption.
- **Enable log file validation** to find if a log file was modified, deleted, or unchanged after CloudTrail delivered the log.
- **Send SNS notification for every log file delivery** to take immediate action.

We also saw the option to stop logging for a trail on the trail's **Configuration** page. Stopping logging will stop any new events being sent to the log, but existing logs will be still available.

There's more...

In this recipe, we queried the logs in S3 directly from the S3 console. For more flexibility when querying CloudTrail logs in S3, we can use Amazon Athena. We will learn how to use Amazon Athena to query CloudTrail logs in the *Using Athena to query CloudTrail logs in S3* recipe of this chapter.

See also

- You can read more about S3 at `https://cloudmaterials.com/en/book/amazon-s3-and-overview-other-storage-services`.

Using Athena to query CloudTrail logs in S3

In this recipe, we will learn how to use Amazon Athena to query CloudTrail logs. Using Athena to query CloudTrail logs provide us with greater flexibility. For example, we cannot filter based on an account ID from the CloudTrail console, even if multiple accounts are sending logs to the CloudTrail's S3 bucket. However, we can use Athena to query for logs from CloudTrail's S3 bucket based on the account ID.

Getting ready

We need to create a trail in CloudTrail to complete this recipe. We can do this by following the *Creating a trail in CloudTrail* recipe of this chapter.

If we are new to Athena, before we can run our queries, we should set up a query result location in Amazon S3, as follows:

1. Go to the Athena service in the console.
2. Go to the **Query Editor** tab. If we are new to Athena, we should see a warning stating that **Before you run your first query, you need to set up a query result location in Amazon S3**:

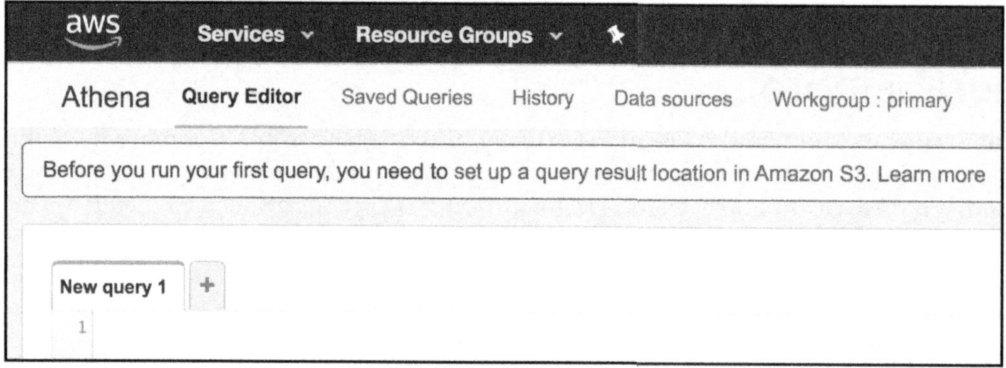

3. Click on the **set up a query result location in Amazon S3. Learn more** hyperlink.
4. Enter a bucket name for the **Query result location** field. I've named my bucket `aws-sec-cb-query-results`:

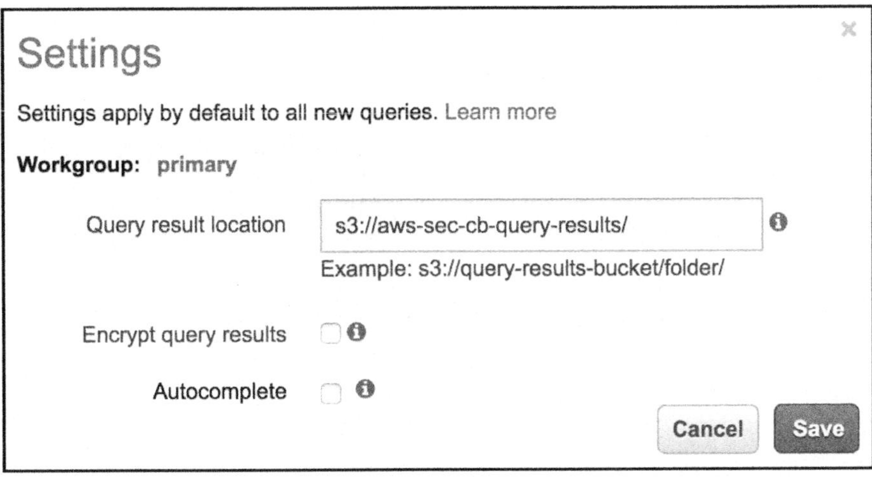

5. Click on **Save**.

How to do it...

We can set up Athena and query CloudTrail logs as follows:

1. Log in to the CloudTrail service in the console.
2. Click on **Event history** from the left sidebar of the CloudTrail dashboard. This will take us to the **Event history** page.
3. Click on **Run advanced queries in Amazon Athena** from the content area. We should see **Create a table in Amazon Athena** with a table creation command for reference.
4. For **Storage location**, select the S3 bucket of our trail.
5. Click on **Create table**. We should see a success message with a link for **Go to Athena**.
6. Click on **Go to Athena**.
7. Go to the **Query Editor** tab. We should get the list of database tables, including the one we created, on the left, and a query editor window on right.

It might take some time for the table to be created and appear on the Athena dashboard after we've initiated its creation from the CloudTrail dashboard. We can manually refresh the table list using the refresh icon in the left sidebar.

8. Click on the button with three dots next to our table and click on **Preview table**:

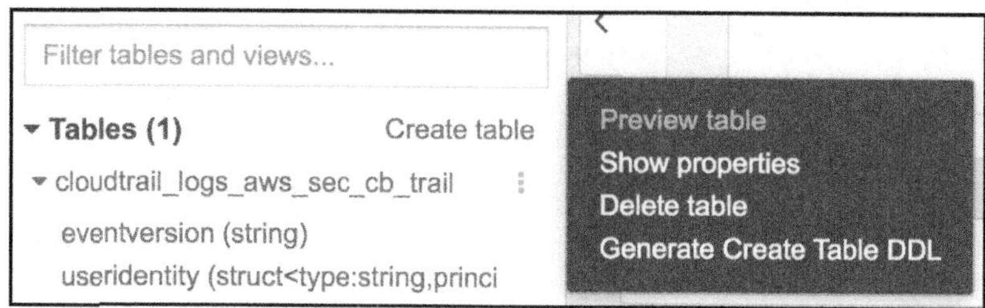

A sample query will be created that we can modify so that it meets our needs:

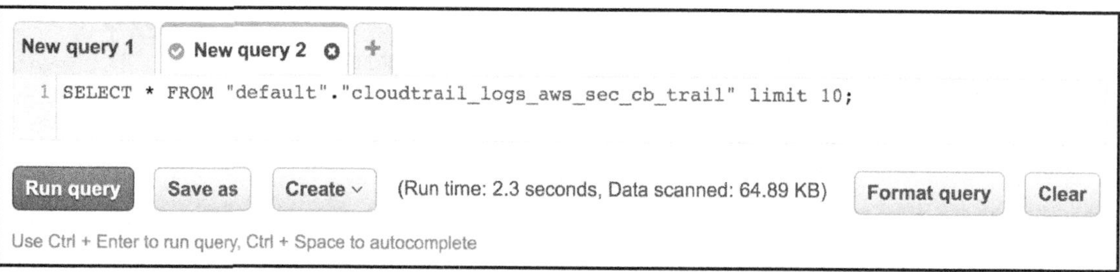

9. I have set the limit to 2 with `SELECT * FROM "default"."cloudtrail_logs_aws_sec_cb_trail" limit 2;`. Click **Run query**. We should see the results shown in the following screenshot:

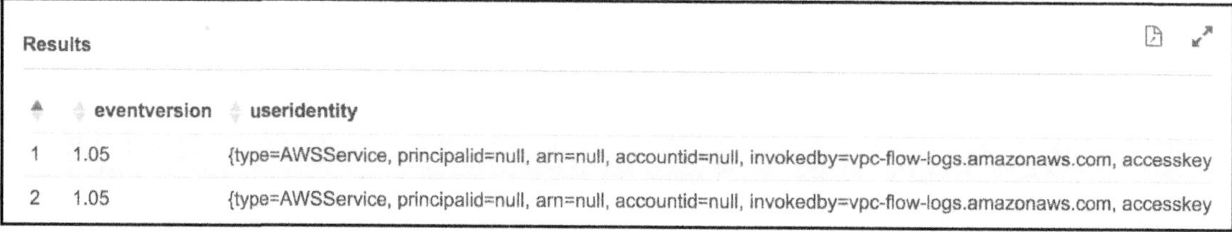

10. Click on the document icon on the top-right corner to download the results in CSV format. We can use the expand icon to display the result in full-screen mode.

How it works...

In this recipe, we used Amazon Athena to query CloudTrail logs in S3. Athena uses queries based on **Structured Query Language** (**SQL**) and creates virtual tables. If we are new to Athena, before we can run our queries, we should set up a query result location in Amazon S3. We clicked on the **Run advanced queries in Amazon Athena** option from within the CloudTrail dashboard and AWS created an Athena table. Then, we went to Athena and ran a preview query. We modified the query and executed it. Finally, we exported the results into a CSV file using an icon from the results screen.

After, we ran the `SELECT * FROM "default"."cloudtrail_logs_aws_sec_cb_trail" limit 2;` query. In this query, the `"default"."cloudtrail_logs_aws_sec_cb_trail"` table was auto-populated when we generated the query. `Select *` selects all the columns, while `limit 2` limits the records that are returned to two.

There's more...

Let's quickly go through some important concepts related to Amazon Athena:

- Athena is a query service provided by AWS to analyze data in Amazon S3 using SQL.
- Athena can only query S3 data and not CloudTrail directly.
- Amazon Athena now supports federated queries. We can run SQL queries across data stored in relational, non-relational, object, and custom data sources, and then store the result in Amazon S3. At the time of writing, this feature is in preview.
- Athena is serverless. We do not have to set up any infrastructure and we only pay for the queries we run.
- Athena, integrated with AWS Glue, allows us to crawl data sources and populate table and partition definitions, and even maintain schema versioning.

See also

- You can read more about Amazon Athena here: `https://aws.amazon.com/athena`.

Cross-account CloudTrail logging

In this recipe, we will learn how to send the CloudTrail logs of one account to another account. By storing logs in a separate account, we isolate the logs from the source account, which will prevent anyone with access to the source account from tampering with the logs. We can provide account-level access to the log account to a limited set of people. Sending logs from multiple accounts to a single account also provides a central place for us to query logs.

Getting ready

We'll need two working AWS accounts to complete this recipe. We will call them log account and logger account. The logger account will send logs to the log account.

Log in to the logger account, which is where logs will be sent, and take note of its account number. The account number can be found in the **Support Center**. We can go to the **Support Center** from the **Support** dropdown, which can be found in the top right corner of our AWS dashboard:

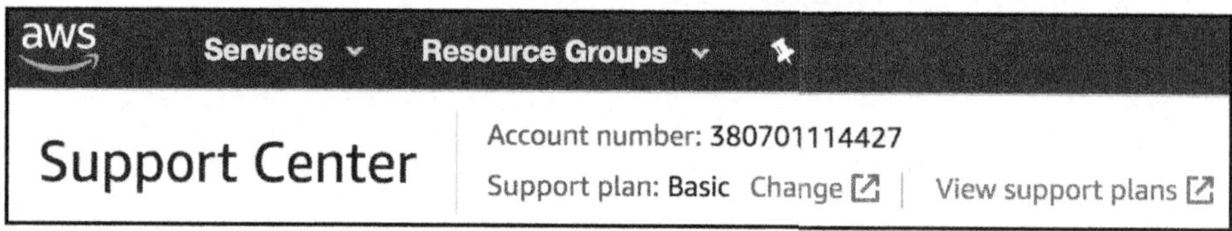

We also need to set up CloudTrail in the log account, which is where all the logs will be stored. We can do this by following the *Creating a trail in CloudTrail* recipe of this chapter.

How to do it...

We can send CloudTrail logs between two standalone accounts as follows:

1. Log in to the log account where logs will be sent to. A trail should have already been configured, as described in the *Getting ready* section.

If you are using AWS Organizations, the steps are simpler and are provided in the *There's more...* section.

2. Go to our trail's bucket and go to its **Permissions** tab. Then, click on **Bucket Policy**. The current policy should allow `cloudtrail.amazonaws.com` to perform the `s3:GetBucketAcl` action on the `arn:aws:s3:::aws-sec-cb-trail` resource. It should also allow `cloudtrail.amazonaws.com` to perform the `s3:PutObject` action on the `arn:aws:s3:::aws-sec-cb-trail/AWSLogs/135301570106/*` resource with a condition that checks if the value of `s3:x-amz-acl` is `bucket-owner-full-control`:

```
{
    "Version": "2012-10-17",
    "Statement": [
        {
            "Sid": "AWSCloudTrailAclCheck20150319",
            "Effect": "Allow",
            "Principal": {
                "Service": "cloudtrail.amazonaws.com"
            },
            "Action": "s3:GetBucketAcl",
            "Resource": "arn:aws:s3:::aws-sec-cb-trail"
        },
        {
            "Sid": "AWSCloudTrailWrite20150319",
            "Effect": "Allow",
            "Principal": {
                "Service": "cloudtrail.amazonaws.com"
            },
            "Action": "s3:PutObject",
            "Resource": "arn:aws:s3:::aws-sec-cb-
trail/AWSLogs/135301570106/*",
            "Condition": {
                "StringEquals": {
                    "s3:x-amz-acl": "bucket-owner-full-control"
                }
            }
        }
    ]
}
```

3. For the statement whose `Sid` starts with `AWSCloudTrailWrite`, change the `Resource` element into a list, and add permissions to write to the log folder that's specific to the logger account. The statement should now look as follows:

```
{
    "Sid": "AWSCloudTrailWrite20150319",
    "Effect": "Allow",
    "Principal": {
```

```
                "Service": "cloudtrail.amazonaws.com"
            },
            "Action": "s3:PutObject",
            "Resource": [
                "arn:aws:s3:::aws-sec-cb-trail/AWSLogs/135301570106/*",
                "arn:aws:s3:::aws-sec-cb-trail/AWSLogs/380701114427/*"
            ],
            "Condition": {
                "StringEquals": {
                    "s3:x-amz-acl": "bucket-owner-full-control"
                }
            }
        }
```

4. Log in to the logger account and create a trail by following the *Creating a trail in CloudTrail* recipe of this chapter, but with the following changes under the **Storage location** heading:
    1. For **Create a new S3 bucket**, select **No**.
    2. For **S3 bucket**, enter the name of the bucket we created in the log account for the trail, which is `aws-sec-cb-trail` in my case:

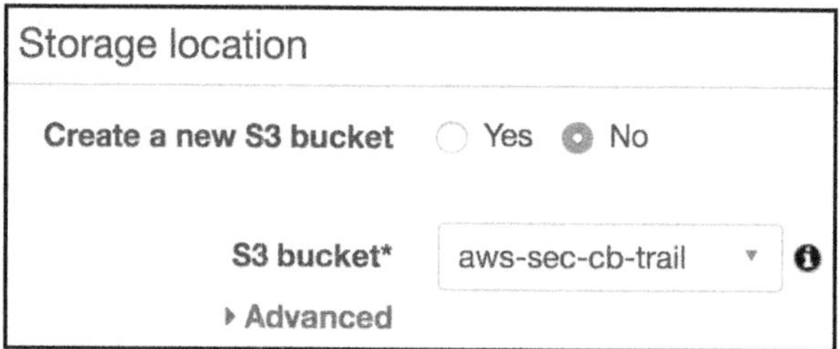

For some API activity, you can launch an EC2 instance. You can do this by following the *Launching an EC2 instance into VPC* recipe in `Chapter 6`, *Working with EC2 Instances.*

5. Log back into the log account and check the logs for the logger account in the trail's bucket in the folder that's specific to the logger account, which is `380701114427` in my case. Within the bucket, the logs should be present in a folder structure similar to `AWSLogs/380701114427/CloudTrail/us-east-1/2019/12/11`. You can examine the logs by following the previous CloudTrail recipes within this chapter.

How it works...

In this recipe, we sent logs from one account – the logger account – into another account – the log account. First, we created a trail in the log account. A bucket policy was created that allowed the CloudTrail service to log to the current account's log folder. We modified the bucket policy to allow the CloudTrail service to log to the logger account's log folder. CloudTrail logs each account's log in a folder specific to that account.

The default bucket policy that was generated by AWS had two statements. The first statement, whose `Sid` starts with `AWSCloudTrailAclCheck`, allows CloudTrail to read the bucket's ACL. The second statement, whose `Sid` starts with `AWSCloudTrailWrite`, gives CloudTrail permission to write to the specified account's folder. Each account logs into a folder that is specific to that account.

After that, we created a trail in the logger account by specifying the same S3 bucket that we specified in the log account. We went back to the log account and verified the logs that were sent from the logger account. Within the bucket, the logs are present in a folder structure similar to `AWSLogs/380701114427/CloudTrail/us-east-1/2019/12/11`, where `380701114427` is the account number of the logger account, `us-east-1` is the region, and `2019/12/11` is the date.

There's more...

In this recipe, we looked at the steps for sending CloudTrail logs from a standalone account into another. If we are using AWS Organizations, we can enable CloudTrail across accounts from the master account by selecting **Yes** for **Apply trail to my organization** while creating a trail:

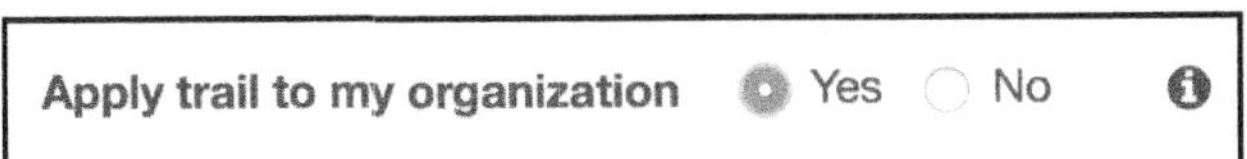

An organization's trail is then created in all the member accounts, which means we don't have to modify the bucket policy, as we saw in this recipe. Enabling this option may lead to additional charges if the member accounts already have trails since only the first trail within a region is free. We learned about AWS Organizations in the *Creating a master account for AWS Organizations* recipe in `Chapter 1`, *Managing AWS Accounts with IAM and Organizations*.

See also

- You can read about AWS Organizations at `https://aws.amazon.com/organizations`.

Integrating CloudWatch and CloudTrail

In this recipe, we will learn how to integrate CloudWatch with CloudTrail. Once integrated, we can create metric filters and alarms within CloudWatch based on CloudTrail logs. We will also learn how to use the CloudFormation template provided by AWS to create a set of alarms within CloudWatch that use CloudTrail logs.

Getting ready

Create a trail by following the *Creating a trail in CloudTrail* recipe of this chapter. I have called my trail `aws-sec-cookbook-trail`.

You can also perform the steps in this recipe while creating a trail by making minor modifications to them.

How to do it...

We can integrate CloudWatch with an existing trail as follows:

1. Go to the CloudTrail service in the console.
2. Click on **Trails**.
3. Click on the name of our trail to go to the trail's **Configuration** page.
4. Scroll down to the **CloudWatch Logs** section. Click on **Configure**.
5. Leave the auto-populated value for **New or existing log group** as is, which is `CloudTrail/DefaultLogGroup` in my case, and click **Continue**.
6. Click **Allow** to give CloudTrail permission to deliver CloudTrail events associated with API activity in our account to our CloudWatch Logs log group. We should see the CloudWatch details in the **CloudWatch Logs** section of our trail's configuration:

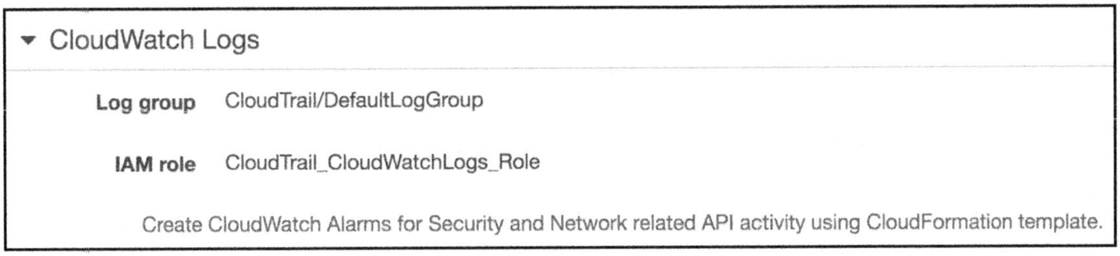

▾ CloudWatch Logs	
Log group	CloudTrail/DefaultLogGroup
IAM role	CloudTrail_CloudWatchLogs_Role
	Create CloudWatch Alarms for Security and Network related API activity using CloudFormation template.

7. Click on the **Create CloudWatch Alarms for Security and Network related API activity using CloudFormation template** link. We will be taken to the **Create stack** page, where the template details will be pre-populated.
8. Click **Next**.
9. On the **Specify stack details** page, provide an email address so that you'll be notified when an API activity has triggered an alarm. Click **Next**.
10. On the **Configure stack options** page, we will use the default selections. Click **Next**.
11. On the **Review CloudWatchAlarmsForCloudTrail** page, review our selections and click **Create stack**. Wait until the status of the stack becomes **CREATE_COMPLETE**. If we go to the **Alarms** page in CloudWatch, we will be able to view the new alarms that were created:

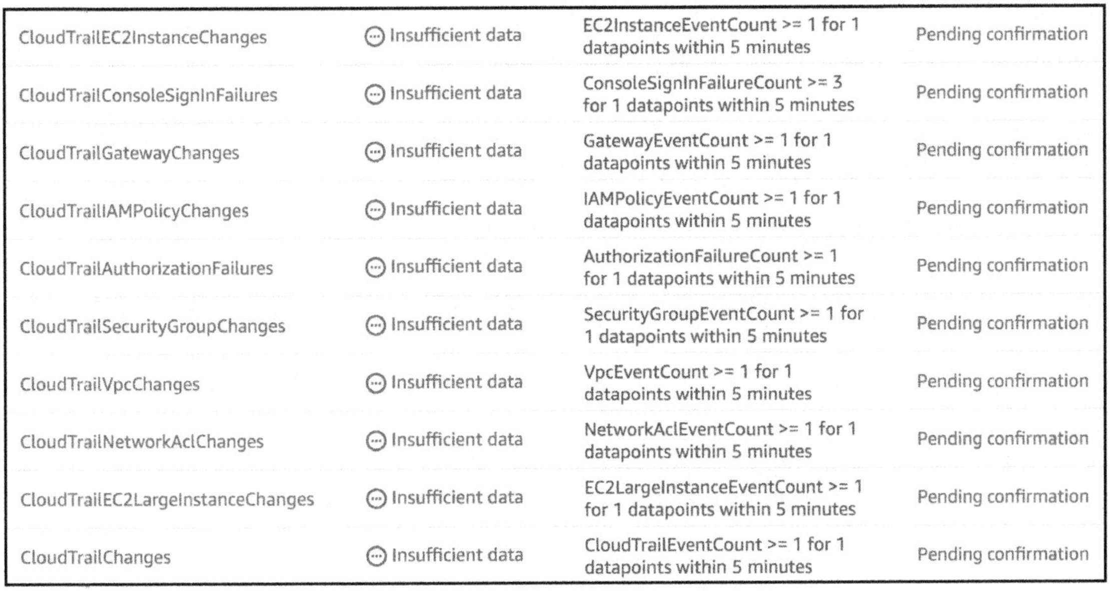

CloudTrailEC2InstanceChanges	Insufficient data	EC2InstanceEventCount >= 1 for 1 datapoints within 5 minutes	Pending confirmation
CloudTrailConsoleSignInFailures	Insufficient data	ConsoleSignInFailureCount >= 3 for 1 datapoints within 5 minutes	Pending confirmation
CloudTrailGatewayChanges	Insufficient data	GatewayEventCount >= 1 for 1 datapoints within 5 minutes	Pending confirmation
CloudTrailIAMPolicyChanges	Insufficient data	IAMPolicyEventCount >= 1 for 1 datapoints within 5 minutes	Pending confirmation
CloudTrailAuthorizationFailures	Insufficient data	AuthorizationFailureCount >= 1 for 1 datapoints within 5 minutes	Pending confirmation
CloudTrailSecurityGroupChanges	Insufficient data	SecurityGroupEventCount >= 1 for 1 datapoints within 5 minutes	Pending confirmation
CloudTrailVpcChanges	Insufficient data	VpcEventCount >= 1 for 1 datapoints within 5 minutes	Pending confirmation
CloudTrailNetworkAclChanges	Insufficient data	NetworkAclEventCount >= 1 for 1 datapoints within 5 minutes	Pending confirmation
CloudTrailEC2LargeInstanceChanges	Insufficient data	EC2LargeInstanceEventCount >= 1 for 1 datapoints within 5 minutes	Pending confirmation
CloudTrailChanges	Insufficient data	CloudTrailEventCount >= 1 for 1 datapoints within 5 minutes	Pending confirmation

We can wait until the alarm state changes to **OK** or **ALARM** and play around with these alarms to learn more about them.

12. Check the email address provided. We should get an email so that we can confirm the subscription. Click on the **Confirm subscription** hyperlink. If you refresh the **Alarms** page, the **Pending confirmation** action should disappear.

How it works...

In this recipe, we integrated CloudWatch with CloudTrail through our trail's settings. CloudTrail asked us for permission to deliver CloudTrail events associated with API activity in our account to our log group. We allowed this from the console. The following permissions were granted:

- **CreateLogStream**, to create a log stream in the log group we specified
- **PutLogEvents**, to deliver CloudTrail events to the log stream

We used the CloudFormation template provided by AWS to set up some CloudWatch Alarms for security and network-related API activity. If we delete the CloudFormation stack, all the alarms will also be deleted.

AWS uses SNS to send notifications and created an SNS topic subscription for us. We had to confirm the email subscription by verifying our email address since SNS will not send notifications until we manually confirm the subscription.

There's more...

In this recipe, we integrated CloudWatch with CloudTrail and used the CloudFormation template provided by Amazon to create some alarms that are related to security and network-related API activity. You can add these alarms to a dashboard by following the *Creating a dashboard in CloudWatch* recipe of this chapter.

See also

- You can read more about CloudFormation here: `https://aws.amazon.com/cloudformation`.

Setting up and using AWS Config

In this recipe, we will learn how to set up and use AWS Config. We can use Config to record and evaluate configurations of our AWS resources. We can create rules that define security standards and find out about resources that do not comply with the security standards. Config also supports the auto-remediation of problems whenever they are detected.

Getting ready

If you want to add an SNS topic for notifications, you can create an SNS topic with an email subscription by following the *Creating an SNS topic to send emails* recipe of this chapter.

For the purpose of testing, we need to have at least one IAM user without MFC enabled.

How to do it...

We can set up and use AWS Config as follows:

1. Go to the Config service in the console.
2. If we are logging in for the first time, we will see a **Getting started** page. Click on **Get started**. We will be taken to the **Settings** page.
3. In the **Resource types to record** section, against **All resources**, select **Record all resources supported in this region** and **Include global resources** (for example, **AWS IAM resources**).
4. In the **Amazon S3 bucket** section, select **Create a bucket**. We will also use the default bucket name that we populated in the **Bucket name** field.
5. In the **Amazon SNS topic** section, select **Stream configuration changes and notifications to an Amazon SNS topic**. For topic, select **Choose a topic from your account** and select the topic we created in the *Getting ready* section.
6. In the **AWS Config role** section, select **Create AWS Config service-linked role**.
7. Click **Next**. We will be taken to the **AWS Config rules** page.
8. Search for and select the `iam-user-mfa-enabled` rule. Click **Next**.

We can add more rules if we want. We can also add rules after completing the setup process.

9. On the **Review** page, review the changes and click **Confirm**. We will be redirected to the **Config Dashboard**. After waiting for some time, the left-hand side of the dashboard should show all the services being monitored. The right-hand side should show the compliance status graph and list of non-complaint rules. We can drill down on these rules for more information:

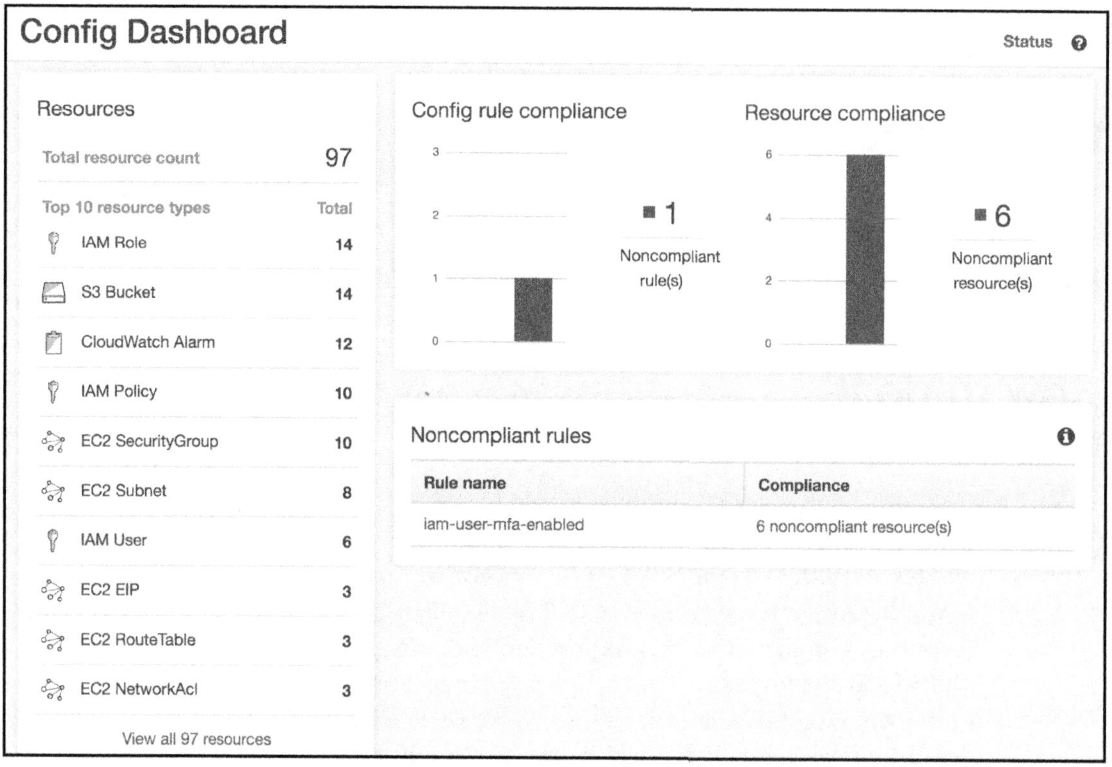

Config Dashboard

Status

Resources

Total resource count	97
Top 10 resource types	Total
IAM Role	14
S3 Bucket	14
CloudWatch Alarm	12
IAM Policy	10
EC2 SecurityGroup	10
EC2 Subnet	8
IAM User	6
EC2 EIP	3
EC2 RouteTable	3
EC2 NetworkAcl	3

View all 97 resources

Config rule compliance

1 Noncompliant rule(s)

Resource compliance

6 Noncompliant resource(s)

Noncompliant rules

Rule name	Compliance
iam-user-mfa-enabled	6 noncompliant resource(s)

Currently, I have the option to try out the newly redesigned AWS Config Console. Once I click on the **Try it out now** link, I can view the new dashboard, which contains the **Resource inventory**, which contains the resources that are monitored on top, followed by compliance details. The exact display options on the console may change from time to time, but the concepts remain the same.

How it works...

In this recipe, we set up AWS Config on our account. We selected **Record all resources supported in this region** and **Include global resources** (for example, **AWS IAM resources**) against **All resources** in order to record for all the resources across all regions. We can also configure recording for specific resources by unchecking **Record all resources supported in this region** and selecting the resources we want in the **Specific types** field.

We enabled SNS notifications to receive email notifications by selecting an SNS topic with an email subscription from our account. We can also choose an SNS topic from another account by selecting the **Choose a topic from another account** option. In the **AWS Config role** section, we selected **Create AWS Config service-linked role**. This role grants read-only access for Config to our AWS resources so that we can record configuration information. The role also grants permission to send information to S3 and SNS.

Here, we selected the `iam-user-mfa-enabled` rule, which is a periodic rule. **Periodic** rules are run periodically, whereas non-periodic rules (configuration changes-based rules) are run immediately when a change is made to an associated configuration.

There's more...

Let's go through some important concepts related to AWS Config:

- Some of the checks that we can do with AWS config include the following: check if MFA is enabled, check if S3 buckets are not public, databases are encrypted, VPC flow logs are enabled, and so on.
- We can write our own custom rules using AWS Lambdas.
- AWS Config can perform auto-remediation actions for a rule. For example, we can change the configuration of an EC2 instance based on a rule. However, AWS may stop and restart the EC2 instance, so we need to consider possible downtime.
- To configure auto-remediation from the new console, we can go to our rule, click on the **Actions** dropdown, and select **Manage remediation**. In the older console, we can do this from the **Choose remediation action** section of our rule, while editing a rule or adding a new rule.
- We can use the same set of Config rules across multiple accounts to ensure they all follow a common set of rules.

- We can create an aggregator in AWS Config to view the AWS resource inventory or Config rule compliance status for multiple accounts and across all regions. In the current console, we can create an aggregator by going to the **Aggregate View** from the left sidebar and then clicking on **Add aggregator**.
- AWS Config is charged based on the number of rules evaluations that are recorded.

The steps for creating a custom rule can be summarized as follows:

1. Create an IAM role that can be used by a Lambda with required permissions. To report back to AWS Config, we need to provide `AWSConfigRulesExecutionRole`. To send logs to CloudWatch, we will need to add `AWSLambdaBasicExecutionRole`. Finally, we need to give access to the service it will monitor (for example, `AmazonS3ReadOnlyAccess` for accessing S3).
2. Create a Lambda by selecting the IAM role we created in the previous step using any of the supported programming languages.
3. Write some code within Lambda in order to evaluate the service parameters that we are monitoring (for example, S3 bucket properties), update a `ResultToken` object per evaluation, and return a list of `ResultToken` objects back to Config. `ResultToken` should consist of the following information: `ComplianceResourceType` (for example, `AWS::S3::Bucket`), `ComplianceResourceId` (for example, bucket name), `ComplianceType` (`COMPLIANT` or `NON_COMPLIANT`), and `OrderingTimestamp`.
4. Within the Config dashboard, we can go to **Rules**, then to **Add rule**, and select **Add Custom rule**. The exact screen names of these options may be different when you do.
5. Set the **Trigger type** to **Configuration changes** or **Periodic**.
6. Next, we can choose a remediation action or notification for our rule.
7. Click **Save**. Our rule should be listed along with the other rules on the **Rules** page.

See also

- You can read more about AWS Config here: `https://aws.amazon.com/config`.

9
Compliance with GuardDuty, Macie, and Inspector

Regularly checking for compliance within our account and being notified if anything is not compliant is an important step toward keeping our account secure. In this chapter, we will learn about some services within AWS that can help us in achieving security by checking compliance, with the help of additional intelligence and rules. We will learn about Amazon GuardDuty, Amazon Macie, and Amazon Inspector, which use machine learning and advanced algorithms to help us in checking for compliance.

This chapter will cover the following recipes:

- Setting up and using Amazon GuardDuty
- Aggregating findings from multiple accounts in GuardDuty
- Setting up and using Amazon Macie
- Setting up and using Amazon Inspector
- Creating a custom Inspector template

Technical requirements

We need a working AWS account.

Code files for this chapter are available at `https://github.com/PacktPublishing/AWS-Security-Cookbook/tree/master/Chapter09`.

Setting up and using Amazon GuardDuty

In this recipe, we will learn to set up and use Amazon GuardDuty. GuardDuty analyzes data from sources such as CloudTrail, VPC flow logs, and DNS logs, and uses machine learning, anomaly detection, and integrated threat intelligence to find malicious activities and unauthorized behavior. GuardDuty can be integrated with CloudWatch and SNS to raise alarms and send notifications. GuardDuty can also aggregate data from multiple accounts.

Getting ready

We need a working AWS account.

How to do it...

We can enable GuardDuty for our account as follows:

1. Go to the GuardDuty service in the console.
2. If we are logging in for the first time, we should see a **Get started** page. Click on **Get started**. We should now see the **Welcome to GuardDuty** screen, as shown in the following screenshot:

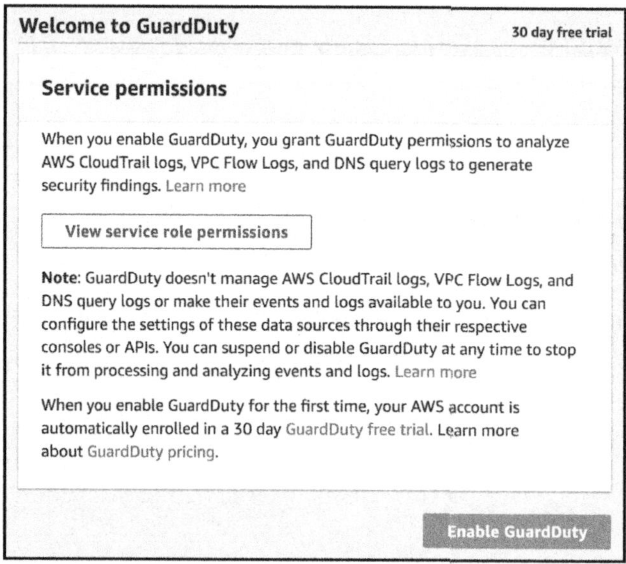

3. Click on **Enable GuardDuty**.

We can see GuardDuty in action using the sample events provided by AWS, as follows:

1. Click on **Settings** from the left sidebar in the GuardDuty dashboard.
2. Click on **Generate sample findings** under **Sample findings**.
3. Click on **Findings** from the left sidebar to go to the **Findings** page. New sample findings will now be generated:

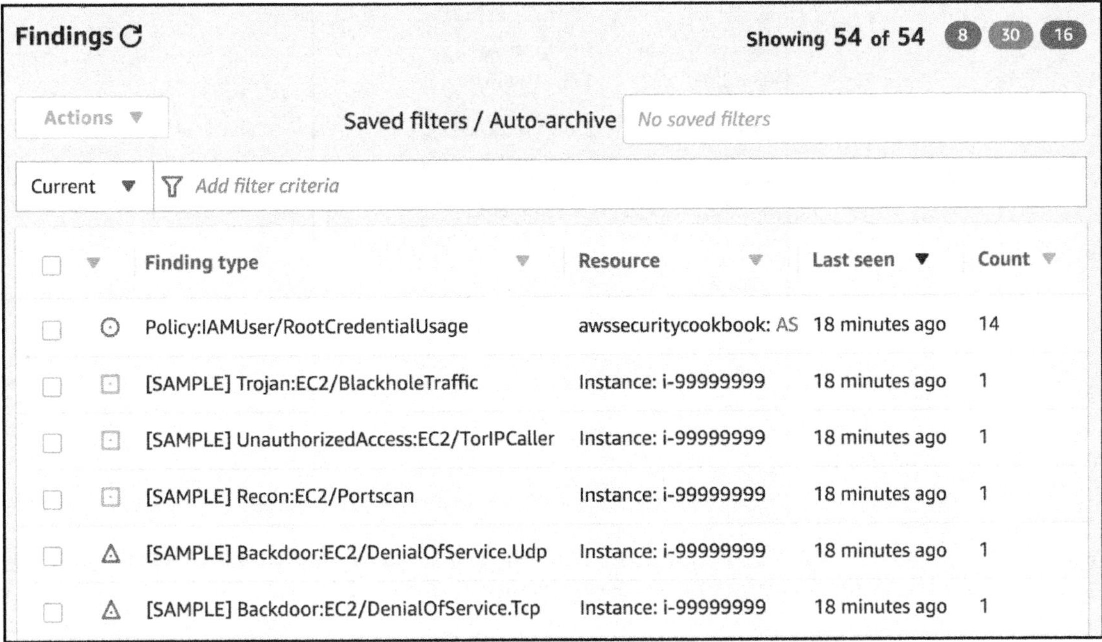

4. Click on any of the events to see additional information provided about that particular **Finding**:

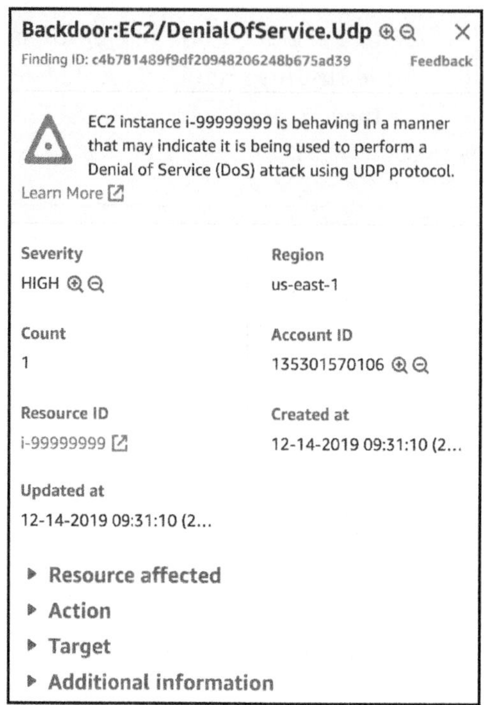

5. We can expand the **Resources affected**, **Action**, **Target**, and **Additional information** sections to understand more about the event.

We can whitelist and blacklist IPs in GuardDuty as follows:

1. Create and upload the following two files, one with trusted IPs and one with threat lists, and upload them into an S3 bucket:
    - `trusted-ips.txt`: A text file with the list of IPs and CIDR ranges we want to trust. Each IP or CIDR range should be on its own line.
    - `threat-lists.txt`: A text file with the list of IPs and CIDR ranges we want to add to the suspicious IP list. Each IP or CIDR range should be on its own line.

   I have used the sample IPs provided by Amazon in their documentation and called my bucket `myguarddutydemo`.

2. Click on **Lists** in the left sidebar.
3. Under **Trusted IP lists**, click on **Add a trusted IP list**.
4. In the pop-up screen named **Add a trusted IP list**, give a name to our list in the **List name** field. For **Location**, enter the S3 URL of our trusted IP list, which is `https://myguarddutydemo.s3.amazonaws.com/trusted-ips.txt` in my case. For **Format**, select **Plaintext**.
5. Click on **Add list**. We should see our list under **Trusted IP lists**.
6. Click the checkbox under the **Active** column against our list. We should see a success message, indicating that the list has been activated, and it may take five or more minutes for the changes to take effect.
7. Under **Threat lists**, click on **Add a threat list**. We should see a pop-up screen named **Add a threat list**.
8. Repeat the steps from *step 4* to *step 6*, but add a threat list instead of a trusted IP list. For the threat list, I will be using the location at `https://myguarddutydemo.s3.amazonaws.com/threat-list.txt`.

How it works...

We first enabled GuardDuty. GuardDuty asked us for the permissions for `ec2:DescribeInstances` and `ec2:DescribeImages`. An actual permissions file is available with the code files for reference. For testing purposes, we then generated sample findings from the GuardDuty console; GuardDuty generated 54 sample events in my case. GuardDuty events are categorized into three severity levels, from lowest to highest, denoted by blue, yellow, and red icons, where blue is the least severe and red is the most severe. Once we click on a finding, we will get additional information about the finding.

We whitelisted and blacklisted a few IP addresses by adding them to the trusted IP lists and threat lists, respectively. GuardDuty will not generate findings for IP addresses that are included in the trusted IP lists. This is done to avoid false alarms, especially from company IP addresses. However, we need to keep in mind that attacks can be internal too. Threat lists consist of known malicious IP addresses. The addresses we provide will be used along with the ones already available with AWS, based on their research and experiences.

We can add an IP or a CIDR range to the trusted IP lists and threat lists in various formats, such as plain text (an IP or a CIDR per line), **Structured Threat Information Expression (STIX)**, **Open Threat Exchange (OTX)** CSV, FireEye iSIGHT Threat Intelligence CSV, Proofpoint ET Intelligence Feed CSV, and AlienVault Reputation Feed. Currently, we can have up to 2,000 lines in a trusted IP list and 250,000 lines in a threat list.

There's more...

Let's go through some important concepts related to GuardDuty:

- GuardDuty can detect compromised EC2 instances by analyzing VPC flow logs—for example, GuardDuty can detect whether an instance is used in a **denial of service** (**DOS**) attack.
- GuardDuty can detect whether our instances have been used for cryptocurrency mining.
- GuardDuty can detect whether our credentials have been stolen by accessing malicious IPs, using EC2 instance profiles outside of EC2, and so on.
- We can aggregate GuardDuty findings across different accounts into one account. We will discuss this in the *Aggregating findings from multiple accounts in GuardDuty* recipe.
- We can export GuardDuty findings across different accounts and regions to an Amazon S3 bucket to simplify the aggregation of all the findings. This is a new feature and is different from aggregating findings across different accounts into one account.
- We can use CloudWatch and SNS to monitor GuardDuty findings and send notifications.
- GuardDuty pricing is based on the amount of data analyzed:
    - For VPC flow log and DNS log analysis, GuardDuty charges us based on the size of the data analyzed.
    - For CloudTrail events, GuardDuty charges us based on the number of events analyzed.

The steps to set up CloudWatch to monitor our findings from GuardDuty can be summarized as follows:

1. Go to the CloudWatch service in the console.
2. Click on **Rules** under **Events** from the left sidebar and to go to the **Rules** page.
3. Click on **Create rule** to go to the **Create rule** page.
4. Under the **Event Source** section, do the following:
    1. Select **Event Pattern**.
    2. Select **Service Name** as **GuardDuty**.
    3. Select **Event Type** as **GuardDuty Finding**.

5. Under **Targets**, do the following:
    1. Click on **Add target**.
    2. Select **SNS topic** from the dropdown.
    3. Select an **SNS topic**. You can create an SNS topic by following the *Creating an SNS topic to send email* recipe in `Chapter 8`, *Monitoring with CloudWatch, CloudTrail, and Config*.
6. Scroll down and click on **Configure details**.
7. In the **Configure rule details** page, provide a **Name** and **Description** for our rule. Click **Create rule**.
8. We can configure and modify the frequency with which GuardDuty updates **CloudWatch Events** (**CWE**) and S3 using the **Findings export options** in the GuardDuty **Settings** page:

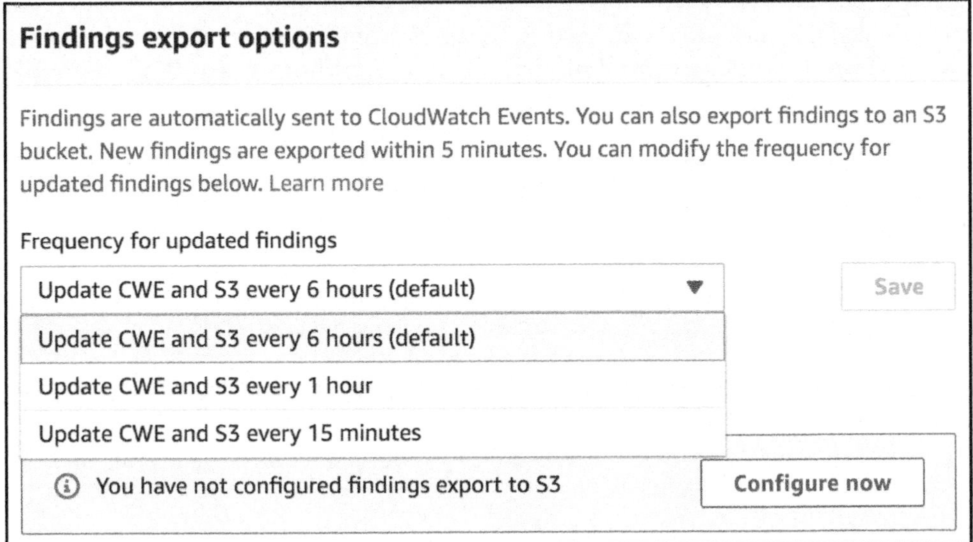

As we have not yet configured findings to export to S3, we are provided with an option to configure this. This is a new feature that was introduced by AWS in 2019.

See also

- For more details on using CloudWatch Events, refer to the *Working with CloudWatch events* recipe in `Chapter 8`, *Monitoring with CloudWatch, CloudTrail, and Config*.
- You can read more about creating a threat intel set for GuardDuty at `https://docs.aws.amazon.com/guardduty/latest/ug/create-threat-intel-set.html`.

Aggregating findings from multiple accounts in GuardDuty

In this recipe, we will configure GuardDuty to aggregate findings from multiple AWS accounts into a single account. Aggregating findings from multiple accounts into a single dedicated account provides a central place to query the findings from all our accounts. We can also make configuration changes in one place for all the accounts.

Getting ready

We need two working AWS accounts. We will call them the main account and the member account. The main account will aggregate logs from the member account and any other accounts we add later.

Log in to the member account and note down its account number. The account number can be found in the **Support Center**, as you saw in the *Getting ready* section of the *Cross-account CloudTrail logging* recipe in `Chapter 8`, *Monitoring with CloudWatch, CloudTrail, and Config*.

How to do it...

We can configure GuardDuty to aggregate the findings from member accounts as follows:

1. Go to the GuardDuty service in the main account console.
2. Click on **Accounts** from the left sidebar.
3. Click on **Add accounts**.

4. Enter the **Account ID** and **Email address** for the member account:

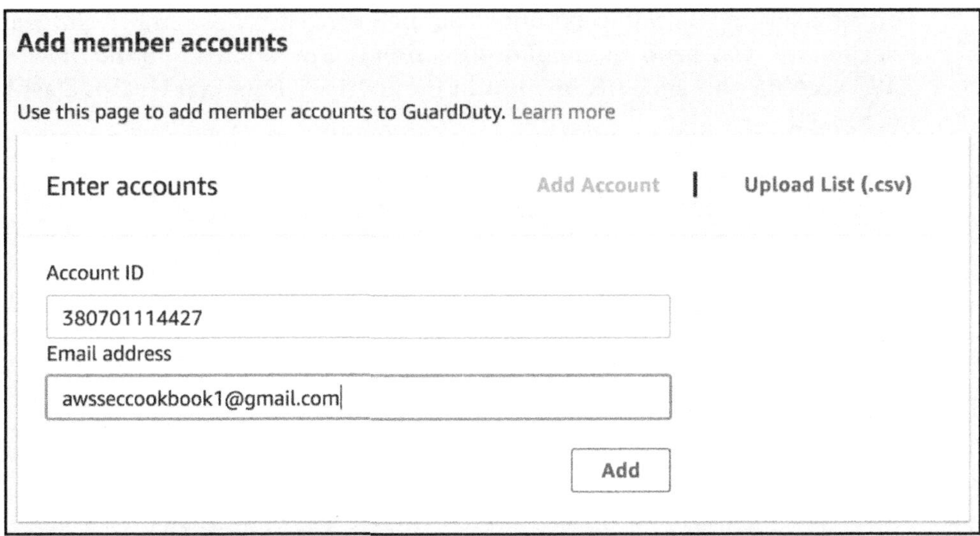

5. Click on **Add**. The account details will be shown under **Accounts to be added**.
6. Click **Next**. We should see our account under the **Accounts** page. The **Status** field will have a link to **Invite** the account we just added:

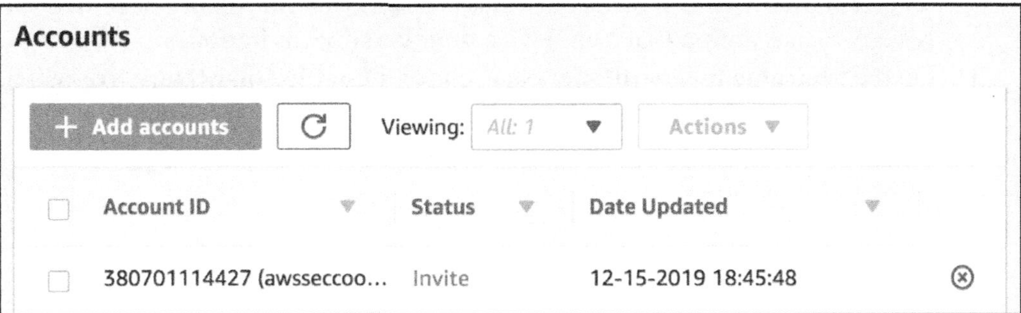

7. Click on **Invite** under the **Status** column. We should get a pop-up screen to add an optional message and email notification to the admin of the other account. If you are handling both the accounts, you may leave this field empty and leave the selection for **Also send an email notification to the root user on the invitee's AWS account and generate an alert in the invitee's Personal Health Dashboard** unchecked:

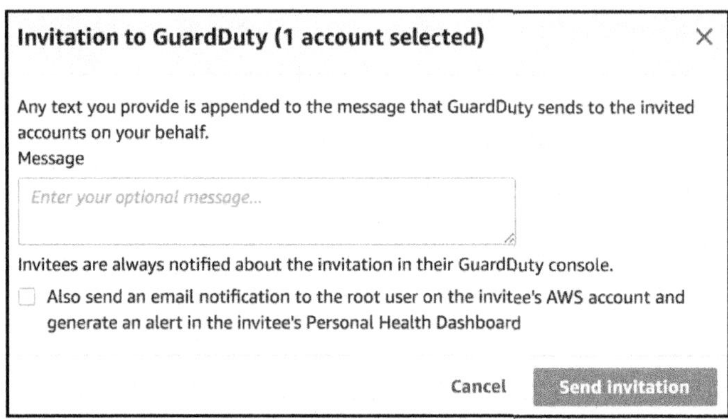

8. Click on **Send invitation**. The **Status** of our account should change to **Invited**.
9. Go to the GuardDuty service in the member console.
10. If we are logging in for the first time, we will get a **Getting started** page. Click on **Get started**. We will be taken to the **Welcome to GuardDuty** page. We should see a message stating that **You have a membership invitation**.
11. On the **Welcome to GuardDuty** page, click on **Enable GuardDuty**. We will be taken to the **Invitations** page:

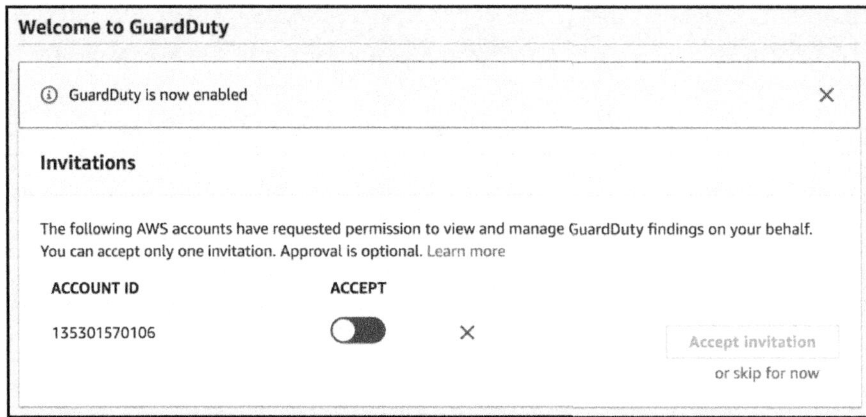

You can also go to the **Invitations** page by clicking on **Invitations** from the left sidebar.

12. Click on the **ACCEPT** button and then click on **Accept invitation**.
13. Click on **Settings** from the left sidebar to go to the **Settings** page and click on **Generate sample findings**.
14. Go to the GuardDuty dashboard in the main account and verify the findings. We should be able to see the findings from our member account.

How it works...

First, we logged in to the main account, which is the account that will aggregate all GuardDuty findings. We then invited a member account. We had already noted down the account ID, and so it should have known the root email address of this account.

We then logged in to our member account and accepted the invitation. After that, we generated sample findings from the member account. Finally, we logged back into our main account and verified that the findings from the member account were now present in the main account.

There's more...

At the time of writing, AWS shows a notification regarding the new **Export findings to an S3 bucket** feature.

New feature: Exporting findings to an S3 bucket
You can now export findings to Amazon S3 to simplify aggregation of all GuardDuty findings across all accounts and regions. In addition to pushing findings out through AWS CloudWatch Events, this gives customers another option for the aggregation and retention of GuardDuty findings across accounts and regions using S3. Learn more

We can now export findings across accounts and regions to an S3 bucket to simplify the aggregation of the findings.

See also

- You can read more about the export findings feature in GuardDuty at `https://docs.aws.amazon.com/guardduty/latest/ug/guardduty_exportfindings.html`.

Setting up and using Amazon Macie

In this recipe, we will learn how to set up and use Amazon Macie. Macie is a machine-learning-powered service in AWS and is used primarily to discover, classify, and protect sensitive data. Macie can analyze data in S3 buckets to find sensitive information, such as **personally identifiable information** (**PII**), API keys, source code, and so on, and then classify them into different security levels. Macie can be used with CloudWatch to raise alarms and send notifications. Macie can also analyze API calls from CloudTrail to detect anomalies.

Getting ready

We need an S3 bucket. The bucket should be in the same region in which we configure Macie. I have created a bucket named `aws-sec-cb-macie-demo` in the `us-east-1` region.

Our S3 bucket should have the following fake sensitive data:

- `Main.java`, which is a Java code file
- `for-macie-demo-only-do-not-use.pem`, which is a key-value pair private file created for this demo

These two files are available with the code files. You may add additional files with fake sensitive data and experiment.

How to do it...

We can configure Macie to discover and classify risks in an S3 bucket as follows:

1. Go to the Macie service in the console.
2. If we are using Macie for the first time, we should see a **Getting Started** page. Click on **Get started**. We should see a screen with options to select the region, view service role permissions, and enable Macie.

3. Select the region as **US East (N. Virginia)** and click **Enable Macie**. We will then be taken to the Macie dashboard:

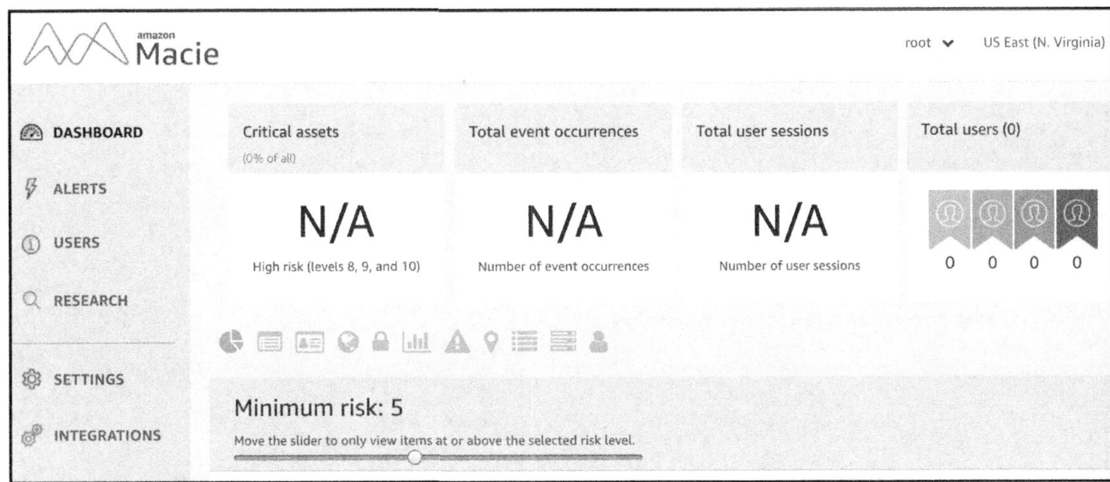

4. Click on **INTEGRATIONS** on the left sidebar. This will show us the list of resources and accounts currently integrated with Macie:

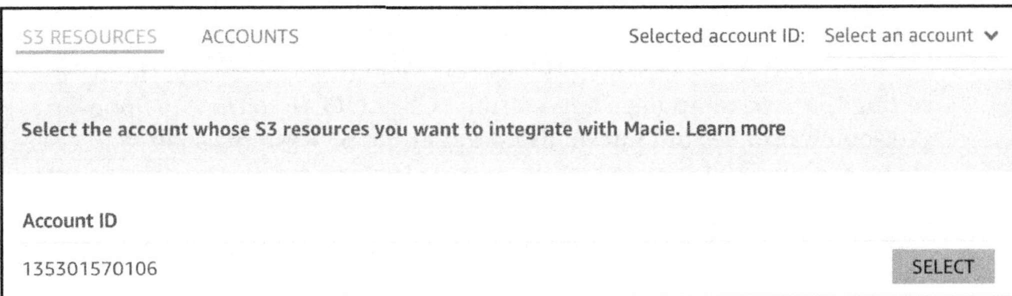

5. Click the **SELECT** button next to our **Account ID**, which is `135301570106` in my case. We should see the following screen:

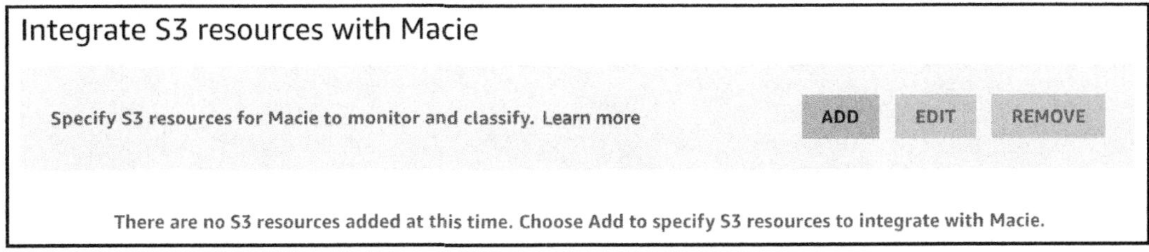

6. Click on **ADD**. Select the bucket we created in the *Getting ready* section. Click on **ADD** to finish adding the bucket. We should see a pop-up page for configuring the classification of existing objects:

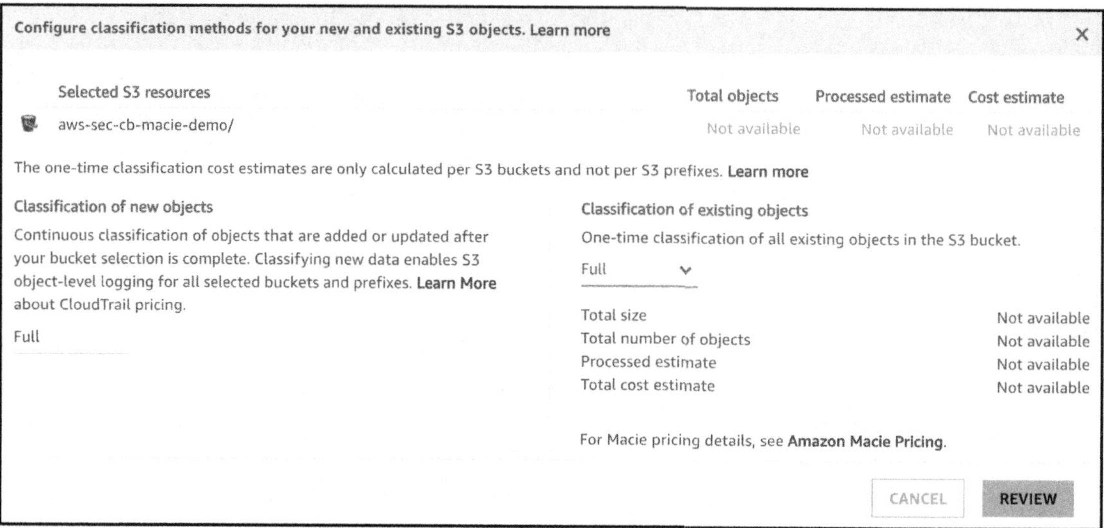

7. For **Classification of existing objects**, select **Full**. Click **REVIEW**. We should see a summary page with options to start classification.
8. Click on **START CLASSIFICATION**. We should see a message stating that our settings have been updated successfully. Click **DONE** to close the pop-up screen. We should now see our bucket listed under the **S3 Resources** tab.
9. Go back to the dashboard by clicking on **DASHBOARD** from the left sidebar and wait for the results of the S3 classification to show. It may take some time, maybe up to an hour, for the results to show in the dashboard, especially for the S3 content classification results. The top part of the dashboard page provides general statistics:

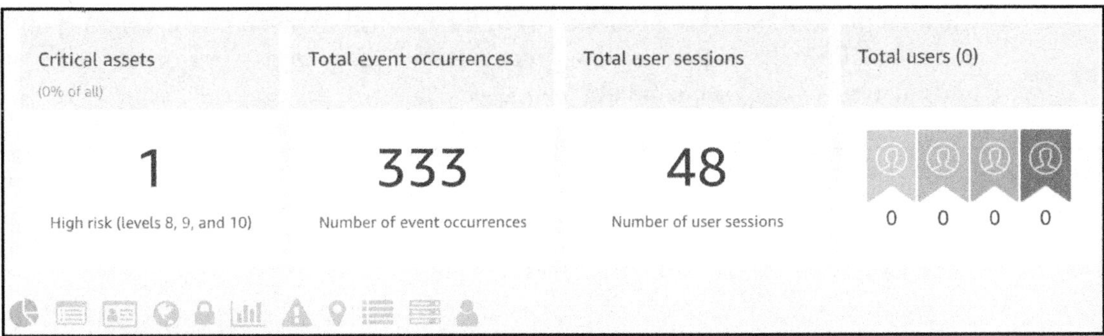

On the lower part of the page, we can see the S3 classification results in chart form:

Minimum risk: 5

Move the slider to only view items at or above the selected risk level.

S3 objects for selected time range - minRisk: (5)

The following graph shows S3 objects grouped into top 20 matching themes for the selected time range. To further investigate your S3 objects, double-click sections of the graph or color chart. **Learn more**

All Data
Range: 0 - 6 months ago
Range: beyond 6 months ago
RSA Private Key
source_code/java

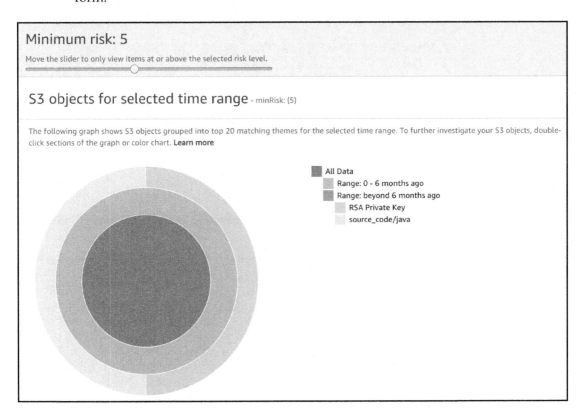

We can use the slider for **Minimum risk** to set a minimum risk level for the search. I have used **5**, which is the default.

10. Click on the number of issues (here, **1**) in the **Critical assets** box. This should take us to the **RESEARCH** page with a prepopulated query of `dlp_risk:[8 TO *]` and the type of data set as **S3 objects**:

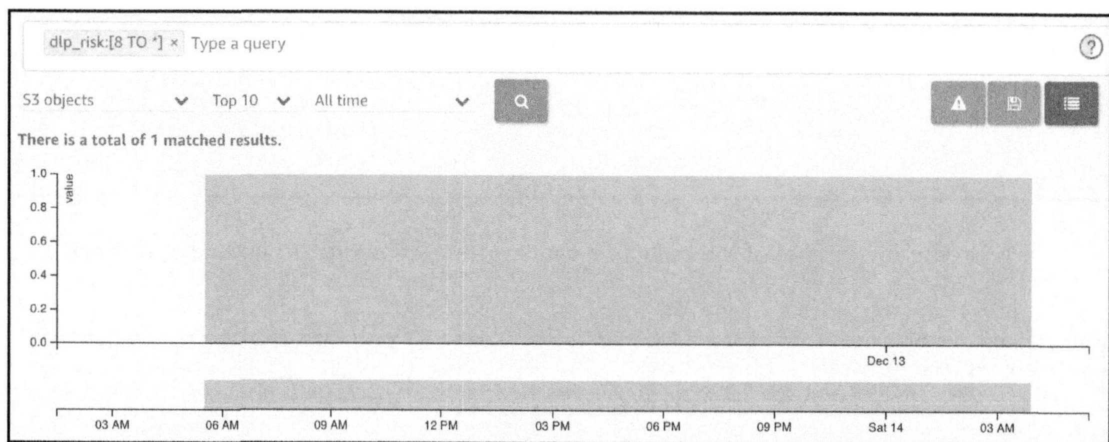

11. Scroll down to the bottom of the page and verify the high-risk items:

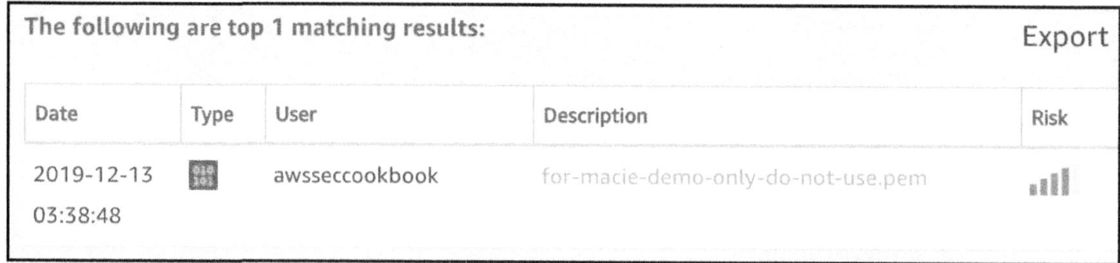

The following are top 1 matching results: Export

Date	Type	User	Description	Risk
2019-12-13 03:38:48		awsseccookbook	for-macie-demo-only-do-not-use.pem	

We can also reach the **RESEARCH** page by clicking on **RESEARCH** from the left sidebar and then run advanced queries to filter out the results we want.

12. Expand the event for additional information about the event, which includes the **Object activity** property. By clicking on the **Search CloudTrail activity** link next to the **Object activity** property, we can get the CloudTrail activity related to this object.

13. Go back to the dashboard and click on the number of events under the **Total event occurrences** box. This will take us to the **RESEARCH** page with a prepopulated query of * and the type of data listed as **CloudTrail data**:

Apart from **S3 object** (*step 10*) and **CloudTrail data** (*step 13*), we can also select **S3 bucket properties** in the query's type dropdown.

14. Go back to the dashboard and click on **ALERTS** in the left sidebar. We can see the alerts raised along with their threat levels, such as **MED** for medium, **CRIT** for critical, and so on:

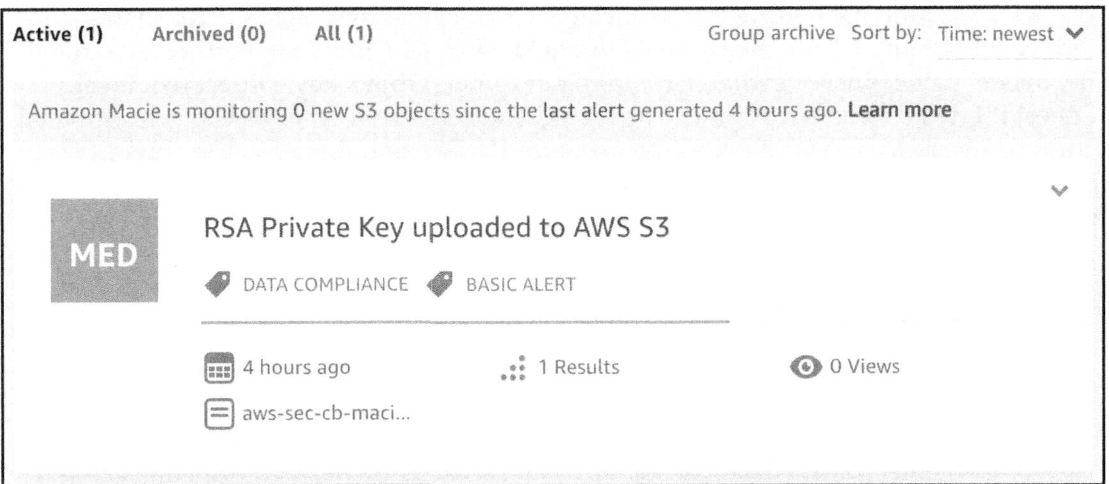

Using the dropdown button on the top-right corner of the alert, we can archive an alert (**Archive**), whitelist the bucket for that alert type (**Whitelist bucket**), or disable the alert for this type (**Edit basic alert**).

How it works...

Macie can be used to analyze S3 buckets and CloudTrail logs. In this recipe, we configured Macie to analyze and classify data in an S3 bucket. We enabled Macie in the `us-east-1` region, as we had created the S3 bucket in the `us-east-1` region. At the time of writing, Macie is available only in US East (North Virginia) and US West (Oregon). While enabling this, Macie also asked for some permissions, mostly permissions for CloudTrail and S3 actions. We went to the **INTEGRATIONS** page and added our S3 bucket. We configured the option to classify the existing objects as well. The configuration page also shows us the tentative cost for analyzing the contents of the bucket. The calculations may not be present or accurate for newly created buckets.

After integrating the S3 bucket, we could see the risks within our dashboard at a certain time. We clicked on **Critical assets** and **Total event occurrences** from the top of the dashboard, which took us to the **RESEARCH** page with a prepopulated query. We could also have clicked on **Total user sessions**. Macie assigns a risk value of between 1 and 10 for the risks it detects. Macie queries within the **RESEARCH** tab, following the Apache Lucene query parser syntax. We can then run advanced queries to filter out the results we want in the **RESEARCH** tab.

We saw the additional information available for an event of the S3 object type in the recipe. This additional information includes fields such as **Type**, **Last modified**, **Account ID**, **Bucket name**, **Bucket owner**, **Path prefix or folder**, **Object key**, **Object risk level**, **Object PII details**, and so on. Similarly, for a CloudTrail event type, we can get additional information, such as **Type**, **Timestamp**, **Account ID**, **Macie unique ID**, **User identity type**, **Source ARN**, **Event type**, **Count of unique event names**, **Event name by error code**, **Error code**, **Event source**, and so on.

There's more...

Let's go through some important concepts related to Macie:

- Macie can be used within enterprises for a variety of use cases. Macie can detect whether sensitive data or source code has been downloaded from unusual IP addresses. Macie can detect which users are causing the most high-risk events. Macie can group events by location and help us detect any activity from unknown locations. Macie can also give a high-level breakdown of the type of CloudTrail events within our account. If we see any unexpected calls, we can drill down to find out the root cause.

- Both Macie and GuardDuty have an overlap of functionalities related to analyzing API calls. Unlike GuardDuty, the focus of Macie is more on access patterns, such as uploading or downloading more data than is normally done. In general, it is more preferable to use Macie alongside GuardDuty for better protection.
- Based on the activity of API calls, IAM users (or roles) in Macie are categorized as follows:
    - **Platinum**: Has a history of making high-risk API calls, probably an administrator or root user
    - **Gold**: Has a history of making infrastructure-related API calls, probably a power user running EC2 instances
    - **Silver**: Has a history of issuing high quantities of medium-risk API calls, such as `Describe*` and `List*` operations
    - **Bronze**: Has a history of lower quantities of `Describe*` and `List*` API calls
- Platinum and Gold users need to be monitored closely for signs of account compromise.
- Macie can be used alongside CloudWatch for raising alarms and sending notifications.
- Macie can aggregate data from multiple accounts. We can add additional accounts from the **ACCOUNTS** tab in the **INTEGRATIONS** page after setting up the required permissions as mentioned.
- Macie currently charges us for S3 content classification and CloudTrail event processing.

The steps to configure notifications for Macie alerts with CloudWatch and SNS can be summarized as follows:

1. Go to the CloudWatch dashboard.
2. Click on **Rules** under **Events** to go to the **Rules page**.
3. Click on **Create rule** to go to the **Create rule page**.
4. Under the **Event Source** section, do the following:
    1. Select **Event Pattern**.
    2. Select the **Service Name** as **Macie**.
    3. Select the **Event Type** as **Macie Alert**.

5. Under **Targets**, do the following:
    1. Click on **Add target**.
    2. Select **SNS topic** from the dropdown.
    3. Select an SNS topic. You can create an SNS topic by following the *Creating an SNS topic to send email* recipe in `Chapter 8`, *Monitoring with CloudWatch, CloudTrail, and Config*.
6. Scroll down and click on **Configure details**.
7. In the **Configure rule details** page, provide a **Name** and **Description** for our rule. Click **Create rule**.

For more details on using CloudWatch Events, refer to the *Working with CloudWatch events* recipe in `Chapter 8`, *Monitoring with CloudWatch, CloudTrail, and Config*.

See also

- You can read more about Macie research queries at `https://docs.aws.amazon.com/macie/latest/userguide/macie-research.html`.

Setting up and using Amazon Inspector

In this recipe, we will learn how to set up and use AWS Inspector. Inspector is a service that performs automated security assessments to find vulnerabilities or deviations from standard practices for applications deployed on AWS. We can check Inspector's findings directly in the console or from the detailed assessment report provided by Inspector.

Getting ready

Create an EC2 instance in the default VPC, within a public subnet within the VPC, using the default VPC security. You can follow the *Launching an EC2 instance into VPC* recipe in `Chapter 6`, *Working with EC2 Instances*.

How to do it...

We can set up Inspector as follows:

1. Go to the Inspector service in the console.
2. If we are logging in for the first time, we should see a **Get started** page. Click on **Get started**.
3. In the **Welcome to Amazon Inspector** page, under the **Assessment Setup** section, select **Network Assessments** and **Host Assessments**. Click on **Run weekly (Recommended)**. This will show us the following confirmation dialogue:

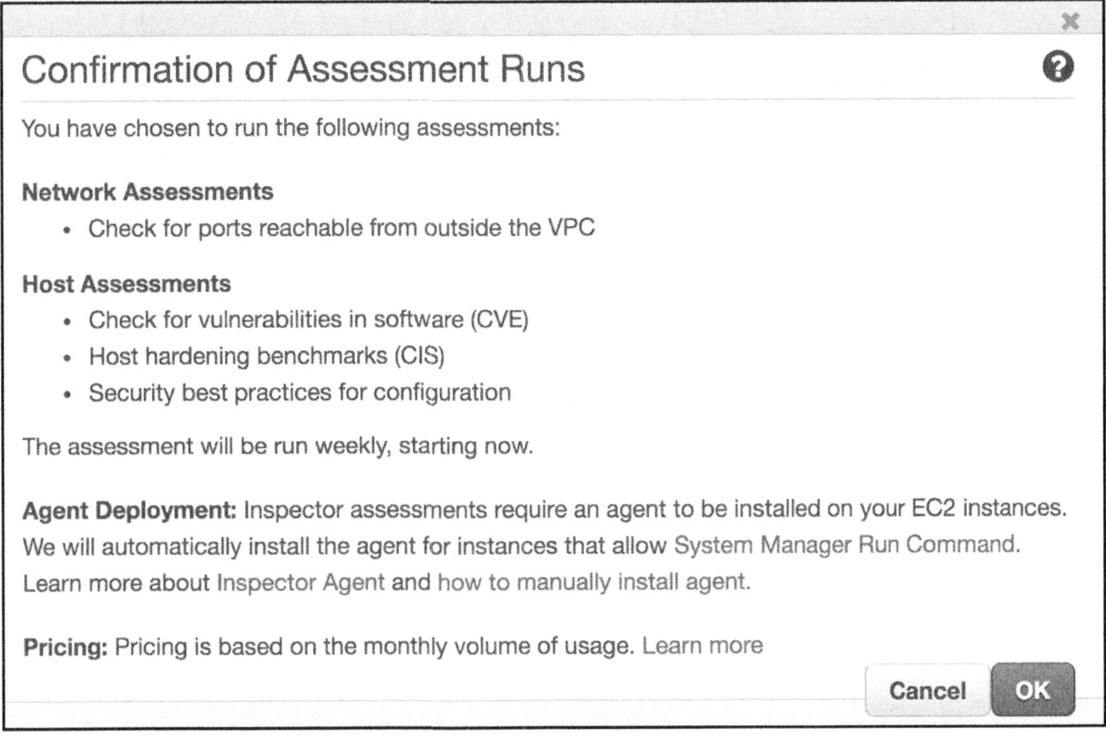

Confirmation of Assessment Runs
You have chosen to run the following assessments:
Network Assessments
Check for ports reachable from outside the VPC
Host Assessments
Check for vulnerabilities in software (CVE)
Host hardening benchmarks (CIS)
Security best practices for configuration
The assessment will be run weekly, starting now.
Agent Deployment: Inspector assessments require an agent to be installed on your EC2 instances. We will automatically install the agent for instances that allow System Manager Run Command. Learn more about Inspector Agent and how to manually install agent.
Pricing: Pricing is based on the monthly volume of usage. Learn more
Cancel
OK

4. Click on **OK**. We should see the following success message:

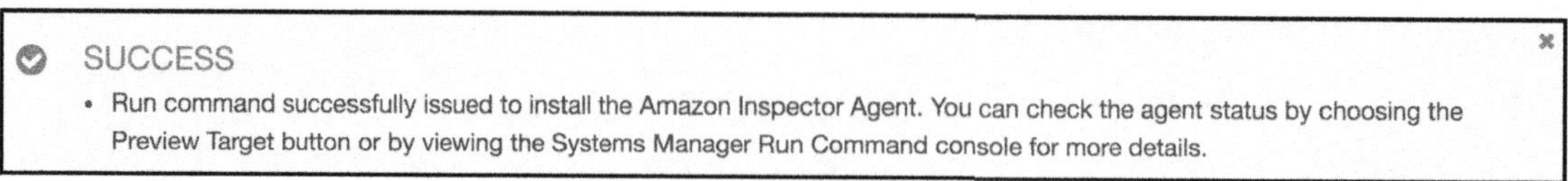

SUCCESS
Run command successfully issued to install the Amazon Inspector Agent. You can check the agent status by choosing the Preview Target button or by viewing the Systems Manager Run Command console for more details.

5. Click on **Dashboard** from the left sidebar. Once the assessment run is completed, we should see the status of the assessment in the dashboard:

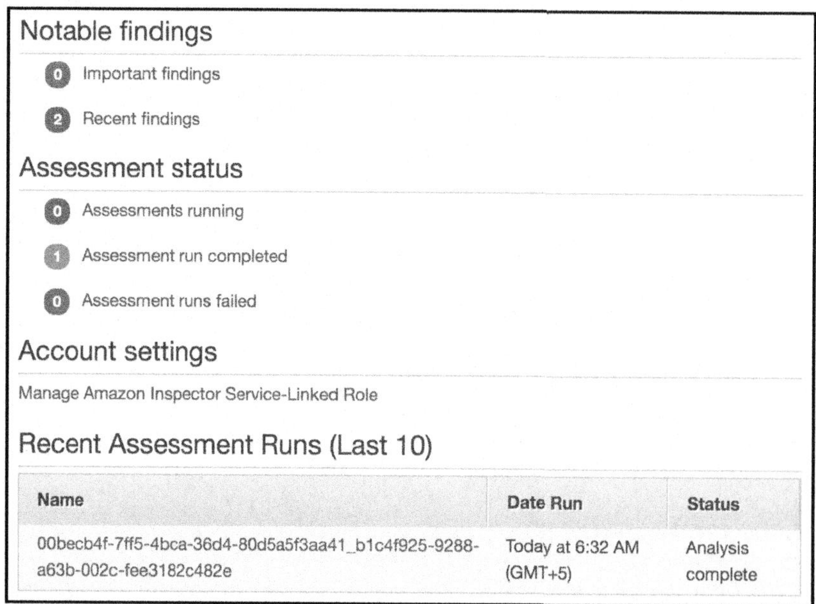

6. Click on the hyperlink under **Name** in the **Recent Assessment Runs** box to see the result of our assessment:

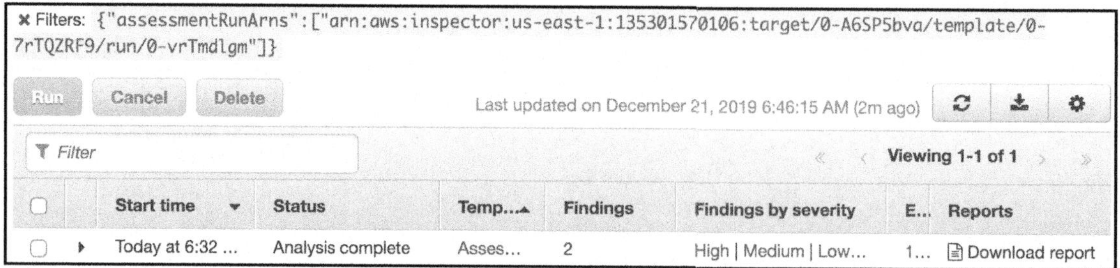

7. Click on the hyperlink (here, there are two) under the **Findings** column to see the findings:

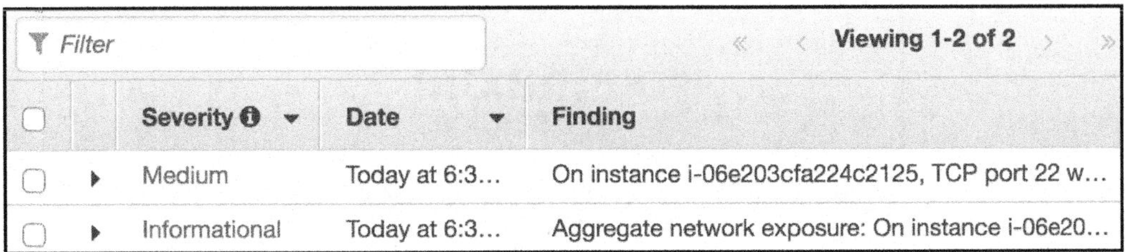

8. We can also click on the hyperlinks specific to a particular severity under the findings by **Severity** column to see only those findings that belong to a particular severity level.
9. Click on the **Download report** hyperlink under the **Reports** column. We should get the following pop-up screen:

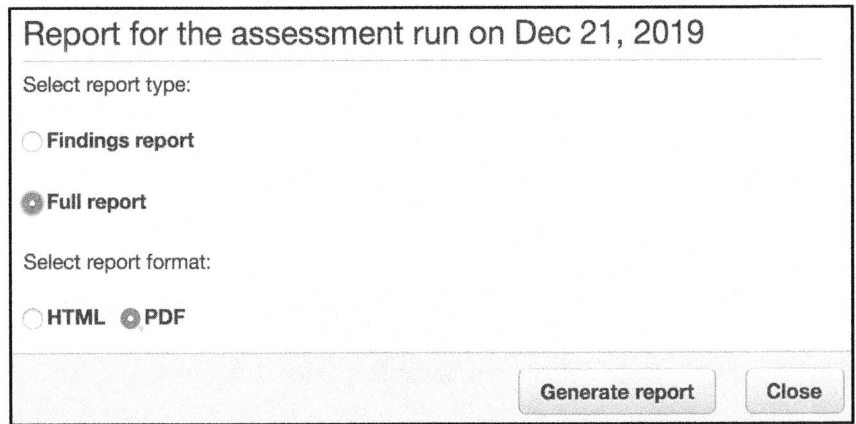

10. Select **Full report**, select **PDF,** and click **Generate report**. We should get a detailed report PDF with a front page that looks like the following screenshot:

Amazon Inspector - Assessment Report

Full Report

Report generated on 2019-12-21 at 01:24:48 UTC

Assessment Template: Assessment-Template-Default-All-Rules

Assessment Run start: 2019-12-21 at 01:02:41 UTC
Assessment Run end: 2019-12-21 at 01:06:34 UTC

The size of the report will vary based on the number of instances we are assessing in your account.

How it works...

While enabling the Inspector, we selected the frequency of inspection as weekly. We can also run it once manually. We selected the types of inspection on EC2 instances as both network assessments and host assessments. With network assessments, AWS performs a network configuration analysis to check for the ports that are reachable from outside the VPC. With network assessments, installing an agent is optional; however, with the agent, AWS will also find the processes that are reachable on the ports.

With host assessments, AWS checks for **common vulnerabilities and exposures** (**CVE**), performs host hardening (CIS benchmarks), and implements other security best practices. With host assessments, we need to install the Inspector agent on the EC2 machines. AWS will automatically install the agent for instances as long as the instances allow Systems Manager Run Command. We learned about Systems Manager briefly in the *Storing sensitive data with Systems Manager Parameter Store* recipe in `Chapter 6`, *Working with EC2 Instances*.

To install Inspector agents on an EC2 machine, the EC2 instances should have SSM Agent installed and there should be an IAM role that permits the Run Command. EC2 Windows instances and Amazon Linux instances come with SSM Agent installed.

There's more...

In the recipe, we scheduled Inspector to run checks weekly. We can manually run checks as follows:

1. Go to the **Assessment templates** page.
2. Select our assessment template.
3. Click **Run**.

The steps to configure notifications for Inspector using CloudWatch and SNS can be summarized as follows:

1. Go to the CloudWatch service in the console.
2. Click on **Rules** under **Events** to go to the **Rules** page.

From the **Assessment templates** page of Inspector, we can click on **Create Assessment Events** to directly go to the **CloudWatch Rules** page.

3. Click on **Create rule** to go to the **Create rule** page.
4. Under the **Event Source** section, do the following:
    1. Select **Event Pattern**.
    2. For **Service Name**, select **Inspector**.
    3. **For Event Type**, select **All Events**.
5. Under **Targets**, do the following:
    1. Click on **Add target**.
    2. Select **SNS topic** from the dropdown.
    3. Select an SNS topic. You can create an SNS topic by following the *Creating an SNS topic to send email* recipe in `Chapter 8`, *Monitoring with CloudWatch, CloudTrail, and Config*.
6. Scroll down and click on **Configure details**.
7. In the **Configure rule details** page, provide a **Name** and **Description** for our rule. Click **Create rule**.

For more details on using CloudWatch Events, refer to the *Working with CloudWatch events* recipe in `Chapter 8`, *Monitoring with CloudWatch, CloudTrail, and Config*.

AWS Inspector is priced as follows: Network assessments are charged based on the monthly volume of instance assessments. Host assessments are charged based on the monthly volume of agent assessments. The more we use it, the more the cost per instance assessment is reduced. Currently, AWS also provides a free trial for 90 days, where the first 250 instance assessments are not charged.

See also

- You can read more about Amazon Inspector assessment targets at `https://docs.aws.amazon.com/inspector/latest/userguide/inspector_applications.html#create_application_via_console`.

Creating a custom Inspector template

In this recipe, we will learn how to create a new assessment template with a custom assessment target for EC2 instances that have a particular tag. In the previous recipe, we created an assessment template with an assessment target for all EC2 instances in our AWS account.

Getting ready

Create an EC2 instance in the default VPC within a public subnet within the VPC using the **default** VPC security group. You can follow the *Launching an EC2 instance into VPC* recipe in `Chapter 6`, *Working with EC2 Instances*.

Add a tag with the **Key** as `Environment` and **Value** as `Prod` for the EC2 instances we need to assess:

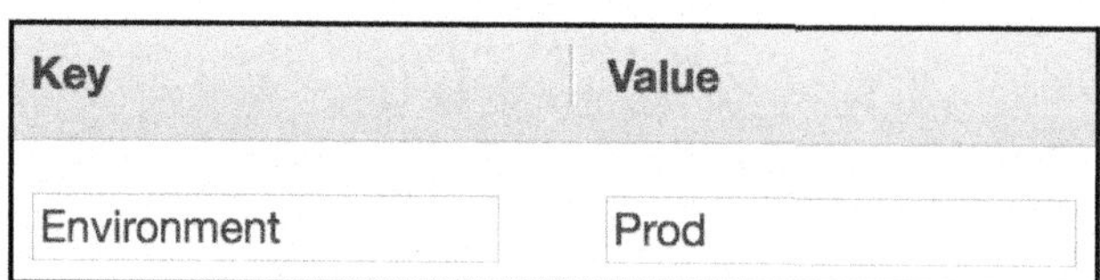

You may use any **Key** and **Value** for the tag and use it accordingly within the following steps. You can also perform an assessment on multiple tags.

Create an SNS topic for Inspector notifications by going through the *Creating an SNS topic to send email* recipe in `Chapter 8`, *Monitoring with CloudWatch, CloudTrail and Config*, but making the following changes while creating the topic:

1. Give a **Name** and **Description** that is specific to our topic. I have given the **Name** as `MyInspectorEmailTopic` and **Description** as `My Email Topic for Inspector`.
2. Click and expand the **Access policy - optional** section.
3. For **Choose method**, select **Basic**.
4. For **Define who can publish messages to the topic**, select **Only the specified AWS accounts**. Enter the value as `arn:aws:iam::316112463485:root`. For **Define who can subscribe to this topic**, select **Only the specified AWS accounts**. Enter the value as `arn:aws:iam::316112463485:root`.

I have provided the ARN that is specific to US East (N. Virginia). To see the complete list of ARNs specific to each region, you can refer to the AWS documentation at `https://docs.aws.amazon.com/inspector/latest/userguide/inspector_assessments.html#sns-topic`.

Lastly, create a subscription and confirm the subscription.

How to do it...

We can create an assessment target as follows:

1. Go to the Inspector service in the console.

If you are logging in for the first time and see a **Get started** page, refer to the *Setting up and using Amazon Inspector* recipe.

2. Click **Assessment targets** from the left sidebar.
3. In the **Amazon Inspector - Assessment Targets** page, click **Create**.
4. For **All Instances**, uncheck **Include all EC2 instances in this AWS account and region**.

5. For **Use Tags**, click on **Add a new key** and select the **Key** and **Value** we created for our EC2 instance in the *Getting ready* section. Our assessment target creation screen should look like the following screenshot:

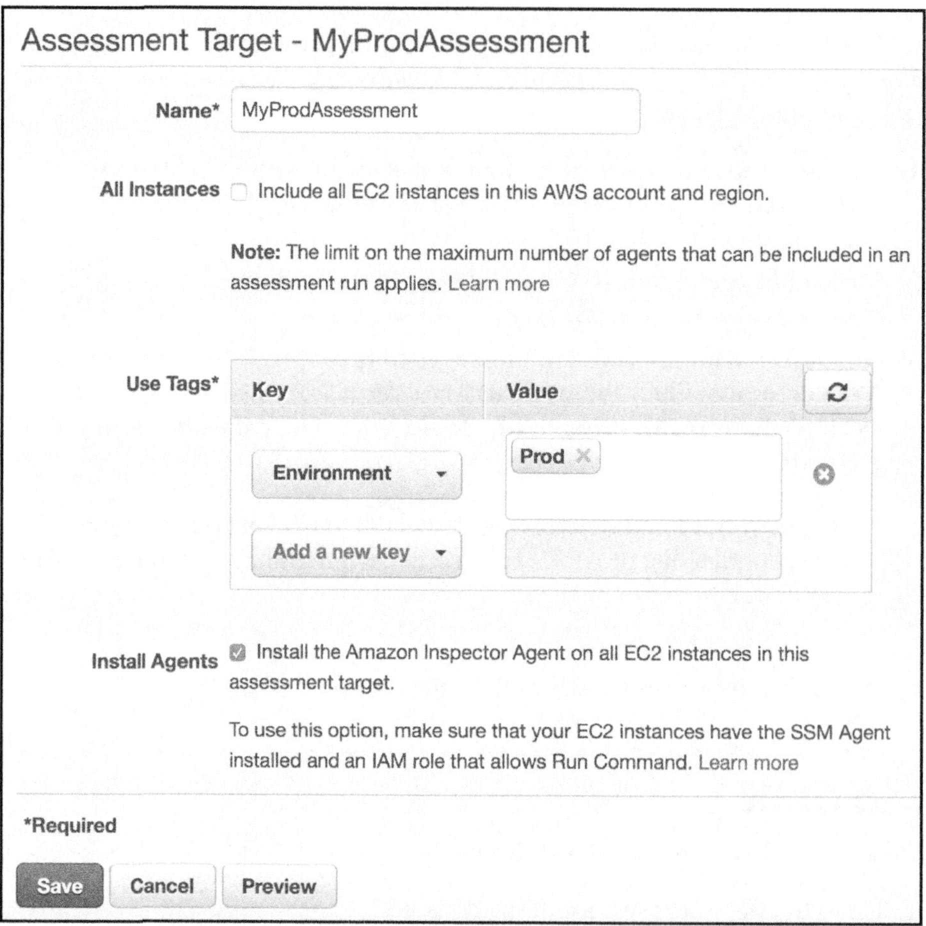

6. Click on **Preview**.
7. In the **Resources for assessment target** screen, verify the instances and click **OK**.
8. Click on **Save**.

We can create an assessment template as follows:

1. From the Inspector service console, click on **Assessment templates** from the left sidebar.
2. Click **Create**.

3. Provide a **Name**.
4. For **Target name**, select the target we created in the previous section:

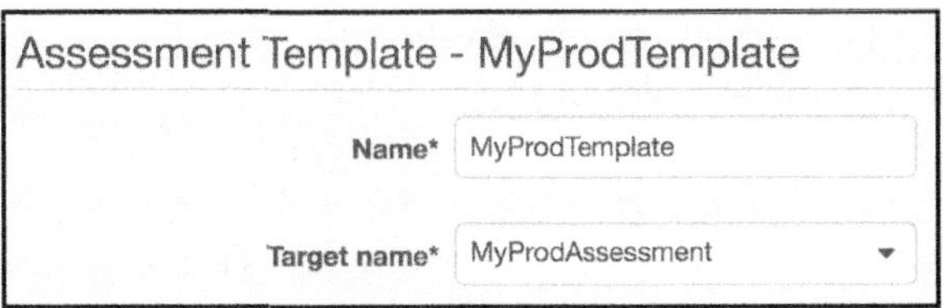

5. Under **Rules packages**, select the following rules: **Network Reachability-1.1**, **Security Best Practices-1.0**, **Common Vulnerabilities and Exposures-1.1**, and **CIS Operating System Security Configuration Benchmarks-1.0**.
6. Leave the **Duration** as **1 Hour**, which is the default:

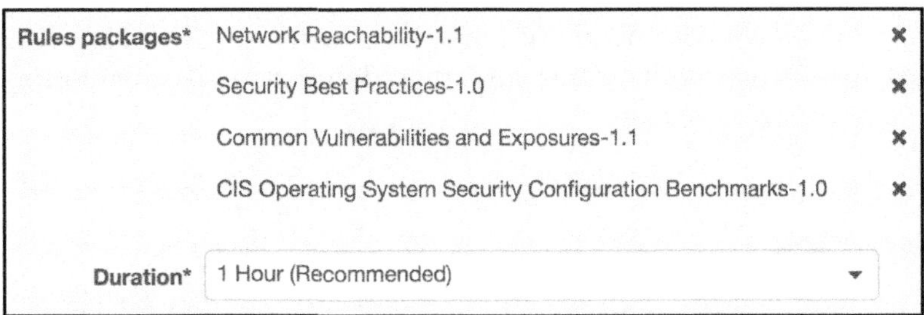

7. For **SNS Topics**, select the SNS topic we created in the *Getting ready* section. Leave the following auto-populated events as is: **Run started**, **Run finished**, **Run state changed**, and **Finding reported**:

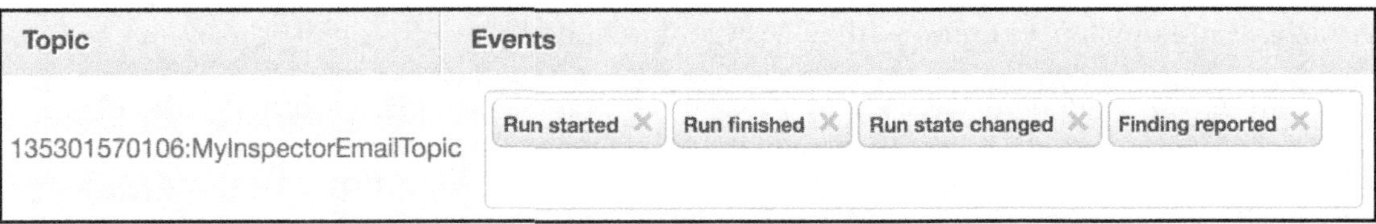

8. For **Tags**, select the **Key** and **Value** we gave for the EC2 instance that we created in the *Getting ready* section.
9. Leave the value for **Attributes added to findings** empty.
10. Set **Assessment Schedule** to **Set up recurring assessment runs once every 7 days**.

11. Click on **Create**.
12. We can either wait for the template to run as per its schedule or we can manually trigger a run as follows:
    1. Go to the **Assessment templates** page.
    2. Select our template.
    3. Click on **Run**.

    In our case, we should see a response similar to the previous recipe if we have only the one EC2 instance we used for the recipe:

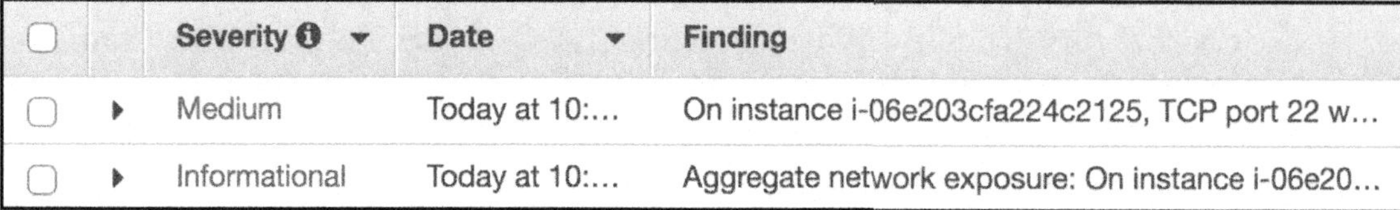

		Severity	Date	Finding
		Medium	Today at 10:...	On instance i-06e203cfa224c2125, TCP port 22 w...
		Informational	Today at 10:...	Aggregate network exposure: On instance i-06e20...

In real-world use cases, we will mostly run the assessment for targeted systems, such as production systems. If cost is not a constraint, then doing an assessment for all instances can make our account more secure.

How it works...

In this recipe, we first created an assessment target. While creating the target, we unchecked **Include all EC2 instances in this AWS account and region** to not target all instances within our account. We then selected the tag of our EC2 instance. We asked AWS to install the Inspector in all the EC2 machines in this target. To install Inspector agents within an EC2 machine, the EC2 instances should have SSM Agent installed and there should be an IAM role that permits the Run Command. EC2 Windows instances and Amazon Linux instances come with SSM Agent installed.

In addition, we created an assessment template with the assessment target we already selected. We selected all of the rules available, which are **Network Reachability-1.1**, **Security Best Practices-1.0**, **Common Vulnerabilities and Exposures-1.1**, and **CIS Operating System Security Configuration Benchmarks-1.0**. We set the duration as 1 hour, which is the AWS recommendation. Other available options are **15 minutes**, **8 hours**, **12 hours**, and **24 hours**. We selected an SNS topic that we created in the *Getting ready* section. We then selected the tag we had created for our EC2 instance.

There's more...

The ARNs for Amazon Inspector rules packages use a different account that is specific to each region. The account number that Inspector rules packages use for US East (N. Virginia) is `316112463485`. Therefore, we created an SNS topic with permission to access this account. If you directly try to use the topic we created in the *Creating an SNS topic to send email* recipe in `Chapter 8`, *Monitoring with CloudWatch, CloudTrail, and Config*, we will get the following error after the template creation:

ERROR

- The Inspector Account was denied access to the requested topic Grant account 316112463485 permission to publish to the topic arn:aws:sns:us-east-1:135301570106:MyEmailTopic

Use the ARN for the regions we want. You can refer to the URLs provided in the following *See also* section for the complete list of regional ARNs.

See also

- You can find the detailed steps for setting up an SNS topic for Inspector notifications at `https://docs.aws.amazon.com/inspector/latest/userguide/inspector_assessments.html#sns-topic`.
- You can find the regional ARNs for Amazon Inspector rules packages at `https://docs.aws.amazon.com/inspector/latest/userguide/inspector_rules-arns.html`.

10
Additional Services and Practices for AWS Security

We looked into many security-related concepts and services throughout this book. There are still more security services and practices that can help us make our AWS infrastructure secure. In this chapter, we will look into some of these additional services and practices that are worth paying attention to. Unlike other chapters, we will not go very deep into these services. You can refer to the documentation of the respective services and check the links provided in the *See also* section for further learning. We will first learn about using AWS Security Hub to work with multiple security services we learned about in previous chapters. We will learn about some security-related managed services not covered before, such as AWS **Single Sign-On** (**SSO**), AWS Resource Access Manager, AWS Secrets Manager, AWS Trusted Advisor, and AWS Artifact. We will look into some security-related features, such as S3 Glacier Vaults. We will also see how we can use security products from AWS Marketplace.

In this chapter, we will cover the following recipes:

- Setting up and using AWS Security Hub
- Setting up and using AWS SSO
- Setting up and using AWS Resource Access Manager
- Protecting S3 Glacier Vaults with Vault Lock
- Using AWS Secrets Manager to manage RDS credentials
- Creating an AMI instead of using EC2 user data
- Using security products from AWS Marketplace
- Using AWS Trusted Advisor for recommendations
- Using AWS Artifact for compliance reports

Technical requirements

We need a working AWS account.

Code files for this chapter are available at `https://github.com/PacktPublishing/AWS-Security-Cookbook/tree/master/Chapter10`.

Setting up and using AWS Security Hub

In this recipe, we will learn to set up and use AWS Security Hub. Security Hub makes use of findings from services such as Config, GuardDuty, Macie, and Inspector to provide a central view from which to manage security alerts and automate compliance checks. Security Hub can do automated compliance checks using the CIS AWS Foundation Benchmarks, which is enabled by default when we enable Security Hub.

Getting ready

Set up one or more of the following services: AWS Config, Amazon GuardDuty, Amazon Macie, and Amazon Inspector, following the recipes in `Chapter 8`, *Monitoring with CloudWatch, CloudTrail, and Config* and `Chapter 9`, *Compliance with GuardDuty, Macie, and Inspector*.

How to do it...

We can set up Security Hub in a region as follows:

1. Go to the Security Hub service in the console. If we are using Security Hub for the first time, we should see a **Getting started** landing page with a **Go to Security Hub** button.
2. Click on **Go to Security Hub**. We should see the **Welcome to AWS Security Hub** page with the **Enable Security Hub** option, and a list of services with **Service Linked Roles (SLRs)** for conducting compliance checks (currently, **Amazon CloudWatch**, **Amazon SNS**, **AWS Config**, and **AWS CloudTrail**) and permissions for importing findings (currently **Amazon GuardDuty**, **Amazon Inspector**, **Amazon Macie**, **AWS Firewall Manager**, and **IAM Access Analyzer**).

3. Click on **Enable Security Hub**. We should see a screen with sections for **Summary, Compliance standards**, and **Insights**. The **Summary** section has tabs for **Insights** and **Latest findings from AWS integrations**. It may take some time for the findings to get updated:

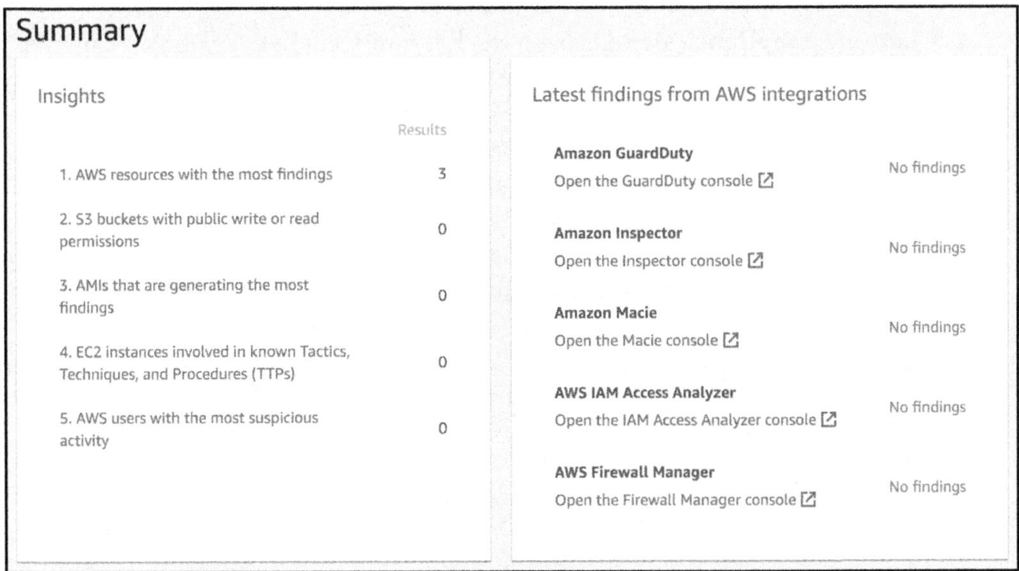

Under **Compliance standards**, there are tabs for **CIS AWS Foundations** and **Resources with the most failed CIS checks**:

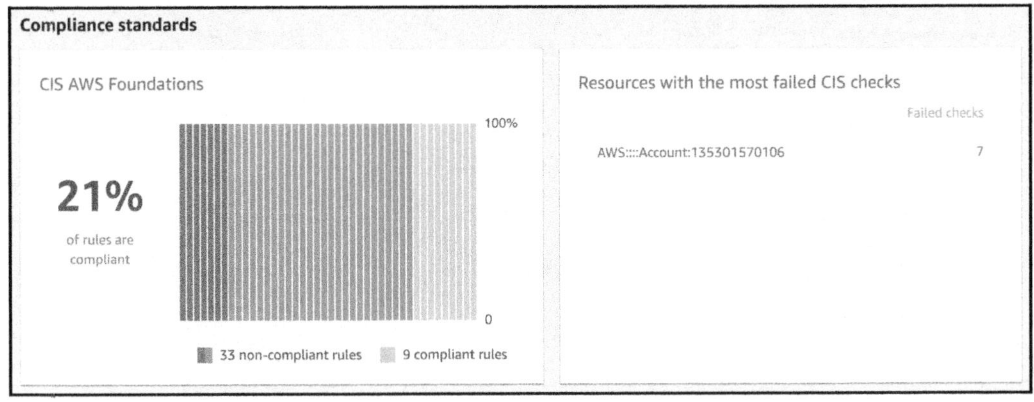

Under the **Insights** section, there are tabs for sections such as **Findings over time by provider**, **Findings over time by severity**, **S3 buckets with the most findings**, **EC2 instances with the most findings**, **AMIs with the most findings**, **IAM users with the most findings**, **Accounts with the most findings (by severity)**, and **Accounts with the most findings (by resource type)**.

4. Click on **Compliance standards** on the left-hand sidebar. Currently, only the CIS AWS Foundations Benchmark controls are monitored under **Compliance standards**. There are about 42 such benchmark controls.
5. Click on **Insights** from the left sidebar to go to the **Insights** page, where we can see the list of insights. There are about 30 insight filters currently available.
6. Click on **Findings** from the left sidebar to go to the **Findings** page, where we can see the list of findings across service integrations. We can filter the list based on various criteria, such as the service that exported the finding or the severity of the finding.
7. Click on **Integrations** from the left sidebar to go to the **Integrations** page, where we can see the list of integrations currently enabled and those that are yet to be enabled. For integrations that are already enabled, we can disable them from the **Integrations** page.
8. Click on **Settings** from the left sidebar and go to the **Usage** tab to see the estimated usage costs:

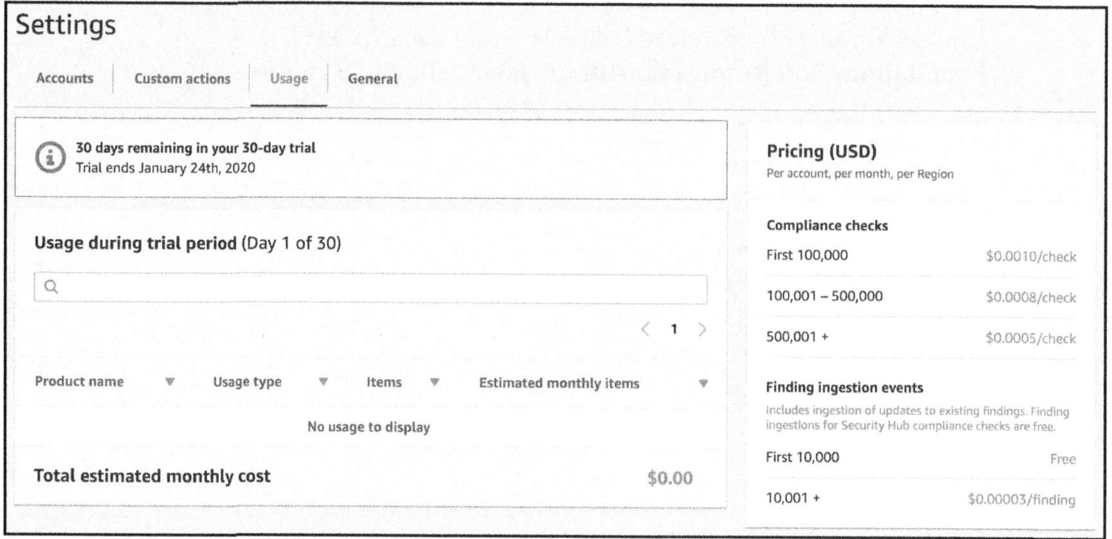

9. Go to the **Accounts** tab in the **Settings** page to add additional member accounts to share their findings with this account. An invitation will be sent to the member accounts and they must accept the invitation.
10. Go to the **Custom actions** tab in the **Settings** page to send selected insights and findings to Amazon CloudWatch Events.

To disable Security Hub, we can go to the **General** tab in the **Settings** page and click on **Disable AWS Security Hub**. However, it is always recommended to have Security Hub enabled for all regions if the cost is not a constraint.

How it works...

While enabling Security Hub from the console, we granted permission for its service integrations. Security Hub conducts compliance checks using the Amazon CloudWatch, Amazon SNS, AWS Config, and AWS CloudTrail services. Security Hub currently imports findings from Amazon GuardDuty, Amazon Inspector, Amazon Macie, AWS Firewall Manager, and IAM Access Analyzer. Security Hub is a relatively new service and the service integrations are expected to increase over a period of time.

A summary of compliance standards and insights is shown in the Security Hub dashboard. We can click on **Compliance standards** on the left sidebar to see the compliance standards monitored. Currently, only the CIS AWS Foundations Benchmark controls are monitored under **Compliance standards**. There are about 42 such benchmark controls. We can click on **Insights** from the left sidebar to see the list of about 30 insights. Insights are saved filters for related findings. We can click on **Findings** from the left sidebar to see the findings from across our services.

From the **Settings** page, we went to the **Usage** tab to verify the expected usage costs. The **Usage** tab also provides us with a summary of pricing. From the **Accounts** tab in the **Settings** page, we can add additional member accounts to share their findings with this account. From the **Custom actions** tab, we can configure the sending of selected insights and findings to Amazon CloudWatch Events.

We can disable Security Hub from the **General** tab of the **Settings** page. After disabling, Security Hub stops ingesting findings and does not conduct new compliance checks. We will lose all existing findings and Security Hub configurations, and can't recover the data later. We can export findings before disabling Security Hub. From the **General** tab of the **Settings** page, we can also see the service permissions used by Security Hub to monitor our data sources on our behalf, as well as the resource policies to simplify how customers subscribe to partner solutions.

There's more...

Let's quickly go through some important concepts around Security Hub and its related services:

- Security Hub is a regional service. If cost is not a constraint, it is recommended to enable it in all regions.
- Security Hub can integrate with third-party security tools such as Alert Logic, Armor, Atlassian Opsgenie, and more.
- We can archive security findings from the **Findings** page so that older ones won't appear on the page.
- The **Center for Internet Security** (**CIS**) provides security standards for different servers, applications, and cloud providers. For example, they provide a set of security standards that are specific to AWS security.
- CIS Benchmarks for AWS can be categorized into four categories: identity and access management, logging, monitoring, and networking.
- IAM Access Analyzer uses logic-based reasoning to analyze resource-based policies in our AWS environment to inform us which resources in our account are shared with external principals.
- AWS Firewall Manager can be used to manage firewall rules across accounts and applications.

Learning about and understanding the CIS security benchmark controls for AWS will provide us a better sense of security while working with AWS infrastructure. These controls can also help us take better decisions at work and even during exams.

See also

- You can read about IAM Access Analyzer at `https://docs.aws.amazon.com/IAM/latest/UserGuide/what-is-access-analyzer.html`.
- You can read about AWS Firewall manager at `https://aws.amazon.com/firewall-manager`.
- You can find the list of CIS security standards supported by Security Hub at `https://docs.aws.amazon.com/securityhub/latest/userguide/securityhub-standards.html`.
- You can find a list of all third-party partners that are integrated with Security Hub at `https://cloudmaterials.com/en/blog-entry/cis-benchmark-controls-available-within-aws-security-hub`.

Setting up and using AWS SSO

In this recipe, we will learn to use AWS SSO. AWS SSO is a cloud service that helps us easily manage SSO access to multiple AWS accounts and other applications.

Getting ready

We need at least two AWS accounts. I will be using a master account and a child account, as set up in the *Creating a master account for AWS organizations* and *Creating a new account under an organization* recipes in `Chapter 1`, *Managing AWS Accounts with IAM and Organizations*.

How to do it...

We can set up SSO from the main account as follows:

1. Go to the AWS SSO service in the console. If we are using AWS SSO for the first time, we should see a **Getting started** landing page.
2. Click on **Enable AWS SSO**. Once AWS SSO is enabled, we should see a dashboard similar to the following:

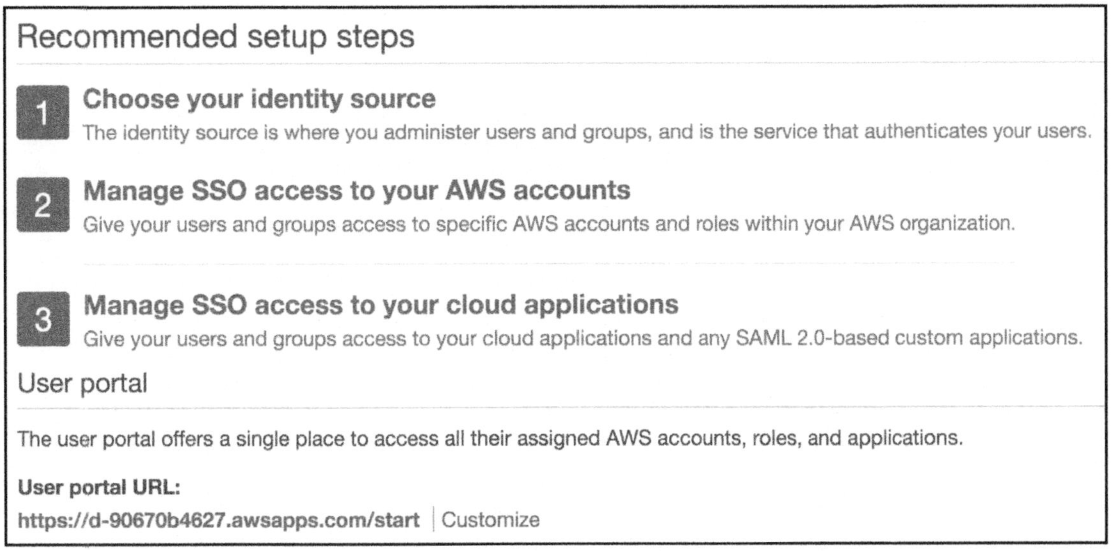

Recommended setup steps

1 **Choose your identity source**
The identity source is where you administer users and groups, and is the service that authenticates your users.

2 **Manage SSO access to your AWS accounts**
Give your users and groups access to specific AWS accounts and roles within your AWS organization.

3 **Manage SSO access to your cloud applications**
Give your users and groups access to your cloud applications and any SAML 2.0-based custom applications.

User portal

The user portal offers a single place to access all their assigned AWS accounts, roles, and applications.

User portal URL:
https://d-90670b4627.awsapps.com/start | Customize

You can also click on **Dashboard** from the left sidebar to reach the **Recommended setup steps** page.

3. Under the **User portal**, click on **Customize** to provide a customized **User portal URL**. Click on **Save** once done:

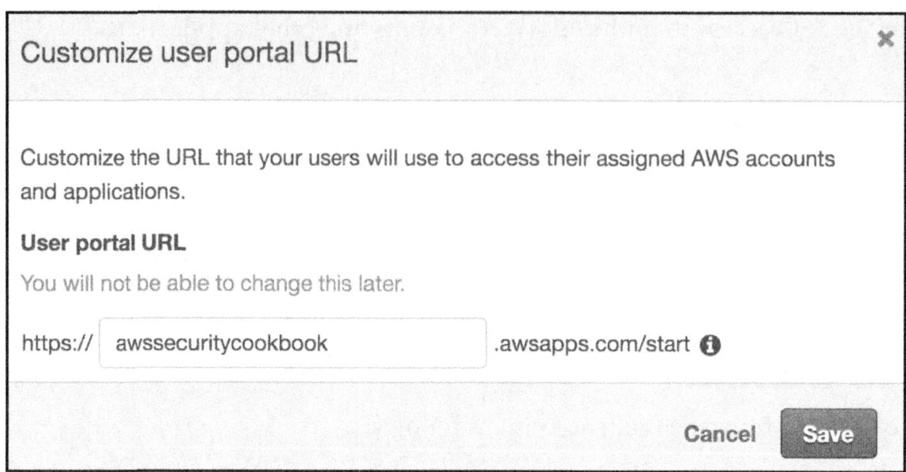

4. We will use the default identity source, which is **AWS SSO**. We can verify this from the **Identity source** section of the **Settings** page. We can reach the **Settings** page using the **Settings** link from the left sidebar or using the **Choose your identity source** option, which is choice **1** in the screenshot for the **Recommended setup steps** we saw in *step 2:*

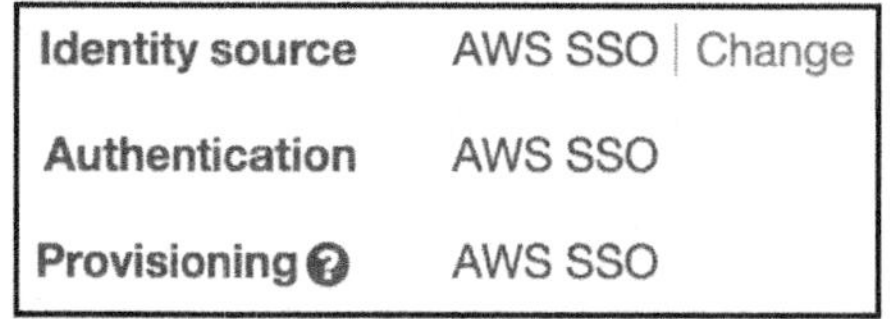

   We can click on **Change** next to the identity source to change the **Identity source**. Currently, the following options are available to select: **AWS SSO**, **Active Directory**, and **External identity provider**.

5. Go to the **AWS Accounts** page. We can reach the **AWS Accounts** page using the **AWS Accounts** link from the left sidebar or using the **Manage SSO access to your AWS accounts** option, which is choice **2** in the screenshot for the **Recommended setup steps** we saw in *step 2:*

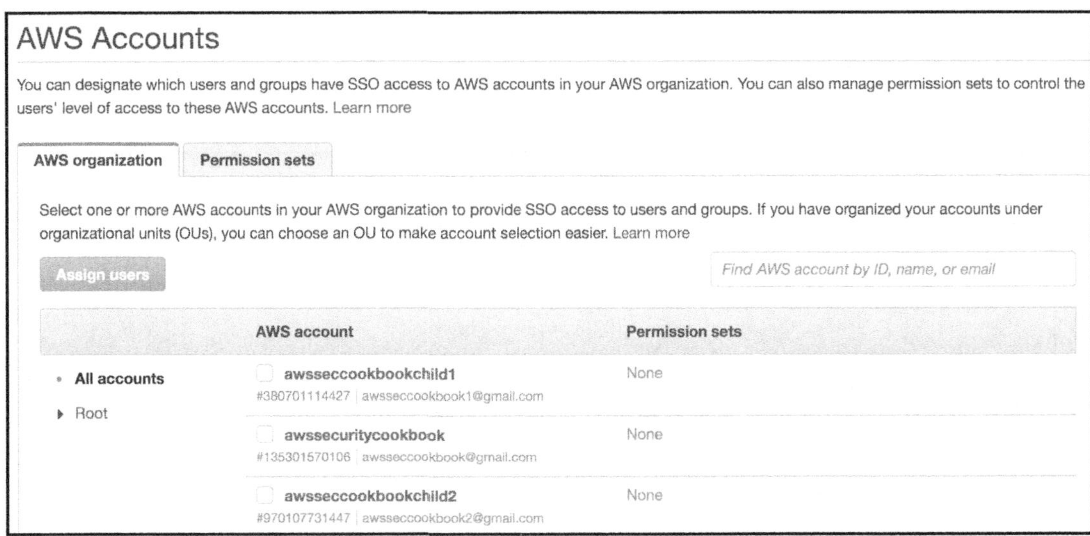

We can designate any users and groups with SSO access to our AWS accounts in our AWS organization.

6. Go to the **Applications** page. We can reach the **Applications** page using the **Applications** link from the left sidebar or using the **Manage SSO access to your cloud applications** option, which is choice **3** in the screenshot of the **Recommended setup steps** we saw in *step 2:*

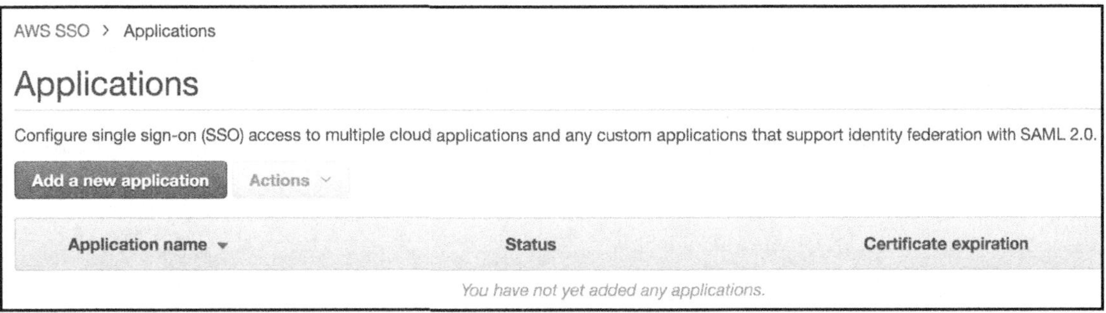

7. Optionally, click on **Add a new application** to select an application from the catalog of pre-integrated cloud applications or to add a custom SAML 2.0 application:

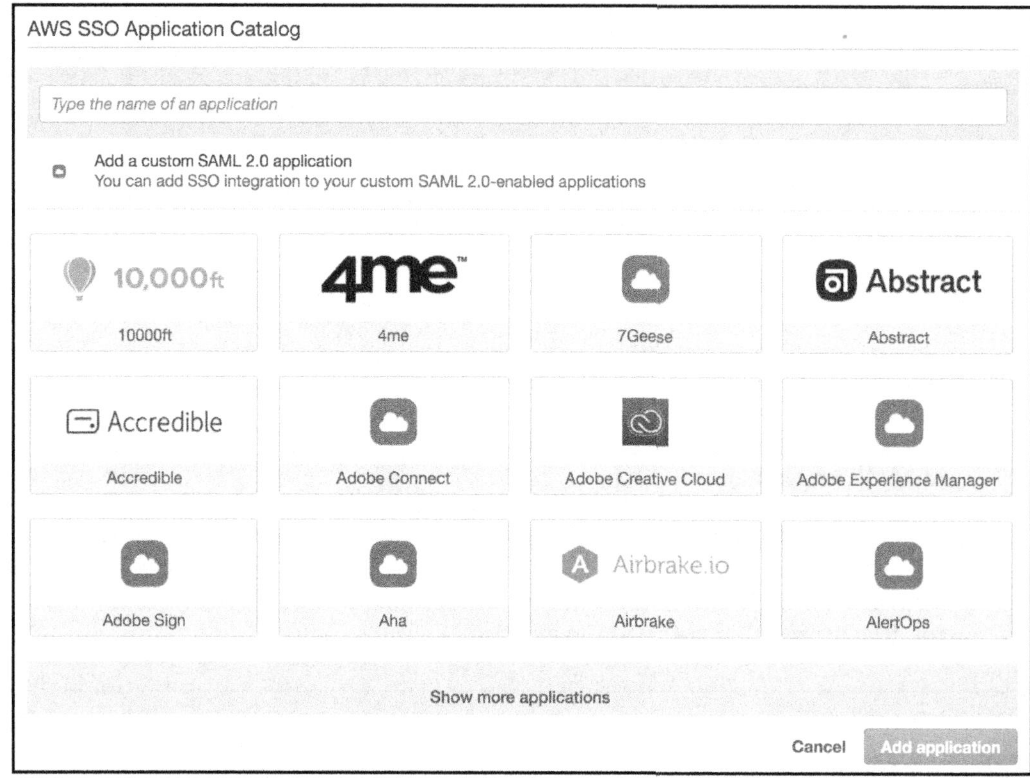

Click on **Show more applications** to see further pre-integrated cloud applications. After selecting, click on **Add application**.

How it works...

When you enable the AWS SSO service from the console, we allow AWS SSO to create roles for each of our AWS Organization member accounts. We also allow each of our AWS Organization member accounts to provide applications access to AWS SSO users.

We used an identity source as AWS SSO. We can also select the **Active Directory** or **External identity provider** options. With the **Active Directory** option, we can use AWS Managed Microsoft AD, or our existing Active Directory using AWS Managed Microsoft AD or AD Connector. With the **External identity provider** option, we can manage users, groups, credentials, MFA, and more with an external identity provider. With the **AWS SSO** and **Active Directory** options, users sign in through the AWS SSO user portal. With the **External identity provider** option, users sign in through the identity provider sign-in page to access the AWS SSO user portal.

There's more...

Some of the important usages of the AWS SSO service are as follows:

- Set up and manage SSO across all our AWS accounts in our AWS Organization, business applications, and custom SAML 2.0-based applications.
- Use SSO access for users and groups in our corporate Microsoft Active Directory instance.
- Give users easy access to AWS accounts and business applications you've authorized through the end-user portal.

See also

- You can read more about AWS SSO at `https://aws.amazon.com/single-sign-on`.

Setting up and using AWS Resource Access Manager

In this recipe, we will learn to use AWS **Resource Access Manager** (**RAM**). AWS RAM enables us to securely share AWS resources with other AWS accounts or within our AWS Organization. The resources we can share include AWS Transit Gateways, Subnets, AWS License Manager configurations, Amazon Route 53 Resolver rules, and more.

Getting ready

If you are using the resource share type as a subnet, you can create a subnet by following the *Creating subnets in VPC* recipe in `Chapter 5`, *Network Security with VPC*.

To select an **organizational unit** (**OU**) to share the resource, you need an Organization set up to use OUs. I will be using an Organization, as set up in the *Creating a master account for AWS Organizations* and *Creating a new account under an Organization* recipes in `Chapter 1`, *Managing AWS Accounts with IAM and Organizations*.

How to do it...

We can set up and use AWS RAM as follows:

1. Go to the AWS RAM service in the console. If we are using the service for the first time, we should be taken to the initial landing page.
2. Click on **Settings** from the left sidebar, select the **Enable sharing within your AWS Organization** option, and click **Save settings**:

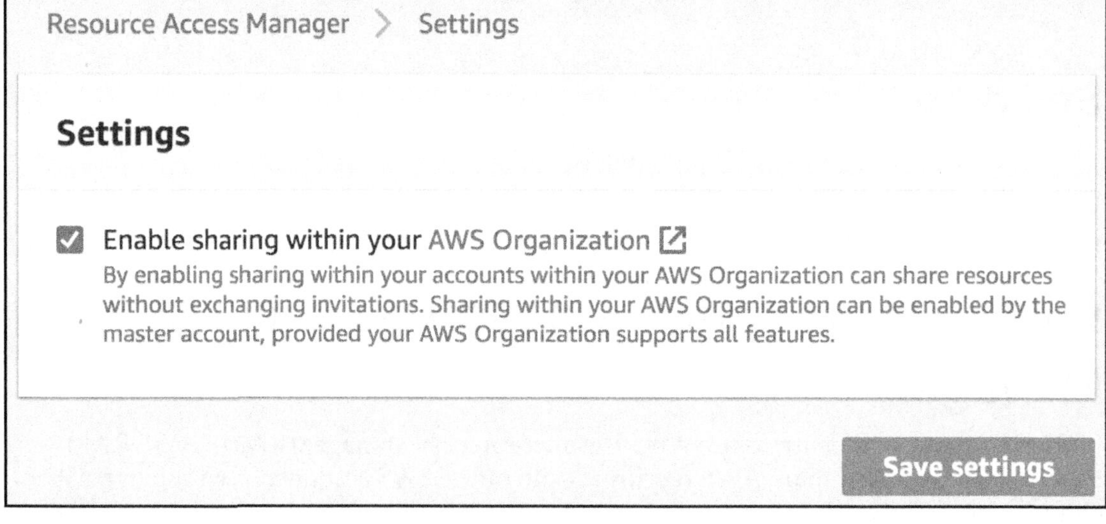

We can only enable sharing with AWS Organizations from the master account.

3. Go back to the AWS RAM dashboard and click on **Create a resource share**.
4. In the **Description** section, provide a **Name** for our resource.
5. In the section titled **Resources - optional**, for **Select resource type**, select **Subnets**. Select a subnet if available. We created subnets in the *Creating subnets in a VPC* recipe in `Chapter 5`, *Network Security with VPC*.
6. In the **Principals - optional** section, add the account number of the account we want to share resources with:

Principals - *optional*

Add principals to the resource share. Principals can be AWS accounts, organizational units, or your organization.

☑ Allow external accounts Info
Provide access to other AWS accounts outside your organization

Show organization structure

Add AWS account number, OU or organization Add

Selected principals

380701114427 ✕
AWS account

We can also click on **Shown organization structure** to select the master account, an OU or accounts under OUs from our AWS Organization. We should see the accounts and OU selected under **Selected principals**.

The account number for an account can be found in the **Support Center** page of the account. In our case, we could simply select the account from the organizational structure itself, but I wanted to show what is possible. We selected the option to allow external accounts. In our particular case, that was also not needed, as we have selected an account within our Organization.

7. Click **Create resource share**.

8. To verify the resource share, log in to the shared account (`380701114427` in my case) and go to the AWS **Resource Access Manager** dashboard. Click on **Resource shares** under **Shared with me** in the left sidebar:

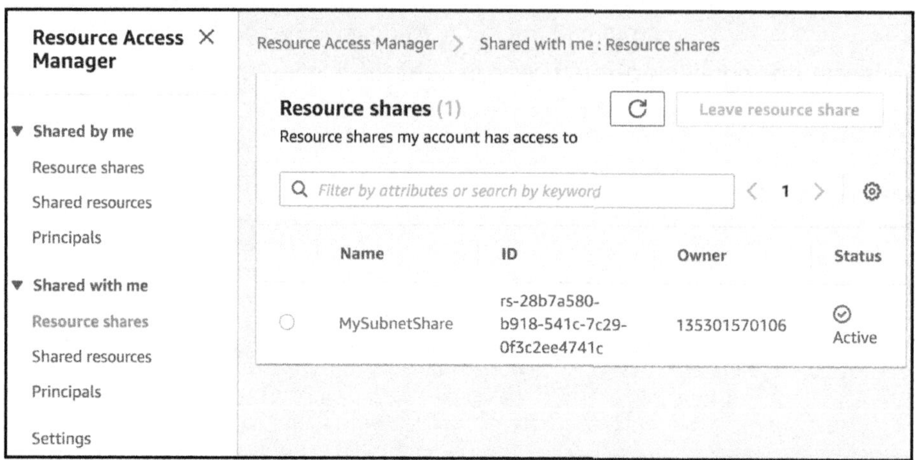

We should see our resource share in the member account. Here, `135301570106` is my master account's account ID.

How it works...

First, we enabled sharing within our AWS Organization. This can be done from the AWS RAM console, as we saw in this recipe, or by using this AWS CLI command: `aws ram enable-sharing-with-aws-organization`. If we do not enable sharing within our AWS Organization, the accounts we add will be considered external accounts, even if they are part of our Organization, and this may result in an error similar to the following screenshot:

Resource share creation has failed.
Resource arn:aws:ec2:us-east-1:135301570106:subnet/subnet-071b1776b379a5e58 can only be shared with principals inside your AWS organization.

We added a resource share for a subnet and shared it with another account within our OU. We added the account ID `380701114427` directly from the console. In our case, we could select the account from the organizational structure itself, but I wanted to show what is possible. We selected the option to allow external accounts. In our particular case, that was also not needed.

There's more...

We shared a subnet resource type with AWS RAM. The following is the list of resource types currently available: **Aurora DB Clusters**, **Capacity Reservations**, **CodeBuild Projects**, **CodeBuild Report Groups**, **Dedicated Hosts**, **Image Builder Components**, **Image Builder Image Recipes**, **Image Builder Images**, **License Configurations**, **Resolver Rules**, **Traffic Mirror Targets**, and **Transit Gateways**.

See also

- You can read more about AWS RAM at `https://aws.amazon.com/ram`.

Protecting S3 Glacier vaults with Vault Lock

In this recipe, we will learn to use Amazon S3 Glacier Vault Lock and the Vault Lock policy. We will create a Glacier vault, as required for this recipe, in the *Getting ready* section.

Getting ready

Create an S3 Glacier vault as follows:

1. Go to Glacier service in the console.
2. Click on **Create Vault**.
3. Select a region and provide a name. I have selected `US East (N. Virginia)`. I have also given the name as `mybackupvault`. Click **Next Step**.
4. Select **Enable notifications and use an existing SNS topic** and click **Next Step**.
5. Provide the **Amazon Resource Name** (**ARN**) of the SNS topic we have already created. We created an SNS topic in the *Creating an SNS topic to send email* recipe in `Chapter 8`, *Monitoring with CloudWatch, CloudTrail, and Config*.
6. Select the job types to trigger a notification, choosing **Archive Retrieval Job Complete** and **Vault Inventory Retrieval Job Complete**. Click **Next Step**.
7. Review and click **Submit**.

How to do it...

We can create a Vault Lock as follows:

1. Go to the Glacier service in the console.
2. Select our vault.
3. Go to the **Vault Lock** tab.
4. Click **Create Vault Lock policy**.
5. Add the following policy statement:

```
{
      "Version":"2012-10-17",
      "Statement":[
       {
          "Sid": "deny-delete-if-archive-age-less-than-year",
          "Principal": "*",
          "Effect": "Deny",
          "Action": "glacier:DeleteArchive",
          "Resource": [
             "arn:aws:glacier:us-
east-1:135301570106:vaults/mybackupvault"
          ],
          "Condition": {
              "NumericLessThan" : {
                   "glacier:ArchiveAgeInDays" : "365"
              }
          }
       }
   ]
}
```

   Replace my account ID of `135301570106` and the vault name of `mybackupvault` with your account ID and vault name. We can also click on **Add a permission** and generate the policy statement.

6. Click **Initiate Vault Lock**. We should see the message shown in the following screenshot:

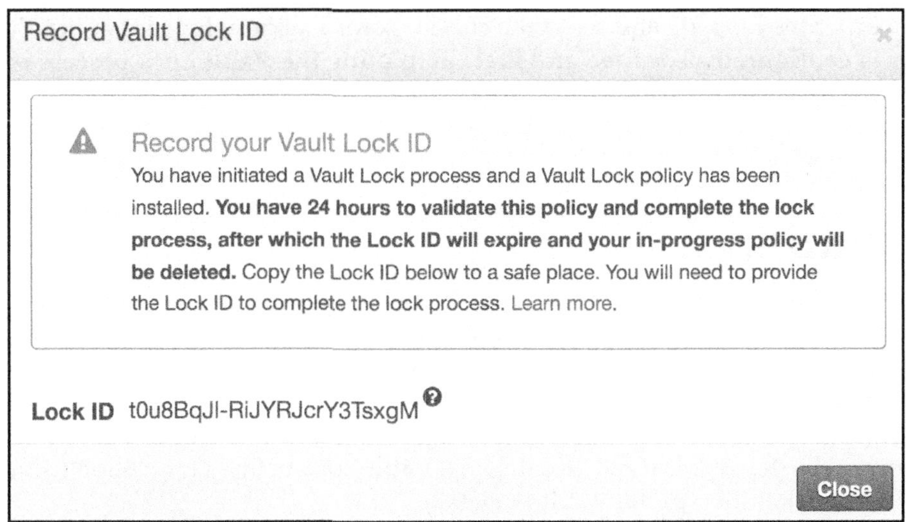

7. Copy the **Lock ID** and store it safely. Click **Close**. We should see our policy details with the Vault Lock status reading **In progress**:

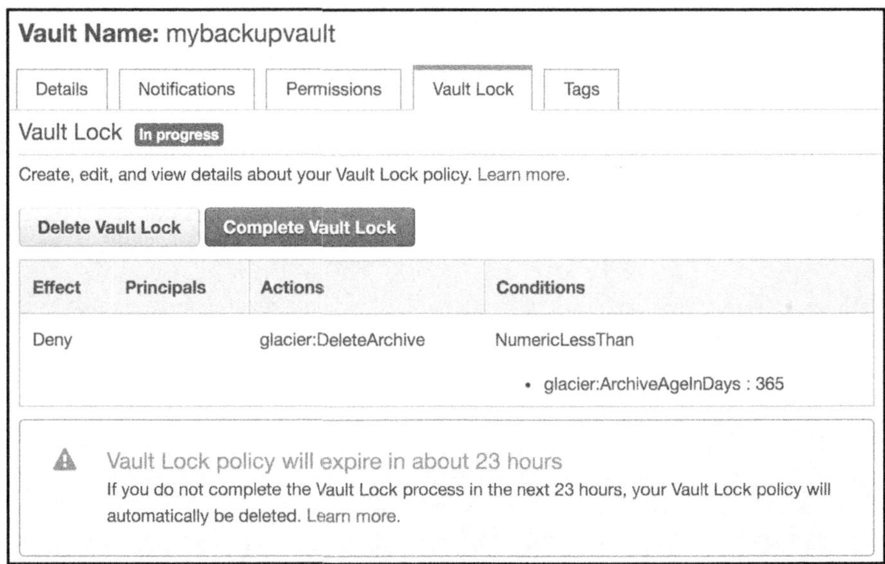

8. After enough validation, and within 24 hours of initiating the **Vault Lock** process, click on **Complete Vault Lock**.

9. Enter the Lock ID and select the checkbox for **I acknowledge that the Vault Lock is configured as desired and that completing the Vault Lock process is irreversible.**
10. Click **Complete Vault Lock**. We should see the status of Vault Lock as **Locked**.

How it works...

After we initiate a **Vault Lock** process, a **Vault Lock policy** is installed and we are provided with a **Lock ID**. We need to validate this policy and complete the lock process within 24 hours using the **Lock ID**. We then completed the **Vault Lock** process by providing the **Lock ID**. Once the **Vault Lock** process is completed, we cannot change the policy. If we do not complete the lock process within 24 hours, the **Lock ID** will expire and our policy will be deleted. We can also delete a Vault Lock before completion using the **Delete Vault Lock** button in the **Vault Lock** tab.

There's more...

We used the **DeleteArchive** action in our policy. The following are all the supported policy actions currently: **AbortMultipartUpload**, **AddTagsToVault**, **CompleteMultipartUpload**, **DeleteArchive**, **DeleteVault**, **DeleteVaultAccessPolicy**, **DeleteVaultNotifications**, **DescribeJob**, **DescribeVault**, **GetJobOutput**, **GetVaultAccessPolicy**, **GetVaultLock**, **GetVaultNotifications**, **InitiateJob**, **InitiateMultipartUpload**, **ListJobs**, **ListMultipartUploads**,**ListParts**, **ListTagsForVault**, **RemoveTagsFromVault**, **SetVaultNotifications**, **UploadArchive**, **UploadMultiPart**, and **SetVaultAccessPolicy**.

See also

- You can read more about the Vault Lock policy here: `https://docs.aws.amazon.com/amazonglacier/latest/dev/vault-lock-policy.html`.

Using AWS Secrets Manager to manage RDS credentials

In this recipe, we will learn to use AWS Secrets Manager to manage RDS credentials. This is a more secure alternative to managing and rotating the RDS credentials manually.

Getting ready

We need a database instance created in RDS for completing the steps in this recipe. I have created an Amazon Aurora database with defaults.

How to do it...

We can configure AWS Secrets Manager to manage credentials of an RDS database as follows:

1. Go to the Secrets Manager service in the console.
2. If we are using Secrets Manager for the first time, we should see the landing page with the **Get Started** section. Click on **Store a new secret**.
3. For **Select secret type**, select **Credentials for RDS database**:

Select secret type Info

Credentials for RDS database

Credentials for Redshift cluster

Credentials for DocumentDB database

Credentials for other database

Other type of secrets (e.g. API key)

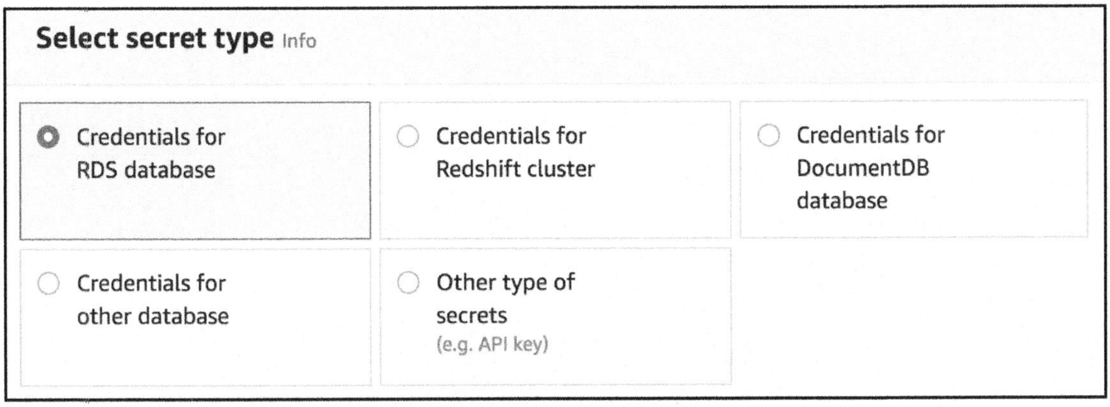

4. Provide the **User name** and **Password**. For the **Select the encryption key** option, select **DefaultEncryptionKey** from the dropdown. We can also use a KMS encryption key we created.
5. For the **Select which RDS database this secret will access** option, select the RDS database for which we want to manage credentials. Click **Next**.
6. Provide a **Secret name** and **Description** for our secret to make finding and managing it easy. Optionally, add any tags. Click **Next**.

7. Under **Configure automatic rotation**, select **Enable automatic rotation**. For **Select rotation interval**, select **30 days**. Select **Create a new Lambda function to perform rotation**. Under the **New AWS Lambda function name**, provide a name for our Lambda. For the **Select which secret will be used to perform the rotation** option, select **Use this secret**. Click **Next**:

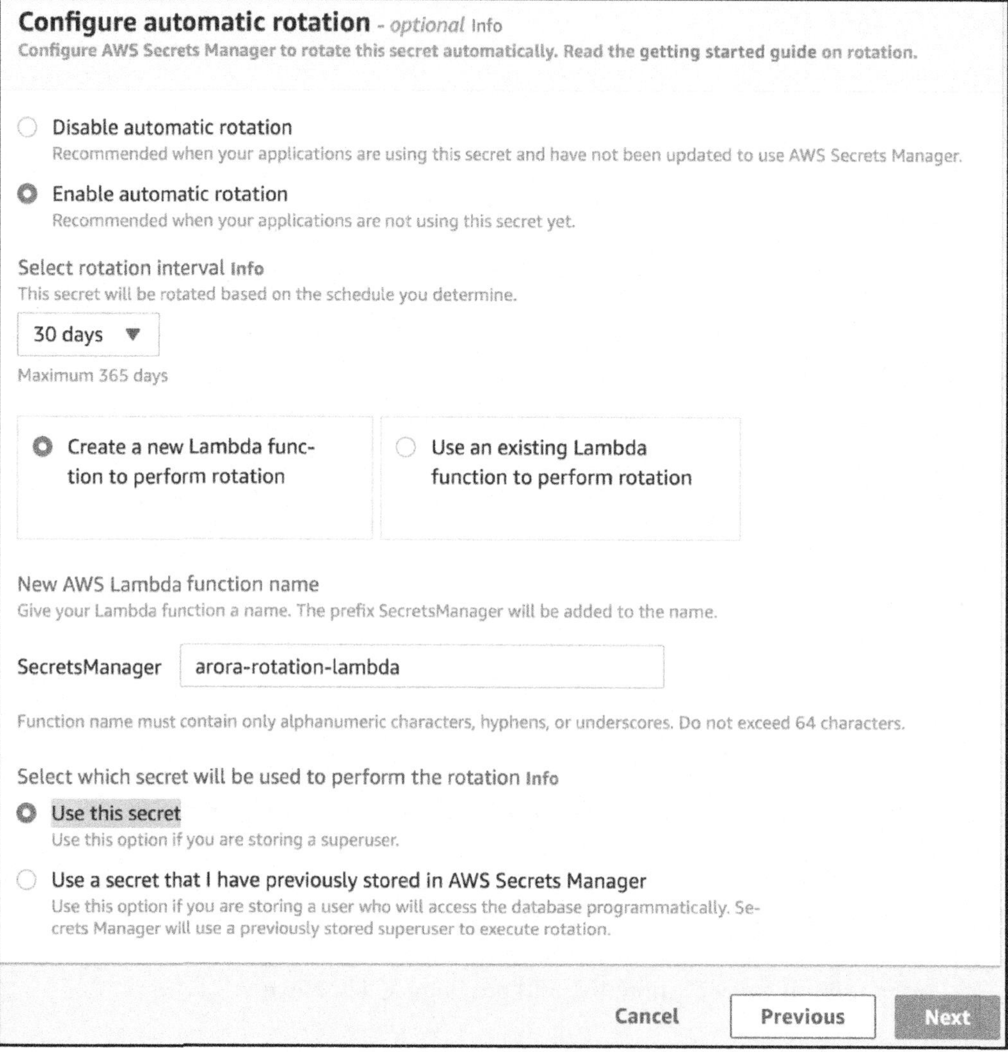

8. Review details on the next screen and click **Store**. We will see a warning that the first rotation will happen immediately upon storing this secret:

> ⓘ The first rotation will happen immediately upon storing this secret.
> Ensure that your applications have been updated to retrieve this secret from AWS Secrets Manager. Get started with the code below. Learn More

The page also has sample code for different languages with which we can retrieve the secret from our application. Currently, there is a sample code for Java, JavaScript, C#, Python3, Ruby, and Go.

We can delete a secret as follows. Go to the secret's configuration. Click on the **Actions** dropdown. Click on **Delete secret**. We must specify a waiting period of between 7 and 30 days before the secret will be deleted.

How it works...

In this recipe, we stored credentials for our RDS database in Secrets Manager. For the secret type, we selected **Credentials for RDS database**. The following are the other secret types currently available in the console: **Credentials for Redshift cluster**, **Credentials for DocumentDB database**, **Credentials for other database**, and **Other type of secrets (e.g. API key)**.

We enabled automatic key rotation with a duration of 30 days. We can also select 60 days or 90 days, or provide a custom period of time up to 365 days. I selected the **DefaultEncryptionKey** for this recipe. Instead, you can use a KMS key you created. We learned about KMS keys in `Chapter 4`, *Key Management with KMS and CloudHSM*.

After configuring a secret, our application can make an API call to Secrets Manager to retrieve the secret programmatically. While storing the secret, AWS provides us with sample code for different languages to retrieve the secret. Currently, there are sample codes for Java, JavaScript, C#, Python3, Ruby, and Go.

We saw a warning that the first rotation will happen immediately upon storing this secret. Therefore, if any of our applications are still using hardcoded credentials and are not updated to use the APIs to get the latest credentials, those applications will fail.

There's more...

AWS Secrets Manager may look similar to AWS Systems Manager Parameter Store. Let's quickly compare Secrets Manager with Parameter Store:

- Secrets Manager is primarily used for storing database credentials, API keys, and SSH keys. Parameter Store is primarily used for storing license codes, configuration data, user-defined parameters, and database strings, and is less commonly used for passwords too.
- Secrets Manager has built-in integration with RDS databases.
- Secrets Manager supports the built-in rotation of secrets for RDS. It also supports the rotation of non-RDS databases using custom Lambdas.
- The parameter store is integrated with AWS Systems Manager.
- AWS Secrets Manager is charged per secret per month and per API call. AWS Systems Manager Parameter Store does not charge for standard parameters, but charges us for advanced parameters based on the number of advanced parameters stored and per API interaction.

See also

- We learned about Parameter Store in the *Storing sensitive data with Systems Manager Parameter Store* recipe in `Chapter 6`, *Working with EC2 Instances.*

Creating an AMI instead of using EC2 user data

In this recipe, we will create an **Amazon Machine Image** (**AMI**) with a web server and then launch an instance from that AMI. Instances from AMIs have faster boot times than instances with the same configuration defined through EC2 user data. In the *Using EC2 user data to launch an instance with a web server* recipe in `Chapter 6`, *Working with EC2 Instances,* we used EC2 user data to update our operating system and set up a simple web server at launch.

Getting ready

Launch an EC2 instance following the *Launching an EC2 instance into VPC* recipe in `Chapter 6`, *Working with EC2 Instances*. SSH into our machine and run the following commands:

```
sudo su
yum update -y
yum install -y httpd
systemctl start httpd.service
systemctl enable httpd.service
cd /var/www/html
echo "<html><h1>My Web Server</h1></html>" > index.html
```

We did this through EC2 user data in the *Using EC2 user data to launch an instance with a web server* recipe in `Chapter 6`, *Working with EC2 Instances*.

How to do it...

We can create an AMI from an EC2 instance as follows:

1. Go to the EC2 service in the console.
2. Click on **Instances**, select our instance, click **Actions**, click **Image**, and click **Create Image**.
3. On the **Create Image** screen, provide a name and description. Use the defaults for the other parameters and click on **Create Image**:

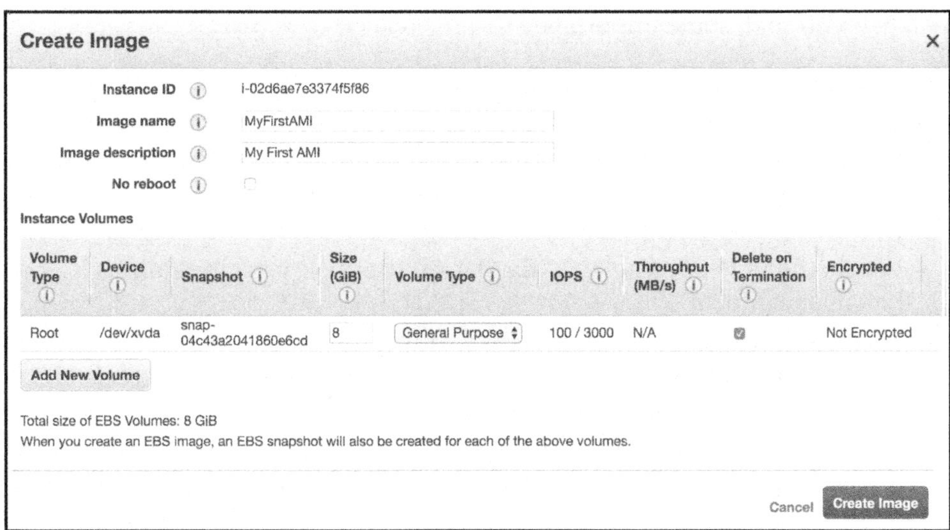

If we go to the AMI list, our AMI should display its initial **Status** as **pending**. Once the **Status** changes to **available**, create a new instance from this AMI. While launching the instance, choose our AMI from the **My AMI** tab.

How it works...

In this recipe, we created an AMI from an EC2 instance. Information related to the launch of an instance, including any Organization-specific configuration, can be saved into an AMI. We used Amazon Linux 2 as our base AMI within this recipe and hence used commands that are specific to Amazon Linux 2. If you are using Amazon Linux 1, you may use the following set of commands instead:

```
#!/bin/bash
yum update -y
yum install -y httpd
service httpd start
chkconfig httpd on
```

We did a similar configuration in `Chapter 6`, *Working with EC2 Instances*, using EC2 user data. Instances from AMIs have faster boot times than instances with the same configuration defined through EC2 user data. This is because we can have packages pre-installed in an AMI, whereas we need to install them at launch with user data.

There's more...

Let's quickly go through some important concepts related to AMIs:

- Multiple EC2 instances can be launched from a single AMI.
- AMIs are specific to a region, but you can copy them across regions.
- While launching an instance, we can choose between the AMIs suggested by Amazon, our own AMIs, AWS Marketplace AMIs, and community AMIs. We can also filter the list based on additional parameters.
- We should only use public AMIs that we trust. We can check ratings for AMIs before using them.
- AMIs are stored in S3. Hence, we will be charged based on S3 pricing, which is also dependent on our free tier eligibility and usage. However, we won't be able to see the AMI or its bucket from the S3 console.
- By default, AMIs are private for our account and region. We can make our AMIs public for other AWS accounts to use, or sell them through AWS marketplace.

See also

- You can read more about AMIs at `https://docs.aws.amazon.com/AWSEC2/latest/UserGuide/AMIs.html`.

Using security products from AWS Marketplace

In this recipe, we will learn to use various security products from AWS Marketplace. Many third-party companies will install and configure their products and solutions on EC2 instances and provide them as AMIs in AWS Marketplace. Marketplace AMIs can be considered EC2 instances with preconfigured software. Alternatively, we can also buy the products directly from these vendors and do the configurations on our own.

Getting ready

We need a working AWS account.

How to do it...

We can find and use security-related AMIs from AWS Marketplace as follows:

1. Go to the EC2 service on the dashboard.
2. Click **Instances** from the left sidebar and click **Launch Instance**.
3. Select **AWS Marketplace** from the left sidebar.
4. Scroll down to the **Security** subheading under the **Infrastructure Software** heading in the main content area.

5. Click on the hyperlink with numbers under the **Security** subheading. As of the time of writing, `701` products are available. We should see the AMIs tagged with security, as follows:

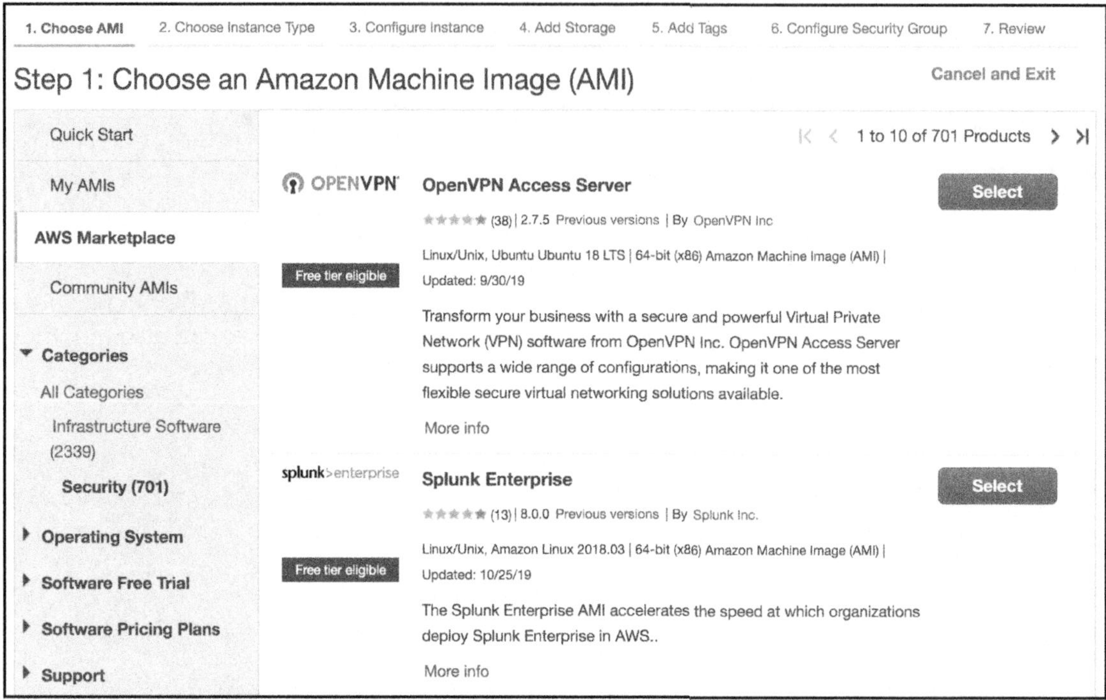

We can further filter results based on parameters such as **Operating System**, **Software Free Trial**, **Software Pricing Plans**, and **Support** from the left sidebar. Once we decide on a product, we can follow the recipes within `Chapter 6`, *Working with EC2 Instances*, to complete launching the instance.

How it works...

AWS may not be able to provide all the security products we need. Many third-party companies have developed products and solutions that complement AWS services for security and compliance. We saw how to find such AMIs in AWS Marketplace. Once we decide on a product, we can launch an instance with that AMI. For more details about the particular product we selected, we can refer to the respective product's documentation.

There's more...

Network packet inspection, also referred to as **Deep Packet Inspection** (**DPI**), inspects packet headers and data contents of packets to detect non-compliant data, viruses, spam, and so on, and can take actions such as blocking, logging, and so on. It combines the functionalities of a traditional firewall with an **Intrusion Detection System** (**IDS**) or an **Intrusion Prevention System** (**IPS**).

AWS WAF, the firewall service in AWS, can check for known exploits such as SQL injection, cross-site scripting, and so on. However, AWS cannot do a complete network packet inspection and lacks the functionality of an IDS and IPS. We can, however, use solutions from AWS Marketplace. There are solutions provided by vendors including Alert Logic, Trend Micro, McAfee, Palo Alto Networks, and Cisco Systems, among others.

See also

- You can read about security products in AWS Marketplace at `https://aws.amazon.com/marketplace/solutions/security`.

Using AWS Trusted Advisor for recommendations

In this recipe, we will learn to use Trusted Advisor. Trusted Advisor is an online tool in AWS that provides recommendations related to cost optimizations, performance, security, fault tolerance, and service limits.

Getting ready

We need a working AWS account.

How to do it...

We can use Trusted Advisor as follows:

1. Go to the Trusted Advisor service in the console. We should see the recommendation categories and basic recommendations on the **Dashboard** landing page:

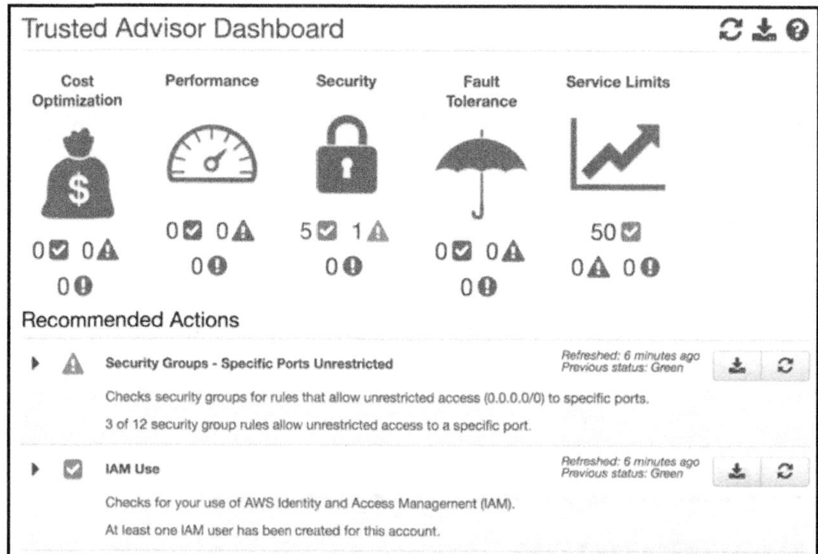

We can click on the **Cost Optimization**, **Performance**, **Security**, **Fault Tolerance**, and **Service Limits** options from the left sidebar to see recommendations only from that category.

2. Expand any recommendations for more details. I have expanded the first recommendation, **Security Groups - Specific Ports Unrestricted**, to see the security groups specified in that recommendation:

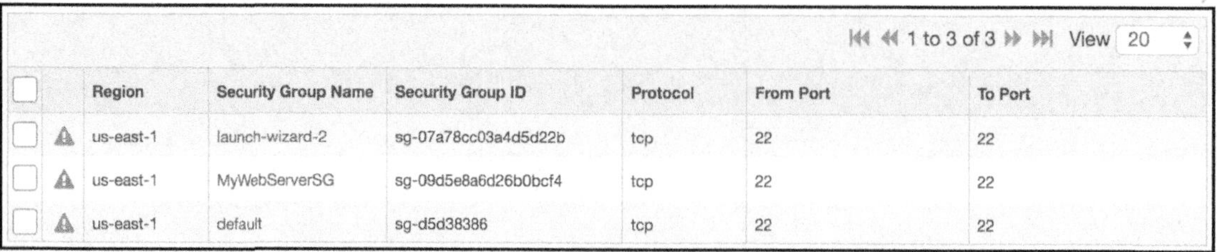

1 to 3 of 3 View 20

Region	Security Group Name	Security Group ID	Protocol	From Port	To Port
us-east-1	launch-wizard-2	sg-07a78cc03a4d5d22b	tcp	22	22
us-east-1	MyWebServerSG	sg-09d5e8a6d26b0bcf4	tcp	22	22
us-east-1	default	sg-d5d38386	tcp	22	22

3. Use the download button next to a recommendation to download the details of that recommendation as an `.xls` file.

There is a download button available on the top of the dashboard home for downloading details of all recommendations.

4. Use the refresh button by a recommendation to refresh it.

There is a refresh button available on the top of the dashboard home for refreshing all recommendations.

5. Scroll down to verify the upgrade section and click the **Upgrade** button to unlock all Trusted Advisor recommendations:

Upgrade your Support plan to unlock all Trusted Advisor recommendations!
You will have access to technical support from a cloud support engineer, with phone and chat support, support API, Identity and Access Management, Architecture support - use case guidance, and more.
Upgrade
Learn More

Clicking **Upgrade** to upgrade the support plan is available for Business and Enterprise AWS support plans.

How it works...

Trusted Advisor provides recommendations related to cost optimizations, performance, security, fault tolerance, and service limits. There are two service levels: the Basic plan, and full Trusted Advisor. The Basic plan is free and covers core checks and recommendations. Full Trusted Advisor functionality is available for the Business and Enterprise AWS support plans.

There's more...

The Trusted Advisor Basic plan currently has no recommendations available under cost optimization, performance, and fault tolerance. For these categories, recommendations are available only with full Trusted Advisor. For the security and fault tolerance categories, there are some recommendations that come with both the Basic plan as well as the full Trusted Advisor.

The recommendations available under security for the Basic plan include the following:

- Specific Ports Unrestricted (Alert)
- Amazon EBS Public Snapshots
- Amazon RDS Public Snapshots

The recommendations available under fault tolerance for the Basic plan include the following:

- Auto Scaling Groups
- CloudFormation Stacks
- DynamoDB Read Capacity

The recommendations available under security for the full Trusted Advisor include the following:

- Unrestricted Access
- IAM Password Policy

The recommendations available under fault tolerance for the full Trusted Advisor include the following:

- Amazon EBS Snapshots
- Amazon EC2 Availability Zone Balance
- Load Balancer Optimization
- VPN Tunnel Redundancy

See also

- You can see more Trusted Advisor recommendations at `https://cloudmaterials.com/en/blog-entry/aws-trusted-advisor-recommendations`.

Using AWS Artifact for compliance reports

In this recipe, we will learn to use AWS Artifact. AWS Artifact is a free, self-service portal for accessing AWS's compliance reports. AWS Artifact can be used to access AWS's security and compliance reports and select online agreements.

Getting ready

We need a working AWS account.

How to do it...

We can use AWS Artifact as follows:

1. Go to the AWS Artifact service in the console.
2. Click on **Reports** in the left sidebar to see the available AWS Artifact reports:

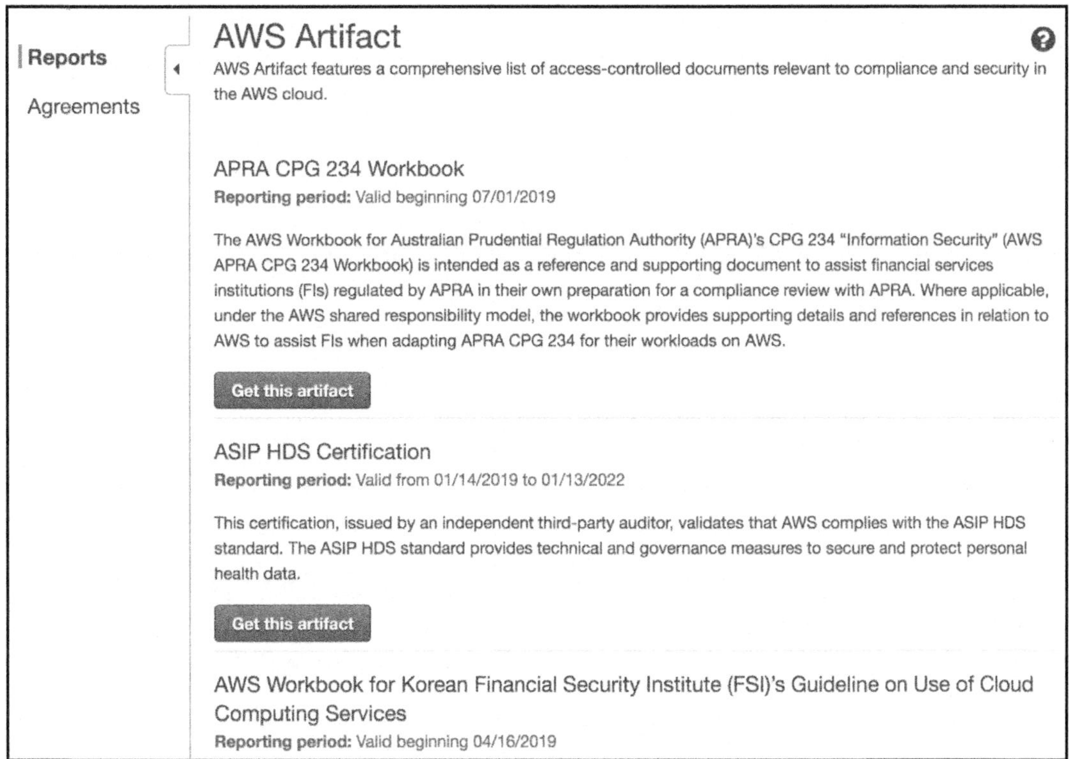

3. Click **Agreements** in the left sidebar to see and approve account agreements and Organization agreements:

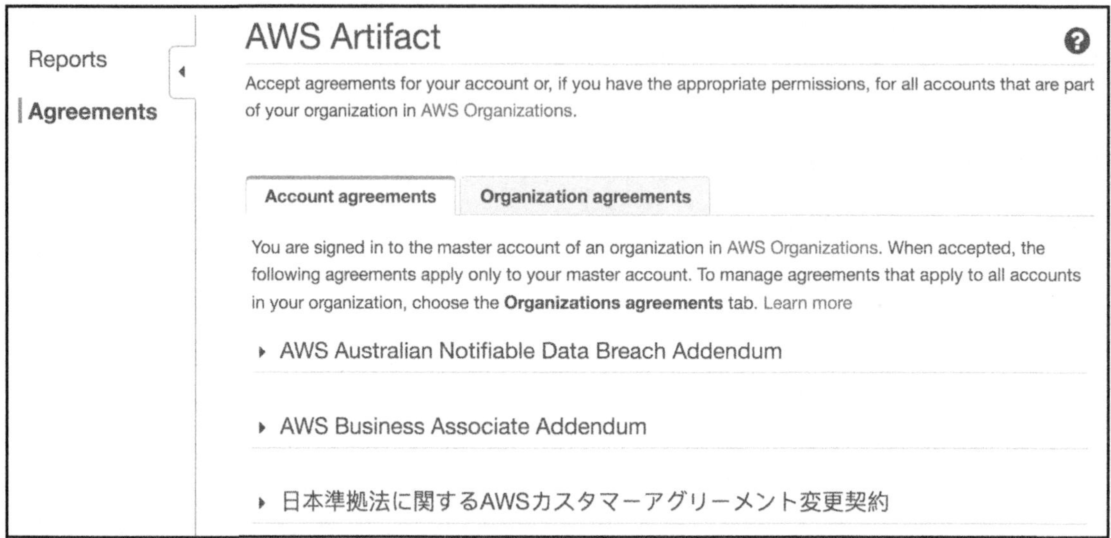

We can click on the **Organization agreements** tab from an Organization's master account to manage agreements for our master account and for all member accounts in our Organization.

4. Click on **Get this artifact** to download the document.
5. If a **Terms and conditions** screen appears, we need to select a checkbox to indicate that we have read and agree to the terms and conditions for the artifact, and click **Accept and download**.

How it works...

We've learned to use AWS Artifact for checking compliance reports. The following are some of the reports currently available with AWS Artifact: **APRA CPG 234 Workbook**, **BioPhorum IT Control Implementation Responsibilities**, **BSP 982 Workbook**, **FedRAMP Partner Package**, **Global Financial Services Regulatory Principles**, **Government of Canada (GC) Partner Package**, **IRAP PROTECTED Package**, **PCI DSS Attestation of Compliance (AOC) and Responsibility Summary**, **Quality Management System Overview**, and **Resiliency of the AWS Region in India**.

There's more...

We saw many AWS services within this book to help us secure our infrastructure on AWS. However, that is not an exhaustive list. AWS also constantly adds more services and features. Let's quickly go through some more services related to security:

- **Amazon Detective** is a service that can help in finding the root cause of potential security issues by analyzing and visualizing security data. As of this writing, this service is in preview.
- **AWS Control Tower** helps us to set up and govern a multi-account AWS environment based on best practices related to security and compliance. End users can provision new accounts following the company-wide compliance policies centrally established, and the cloud administrators can see a complete overview of the landing zone. A landing zone is the container for all of our OUs, accounts, users, and other resources that need to be compliant. Landing zones should be in a non-member account of an organization.
- **AWS License Manager** helps us in managing licenses from third-party vendors, such as Microsoft, Oracle, and SAP when we bring them to AWS. We can control their usage and even set customized rules on their usage for different groups of users.
- **AWS Personal Health Dashboard** is a service available to customers with the Premium support plan to monitor, manage, and optimize their AWS environment.
- **AWS Well-Architected Tool** is a management service based on the AWS Well-Architected Framework. We can define workloads against current AWS best practices and this tool will provide guidance on how to improve our cloud architectures.

See also

- You can read about AWS Artifact at `https://aws.amazon.com/artifact`.
- You can find updated recipes about AWS services at `https://cloudmaterials.com`.

Other Books You May Enjoy

If you enjoyed this book, you may be interested in these other books by Packt:

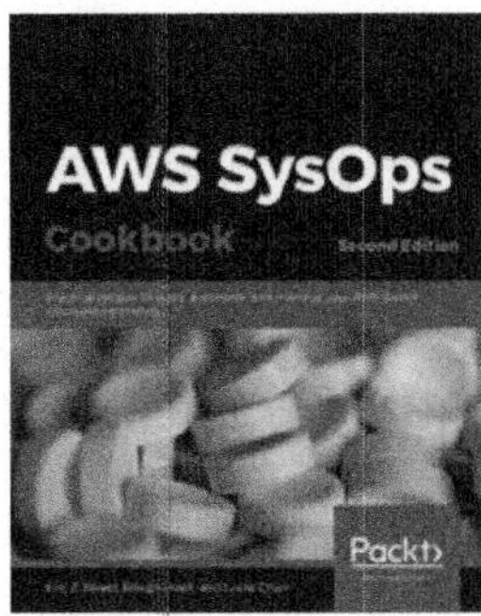

AWS SysOps Cookbook - Second Edition
Eric Z. Beard, Rowan Udell, Lucas Chan

ISBN: 978-1-83855-018-9

- Secure your account by creating IAM users and avoiding the use of the root login
- Simplify the creation of a multi-account landing zone using AWS Control Tower
- Master Amazon S3 for unlimited, cost-efficient storage of data
- Explore a variety of compute resources on the AWS Cloud, such as EC2 and AWS Lambda
- Configure secure networks using Amazon VPC, access control lists, and security groups
- Estimate your monthly bill by using cost estimation tools
- Learn to host a website with Amazon Route 53, Amazon CloudFront, and S3

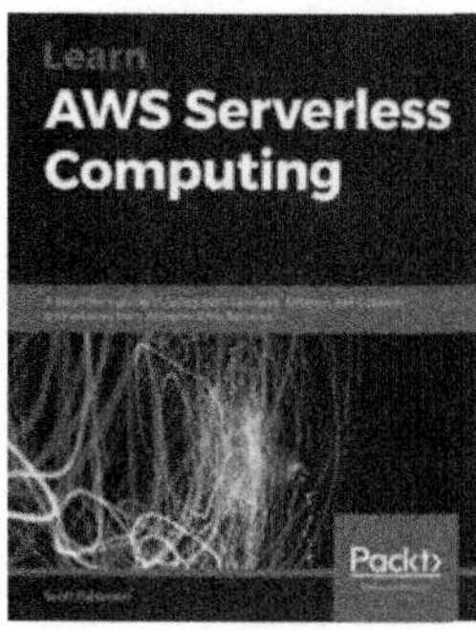

Learn AWS Serverless Computing
Scott Patterson

ISBN: 978-1-78995-835-5

- Understand the core concepts of serverless computing in AWS
- Create your own AWS Lambda functions and build serverless APIs using Amazon API Gateway
- Explore best practices for developing serverless applications at scale using Serverless Framework
- Discover the DevOps patterns in a modern CI/CD pipeline with AWS CodePipeline
- Build serverless data processing jobs to extract, transform, and load data
- Enforce resource tagging policies with continuous compliance and AWS Config
- Create chatbots with natural language understanding to perform automated tasks

Leave a review - let other readers know what you think

Please share your thoughts on this book with others by leaving a review on the site that you bought it from. If you purchased the book from Amazon, please leave us an honest review on this book's Amazon page. This is vital so that other potential readers can see and use your unbiased opinion to make purchasing decisions, we can understand what our customers think about our products, and our authors can see your feedback on the title that they have worked with Packt to create. It will only take a few minutes of your time, but is valuable to other potential customers, our authors, and Packt. Thank you!

Index

A

B

C

D

E

F

G

H

I

J

K

L

M

N

O

P

R

S

T

U

V

W

Printed in Great Britain
by Amazon